Disability and the Law

of related interest

Community Care Practice and the Law
Michael Mandelstam with Belinda Schwer
ISBN 1 85302 273 X

Children with Special Needs
Assessment, Law and Practice – Caught in the Acts, 3rd edition
John Friel
ISBN 1 85302 280 2

Young Adults with Special Needs
Assessment, Law and Practice – Caught in the Acts
John Friel
ISBN 1 85302 231 4

Legislating for Harmony
Partnership under the Children Act
Edited by Felicity Kaganas, Michael King and Christine Piper
ISBN 1 85302 328 0

Disability and the Law

Jeremy Cooper and Stuart Vernon

Jessica Kingsley Publishers
London and Bristol, Pennsylvania

First published in the United Kingdom in 1996 by
Jessica Kingsley Publishers Ltd
116 Pentonville Road
London N1 9JB, England
and
1900 Frost Road, Suite 101
Bristol, PA 19007, U S A

Copyright © 1996 Jeremy Cooper and Stuart Vernon

Library of Congress Cataloging in Publication Data
Cooper, Jeremy, Barrister,
Disability and the law / Jeremy Cooper and Stuart Vernon.
p.   cm.
Includes bibliographical references and index.
ISBN 1-85302-318-3 (PB)
1. Discrimination against the handicapped--Law and legislation-
-Great Britain. 2. Handicapped--Legal status, laws, etc.--Great
Britain. I. Vernon, Stuart. II. Title.
KD737.C66
342.41'087--dc20
[344.10287]   96-13407
                                               CIP

British Library Cataloguing in Publication Data
Cooper, Jeremy, 1950-
Disability and the law
1.Physically handicapped - Legal status, laws, etc. - Great
Britain 2. Mental health laws - Great Britain
I. Title II. Vernon, Stuart
344.1'04322
ISBN 1-85302-318 3

Printed and Bound in Great Britain by
Athenaeum Press, Gateshead, Tyne and Wear

Contents

Acknowledgements

We are delighted to record our thanks to others for their help and encouragement. The idea for this book was generated largely by discussions surrounding our teaching at the University of East London and subsequently by the support of Jessica Kingsley Publishers for our proposal. Research funding provided by the Southampton Institute allowed us to begin the writing of the manuscript and colleagues at both institutions, and elsewhere, have sustained us and the project over many months. In particular we wish to record our gratitude to Richard Whittle and Ian Wheaton for their valued support in the early stages of the books preparation, and to Howard Davis, Clare Picking, Michael Mandelstam, Belinda Schwehr and Raymond Youngs for specialist advice. Errors remain our responsibility. We also wish to record our gratitude to Disability Awareness in Action for permission to reproduce copyright material in Appendix II.

Many authors will know of the problems concerning joint writing projects; we are pleased to report that our friendship remains intact despite the challenges provided by the use of different word processing software and the attendant and continuing loss of footnotes in the process of conversion. Particular thanks go to Irene Clark at Southampton Institute who put the manuscript and the bibliography together on one disk and fought the battle of the footnotes on competing software with grace and humour.

Personal thanks go to our families for their love and for much else; to Sue, Kate, Laura, Clare, Juliet and Doug.

This book is dedicated to all people with disability.

St Margarets and Netley Abbey
May 1996

CHAPTER ONE

DISABILITY AND DISABILITY LAW

> At the core of traditionally held attitudes to people with disabilities is the belief that a disability renders one substantially incapable of enjoying life. Blindness, deafness, reliance upon a wheelchair and the like are typically perceived as individual tragedies unjustly imposed upon the undeserving. Those suffering from these conditions deserve pity, for they have been robbed of the fullness of life, they are not whole persons. (Lepofsky and Bickenbach 1985)

The above statement encapsulates with some poignancy the core of the problem of disability in contemporary society. This book will examine the problem from the perspective of the lawyer to test its validity. It is clear that the last few years have generated considerable public debate concerning the issue and incidence of disability. Legislative reform within this period has provided for the reorganisation of the health service, the introduction of the care in the community initiative and significant social security benefit changes. Public interest and concern has been heightened by these changes and by other events, in particular by the unsuccessful attempt to get civil rights legislation onto the statute book in 1994. This interest and concern needs to be informed by an understanding of the debate concerning the description and definition of disability. The pursuit of an accepted understanding or definition both of disability, and consequently of disability law, is fraught with difficulty and dispute. This first chapter will identify and discuss these difficulties and disputes.

DISABILITY

The late 1980s and early 1990s saw the publication of a number of government sponsored reports within, and related to, the issue of disability. Of primary importance was the *Survey of Disability in Great Britain* undertaken by the Office of Population, Censuses and Surveys (OPCS) between 1985 and 1988 and published as a series of four reports in 1988. The surveys used a functional definition of disability by their concentration on the incidence of 'impairment.'[1] This methodology and the findings of the surveys have been criticised by the Disability Alliance, among others, as underrepresenting the incidence of disability in Great Britain.[2] The survey reports were published at a time of considerable public concern about issues surrounding disability, residential care and the wider context of care in the community.

Three other major reports were published in 1988. All were concerned with issues surrounding disability. The Griffith Report, *Community Care: an Agenda for Action* (Griffith 1988) identified confusion in responsibility for community care which was shared between local and national government, the national health service, the voluntary and private sector and informal carers and proposed that local authorities take over lead responsibility for the organisation and provision of community care services. The Wagner Report, *Residential Care: A Positive Choice* (Wagner 1988), emphasised a positive role for residential care arguing that it should be seen as part of community care. The report by the Social Security Advisory Committee, *Benefits for Disabled People: A Strategy for Change* (1988), proposed the introduction of an integrated Disablement Allowance which would provide an element of income maintenance for people of working age who were incapable of work and help towards the extra costs imposed by a person's disability.

The public debate generated by these reports was further fuelled by pressure groups in the field, particularly by the campaign for a unified and comprehensive disability benefit run by, among others, the Disability Income Group and the Disability Alliance.[3] Together they provided a public focus for concern and a case for legislative reform. In response the government published its White Paper, *Caring for People* in November 1989 (HMSO 1989), and a review of disability benefits in January 1990. The White Paper formed the basis of the *National Health Service and Community Care Act 1990 (NHSCCA)* which legislated for the reorganisation of the National Health Service and the provision of community care services. The review of benefits led to the introduction of the Disability Living Allowance and Disability Working Allowance in April 1992.

The Law Commission, working independently of these initiatives, published an important consultation paper in 1991: *Mentally Incapacitated Adults and*

---

1   Gooding defines impairment as 'the functional limitation within the individual caused by physical, mental, or sensory factors.' Such a concentration establishes a functional definition of disability. She distinguishes impairment from disability: 'a disability is the loss or limitation of opportunities to take part in the normal life of the community on an equal basis with others imposed on people with impairments by physical and social barriers' (Gooding 1994, p.1).

2   The Disability Alliance has criticised the surveys on the following grounds: Northern Ireland was excluded from the survey; a postal questionnaire was used; the definition of disability used excludes a number of people with disabilities (those who have an impairment which does not affect their everyday activities – because it is controlled by medication – are not included); and a particular disability threshold was chosen.

3   For more information on both of these organisations see Chapter Ten p.259.

Decision-Making: An Overview, (Consultation Paper 119) and a more specific series of papers in 1993, *A New Jurisdiction* (Consultation Paper 128) *Medical Treatment and Research* (Consultation Paper 129) and *Public Law Protection* (Consultation Paper 130). The policy aims of any reform have been identified by the Law Commission in the following terms (Law Commission 1993, p.7):

i) that people are enabled and encouraged to take for themselves those decisions which they are able to take;

ii) that where it is necessary in their own interests or for the protection of others that someone else should take decisions on their behalf, the intervention should be as limited as possible and concerned to achieve what the person himself would have wanted; and

iii) that proper safeguards be provided against exploitation, neglect, and physical, sexual or psychological abuse.

Thus, in a short space of time the issue of disability had become a matter of significant public debate and concern. The OPCS Surveys and Reports were central to this debate, although as has already been identified, they have been subject to criticism. The surveys had been commissioned by the Department of Health and Social Security in 1984 to 'provide the evidence for a comprehensive review of benefits for sick and disabled people' (Hansard, 4.3.87, Col 623). Four surveys were undertaken: adults in private households, children in private households, adults in communal establishments and children in communal establishments.

The first report, *The Prevalence of Disability Among Adults,* identified a figure of 6000–202,000 disabled adults in Great Britain. The survey used a 10 point scale of severity and a functional definition of disability (in which a person's functional limitation is used to define their disability and its extent) to establish its findings. Though it has been suggested that the total figure thus identified highlighted 'the systematic underestimation of the prevalence of disability which was enshrined in previous government research' (Abberley 1992, p.139), the methodology by which it was calculated and the definition of disability used have both been the subject of much criticism.

The fundamental problem at the root of the OPCS definition of disability is that only those people whose lives are restricted by their inability to carry out the normal range of activities are included in the survey... The report also makes it clear that people who have an impairment which does not affect their everyday activities – because it is controlled by regular medication – are not included. (Robertson 1989, p.1)

Other criticism of the surveys is more conceptual and reflects the debate concerning the ways in which disability is understood and defined.

This debate, which is itself an important element of the 'politics of disability' (Oliver and Zarb 1989, p.221) can be characterised by identifying alternative definitions of disability. Barton contrasts a 'medical' model of definition with a 'social' or 'political' model (Barton 1993). Within a 'medical' model, he argues:

> Terms such as 'cripple' or 'spastic' reinforce an individualised definition in which functional limitations predominate. Thus, disability is viewed in terms of an individual's personal inability to function... This type of perspective legitimates an individualised, homogenised and static view of disability. It assumes an idealised notion of 'normality' against which disabled people are being constantly compared. 'Able-bodiedness' is seen as the acceptable criterion of 'normality'. (Barton 1993, p.237)

In seeking to define an alternative 'social' or 'political' model Barton goes on to argue that:

> Recognising the importance and exploring the origins of difference in the lives of disabled people compared to the rest of the community, are thus fundamental elements in a social theory of disability. Disability is thus a social and political category in that it entails practices of regulation and struggles for choice, empowerment and opportunities. (Barton 1993, p.238)

A similar point is made by Gooding in her distinction between 'impairment' and 'disability'. *Impairment* relates to a functional limitation caused by physical, mental or sensory factors, whilst *disability* is the restriction of opportunity to participate in normal life which is imposed on people with impairments by physical and social barriers.

> The vital feature of this definition of disability is that it distinguishes between the functional restrictions which are inherently associated with certain impairments (difficulty in walking, seeing, hearing, etc.) and those which stem from avoidable social restrictions. These restrictions may be social – refusal of entry to cinemas, clubs or employment – or environmental – stairs, poor lighting or lack of audio aids. (Gooding 1994, p.1)

The recognition of a 'social' or 'political' context for defining disability has also been used for criticising the financial focus adopted by pressure groups such as the Disability Alliance and the Disability Income Group in their campaigning for a comprehensive disability benefit.[4] Oliver and Zarb argue that a concentration on the poverty of disabled people examines a *symptom* sometimes at the expense of exposing the *oppression* of disabled people by society as the cause of their poverty (and of much else of their life experience) (Oliver and Zarb 1989).

Such criticism also identifies the development of other, more overtly political, strategies within the disability movement that have challenged the model of single issue pressure group politics.

---

4   The validity and power of this campaign had been considerably enhanced by the link
     between disability and poverty established by the second OPCS Survey and the
     recommendation of the Social Security Advisory Committee for an Integrated
     Disablement Allowance in its report *Benefits for Disabled People: A Strategy for Change.*

Disabled people are different and many believe that by recognising the importance of their own definitions they can take pride in their difference (Barton 1993, p.243).

Such an analysis of disability was evident in the campaign to get the Civil Rights (Disabled Persons) Bill 1994 onto the statute book. The Bill and the political debates surrounding its attempted passage are dealt with in some detail in Chapter Three.

Gooding has identified the way in which powerful understandings of disability are constructed. By charting the 'historical production of disability' she is able to show that: 'the distinctive category "the disabled" is the product of recent nineteenth and twentieth-century development' (Gooding 1994, p.13)

By reference to a number of writers (Finklestein 1980, Oliver 1990, and Doyal with Pennell 1979) she argues that the growth and consolidation of capitalism effectively excluded many disabled people from the production process and thereby from access to waged labour. Support for individual disabled people and possibly for their carer families was provided for (to a greater or lesser extent) by the emergence of the welfare state. Such available support is both financial (the social security system) and social (for example, personal care provided within the family and by community and residential care).

The distribution of such support is based upon the concept of need which, Gooding argues, constructs a relationship of dependency between disabled people and the welfare state, which is mediated through the work of the professionals employed within the welfare state.

> In the legislation establishing the new welfare system the key concept used when referring to disabled people was that of 'need'. However, control over defining the needs of disabled people, and stipulating how these needs would be met, was placed in the hands of professionals, often medical professionals. This system is based on the assumption that disabled people are incapable of running their own lives, and forces them to become passive recipients of those services which other people think they ought to have. (Gooding 1994, p.18)

The centrality of the concept of 'need' and the disempowerment of disabled people that is a consequence, have dominated much of the particularly post-war experience of disabled people. More recently this experience has been challenged by the emergence of a more radical politics of disability, the conception and advocacy of 'disability rights', concepts of citizenship and by government through the charter movement.

Coote identifies social rights as encompassing rights to health care and other welfare services (Coote 1992) and argues for their individual enforcement. The enforcement of such rights she sees as a powerful element of empowerment and of citizenship. As such, social rights are of manifest importance to disabled people.

> Citizenship entails being able to participate in society, to enjoy its fruits and to fulfil one's own potential, and it follows that each individual citizen must be

equally able (or 'empowered') to do so. This suggests two things: first, that all individuals must have equal access to education, health care and other services necessary to give them an equal chance in life. Second, no-one should be subject to unfair discrimination. As the IPPR (Institute for Public Policy Research) has argued elsewhere, there should be added to existing legislation against sex and race discrimination, a law against discrimination on the grounds of disability. A substantial lobby for such a law had developed by the early 1990s, chiefly among groups of disabled people. They were seeking a model of welfare built not on need and philanthropy, but on equal citizenship as a means to self-determination. (Coote 1992, p.4)

The debate surrounding the concept of citizenship and its relationship to 'rights' is an important element of the wider 'politics of disability'. Recent government social policy in the United Kingdom has emphasised the context of responsibility and minimised the importance of rights within a wider debate concerning citizenship. In the realm of social welfare such an understanding minimises the role of the state and emphasises the responsibilities of the individual. The concept of a right, with its implicit notion of a legitimate call on the responsibilities of the state for and to the individual, is seen as creating a culture of dependency, whilst the notion of individual responsibility is lauded as encouraging autonomy and providing a platform for self-determination.

> The (political) Right has turned commonly accepted notions of citizenship on their head and exchanged the language of entitlement for that of obligation and responsibility: the obligation of citizenship that must be imposed on the poor to reduce their dependency on the benefits culture. (Lister 1990, p.7)

An alternative, though sometimes linked response to disempowerment as a consequence of welfarism is the 'charter movement', exemplified by the publication of the Citizen's Charter (HMSO 1991). A major objective of this charter is the availability of essential services (including education and health) to all. The charter asserts that attainment of this objective is best provided by personal choice over welfare services with a safety net for those unable to exercise such choice. Empowerment comes through the exercise of choice. The charter downplays the importance of social rights whilst acknowledging that the 'poor and the needy' will require help.

> There is room for philanthropy in this view of the world, which acknowledges that the poor and needy are still with us and must be helped — preferably by individual volunteers and independent charities. (Coote 1992, p.5)

The ideological undermining of the legitimacy of rights and the promotion of the notion of responsibility has been reflected in important aspects of welfare state policy for disabled people. The role of the family, the voluntary and the charitable sector is emphasised in policy discussions concerning the provision of care in the community and is now a principle of legislation. A significant proportion[5] of community care services is, by virtue of the provisions of the

---

5   Currently 85 per cent.

National Health Service and Community Care Act 1990, to be provided on a contractual basis by the private, charitable and voluntary sectors. The impact of such developments in policy has been enormous.

Related themes emerge in social security policy and are again significant. The principles of universality in social security benefits (such as applies to child benefit) and of the link between contributions and benefit entitlement are under attack through an increase in targeting via means testing and from other increasingly restrictive criteria, for example those to be used to define 'incapacity for work' in the new Incapacity Benefit. The concept of 'entitlement' has itself been replaced by 'discretionary decision making' in the administration of the cash-limited Social Fund, which now operates as a minimal social security safety net and as an significant funder of grants and loans in support of care in the community.

> These beneficiaries are being increasingly stigmatised as 'dependent on the benefits culture'; the citizenship ideal of universalism is receding even further as means-testing is now promoted as a positive virtue in its place; the social fund marks a retreat from a commitment to welfare rights and, instead, increased reliance on charity in an attempt to reduce poor citizens' expectations of their legitimate claims on the State; and the growing emphasis on private provision, subsidised by public tax relief, could signal the final collapse of the post-war tradition of welfare citizenship if use of State provision comes to signify membership of a social minority rather than citizenship. (Lister 1990, p.66)

Nonetheless the language of rights is still available and is utilised. It carries with it a powerful currency of belief in the notion of entitlement. Disabled people (and many others) are frequently told by government and other public and quasi-public bodies that their interests and claims are provided for through a corpus of rights, for example, rights to social security benefits, to housing, residential accommodation, to personal and nursing care, to mobility and to appropriate independence and self-determination. However, the contemporary reality for disabled people is often more problematic. Few if any of these rights are absolute or unconditional. They are often significantly limited. The means testing of benefits, the plethora and increasing stringency of conditions attached to entitlement and the level of payment inevitably consign many disabled people to life on or just above the poverty line. The funding of community care and the cost of domiciliary and residential care mean that considerable responsibilities for the personal care of disabled people are organised and undertaken by families and through the voluntary and charitable sector.

Consequently, the situation and life experience of many disabled people may be understood as a denial of full citizenship in the sense that they are refused a significant range of the rights attached to a comprehensive notion of individual citizenship and are therefore unable to discharge the responsibilities currently ascribed to such a status. Drawing on the work of pressure groups Lister draws an analogy between the undermining of social citizenship rights for the unemployed with the position of disabled people.

> The CPAG (Child Poverty Action Group) has criticised both economic policies which have eroded the key post-war citizenship right to employment (for men at least) and social policies which have treated the unemployed 'as if they were an inferior caste'. Similarly the Disability Alliance, of which CPAG is a member, has repeatedly drawn attention to how failure of social policies has meant the continued exclusion from full participation for many people with disabilities. (Lister 1990, p.51)

The ability to enforce social rights is important. It is this aspect of social rights which receives little recognition in the Citizens' Charter. The principles of non-discrimination and accessibility to buildings and to services both feature in the Citizen's Charter, though there is no clearly established means of enforcement. The subsequent refusal of government to legislate for the enforceability and realisation of these principles in the field of disability by the defeat of the Civil Rights (Disabled Persons) Bill in Parliament can be seen both as a powerful denial of their status as rights and a denial of full citizenship for disabled people. Such a conclusion is all the more difficult for disabled people to accept, when the need for the existence of the Commission for Racial Equality and the Equal Opportunities Commission and for their attendant legal powers of enforcement has been almost universally accepted for some considerable time. The legal work that both commissions undertake is seen as both legitimate and necessary in the continuing fight against discrimination on the grounds of race and gender.

In a powerful assertion of the status of social rights, Plant identifies the importance of enforceability in establishing such rights and by so doing identifies a number of themes which we will discuss in the second part of this chapter, which seeks to identify the nature and character of 'disability law'.

> The assumption has been that the general provision of public services is what social rights require, but equally it is clear that these have not led, by and large, to individually enforceable rights. The point also links to professional power and discretion. If individuals do not have enforceable rights and the distribution of services is to a large degree at the discretion of professional providers, then the providers of services have every incentive to provide them on terms that suit them – rather than seeing themselves as responding to the rights of individuals to a set of services or resources. The idea of rights therefore can be seen as a way of empowering the citizen in the public sector in relation to those services which are provided, in response to the idea that there is a social dimension to citizenship. (Plant 1992, p.26)

Thus far we have sought briefly to trace how the issue of disability became a matter of public concern. Of particular significance in this process has been the publication of a number of significant reports which had important consequences for disabled people. The OPCS surveys utilised a functional definition of disability which concentrated on the individual impairment of a disabled person. The assumptions implicit in such an understanding have been criticised by commentators writing within a perspective that recognises the politics of disability. Individualised or medical models of disability are rejected by such writers in favour of social or political definitions which assert that disability is a social and political construct. They argue for the recognition and acceptance of disabled people by society as they are.

The construction of a notion of disability through history as charted by Gooding (Gooding 1994) shows how the welfare state has provided for the needs of disabled people within a relationship of dependency. The dominant post-war theme of dependency has recently been challenged by the growth of the disability rights movement, by discussions surrounding citizenship and by government sponsorship of the charter movement. The importance of the assertion of disability rights is recognised by the discussion concerning the enforceability of both social rights to welfare benefits and social services, and to the public and civil rights identified in the Civil Rights (Disabled Persons) Bill 1994. The establishment of such rights could have been an important step toward empowerment and citizenship for disabled people.

However, within the failure of the 1994 bill there seems to have been a recognition by government, and by the public at large, of the legitimacy of the concept of disability rights. As part of the price paid for undermining the bill the government proposed to come forward with its own legislation and after a short period of public consultation introduced its own Disability Discrimination Bill.[6] The bill became law in November 1995, and the government will start to implement parts of it at the end of 1996. Though its provisions fall some way short of those in the 1994 bill, it remains possible that the rights established and the duties imposed by this piece of legislation will provide positive gains for disabled people.[7]

DISABILITY LAW

From a legal perspective the issue of rights always involves the related discussion on entitlement and enforcement. Many of the rights 'enjoyed' by disabled people and other welfare state claimants are at best equivocal in a legal sense. They are only 'enforceable' through processes that are qualitatively different and often inferior to those available to protect more traditional property and personal rights such as those available in the law of contract and land law. This comment, and the related argument that disabled people have access only to a 'second class' legal system, will be recurrent themes throughout this discussion of 'disability law.'

---

6   For detailed discussion of the passage of these bills see Chapter Three, p.77 et seq.

7   For an account of the general duties established under this new law see Chapter Three, pp.83–88; for specific duties in relation to the law see Chapter Five, pp.129–133 (Employment) and p.163 (Goods and Services), Chapter Eight, p.216 (Mental Impairment) and Chapter Nine, p.254 (Education).

Defining the phrase 'disability law' and specifying the subject matter of such a category of law is a task of some considerable difficulty. Within the worlds of legal practice and legal scholarship there are a number of well established 'subjects' and areas of work such as criminal law and family law. Each has, over a period of time, built up an accepted subject matter and defined criteria for recognising its own boundaries and therefore for identifying developments as being within or outside its field of interest. This is not the case with 'disability law'. The phrase itself has no established currency or an accepted meaning. As yet there are no agreed subject specifications or agreed criteria for identifying law or legal developments as being within the field of 'disability law'. In this section we will explore some of the criteria for demarcating a 'disability law' and identify a possible content for consideration. Some of our comments will therefore be speculative but are intended to examine first the obvious proposition that 'disability law' is characterised by its designed or incidental application to disabled people, and second by the tendency that in operation it often reflects, confirms and consolidates the disadvantage of disabled people and of discrimination against them. Indeed Gooding goes as far as to suggest that: 'the law is not an impartial arbiter, but colludes with, and indeed itself perpetrates, discrimination' (Gooding 1994, p.xvii).

Rights, powers and duties

We start with the assertion that within English law there is a formal legal equality within which all people have the same legal rights, powers and duties. But even the most superficial examination of this proposition identifies the unequal legal status of some disabled people. For example, the validity, and therefore enforceability, of most contracts in law specifies a condition of legal capacity or competency; there is a requirement of the chronological age of majority and mental capacity to make a will, or to own and convey land, and a test of intellectual competency to consent to or refuse medical treatment. It becomes apparent therefore that people with a learning disability may not enjoy access to the same set of legal rights available to people with a physical disability or to other people.

Conversely some legal rights are available only for people with a disability. Such rights include the ability to claim social security benefits that relate specifically to disability, such as Disability Living Allowance and the right to request an assessment under the Disabled Persons (Services, Consultation and Representation) Act 1986 for the provision of aids and adaptations to the living accommodation of a disabled person.

Within a legal discourse the concept of a right has a generalised rather than specific meaning. The ability to claim a social security benefit designed to provide for particular consequences of disability may be understood as a 'positive' right. In addition to such 'positive' rights there are other consequences of disability, particularly of mental disorder, which involve an element of paternalistic protection which can be conceptualised as both a restriction on absolute autonomy and a right to protection. Examples would include the jurisdiction of the Court of Protection to administer the property and financial affairs of a person diagnosed as suffering from a mental disorder within the terms of the Mental Health Act 1983.

The law also establishes a number of *powers and duties* which relate to disabled people. Duties are mandatory requirements established by law whilst powers are discretionary, conditional or enabling provisions within which there is an element of discretion concerning performance. The National Assistance Act 1948 provides an example of the distinction between duties and powers. Section 21 establishes a duty on local authorities to provide residential accommodation to those who are resident in their area who are in need of care and attention because of age, illness, disability or other circumstances; there is only a a discretionary power to provide such accommodation for people who are not ordinarily resident in the local authority area.

Though duties are mandatory legal requirements their performance may be subject to discretion. For example, The National Health Service and Community Care Act 1990 imposes a duty on local authorities to assess needs for community care services though the manner of assessment is not specified in the Act. Consequently, local authorities have a discretion in the design of their assessment procedures though this discretion will in turn be influenced by guidance issued by the Department of Health and the Social Services Inspectorate.

In one sense legal duties establish concomitant legal rights. Thus the *duty* to assess under the Disabled Persons (Services, Consultation and Representation) Act 1986 establishes a *right* to be assessed. The reality of English law is that duties are prescribed in legislation and often defined in subsequent case law, whilst the rights that such duties establish are frequently not defined within legislation and are therefore much more difficult to identify and determine with accuracy.

This difficulty is necessarily associated with the nature and character of English law which has no overarching written corpus of individual legal rights, much less of disability rights. Thus, strictly, the only 'legal' rights which individuals have are those that have been established by statute or through the articulation of rules of law by the courts. Consequently, there are some alarming gaps in general law and in the law as it relates to people with a disability which become apparent only when a particular issue or problem presents itself. An example of this is provided by a recent case[8] which was concerned with the

---

8   Re F [1990] 2 AC 1.

legality of an operation to sterilise an adult woman with severe learning disability. The woman was aged 36, but had the verbal capacity of a two-year-old, and the mental capacity of a child aged four to five. She had formed a relationship with a male patient which involved a sexual element and there was general concern that pregnancy would be disastrous and that other forms of contraception, for a number of reasons, were inappropriate. The woman's mother applied to the High Court for a declaration that an operation to sterilise her daughter would not be unlawful, despite the absence of her daughter's consent, something which the latter was clearly incapable of giving or under-standing. The extent of her daughter's learning disability was such that she did not, and never would have in law, sufficient competency to be able to give her own consent to the operation and English law provided no other way in which the necessary consent could be obtained. The courts were required to establish a legal principle for such medical intervention and a procedure for future cases. The House of Lords held that the 'patient's best interests' were to be the criteria for such medical interventions. The procedure for establishing such a criteria for a proposed sterilisation would most often be an application to the High Court for a declaration that such an operation would not be unlawful in the absence of the patient's consent where the patient is incapable of providing such a consent.

Establishing the subject matter of 'disability law'

The primary category of 'disability law' is established by those duties, rights and powers established by the law specifically to legislate for disabled people and for the consequences of disability. Examples are easy to identify and include statutes such as the National Assistance Act 1948 and the Chronically Sick and Disabled Persons Act 1970. The former provides, among other things, a definition of the categories of disability and a duty on local authorities to provide for residential care. The latter requires local authorities to, among other things, provide assistance in arranging, or carrying out, adaptations to a person's home, or the provision of additional facilities to secure their greater safety, comfort or convenience. This duty is owed to people who are identified as disabled by reference to the categories established in the National Assistance Act 1948. Such provisions have a direct and designed impact upon the lives of disabled people; such a category of law might be termed *direct disability law*. Civil rights legislation concerning disabled people would, if introduced, be an important example of this category of 'disability law'.

There are particular aspects of disability law that provide for the exercise of compulsory powers against disabled people. The Mental Health Act 1983 specifies circumstances in which patients may be compulsorily admitted to, and detained in, hospital and circumstances in which treatment for their mental disorder may be administered without their consent.[9] The National Assistance Act provides for the compulsory (i.e. if necessary, forced) removal of people from their own home in circumstances where they are unable to care for themselves.[10] The use of such paternalistic powers raises moral, ethical and civil liberties questions, though the rationale for the exercise of such powers is most often the best interests of the person concerned or the protection of the public.

Direct and indirect disability law

Other categories of 'disability law' can be established by identifying law, be it statute or case law, that has a particular impact on disabled people even though it was not designed specifically for disabled people. Such a category might be identified as 'indirect' disability law. An example is provided by the Social Security Act 1986 which, among other things, established the Social Fund. Grants and loans from the fund can be made in respect of community care expenses. As such, many of the applications for payments will come from disabled people. Similarly, the common law rule requiring a valid consent to medical treatment has a particular impact on people with a learning disability, for the rule requires the patient to be able to understand information about the operation that is communicated to them as a pre-condition of a valid consent.

The distinction between 'direct' and 'indirect' disability law is often not as clear as these examples might indicate. The National Health Service and Community Care Act 1990 establishes a duty on local authorities to provide particular community care services to those assessed as needing them. Though the category of those to be assessed does not use disability as a defining characteristic there is no doubt that a substantial number of people assessed for community care services and provided with them, will be disabled people.

Some aspects of social security legislation provide an illustration of how 'direct' and 'indirect' disability law may co-exist within a single legislative framework. One example is Income Support, which provides a personal allowance for claimants whose resources do not meet their requirements as specified by the benefit.[11] This personal allowance may be supplemented by weekly premiums to take account of the extra costs associated with bringing up children, old age and disability. The basic personal allowance is not designed specifically for disabled people though the fact that a significant proportion of income support claimants will be disabled people reflects the link between poverty and disability established by the OPCS Surveys. Four of the premium

---

9   See sections 2, 3 and 4 which specify the criteria within which patients may be admitted to hospital without their consent. Part IV of the Act contains provisions relating to treatment. Section 58 provides for circumstances in which treatment for a mental disorder may be administered without consent.

10   s 47 NAA 1948.

11   This matter is dealt with in greater detail in Chapter Six.

categories are specifically designed to take account of the extra costs of disability.

The criteria of direct and indirect applicability as a defining characteristic of disability law helps to facilitate the identification of a subject content. This content will be discussed in some detail in the following chapters but we will identify the core range of sources of disability law below.

The range and origins of disability law
Statute law and guidance

Of major significance in constructing the corpus of disability law are the numerous statutory provisions which establish social services and community care duties on local authorities and provide them with appropriate powers. The range, scale and detail of this legislation will be addressed in detail in Chapter Four. Legislation of this nature is normally linked to local government responsibility. However, some statutory provisions take disability law outside the sole responsibility of local government to include, for example, health service provision for disabled people under the National Health Service and Community Care Act 1990; the provision of mental health services under the Mental Health Act 1983, including the jurisdiction of the Court of Protection, and the operation of the social security system under a substantial number of complex statutes and regulations.

Legislative provisions often require interpretation. In practice this interpretation takes place on a daily basis by those administering and working within the legislation. Information on the meaning and implications of legislation and on models of good practice to be adopted under this umbrella is frequently provided by central government departments in the form of official Guidance and Circulars. Examples include the *Code of Practice* issued under the Mental Health Act 1983 to provide guidance to those working in the mental health field on 'how they should proceed when undertaking duties under the Act' (Department of Health and Welsh Office 1993) and *Care Management and Assessment: a Practitioner's Guide*, issued by the Department of Health in 1991, to facilitate the development of care management and assessment procedures under the National Health Service and Community Care Act 1990. Although such guidance does not itself have the force of law it has significant status such that its contents should be included in any identification of 'disability law.'[12]

'Disability law-making' by the courts

Acts of Parliament and Statutory Instruments are subject to interpretation by the courts. When these decisions are made by the senior appeal courts in the English legal system they will form the basis of a binding precedent with the status of a legal rule. A recent example in the field of 'disability law' is provided

12 See Chapter Four, p.90.

by the House of Lords decision in a case[13] where C, who was blind and required assistance when walking in unfamiliar surroundings as he risked injury unless guided, claimed attendance allowance under the 1975 statute, the Social Security Act. His claim was refused on the basis that such assistance was not 'attention in connection with his bodily functions' as is required by the relevant section of the statute. The House of Lords allowed his appeal holding that the word 'attention' denoted a 'personal service of an active nature'. The guidance that C required was active and therefore fell within the meaning of 'attention' to the bodily function of seeing or walking. The role of the courts in defining the content and meaning of disability law through statutory interpretation should clearly not be underestimated.

Some aspects of disability law are within the province of the common law in the sense that the law involved is not the subject of statute but has been developed by the judges through case law. The case establishing the law concerning the giving of consent to sterilisation operations for adult women with learning disabilities has already been discussed,[14] and is a good example of the development of principles of disability law through the common law. Another example is provided by the case involving a football supporter, Tony Bland, rendered into a 'persistent vegetative state' following his crushing in the crowd at the Hillsborough Disaster. In this case the House of Lords applied the principle of 'the patient's best interests' to establish the circumstances in which doctors could cease treating a patient in 'persistent vegetative state' thereby allowing that person to die.[15]

The principle of the patient's best interests, established in the Tony Bland case, now constitutes an important precedent for the care and treatment of patients who do not have sufficient capacity to consent to their own health care. In particular, these criteria in cases involving patients in persistent vegetative state have recently been applied in the tragic case of a 27-year-old Welshman, who suffered irreversible brain damage following an operation to remove his wisdom teeth (*The Times*, 18 November 1995). He was now blind, mute, incapable of recognising friends or family, and confined to be daily strapped into a wheelchair to control his uncontrollable body jerks. The High Court, having reviewed the evidence, acceded to the request of his devoted parents and sister that he be allowed to pass away in peace and dignity, and gave their permission for the withdrawal of water, nutrition and other treatment.[16]

---

13 Mallinson v Secretary of State for Social Security [1994] 1 W.L.R. 630.
14 See p.12.
15 Airedale National Health Service Trust v Bland [1993] 2 WLR 316, see also now the case of parents who sought to apply the same principle to their two-year-old child who was blind, deaf and brain damaged and whom they believed to be in permanent pain.
16 See further Chapter Eight.

The nature and character of disability law

Disadvantage is often acknowledged to be a consequence of disability and it is instructive to evaluate aspects of the law that impact upon disabled people to see whether they evidence characteristics that amount to something that might be termed 'legal disadvantage'. Let us focus upon the status of particular 'disability law' rights and duties; the procedures for their enforcement and the nature of remedies provided; and the forum for enforcement and access to legal services.

The status of disability law rights and duties

The fact that legal rights are most often identifiable within the definition of a statutory duty is significant. Statutory duties are frequently defined in general terms and are therefore subject to interpretation and discretion in their performance. In the area of social services legislation, which has, by definition, a significant impact upon disabled people, statutory duties 'read more like general duties to provide certain services for people in the area than duties owed to particular individuals' (Hoggett 1990, p.307).

The difficulty of establishing an individual legal action based upon the breach of statutory duty by a local authority has recently been confirmed by decisions in the Court of Appeal and the House of Lords.[17] Such general duties are therefore unlikely to establish individual legal rights, a factor which disadvantages disabled people who are, or would be, significant consumers of local authority social services. This disadvantage is confirmed if the provision made for supposed remedies where duties remain unperformed, or are improperly performed, is inadequate.

Procedures for enforcement of disability law and the nature of remedies provided

It seems that this principle of non-enforcement by action for damages on the grounds of breach of statutory duty is re-enforced where statute specifically provides other methods for challenge. Identification and examination of these alternatives illustrates their limitations as a means of enforcing duties and establishing rights to services designed to provide for some of the consequences of disability.

Lord Justice Staughton's judgement in the Court of Appeal in the same case identified the alternative means of enforcing section 17(1) of the Children Act 1989 which imposes a 'general' duty on local authorities (a) to safeguard and promote the welfare of children within their area who are in need.

> In the first place, the members and employees of a local authority will know of that section; it is to be hoped that they will enforce it upon themselves. Secondly if they do not, the Secretary of State or Members of Parliament or the National

---

17   X and Others (Minors) v Bedfordshire CC, M (A Minor) v Newham London BC, E (A Minor) v Dorset CC, (1995), 3 All E.R. 353.

Society for the Prevention of Cruelty to Children can draw their attention to the duty and any specific need for it to be observed. Newspapers can do the same; and there is the sanction of severe criticism by the press or a public inquiry when an error is made. There is the local government – ombudsman. There are also the remedies of public law. These are invoked, for example, in relation to statements under section 7 of the Education Act 1981, which deal with the special educational needs of particular children. Finally the Children Act 1989 itself contains its own remedies. Section 26(3) provides that every local authority shall establish a procedure for considering representations and complaints. By section 84 the Secretary of State may declare a local authority to be in default if it has failed to comply with any duty under the Act, and give directions to ensure compliance.[18]

Although these procedures relate to the enforcement of a general duty under the Children Act 1989 they could equally apply (with appropriate references) to the duty under section 29 of the National Assistance Act 1948, a duty to promote the welfare of disabled people, and to many other duties established in 'social services' legislation. This matter will be dealt with at length in Chapter Four.[19]

It is likely that where statutory 'disability law' establishes a specific procedure for the enforcement of its duties complainants will be required to utilise that procedure and will be denied an action for damages on the basis of breach of statutory duty. For a full description and evaluation of these alternative enforcement procedures which are primarily Internal Complaints Procedures, Local Government Ombudsmen and application to the High Court for Judicial Review, see also Chapter Four.

The forum for enforcement and access to legal services

The courts are rarely the forum for enforcing disability law rights. The difficulties of pursuing an action for breach of statutory duty through the court system have already been identified and though important, judicial review is limited in its availability and by its discretionary remedies which are directed at procedural defects in decision-making. Comment has already been made concerning complaints procedures and the work of the Commissioners for Local Administration and their utility as a forum for the establishment and enforcement of disability law rights.[20]

Switching the focus from community care and other social services to the social security aspect of disability law immediately identifies statutory tribunals

---

18 Reference to the public law remedies available under section 7 of the Educational Act 1981 is presumably a reference to the now replaced right of a parent to appeal against the provision proposed in a statement of special educational needs to a local authority appeal committee and ultimately to the Secretary of State. This right has now been replaced by appeal to a Special Educational Needs Tribunal.

19 See Chapter Four, pp.113–4.

20 See Chapter Four, p.114 et seq.

as another important forum for the adjudication of disputes concerning disability law. Though tribunals have a long history their growth is inextricably linked to the establishment of the post-war welfare state. Government sought to provide an appropriate forum for the resolution of disputes arising from the administration of the welfare state which was sensitive to the interests of the executive, appropriate for those who would appear before them by being cheap, speedy and informal and largely insulated from the formally legalistic influence of the judiciary (Wade 1988). *The Report of the Committee on Administrative Tribunals and Enquiries 1957*[21] was, however, clear in its conclusion that tribunals should be properly understood as being part of the adjudicative system rather than an adjunct of executive administration. The report specified principles of due process and natural justice by requiring tribunals to be characterised by openness, fairness and impartiality. These themes were legislated for in the Tribunals and Inquiries Act of 1958 and in successive statute, and the tribunal system has since been subject to a process of legalisation and judicialisation.

Nonetheless, there is still some disquiet concerning the quality of justice provided by the tribunal system though criticism may also be taken to reflect the unavailability of legal aid for representation before the majority of tribunals (Lister 1990). If disabled people have disproportionately to rely on tribunals for resolution of disputes concerning claims for disability benefits and services then any claim that they are experiencing and receiving inferior justice should be a cause for concern.

An identification of the wide range of specialist tribunals that hear appeals concerning disability law demonstrates the importance of this system of adjudication for disabled people. Within the social security field disabled people may have appeals heard by Social Security Appeal Tribunals, Disability Appeal Tribunals and Medical Appeal Tribunals. Patients detained under the Mental Health Act 1983 may appeal to a Mental Health Review Tribunal for their release; parents of children with special educational needs may appeal to the Special Educational Needs Tribunal against assessment and statementing decisions by local education authorities. Decisions concerning an application for a vaccine damage payment can be challenged before a Vaccine Damage Tribunal.

Research into the tribunal system has largely centred on Industrial Tribunals and what are now the Social Security Appeal Tribunals. Kathleen Bell in her study *Tribunals in the Welfare State* was critical of the Supplementary Benefit Appeal Tribunals, doubting that they provided machinery within which citizens could exercise their rights more effectively (Bell 1969). More recent research for the Lord Chancellor's Department has highlighted the disadvantaged position of the unrepresented claimant before tribunals, including Social Security Appeal Tribunals.

---

21   Cmnd. 218.

Research...suggests that without the benefit of advice or representation, applicants face considerable obstacles in preparing and presenting their case. In the period before the hearing, there may be difficulties in understanding the stages in the appeal process, and the literature that comes from the tribunal. Without advice about the relevant law, applicants may fail to collect together the information and evidence necessary to establish their case. Most importantly, at the hearing stage unrepresented applicants may have difficulty in getting their story across and in understanding the relevance of regulations and case law; and finally, unrepresented applicants may fail to understand why and how the tribunal have reached their decision. (Genn 1994, p.8)

The difficulties identified by Genn will be exacerbated where the appellant has a learning disability, a sensory disability, or where there are access difficulties. Disabled people may therefore experience added disadvantage though particular tribunal systems are sensitive to these issues, for example Disability Appeal Tribunals can be heard in the home of the disabled appellant.

It is clearly established from tribunal research that the chances of a successful appeal are greatly improved by representation and attendance at the hearing (Lister 1990). Consequently, The Disability Alliance ERA, among others, has identified possible sources of help for disabled appellants in circumstances where traditional legal services are often unavailable. These include law centres, Citizens Advice Bureaux, welfare rights and tribunal representation units (Disability Alliance ERA 1994).

Such practical advice is important and necessary to enable disabled people to make the best use of the tribunal system. However, it may be argued that the absence of legal aid for tribunal representation exacerbates the problems faced by disabled people appearing before tribunals and establishes the necessity for such alternative help. The tribunal system and the welfare state schemes that generate the appeals they decide, have in recent years undergone a process of legalisation and judicialisation (Wikely and Young 1993). Such a development has increased the need for the extension of legal aid to cover representation before tribunals which are increasingly adopting a more judicialised procedure for their hearings and are adjudicating on issues which are now much more often subject to formal legal rules.

There are, however, alternative responses to the challenge posed by such developments. Though the tribunal system is the forum for the establishment of many disability law rights, the inquisitorial and enabling procedure adopted by tribunals may be alien to lawyer advocates trained and experienced in the adversarial method. Equally, disability law expertise is not over-represented in the traditional legal profession. These factors, together with the current legal aid position, have helped to generate a significant number of expert 'welfare rights' workers and representatives who have the appropriate skills for tribunal advocacy. In such a circumstance the call for legal aid to be extended to tribunal representation by lawyers needs to treated with some care. It may be more appropriate to argue for the payment of legal aid to appropriately qualified non-lawyer tribunal representatives or to finance disability law services, including tribunal representation, in some way other than through the use of legal aid to finance what are essentially private legal services.[22]

If disability law rights are to be established and enforced through the use of law, access to the legal system and the availability of legal services are important threshold issues. The established link between disability and poverty indicates that many disabled people are not able to afford the services of a lawyer. In such circumstances access to legal services is provided through the legal aid system and through alternative legal and quasi-legal services developed to facilitate access to the legal system. The availability of such services, particularly that of representation, is important. Research carried out for the Lord Chancellor's Department has established that representation at a tribunal hearing significantly increases the probability that appellants will succeed at their tribunal hearing (Genn and Genn 1989). Given this finding two other conclusions of the report are significant and worrying. There is a very low rate of representation at social security tribunals, excluding family and friends, and where there is representation the probability of a successful appeal rises significantly.

Two particular aspects of the statutory legal aid scheme are of relevance to disability law. The Legal Advice and Assistance Scheme, otherwise known as the green form scheme, provides free advice and assistance on any matter of English law to those people who satisfy very strict financial eligibility tests. The scheme does not extend to paying for representation before tribunals such as Social Security Appeal Tribunals and Disability Appeal Tribunals though it would cover the cost of preparing for a tribunal. The scheme provides for up to two hours of legal preparatory work, though this can be extended. The restricted coverage of the green form scheme is significant given the findings of the research into the impact of tribunal research outlined above (Genn and Genn 1989). Assistance By Way of Representation (ABWOR) provides for free legal representation before Mental Health Review Tribunals for patients detained under the Mental Health Act 1983 who are seeking their release from detention.

The structure and coverage of the legal aid scheme acts as a disincentive to the involvement of the legal profession in work to establish and enforce disability law rights through the tribunal system. Consequently many solicitors will be unfamiliar with disability law in general and with the social security aspects in particular. Expertise born of experience is more readily found in

---

22 Recent proposals from the Lord Chancellor's Department suggest that legal aid funding might be extended beyond the private legal profession to include Citizens' Advice Bureaux and other advice and welfare rights agencies. If these proposals were to be introduced such finance could be used to fund a significant amount of tribunal representation by such agencies (Abraham 1995).

citizens advice bureaux, the law centre movement, welfare rights organisations and the disability pressure groups and charities.

Disability that arises from an accident may lead to an action for damages on the basis that the accident and consequent injury was caused by the negligent actions of another person. Personal injury litigation is an important aspect of the civil law and can be financed by an application for civil legal aid. Such an application will be decided by the Legal Aid Board on the basis of a means test and a 'merits' test.

SUMMARY AND CONCLUSIONS

This section has considered the nature, character and content of disability law. Much of the comment in this chapter implies an acceptance of the legitimacy of a rights-based response to the disadvantage and disempowerment experienced by disabled people. In turn it also accepts the utility of enforceable legal rights as an appropriate medium for such a response. It is therefore necessary to examine the validity and utility of such a law/rights discourse for the disability movement and for individual disabled people, particularly when Gooding contends that: 'the law is not an impartial arbiter, but colludes with, and indeed itself perpetrates, discrimination' (Gooding 1994, p.xvii).

What is the utility of legal rights in the work of the disability movement against disempowerment and discrimination? The claims of law to universality, equality and impartiality underpin arguments for change which utilise enforceable legal rights as the agency of change. Gooding accepts that these characteristics impose a formal legal equality upon situations of structural inequality and acknowledges the consequences:

> I agree that the formal equality model is fundamentally flawed because it does not recognise, or seek to redress structural inequalities. Furthermore, because it fails to do so this model cannot succeed in redressing inequality, and risks compounding the problem by legitimating inequality through its false account of equality. (Gooding 1994, p.32)

In challenging this rather bleak position it is important to identify the important power of the law/rights based discourse for the disability movement. It has been the accepted model of race and gender equality legislation, and legislation is the current focus for the continuing campaign for civil rights for disabled people. In their response to the government's consultation document on measures to tackle discrimination against disabled people The Royal Association for Disability and Rehabilitation (RADAR) identifies the position of the *Committee on Restrictions against Disabled People* (CORAD):

> On balance, anti-discrimination legislation on the grounds of disability would achieve the aim of integrating disabled people into society more effectively and cheaply than any other solution: that its effect in establishing an acceptable norm for the treatment of disabled people, and in bringing into the open arguments in favour of equal rights would have a beneficial effect on public opinion that would

outweigh any antagonism that might result: and that only legislation offers a real opportunity for disabled people to overcome barriers of prejudice and indifference and to take their proper place in society. (Royal Association for Disability and Rehabilitation 1994, p.5)

Though this comment relates to anti-discrimination legislation, its acceptance of the utility of a law/rights discourse is equally applicable to other areas of disability law, particularly where such a discourse is, in a sense, imposed by the existence and administration of current law. Gooding, however, argues that an adoption of a law/rights discourse should not exclude a broader policy or political context to change and may itself be an element of a strategy for policy change (Gooding 1994).

An example of the use of such a strategy is provided by RADAR's campaign concerning section 2 of the Chronically Sick and Disabled Persons Act 1970, which imposes duties on local authorities to provide a number of services for disabled people to facilitate their ability to live in their own homes.

The immediate aim being to ensure that all disabled people receive the services to which they have a statutory right. In the longer term the objective is to clarify once and for all the mandatory nature of Section 2 of the 1970 Act, and to ensure that SSDs (social services departments) are aware of and fulfil their duties under the legislation. (Royal Association for Disability and Rehabilitation 1994, p.2)

The law plays an important role in shaping the everyday life experience of disabled people. If that experience is characterised as disempowering and discriminatory then the nature, substance and operation of the law is an element of that disadvantage. None the less, the rights, powers, duties, benefits and services established by and within the law can be tested by the use of law to seek their definition and enforcement, to improve the individual circumstances of disabled people and as part of the response to and fight against disadvantage.

How, then, are we to assess the politics of the Disability Discrimination Act 1995? The existence of the Act is itself a significant representation of the consequence of the rights discourse and of the symbolic power attached to such rights when they are represented by the specifically legal language of rights and duties utilised in legislation. The Act, and the consultation and parliamentary process leading up to it,[23] presented and continues to present a challenge to the disability movement. The analysis presented by Barnes and Oliver before the Act had been published as a bill, argued for continued political action beyond any legislative programme.

Even fully comprehensive and enforceable civil rights legislation will not, by itself, solve the problem of discrimination against disabled people. This is because, like racism, sexism, heterosexism and other forms of institutional prejudice, discrimination against disabled people is institutionalised in the very fabric of British society. It encompassed direct, indirect and passive discrimination. It has its roots in the very foundations of western culture. It is evident in our abortion

---

23 For further discussion of these debates see Chapter Three, p.77 et seq.

laws, our education system, the labour market, the benefit system, the health and social support services, the built environment – housing, transport and public buildings – the leisure industry, the media, and the political system. (Barnes and Oliver 1995, p.114)

With the Act now on the statute book and with implementation subject to order by the Secretary of State, the politics of disability has to take account of both its existence and its provisions. The tenor of the dominant response to the provisions of the Act, is neatly summarised by the headline above a short review of the legislation in Community Care, 'Too Little Too Late' (1996, p.19). Though the legislation provides nothing like a comprehensive package of civil rights for disabled people it nonetheless represents a partial recognition of the legitimacy of the argument for such rights. Herein lies a dilemma for the disability movement, a dilemma presented not by a universal adoption of a disability rights or law discourse within the movement, but by the fact that the very existence of the legislation established such a discourse at the centre of the debate.

Writing about the demise of the Civil Rights (Disabled Persons) Bill, Barnes and Oliver identify, then analyse the dilemma:

> Our analysis suggests that the achievement of civil rights for disabled people will involve political struggles which go beyond campaigns for legislation. These will include consciousness raising, direct action, the strengthening of democratic and accountable organisations, and the promotion and control of research. They may also involve making political compromises with politicians and governments, and they may require co-operation with non-representative and non-accountable disability organisations. But within the context of the civil rights campaign, it is the other issues which raise key questions and dilemmas for the movement. To get too close to the Government is to risk incorporation and end up carrying out their proposals rather than ours. To move too far away is to risk marginalisation and eventual demise. To collaborate too eagerly with the organisations for disabled people risks having our agendas taken over by them, and having them presented both to us and to politicians as theirs. To remain aloof risks appearing unrealistic and/or unreasonable, and denies possible access to much needed resources. (Barnes and Oliver 1995, p.115)

The implementation of the Act will have far-reaching consequences for disabled people and will inevitably influence the politics of disability and the development of the disability movement. We have already argued for the value of the legal rights discourse. Inevitably this discourse, as represented by the Act, will determine, in part, the everyday experience of many disabled people, and the challenge will be to identify how that experience will continue to be characterised by discrimination and the denial of full civil rights despite the implementation of the Act. Such an analysis should form part of demands for legal, social and political reform and change.

CHAPTER TWO

ENFORCING CIVIL RIGHTS FOR PEOPLE WITH DISABILITIES

The Framework of International Law

In 1981, at the end of the International Year for Disabled Persons, Maria Saulle, the Italian Minister of Foreign Affairs wrote as follows:

> I do not expect, of course, the problems of the disabled to be resolved within one year, but I feel that this special year will help to awaken the awareness of many persons, communities, organisations, etc. about their plight and it will show them the way, and encourage them, to work and fight for the rights of this section of society.

And she did indeed have cause for optimism. A highly successful International Year of campaigns and consciousness raising on disability issues was now to be followed by the United Nations Decade of Disabled Persons to reflect the view of the Secretary General that the plight of disabled people across the globe was the 'world's hidden emergency'.

Despite this new optimism, by 1987, the Mid-Term Evaluation of the UN Decade of Disabled Persons had reported that:

> Very little progress has been made throughout the world, especially in the least developed countries, where disabled people are doubly disadvantaged by economic and social conditions. The situation of many disabled people may indeed have deteriorated in the last five years.[1]

In the next two chapters we will examine in detail the evolution of the civil rights for the disabled movement across the globe over the past 15 years, in order to describe the function and potential of the 'rights' concept, as manifest both through international and domestic (national) law, to provide help and

---

1   Available from United Nations Office in Vienna 1987, cited in DAA 1995, p.3.

support to disabled people in their struggle for equality. In this chapter we focus first on international law.

THE GLOBAL PERSPECTIVE

The concept of *sovereignty* allows every state far-reaching freedom to treat its nationals as it sees fit, unhampered by so called 'universal norms' of international law regarding minimum standards of behaviour. The history of the 20th century is littered with the graveyards of the many millions of people who have suffered the consequences of the abuses of this concept and yet it remains at the heart of constitutional democracy. Notwithstanding the strength of this constitutional doctrine, whose origins are lost deep in the mists of time, global revulsion at the excesses of the destruction unleashed by the second world war by nation states harbouring evil beneath the veil of sovereignty, has enabled the gradual development of a countervailing system of international law seeking to lay down the minimum standards of behaviour that the international community will consider as acceptable in the relations between a state and its citizens. Numerous declarations, conventions, covenants, and protocols have been painstakingly drawn up in a wide range of international fora since 1945, in an attempt to influence nation states to lay down an irreducible minimum of basic human rights their citizens should be entitled to enjoy.

Human rights are both universal and particular, applying in turn both universally, and to specific minorities. In this context it should not be forgotten that, in the words of Theresia Degener: 'Disabled people are the largest minority in the world encompassing more than 500 million people, of which two thirds live in developing countries' (Degener in Degener and Koster-Dreese 1995, p.9; Despouy 1991, p.1).

Disabled people may suffer from an inferior quality of life either because they are not afforded the same benefits that a universal human right affords to those who are not disabled, or because rights which are particular to them, as a minority, are not enforced. The competition between these two positions is intense, but the Secretary General of the United Nations expressed the preferred and more uplifting view in 1992, when he declared that: 'Disabled persons are first and foremost citizens with equal rights and obligations and only secondarily users of social services' (Secretary General UN 1992, para.15).

In this chapter we shall review the range of international law instruments that raise issues relating to the rights of disabled people, and examine the extent of their actual or potential impact in individual 'sovereign' countries, including the United Kingdom.[2] We shall further see how in the case of the countries of

---

2   A number of global studies of this issue have recently emerged. Of particular interest are
     Degener and Koster-Dreese 1995; Gaff 1994, and Human Rights and Equal
     Opportunities Commission 1993.

the European Union, the traditional concept of sovereignty has itself been challenged, as transnational law (in this case, European Union law) has intruded into the domestic laws of the individual states of the Union, and laws have been passed that have called into question the supremacy of state sovereignty, replacing to a significant extent the *sovereignty of the nation state* with the *sovereignty of the European Union.*

Despite the significant developments referred to above, most international lawyers would willingly concede that the framework of international law has in general terms largely failed to find a solution to the problem of the enforcement of the norms that it has managed to lay down through the processes of negotiation and debate. This is not to state that international law is therefore a worthless tool of reform for disabled groups. It is merely to enter a caveat of caution. It remains a fact that in the majority of cases, the protection of human rights through international obligations is only binding on states that have signed the relevant international convention, which can only be a voluntary act. Even when a signature has been obtained, enactment of the terms of the instrument is ultimately a question of political will on the part of the state in question, as a reflection of the wider social and political values operating within that state. It is also the case that an unwillingness to sign an international agreement does not necessarily mean an unwillingness to put its philosophy into practice. Thus, although the United States is only a rare signatory to international conventions and covenants,[3] its record on human rights remains superior to many of the states who jostle across the world's stage to be the first to sign the treaties and conventions that set out the human rights norms that civilised countries are supposed to follow, but do little to uphold these norms.[4]

Notwithstanding the cautionary caveats contained in the above paragraphs, international human rights law nevertheless provides the best framework that we have, within which the debate regarding what constitutes the basic minimum standards of behaviour of the state towards the individual can be conducted, including the place of the rights of the disabled, and furthermore it sets standards against which the conduct of a particular state can be judged. And in certain circumstances, international law can also be used to *enforce* standards within a nation state as will be seen later in this chapter.[5]

---

3   The United States only signed the ICCPR (see p.29) in 1992, and then its signature was
     subject to a number of formal reservations and understandings. At the time of writing it
     has still refused to sign the ICESCR (see p.29).

4   It is worth noting that as of 30 June 1994, 129 countries have ratified the ICESCR,
     including countries that are not obviously identified with enlightened policies regarding
     human rights, such as, for example, Iraq, Croatia, Bosnia Herzegovina, Kenya and
     Rwanda. In these circumstances it is argued by some that signing is of little consequence,
     without a commitment to enforce.

5   See p.30 et seq, p.49 et seq.

Human rights law

Human rights can be generally divided into three categories (normally described as *generations*), as follows:

1. Civil and political rights

   This first *generation* of human rights includes the right to life, the right to freedom of opinion, the right to a fair trial, and the right to protection from torture, slavery and violence. Rooted in the political revolutions of America and France that took place at the end of the 18th century, they found their initial expression in various proclamations of the Rights of Man associated with these revolutions, in particular in the American Declaration of Independence of 1776, in the writings of Tom Paine (Paine 1791), and the French Declaration of the Rights of Man of 1791. Considered by all civilised societies to be fundamental rights, they are also the bundle of rights that are normally described as our basic civil liberties, without which the human condition becomes intolerable. John Rawls, perhaps the most famous of all contemporary human rights philosophers, delimits the scope of first generation rights in the following way: 'Each person is to have an equal right to the most extensive, total system of equal basic liberties compatible with a similar system of liberty for all' (Rawls 1971, p.11).

2. Economic, social and cultural rights

   This second *generation* of human rights reflect the higher aspirations of humankind to a quality of life that justifies the suspension of other personal liberties by handing over to the state the monopoly on the regulation of coercive force, and the power to make laws. The philosophical origins of such a view are to be found in the writings of the 17th century British philosopher, John Locke, who argued that in a civil society citizens, driven by the basic need to protect their lives, their liberties and their property, make a contract with the state to hand over certain powers, such as the use of coercive force, in exchange for the protection of such liberties (Locke 1698). This generation of human rights is less clearly defined than the first generation, but includes the right to work in just and favourable conditions, the right to social protection, the right to an adequate standard of living, the right to the highest possible standards of physical and mental health that a given society can afford, the right to education, the right to enjoy the benefits of cultural freedom and scientific progress and *the right to enjoy all such rights free of discrimination* (our italics).[6] This series of rights is deliberately defined as a *second generation* of rights because on the deepest level of

---

6   ICESCR Article 2 (2).

core human values it could be argued that they are less 'fundamental' to the survival of a civilised society. Conversely, however, it can be argued that the contract upon which the granting by the individual of power and authority to the state is implicitly brought into question, if the state is unable to provide the basic framework at least to develop these rights. For, in the words of the founding fathers of the American Constitution:

> We hold these truths to be self evident, that all men are created equal, that they are endowed by their creator with certain unalienable rights, that among these are life, liberty and the pursuit of happiness, that to secure these rights governments are initiated among men, deriving their just powers from the consent of the governed, and that wherever any form of government becomes destructive of these ends, it is the right of the people to alter or abolish it. (Jefferson 1776)

Disability rights activists should be particularly encouraged to adopt this approach, as it is clear from a reading of the human activities 'protected' by the second generation rights that are set out in the International Covenant on Economic, Social and Cultural Rights (The ICESCR) (see page 29 and Appendix I) that many of them lead to the heart of the issues of the discrimination that is so often articulated by disability rights activists in the language of civil rights (Dredger 1989).

3. Development rights

This third generation of rights is still contested and controversial, and is rooted in the law and development movement. Whilst no mention was made of development rights in the Universal Declaration of Human Rights of 1948, they have played an ever-increasing part in human rights debate in the past 20 years. Contained in this group of rights are the right to peace and security, the right to economic autonomy, and the right to development itself. The attestation of these rights stands uncomfortably in a century in which over 90 million people have died through warfare, in which death by famine, disease and starvation continues to haunt the globe, and in which the spider's web of the economic globalisation movement allows little prospect of economic autonomy to most of the small nations of the world. Despite this, the movement to establish development rights alongside the first and second generation of human rights remains strong and buoyant, and continues to grow apace, against all odds. (See McGoldrick 1991 and Craven 1995)

The development of a philosophy of human rights over the past 300 years is thus real and continuing. But how has the international community set about developing a jurisprudential and thereafter a legal framework through which these rights can be upheld, and, if necessary, enforced?

The work of the United Nations

The starting point for any analysis of the function of international human rights law in the late 20th century must still be the United Nations, and in particular the Universal Declaration of Human Rights (UNDHR), which was adopted by the General Assembly of the United Nations on 10 December 1948, and has remained ever since the touchstone for human rights policy and development. The UNDHR, whilst not legally binding on any state or person, nevertheless retains enormous symbolic force as an agreed statement of, in the words of Eleanor Roosevelt, the 'common standard of achievement for all peoples of all nations.' (Roosevelt 1948). Most of the new constitutions of the world drafted since 1948 contain the tenets of the UNDHR as central to their existence. With the exception of development rights, all of the human rights summarised above are to be found in the body of the UNDHR.

The rights and freedoms contained in the UNDHR have been articulated with even greater precision in subsequent *international covenants*, which are treaties, and which therefore do have legal force in respect of those countries who voluntarily sign the covenant. The two principal covenants in this respect were both drawn up in 1966 and both came into force in 1976. They are as follows:

1. The International Covenant on Civil and Political Rights (ICCPR)

    This covenant is essentially directed towards the upholding of *first generation rights* and imposes obligations upon states, immediately upon ratification by that state in respect of the right to life, liberty, security, equality before the courts, peaceful assembly, marriage and having a family, freedom of association, conscience, thought and religion.

2. The International Covenant on Economic, Social and Cultural Rights (ICESCR)

    This covenant directed towards *second generation rights* obliges contracting parties (i.e. states who ratify the covenant) to take steps to the maximum of their available resources, with a view to achieving progressively the full realisation of the right recognised in the covenant.[7] As it is undoubtedly the more important of the two covenants as far as disability rights are concerned, the full text of the covenant is contained in Appendix I.[8] It includes considerable detail in respect of such things as medical services, employment rights, social security, family protection, child protection, physical and mental health, education and the enjoyment of a common cultural heritage. Most significant of all for our

---

7   ICESCR Article 2(1).

8   For a detailed account of the working of the ICESCR consult Craven 1995.

purposes, it includes the important articulation of *the expectation that all such rights will be exercised without discrimination of any kind as to race, colour, sex, language, religion, political or other opinion, national or social origin, property, birth or other status.* [our italics][9]

The question that arises from the above statement is, can the term 'other status' be deemed specifically to include 'disability'? It is argued by some that the list is exhaustive and therefore the exclusion of the word 'disability' is intentional (see, for example, Bayefsky 1990, p.5 and Klerk 1987). The alternative (and we believe the better) view is that the requirement that rights be exercised 'without discrimination of any kind', clearly applies to discrimination on the grounds of disability, despite the failure explicitly to mention disability on the section of the Article. This view has been explicitly upheld by authority.[10]

Implementation of the covenants

Whilst both covenants remain powerful points of reference for groups cam-paigning to improve the human rights of their particular constituency (and we shall come shortly to the relevance of these various covenants to those campaigning for people with physical or mental disabilities) perhaps the more important question is what sort of implementation machinery and procedures, if any, are attached to these covenants?

Common to both the covenants is a provision that all contracting states (i.e. those who have ratified the treaty, hereafter referred to as State Parties) must submit periodic reports regarding the implementation of the provision of the covenants to the United Nations.

In the case of the ICCPR, the report is to the Human Rights Committee of the United Nations, which is an independent committee of 18 elected repre-sentatives, of 'high moral character and recognised competence in the field of human rights',[11] who study the reports and transmit through the Secretary General of the United Nations 'such *general comments* as they may consider appropriate to the state parties'.

In the case of the ICESCR, the periodic reports are submitted to a direct organ of the United Nations, the Economic and Social Council (ECOSOC), via the Committee on Economic, Social and Cultural Rights, which was created in 1985, with a similar mix of human rights experts as those appointed to the Human Rights Committee,[12] who make similar *general comments* in the light of the reports.

---

9   ICESCR Article 2 (2).
10 See Draft General Comment on Persons with Disabilities, E/C.12/1993/WP.26 at 2, para.5; Standard Rules on the Equalisation of Opportunities for Persons with Disabilities, GA Resnm 48/96 (20 December 1993), 48 UN GAOR, Supp (no.49) (1993) and also Despouy (1991).
11 ICCPR, Article 38 (1) (2).

The procedures for generating and acting upon the *general comments* are still in the process of evolution, but considerable progress has been made in this respect. Commenting on the work of the Committee charged with implementing the ICESCR, Craven writes as follows:

> It is undoubtedly the case that in the relatively short period of time that the Committee on Economic, Social and Cultural Rights has been charged with monitoring the implementation of the Covenant, it has transformed the supervision system beyond recognition. The Committee's work has been marked by a series of procedural reforms, undertaken swiftly and with relative ease, that places it in the position of having one of the most developed and potentially effective reporting mechanisms of all the human rights supervisory bodies. Notably the Committee has undertaken to receive both written and oral information from non-governmental organisations, has adopted the procedure of making State-specific concluding observations following its consideration of State reports, conducts general discussions with experts from other fields and organisations, and drafts general comments to further an understanding of the normative content of the rights in the Covenant and the reporting obligations. (Craven 1995, pp.102–3)

In neither case, however, is the role of the Committee that of a 'court'. i.e. neither Committee is expected to sit in judgement on offending states. Rather,

> It is thought that the Committee should play a facilitative role in assisting States in their realisation of rights, especially through filtering requests for international co-operation and technical assistance, and providing States with advice. *In particular, it has been felt that the Committee should play the role of a catalyst in encouraging States to make it possible for national organisations to participate in the implementation of the rights.* [our italics] (Craven 1995, p.57)

If, for example, a State Party is not yet able to guarantee the upholding of all the rights set out in the relevant covenant at the time of signature, they must undertake the following:

> To take the necessary steps…to…adopt such legislative or other measures as may be necessary to give effect to those rights recognised in the covenant (ICCPR)
>
> AND
>
> To ensure that any person whose rights of freedom (as recognised in the covenant) are violated, shall have an effective remedy (ICCPR)
>
> To take steps *to the maximum of its available resources* (our italics) with a view to achieving progressively the full recognition of the rights recognised in the covenant (ICESCR)

In addition to the above procedures, since 1970, under Resolution 1503, the UN Commission on Human Rights has a further wide power by its own initiative to investigate any complaints that suggest the existence of a consistent pattern of gross and reliably attested violations involving many people over a

---

12   ECOSOC Resolution 1985/17.

long period. It can also from time to time carry out thematic investigations of alleged human rights violations in a country or countries, through its own specially appointed working groups or individual rapporteurs.[13] Under this head it can also test the status of any particular right at any given time.

Related to this right to appoint individual rapporteurs to investigate country specific allegations of violations, the UN also has residual powers to appoint Special Rapporteurs on generic issues, which opportunity it took with respect to disability in 1984 when Leandro Despouy was appointed Special Rapporteur on Human Rights and Disability.[14] The mandate[15] of the Special Rapporteur was: 'To carry out a thorough study of the causal connections between serious violations of human rights and fundamental freedoms and disability, focusing on recommendations and/or progress achieved in remedying that situation.'

The mandate also included a request to make an in-depth analysis of all forms of discrimination against disabled persons, as well as the existing or possible relationship between the system of apartheid and discrimination.

His Final Report was presented in August 1991 and endorsed by the UN Human Rights Committee (Despouy 1991). It demonstrated forcefully that the human rights of disabled people were being systematically and seriously violated in both the generations of human rights supposedly protected by the ICCPR and the ICESCR. It urged that internal (domestic) legislation should be adapted to international norms and guidelines concerning the treatment of disabled people, and that existing international monitoring bodies, such as the Human Rights Committee, and the inter-American Commission on Human Rights, should be more proactive in supervising the implementation of such covenants as the ICCPR, which the Report believed had much to offer in support of the rights of disabled people. It recommended the establishment of non-governmental organizations (NGOs) formed by disabled people or defending their interests. Regrettably, little attention was paid to the findings of the report both within and without the UN.

Application to disability issues

So, in the light of the above outline and the concerns of Despouy, what assistance can those campaigning for the improvement of the right of those

---

13   Under this provision and enquiry into racism and equality laws in the United Kingdom was carried out early in 1995 by the UN special inspector (rapporteur) on racism, Mr Maurice Glegle-Ahanhanzo, who visited Britain for 11 days in order to investigate allegations of widespread and unchecked racism in British society. In principle such an investigation could also be carried out with respect to discrimination on grounds of disability.

14   Appointment made by Sub-Commission on Prevention of Discrimination and Protection of Disability.

15   Commission on Human Rights Resolution 1984/31, Economic and Social Council Resolution 1984/26, Sub Commission Resolution 1984/20.

with disabilities draw from the two principal human rights covenants cited above?

ICCPR

As far as the ICCPR is concerned, probably the most significant clause is contained in Article 26, which guarantees equality of treatment without unfair discrimination:

> All persons are equal before the law and are entitled without any discrimination to the equal protection of the law. In this respect, the law shall prohibit any discrimination and guarantee to all persons equal and effective protection against discrimination on any grounds.

This clause has been described by the UN Human Rights Committee (see above) as a 'free standing guarantee'. Whilst the Human Rights Committee has no enforcement powers it can exert strong moral pressure through the organs of the United Nations, once it has established the existence of serious infringements or violations (see Wadham and Leach 1995). In addition, where a state party signs the Optional Protocol to the ICCPR, it thereby recognises the competence of the Human Rights Committee to receive and consider communications from *any individual* who is subject to the jurisdiction of the state in question. Once the Human Rights Committee has received a complaint under this Protocol, it will first ascertain that the complaint is not already being investigated under another form of international investigation, and that all domestic complaints procedures have been exhausted. Having consulted all parties in question it will then consider the complaint in closed session, and forward its findings to the complainant and to the state in question. At the time of writing however, the British Government has not yet agreed to sign the Optional Protocol, a matter causing concern to human rights groups in the United Kingdom (see Wadham and Leach 1995, Foley 1995).

When we look at the specific rights that the ICCPR sets out to protect and guarantee, a number appear to be of actual or potential relevance to disabled people of which the following are illustrative:

- No-one shall be subjected to torture or to cruel, inhuman or degrading treatment or punishment (Article 7).
- No-one shall be subjected without his free consent to medical or scientific experimentation (Article 7).
- Everyone has a right not to be subjected to arbitrary and unnecessary arrest or any other kind of institutional abuse (Article 9).
- No-one shall be subjected to arbitrary or unlawful interference with his privacy, family, home or correspondence, nor to unlawful attacks on his honour or reputation (Article 17).
- States must recognise the right of men and women of marriageable age to marry and to found a family (Article 23).

- States must recognise the right of everyone to take part in the conduct of public affairs, directly or through freely chosen representatives, to vote, and to have access, on general terms of equality, to public service in their country (Article 25).

ICESCR

The articles of the ICESCR are even more closely identified with potential discrimination on grounds of disability, though the reference in the preamble to 'constraints imposed by resources' provides a let out clause for national governments, that is hard to counter. Notwithstanding the problems generated by this clause, a number of the articles of the ICESCR can be invoked as political lobbying material, to bring pressure to bear on government, by those campaigning for improvements in the lives of people with disabilities. Of central importance to such an approach is Article 3 of the ICESCR whereby all the contracting parties to the Covenant undertake to ensure the equal right of men and women to the enjoyment of all the economic, social and cultural rights set out in the Covenant. It follows that if disabled citizens of a contracting state are prevented from enjoying the same economic, social and cultural rights as able-bodied citizens, that state is *de facto* in breach of the Covenant. Of particular relevance in this respect are the Articles recognizing:

- the right of everyone to just and favourable conditions of work, ensuring a decent living for themselves and their families, and equal opportunity to be promoted to an appropriate higher level (Article 7)
- the right of everyone to the enjoyment of the highest attainable standard of physical and mental health (Article 12)
- that higher education should be made equally accessible to all, on the basis of capacity, by every appropriate means (Article 13)
- the right of everyone to take part in cultural life (Article 15).

Mention has already been made of the key overarching provision, contained in Article 2 (2), namely the expectation that all such rights will be exercised without discrimination of any kind as to race, colour, sex, language, religion, political or other opinion, national or social origin, property, birth *or other status*.

There is currently no equivalent Protocol to that described above under the ICCPR allowing *groups and individuals* to petition the Committee directly with regard to alleged violations of the ICESCR. Such an option does, however, remain under serious consideration, and there is general agreement that such an Optional Protocol would be a beneficial development.[16] Assistance for campaigners for improvements in the rights of people with disabilities can also be found in the pronouncements of the Economic and Social Council (ESC)

---

16   See Konate, E/C.12/1991/SR.13 at 10, para.51; Bonoan-Dandan,
     E/C.12/1991/SR.14, qt 14. para.67 and generally Craven (1995) pp.98–102.

itself, for example, in the 1975 Resolution of the ESC on the prevention of disability and the rehabilitation of disabled persons.[17] More significantly it will be demonstrated below that the wording of subsequent specific UN Declarations regarding the rights of disabled persons, explicitly appears to include disabled persons within the ambit of the fundamental rights guaranteed within the two covenants above.[18]

International conventions

A number of further international conventions – which, like covenants, are treaties which bind those states which sign up to them – have been concluded under the auspices of the United Nations since 1966, each with its own reporting systems, in the wake of the two principal covenants outlined above, to consolidate still further its programme of human rights protection. Of particular note in this regard are the Convention on the Elimination of All Forms of Racial Discrimination (1963), the Convention on the Elimination of All Forms of Discrimination Against Women (1979) and the Convention on the Rights of the Child (1989). Whilst none of these Conventions deals primarily or specifically with discrimination against people with disabilities, each contains articles and provisions that can be implicitly extended to this group. For example, indirect discrimination on grounds of race has been argued to exist in the provisions of the Mental Health Act 1983, allowing police to arrest a member of the public appearing to them to be suffering from a mental disorder in a public place (Mental Health Act 1983, MIND 1993, Cooper 1994, Chapter 5); and the Invalid Care Allowance, paid to people caring full time for disabled relatives or friends was held in its original form to breach the Convention on the Elimination of All Forms of Discrimination Against Women because it excluded from its ambit married women who were caring for a disabled relative (Smith 1986, p.277).

The enforcement procedure attached to the Convention on the Elimination of All Forms of Racial Discrimination is of particular interest, as it allows, in addition to the normal reporting procedures, for an optional system of individual petition whereby an individual or group, can go directly to the relevant Enforcement Committee within the United Nations, a body of 18 independent experts, alleging that their rights guaranteed by the Convention have been violated. This right of individual petition must, however, be accepted by the relevant State party for it to be invocable by an individual or group.[19]

---

17   ESC Resolution 1921 (LVIII) 6 May 1975.

18   See p.36 et seq.

19   For an example of a successful use of individual petition under this convention see
     Yilmaz-Dogan v The Netherlands C.E.R.D. Report, G.A.O.R., 43rd Session, Supp.18,
     p.59 (1988).

The Standard Rules on the Equalisation of Opportunities for Persons with Disabilities (see Appendix II), adopted by the United Nations General Assembly in 1993[20] are perhaps the most promising and significant international expression of standards that can be used by disability rights campaigners to further their cause by putting moral pressure on government to conform to internationally agreed norms. They are dealt with below in more detail.[21]

Declarations

Another form of United Nations activity in its work to strengthen the civil rights of citizens across the globe is the use of the Declaration. Declarations are a device whereby member states of the United Nations General Assembly seek to 'register a consensus of opinion, or a direction in which sentiment is moving' (Nicholas 1975, p.117). They probably represent the Bagehot conception of 'the highest truth that people will bear' and they do not receive any concomitant powers of enforcement (Bagehot 1867). Nevertheless, as instruments of principle they are highly valued and effective tools for argument and persuasion, and it has been noted by more than one commentator that Declarations have often led to treaties.[22] Of special interest in this respect are three particular Declarations, the Declaration on Social Progress and Development which was proclaimed by the General Assembly of the United Nations on 11 December 1969;[23] the Declaration of the Rights of Mentally Retarded Persons which was proclaimed by the General Assembly of the United Nations on 20 December 1971;[24] and the Declaration on the Rights of Disabled Persons which was proclaimed by the General Assembly of the United Nations on 9 December 1975.[25]

1. Declaration on Social Progress and Development

    This important declaration specifically proclaims in Article 11 (c) the necessity of protecting the rights and assuring the welfare of children, the aged and the disabled, and the protection of the physically and mentally disadvantaged.

---

20   Resolution 48/96 20 December 1993.
21   See p.41 et seq.
22   Newman, for example (Degener and Koster-Dreese 1995, p.5) has noted the preambular paragraphs in the Two Covenants, and the UN's Racial, Women's, Children's and Torture Treaties. He also suggests that 'experience in monitoring the UN's 1993 Equalisation Rules for the Disabled may well lead to a consensus that additional treaty law is needed' *ibid.*
23   Resolution 2542 (XXIV).
24   Resolution 2856 (XXVI).
25   UN Resolution 3447 (XXX).

2. Declaration of the Rights of Mentally Retarded Persons

This declaration makes a number of important statements regarding 'mentally retarded persons' (i.e. those with learning disabilities):

> The mentally retarded person has, to the maximum degree of feasibility, the same rights as other human beings (Article 1); a right to proper medical care and physical therapy and to such education, training, rehabilitation and guidance as will enable him or her to develop his ability and maximum potential (Article 2); a right to economic security and to a decent standard of living (Article 3); a right to perform productive work or to engage in any other meaningful occupation to the fullest possible extent of his capabilities (Article 3); wherever possible, he or she shall live with his or her own family or with foster parents and participate in different forms of community life (Article 4); the family with which he or she lives should receive assistance (Article 4); if care in an institution becomes necessary, it should be provided in surroundings and circumstances as close as possible to those of normal life (Article 4); the right to a qualified guardian when this is required to protect his or her personal well-being and interests (Article 5); the right to protection from exploitation, abuse and degrading treatment (Article 6); if prosecuted for any offence the right to due process of law with full recognition being given to his or her degree of mental responsibility (Article 6); if restriction of freedom becomes necessary, the procedures used must contain proper legal safeguards against every form of abuse, must be based upon an evaluation of the social capability of the person by qualified experts, and must be subject to periodic review and to the right of appeal to higher authorities. (Article 7)

3. Declaration on the Rights of Disabled Persons

This is a very important point of reference for disability rights campaigners who are seeking a statement of the general principles of decency and protection that international law expects of nation states in the policies and attitudes they adopt towards their citizens with mental or physical disabilities. As explained above a Declaration is *not* a legally enforceable document, but it is a statement with powerful moral, ethical and political weight. It contains a range of clear statements of right and principle providing a blueprint for any civilised society in this respect. What is astonishing is that this Declaration appears to have been so little used, to date, by campaigners both in the United Kingdom and abroad. After the normal caveat regarding 'limited resources,'[26] the Declaration calls for national and international action to ensure that it will be used as a common basis and frame of reference for the protection of the rights it goes on to proclaim. After a preliminary definitional paragraph,[27] the

---

26 As with all the second generation declarations, a recognition that these rights require resources as well as commitment is always contained in the preamble, thus in this case we find the phrase, 'aware that certain countries, at their present stage of development, can devote only limited efforts to this end'.

27 For general problems of definition see Chapter One.

Declaration sets out in 12 powerful paragraphs a statement of the rights of disabled persons defining what should be the norms of a civilised society for the remainder of the century and beyond. Not only does the Declaration set out the norms, it also clearly links disability with the fundamental first and second generation rights guaranteed in the two Covenants described above, and thus strengthens the case for their enforcement through the reporting and monitoring procedures associated with those Covenants.

Thus the Declaration states that disabled persons:

- Have the inherent right to respect for their human dignity, defined as first and foremost the right to enjoy a decent life, as normal and full as possible.
- Have the same civil and political rights as other human beings.
- Are entitled to the measures designed to enable them to become as self-reliant as possible.
- Have the right to medical, psychological and functional treatment, including prosthetic and orthotic appliances, to medical and social rehabilitation, education, vocational training and rehabilitation, aid, counselling, placement services and other services which will enable them to develop their capabilities and skills to the maximum and will hasten the process of their social integration or reintegration.
- Have the right to economic and social security and to a decent level of living.
- Have the right, according to their capabilities, to secure and retain employment or to engage in a useful, productive and remunerative occupation, and to join trade unions.
- Are entitled to have their special needs taken into consideration at all stages of economic and social planning.
- Have the right to live with their families or with foster parents and to participate in all social, creative or recreational activities. No disabled person shall be subjected, as far as his or her residence is concerned, to differential treatment other than that required by his or her condition or by the improvement that he or she may derive therefrom. If the stay of a disabled person in a specialised establishment is indispensable, the environment and living conditions therein shall be as close as possible to the normal life of a person of his or her age.
- Shall be protected against all exploitation, all regulations and all treatment of a discriminatory, abusive or degrading nature.
- Shall be able to avail themselves of qualified legal aid when such aid proves indispensable for the protection of their persons and property. If judicial proceedings are instituted against them, the legal procedure applied shall take their physical and mental condition fully into account.
- Shall (together with their families and communities) be fully informed by all appropriate means, of the rights contained in this Declaration.

International years, days and summits
International years

International years provide for a sustained programme of action directed towards longer term outcomes. They also have the particular advantage of directly enabling the participation of disabled people in activities and campaigns that raise awareness and influence policy. 1981 was the International Year of Disabled Persons, which was followed by a decade of activities directed towards disabled people. One of the long-term outcomes of this designation was the World Programme of Action concerning Disabled Persons, adopted by the General Assembly of the United Nations in 1982.[28] This programme specifically exhorted governments to

> actively seek out and encourage in every possible way the development of organisations composed of or representing disabled persons...establish direct contacts with such organisations, and provide channels for them to influence government policies and decisions in all areas that concern them.

Although it is ECOSOC that has formal responsibility for the social and economic work of the United Nations, and its work on disability is subsumed under this head, much of the work in this field has been devolved to the Centre for Social Development and Humanitarian Affairs, based in Vienna.[29] The United Nations Disabled Persons Unit was based for a long time in this Centre.[30] This Unit has a number of important functions including the organisation of a programme of technical co-operation activities, advisory services to governments, and management of the Voluntary Fund for the UN Decade of Disabled Persons, which ran from 1983 until 1992.[31] It also carries out research on disability issues and produces a number of manuals, guidelines, policy documents and information sheets, including its own *Disabled Persons Bulletin*.

International days

Another awareness raising mechanism utilised by the United Nations and other international organisations is the use of the *special day*. At the end of the United Nations Decade of Disabled Persons (1983–1992) the General Assembly proclaimed that 3 December should be observed each year as the International

---

28 Resolution A/37/52, 3 December 1982.

29 UN Office at Vienna, Vienna International Centre, Room E 1323, PO Box 500, A-1400, Vienna, Austria.

30 The current address of the United Nations Disabled Persons' Unit is c/o the Department for Policy Co-ordination and Sustainable Development, UN, Room DC2–1302, New York, NY 10017.

31 The UN Decade of Disabled Persons officially ended in April 1992 at the 3rd World Congress of Disabled Persons' International, which was held in Vancouver, Canada from 21–26 April. Major contributions to this Congress are documented in *Equalisation of Opportunities*, Proceedings of the World Congress.

Day of Disabled Persons, to be organised by the UN Commission for Social Development. Proclamation of the Day has three purposes:[32]

- To commemorate the anniversary of the adoption by the General Assembly of the World Programme of Action concerning disabled persons.

- To ensure continued promotion of disability issues beyond the United Nations Decade of Disabled Persons and to further the integration into society of persons with disabilities.

- To promote increased awareness among the population regarding gains to be derived by individuals and society from the integration of disabled persons in every aspect of social, economic and political life.

Various methods have been used to bring this idea to the attention of member states outside the forum of the General Assembly, including the creation (within the European Union) of the European Disabled Persons' Parliament, and a resolution by the UN Commission on Human Rights which 'appealed to member states to highlight the observance of the International Day, with a view to the achievement of the full and equal enjoyment of human rights and participation in society by persons with disabilities'. Backing up this resolution, the Secretary General wrote to the ambassadors of all member states on 4 March 1994, in the following terms:

> The Secretary General is requested in resolution 48/97 to report to the Commission for Social Development, at its 34th Session, on measures taken by Member States to observe the International Day of Disabled Persons. The Secretary General would be grateful if His/Her Excellency would advise him of the measures taken to observe the International Day, by 16 December 1994, in order that the information be included in the report of the Secretary General to the 34th session of the Commission for Social Development.

In April 1995, the Secretary General published his Report, which monitored international plans and programmes of action arising from the International Day.[33] A huge number of events had taken place at locations across the globe. Central to these events was the publication on 3 December 1994 through the European Parliament of the *Report of the Human Rights Meeting* which had taken place two months previously at the European Parliament Building in Brussels.[34] At this meeting an important debate had taken place between 24 European and national disabled people's organisations[35] on the four key topics of:

---

32 Resolution 1992/47/3; Resolution 48/97; Resolution 1993/29; Resolution 48/97.

33 Report of the Secretary General on Monitoring of International Plans and Programmes of Action.

34 Published by the Disabled Peoples' International, for the Disability Forum, as *The Report of the Human Rights Plenary Meeting*, Rapporteur Paul Fagan, Editor Julie Marchbank.

35 A full list of the participants at this important gathering is available from Disability Awareness in Action.

- defining disability
- bio-ethics, eugenics and euthanasia
- independent living
- sexuality.

The Report was the focus of discussions on the International Day in a number of countries including the United Kingdom, where it was presented by the British Council of Organisations of Disabled People to the All-Party Disablement Group, and in France where it was presented to the Parliamentary Intergroup on Disability.[36] Elsewhere programmes of activities in support of disabled people and their organisations were recorded as far afield as Bahrain, Burkina Faso, Cameroon, Congo, Cyprus, Germany, Guinea, Kenya, Mauritius, Morocco, Netherlands, Norway, Pakistan, South Africa, Saint Lucia, Switzerland, Syrian Arab Republic, Turkey, United Republic of Tanzania, Uganda, and the United States of America. The Report concluded as follows:[37]

> Information received suggests that both Governments and organisations of disabled persons have benefited from the opportunity to mark the International Day and promote the World Programme of Action concerning Disabled Persons and Disabilities. The expanded role being played by non-governmental organisations is of note, particularly that of organisations of disabled persons, in furthering the objectives of the World Programme of Action and wide dissemination of the Standard Rules.[38]

An equally eclectic range of events took place on the same day a year later in 1995, with a new set of countries entering the global community of observers, including Barbados, Chile, China, Romania, Singapore, Sri Lanka, Sudan, Taiwan, and Zimbabwe.[39] The most important outcome of the 1995 event in Brussels was the publication of a powerful document entitled *Invisible Citizens* (Secretariat of European Day of Disabled People 1995), which reveals the extent to which the rights and status of disabled people have been left out of European Treaties and argues the case for amends to be made in this respect in the revised Maastricht Treaty that is likely to result from the European Union Intergovernmental Conference due to take place in 1996 (Waddington 1995).

The standard rules

One of the most important outcomes of all this activity has been the adoption by the United Nations of the Standard Rules on the Equalisation of Opportunities for Persons with Disabilities (see Appendix II). Commenting on the status of the Rules, the pressure group, Disability Awareness in Action (DAA) observed as follows (DAA 1995):

---

36 *Disability Awareness in Action Newsletter 23* January 1995, p.1.
37 Supra fn.34, p.13.
38 Report of the Human Rights Plenary Meeting supra fn.34.
39 *Disability Awareness in Action Newsletter 33*, p.5.

Although States cannot legally be forced to carry them out, the Rules should become an accepted standard internationally when they are used by a large number of States. They offer an international instrument with a monitoring system to help make sure the Rules are effective. There is more detailed guidance than ever before to what is needed. They require a strong political and practical commitment by States to take action for equalisation of opportunities for disabled people.

Indeed, it would be possible to go further still and argue that if the Rules are applied by a large number of states with the intention of respecting them as rules in international law, they will become part of what is generally described as international customary law, i.e general principles of law recognised by civilised nations (Newman 1995, p.5 fn.3).

The international monitoring of the implementation of the Rules will be co-ordinated through the United Nations Commission for Social Development. The first Special Rapporteur charged with developing a monitoring mechanism is Bengt Lindqvist, a visually impaired, Swedish ex-minister for Social Services who has been an active disability rights campaigner for many years.[40] He will be advised and guided by a Panel of Experts (10 in total) two each from Disabled Peoples' International (DPI), the International Leagues of Societies for Persons with Mental Handicap (ILSMH), the World Blind Union (WBU) and the World Federation of the Deaf (WFD), and one each from Rehabilitation International and the World Federation of Psychiatric Users.[41]

The Rules are grounded on the belief that equal participation of disabled people in society is only possible where the following four pre-conditions are met:

Rule 1: States should take action to raise awareness in society about persons with disabilities, their rights, their needs, their potential and their contribution.

Rule 2: States should ensure the provision of effective medical care to persons with disabilities.

Rule 3: States should ensure the provision of rehabilitation services to persons with disabilities in order for them to reach and sustain their optimum level of independence and functioning.

Rule 4: States should ensure the development and supply of support services, including assistive devices for persons with disabilities, to assist them to increase their level of independence in their daily living and to exercise their rights.

---

40   Special Rapporteur of the Commission for Social Development on Disability, Swedish
     Parliament, S-100 12 Stockholm, Sweden.
41   The key organisations can be contacted at the following addresses:
         DPI, 101–7 Evergreen, Winnipeg, R3L, 2T3, Canada
         ILSMH, Galeries de la Toison d'Or, 29 Chaussee d'Ixelles, #393/35, 1050
         Bruxelles, Belgium.
         WBU, Secretariat, 58 Avenue Bosquet, 75007 Paris, France.
         WFD, PO Box 65, SF-00401 Helsinki, Finland.

The Rules go on to identify eight target areas of life in which principles of equality regarding those with disabilities ought to be concentrated. The eight areas are:

Accessibility, Education, Employment, Income Maintenance and Social Security, Family Life and Personal Integrity, Culture, Recreation and Sports, and Religion.

Finally, the Rules outline a variety of processes through which such equality can be achieved, including legislation, policy making and planning, the dissemination of more detailed information and research, personnel training, national monitoring systems, greater recognition of the role of disabled persons' organisations, and greater international co-operation.

International summits

Another very effective forum for debate, consciousness raising and collaboration on disability issues between states and organisations across frontiers is the International Summit. The World Summit on Social Development, held in Copenhagen in March 1995 was one such example. Summits of this nature require a long and detailed planning process that affords the time for pressure groups to carry out extensive lobbying to ensure the maximum negotiable space for promoting their cause at the Summit. Thus, a variety of pressure groups and NGOs associated with disability, finding themselves unhappy with the lack of space afforded to disability issues by the early stage planners of the 1995 summit, lobbied the United Nations directly, with a view to raising the profile of disability issues at the Summit. At the Summit planning meeting in New York, in August 1994, the groups agreed that disability should have a higher visibility at the Summit than was at that stage being proposed in the Draft Declaration and Programme of Action being prepared for the Summit. Consequently the group submitted to the drafting committee for the Summit, the following statement:[42]

> The disability international non-governmental organisations know from the direct experience of their members that disabled people are the poorest of the poor-segregated and isolated in their communities. The three core issues of the Social Summit (alleviation of poverty, integration and employment) are particularly relevant to disabled people everywhere. Disabled people demand that the Summit addresses their needs. Disabled people are a significant proportion of every group in the world. The resulting experience of discrimination and oppression makes it imperative that disabled people are included wherever there is reference to marginalised, disadvantaged or impoverished people. There should also be particular recognition of disabled people's experience of social apartheid,

---

42 *Disability Awareness in Action (DAA) Newsletter 20*, September 1994, p.1. The statement was 'respectfully submitted by Disabled People's International, the International Council for the Education of People with Visual Impairment, the International League of Societies for Persons with Mental Handicap, the Nordic Council of Disabled People, Rehabilitation International, the World Blind Union and the World Federation of the Deaf'.

the exciting solutions that disabled people have found for themselves and the monitoring and evaluation mechanisms put in place by the UN itself in the Standard Rules on the Equalisation of Opportunities for People with Disabilities, which were declared by the General Assembly in 1993 by way of an international instrument which though not compulsory set out a strong moral and political case for states to ensure the equalisation of opportunities for those with disabilities into the 21st century.

The Summit duly took place, but most disability rights activists who attended were disappointed by the level of awareness of disability issues. One commentator, for example, wrote as follows after the Summit: 'It could have been a wonderful opportunity for dramatic change, but, as usual, the dynamics of politics ensured that very little happened.'[43]

There was, however, an important policy statement made to the Summit at the Plenary meeting by Liisa Kauppinen, General Secretary of the World Federation of the Deaf, on behalf of the international grouping of disability non-governmental organisations (NGOs), which is set out below in full:[44]

According to the United Nations, one person in ten has a disability and all of us will be affected by disability for a shorter or longer period at some time in our lives. Today, I am speaking on behalf of all organisations of disabled people represented at this global event. We are people first, and only secondly do we have a disability. We reject the label of 'vulnerable' as it appears in the documents of the Summit; we are fellow citizens, with equal rights and responsibilities. What makes us disadvantaged are the obstacles we face in society and its physical, social, economic, cultural and political structures. We look to this Summit to break down the barriers to our full participation and equality.

All the themes of this Summit are highly relevant to us. We are the poorest of the poor in most societies. Disability increases poverty and poverty increases disability. It is women who bear a particular burden of poverty, both as carers and as disabled persons. Two thirds of disabled people are estimated to be without employment. Social exclusions and isolation are the day-to-day experiences of disabled persons. Too many must live in institutions. We cannot and we will not tolerate such conditions any longer. Disabled people must be included in the decisions, and above all, in the follow-up of the implementation of the plan of action this Summit.

Every paragraph and every sentence of the International Human Rights Conventions and other legal instruments apply to disabled people as well as to non-disabled people. But now we also have the United Nations Standard Rules on the Equalisation of Opportunities for Persons with Disabilities. The Special Rapporteur, Mr Bengt Lindqvist, has written to all governments asking some basic questions about their policy towards the Standard Rules. So far, only 15 governments have responded. The disability NGOs call on every government

---

43 Quotation from Rachel Hurst, Project Director, Disability Awareness in Action, quoted in *Newsletter 25*, p.1.

44 Statement to Copenhagen Summit on Behalf of World Federation of the Deaf, the World Blind Union, the International League of Societies for Persons with Mental Handicap, Rehabilitation International, and Disabled Peoples' International.

representative here to support the full implementation of the Standard Rules in their country.

Governments need their national NGOs in working for a better future for disabled people. Governments also need to ensure that a percentage of their development funding goes to grassroots projects empowering disabled people. The United Nations needs the international NGOs. It is the NGOs that work at the grassroots, with people, with public authorities and with the United Nations to create a better life for disabled people and to realise the goals of this Summit. We, disabled people ourselves, need to be empowered to combat poverty, unemployment and social exclusion. The United Nations itself must set a better example: it could employ many more qualified disabled people; it could provide better access to United nations meetings; it could provide documentation in Braille or on tape; it could recognise Sign Language as an official UN language.

Ladies and gentlemen, only as equals can we, disabled people, contribute our full potential to social development. Equal opportunities can only be realised if society adapts itself to the diversity of its members. A society good for disabled people is a better society for all.

One of the more positive outcomes of the Summit was the publication of the UNESCO sponsored report *Overcoming Obstacles to the Integration of Disabled People.*[45] The report concludes that despite considerable national developments of this nature (DAA 1995A)[46]: 'There are few long-term improvements to the horrifying statistics of discrimination, poverty and isolation.'

It does, however, set out a number of practical agendas, stressing the vital importance of including disabled people themselves in the forefront of campaigns to improve their situation:[47]

- Disabled people must be fully involved in the conceptualisation, analysis and discussion of solutions and in the development of policies and programmes.

- There must be adequate funding of organisations of disabled people.

- Legal frameworks should be created to support disabled people's equal rights and integration into mainstream policies, rather than perpetuating the restrictive concepts of income maintenance and segregated services.

- Disabled people should be part of all development and empowerment policies and programmes, in addition to specifically targeted programmes, receiving an appropriate share of all resources.

United Nations agencies

In their 1995 report to the World Summit on Social Development in Copenhagen, the pressure group Disability Awareness in Action reflected on the UN agencies in the following terms (DAA 1995A, at 35):

---

45   Published by and available from Disability Awareness in Action ISBN 1 898037 15 9.
46   Report p.77.
47   *ibid.* p.77–8.

The United Nations agencies have played a substantial role in the international disability field. Throughout the Decade, annual inter-agency meetings allowed discussion of policy and programmes between the agencies and the international non-governmental organisations related to disability. These meetings raised the priority of disability programmes within the agencies and stimulated action. The exchange of information and the networking that took place were as valuable as many of the programmes themselves. indeed, it is regrettable that these meetings have been discontinued. The agencies have also produced important international instruments in specific areas.

The most important UN agencies for these purposes are probably the ILO (International Labour Organisation), UNESCO (The United Nations Educational, Scientific and Cultural Organisation) and the WHO (World Health Organisation).

The International Labour Organisation (ILO)[48]

In 1991, The UN Special Rapporteur on Disability, wrote of the ILO in the following terms (Despouy 1991, p.11 para.50):

> Since its establishment over 70 years ago, the ILO has never ceased to advocate that disabled persons, whatever the cause or nature of their disability, should be afforded every opportunity for vocational rehabilitation, including vocational guidance, training or readaptation as well as opportunities for employment, whether open or under sheltered conditions.

Thus, whilst the term 'human rights' does not appear in the ILO Constitution (see generally ILO 1968), it has nevertheless been one of the few specialised UN organisations which has adopted a specific profile on human rights within the sphere of its activity, primarily labour and employment. This profile has been manifest in particular through its Conventions.

1. **Convention 111 Concerning Discrimination in Respect of Employment and Occupation.**
   This Convention was adopted by the ILO in 1958, and came into force in 1960.

   Under this Convention a ratifying country undertakes to declare and pursue a national policy designed to promote, by methods appropriate to national conditions and practice, equality of opportunity and treatment in respect of employment and occupation, with a view to eliminating any discrimination in respect thereof.[49]

   The United Kingdom has not ratified this Convention.

2. **Convention 142 Concerning Vocational Guidance and Vocational Training in the Development of Human Resources.**
   This Convention was adopted by the ILO in 1975 and came into force

---

48   International Labour Organisation, 4 Route des Morillons, CH-1211, Geneva 27,
     Switzerland.
49   Article 2.

in 1977. Under this Convention a ratifying country agrees to establish and develop open, flexible and complementary systems of general, technical and vocational education, educational and vocational guidance and vocational training, whether these activities take place within the formal education system, or outside it.[50]

The United Kingdom has ratified this Convention.

3. **Convention 159 Concerning Vocational Rehabilitation and Employment (disabled Persons) and Recommendation no.168.**
    This Convention was adopted by the ILO in 1983 and came into force in 1985. Under the Convention a ratifying country agrees to adopt a national policy on vocational rehabilitation and employment of disabled persons, not only in specialised institutions and sheltered workshops, but alongside non-disabled people in mainstream training centres and in open employment, to put such a policy into action and regularly to review and monitor its implementation.[51] This Convention was of particular importance during the UN Decade of Disabled Persons, that has already been referred to above.[52] A number of projects were set up at this time under the auspices of the ILO, aimed at the 'deinstitutionalisation, mainstreaming and normalisation of disabled persons within the labour market' (Degener 1995, p.21) particularly in Africa and Indonesia (Momm and Konig 1989; Stace 1987).

The United Kingdom has not ratified this Convention.

The United Nations Educational, Scientific and Cultural Organisation (UNESCO)

The primary concern of UNESCO is the promotion and protection of cultural rights. According to its Constitution,[53] the purpose of UNESCO is:

> To contribute to peace and security by promoting collaboration among the nations through education, science and culture in order to further universal respect for justice, for the rule of law and for the human rights and fundamental freedoms which are affirmed for the peoples of the world, without distinction of race, sex, language or religion, by the Charter of the United Nations.

CONVENTION AGAINST DISCRIMINATION IN EDUCATION

This Convention was adopted by UNESCO another important UN agency in 1960 by the General Conference of the UN Educational, Scientific and Cultural Organisation and came into force in 1962.

---

50 Article 2.
51 For an account of the history of this Convention and Recommendation and a discussion on ways in which it might be implemented see ILO 1992.
52 Supra p.39.
53 Article 1.

The Convention reformulates the UNDHR statement that: 'discrimination in education is a violation of the right of every person to education' and declares that 'discrimination in education includes depriving any person or group of persons of access to education of any type or at any level...or limiting any person or group of persons to education of an inferior standard...or inflicting on any person or group of persons conditions which are incompatible with the dignity of man.'[54]

It has been ratified by the United Kingdom.

The World Health Organisation (WHO)

Although the WHO has been criticised for failing to define health as an international human right (Leary 1993), it nevertheless is appropriate to include it in a review of the various international bodies that can play a part in engaging the international community in a rights-based discourse concerning disability. As the primary role of the WHO is the exchange of information and knowledge with regard to health matters (public and private), it will come as no surprise that the WHO is associated primarily with the 'medical model' definition of disability.[55] As a consequence, the resolutions and reports of the policy-making organs of the WHO have in recent years referred to only two solutions to disability, rehabilitation or prevention.[56] More promising, however, was the publication in 1990 of a report sponsored by WHO-Europe, on health and social legislation for disabled persons in 25 European Countries, which presents a far more progressive picture in those countries of a shift of emphasis away from the 'medical model' towards a human rights issue (Pinet 1990). Finally, reference should be made to the WHO Declaration of Alma Ata in 1978, which recognised the right to health for all, and the importance of promoting community-based projects.

THE EUROPEAN PERSPECTIVE

Within Europe, a further tranche of transnational law operates to set norms, and create enforcement procedures designed to guarantee the fundamental human rights of individual citizens. There are essentially two transnational law enforcement systems operating in the continent of Europe, over and above the global framework of international human rights law outlined earlier in the chapter. The first system is the manifestation of the work of the Council of Europe, through the European Convention for the Protection of Human Rights and Fundamental Rights, which is enforced through the European Commission and

---

54 Article 1.
55 See generally Chapter One, especially pp.3–5.
56 WHO Resolution WHA 42.28, 19 May 1989; WHO Report EB89/15 and 9 December 1991; WHO Resolution EB89.R7, 27 January 1992; Report A45/6, 10 April 1992; WHO Resolution WHA 45.10, 11 May 1992

Court of Human Rights in Strasbourg. The second system is one of the manifestations of the European Union, whose overarching system of laws and procedures operates within each of the legal systems of the Union, and is ultimately enforceable via the European Court of Justice in Luxembourg. In addition to these two formal systems of regulation and advancement, there are a number of informal or semi-formal organisations that also offer some kind of quasi-legal or strong lobbying function at the centres of political power. For example, since December 1993, a shadow European Parliament has been in existence, known as the European Disabled People's Parliament,[57] which has an increasingly powerful and effective function in bringing disabled people's perspectives to the attention of members of the European Parliament and officials of the European Union.

Let us begin with an examination of the two official law enforcement systems, and examine each of these in turn.

1. European Convention on Human Rights and Fundamental Rights (ECHR)

The Council of Europe is an inter-governmental organisation established after the Second World War, with 10 original members (now 27 and likely to rise to 39 during 1996) in response to the international political, social, economic, and ethnic traumas unleashed on the continent of Europe by that war (Robertson and Merrills 1993). The aim of those establishing the Council of Europe was 'to safeguard and realise ideals and principles of common heritage and to facilitate economic and social progress' (Wallace 1992, p.206). Whatever its original intentions may have been, the work of the Council is now devoted almost exclusively to the operation of the system of human rights enforcement whose principles find their expression in the ECHR, which was created by the State Parties in 1950, and came into force in 1953. When the foreign ministers of the member States of the Council met to sign the treaty creating the ECHR their aim was to lay the foundations for the new Europe which they hoped to build on the 'ruins of a continent ravaged by a fratricidal war of unparalleled atrocity' (Robertson and Merrill, p.1).

The ECHR sets out a number of human rights which its parent body, the European Commission on Human Rights (The Commission)[58] is dedicated to uphold amongst all the contracting states of the Council of Europe. These rights are primarily in the category of 'first generation rights,'[59] and closely mirror those set out in the ICCPR. Thus, the ECHR guarantees:

---

57 See supra p.54.

58 Under the existing arrangements the function of the Commission is, in the first instance, to endeavour to settle any dispute that is referred to it, by a process of conciliation. Only if conciliation fails is there the possibility of a referral to the Court.

59 See supra p.27.

- the right to life
- freedom from torture, inhuman or degrading treatment and punishment
- freedom from slavery and forced labour
- the right to liberty, security of persons and freedom from detention, except by due process of law
- the right to fair administration of justice
- respect for privacy and private life, home and correspondence
- freedom of thought, conscience and religion
- freedom of expression and opinion
- the right to peaceful assembly and association
- the right to marry and found a family
- the right to an effective remedy when a right or a freedom has been violated
- the right to enjoy all the above rights and freedoms without discrimination on any grounds.

This last right is of particular interest for our purposes, because although it does not specifically mention discrimination on grounds of disability, its use of the phrase 'any discrimination' implicitly includes such discrimination.[60]

This list of rights has been added to by a series of Protocols. Thus Protocol 1 includes a right to property, a right to vote and rights in respect of education. Protocol 6 (which the United Kingdom has not agreed to) abolishes capital punishment.

Article 25 of the ECHR enables any state party to recognise the jurisdiction of the Commission to examine petitions from either individuals or groups from that state alleging the state to be in contravention of the convention. Thus, the right of an individual/group to petition the ECHR, in addition to the right of a state to do so, is specifically recognised. Although the United Kingdom has recognised this right since January 1966, the fact remains that at present the ECHR has no *direct* effect on English law, as it has not been directly incorporated into domestic law by legislation.

If an individual wishes to assert a breach of the Convention, they have to do so via the European Commission on Human Rights in Strasbourg. Even though legal aid is not available directly through the UK system to support such an application, the Commission does run its own financial support scheme.[61] A favourable result may then lead to a change on English law to reflect the ruling. This is because the United Kingdom government, in the name of the Crown, is a signatory to the Convention, and as such has agreed to ensure

---

60   The actual phrase incorporated into the Convention is 'discrimination on any ground...such as sex, race, colour, language, religion, political or other opinion, national or social origin, association with a national minority, property or other status'.

61   Legal Aid Handbook Notes for Guidance 1995 para.19.01 at 171. London: Legal Aid Board.

that the rights expressed in the Convention are effectively protected by the law of the United Kingdom. If the Court of Human Rights finds that United Kingdom law is failing to protect the Convention rights then the government is required to seek an Act of Parliament to change the law. The procedure is, however, slow, cumbersome and lengthy. Furthermore, although the Convention may also influence the way in which the United Kingdom courts interpret existing statutes, and supervise administrative decisions and actions, the British courts have made it plain that if an Act of their own Parliament is entirely clear in its meaning, it will be enforced even if that meaning is inconsistent with the Convention.[62] The problems generated by the UK government's unwillingness to accept the ECHR as part of our domestic law[63] may soon be alleviated, however, by virtue of the impact of European Union law, discussed below.

The ECHR has three levels of enforcement machinery, the Commission, the Court and the Committee of Ministers. Most of the detailed enforcement work is carried out by the first two bodies, the third body being the executive (political) organ of the Council of Europe, composed of a government minister from each of the contracting states. Under Convention procedures either a contracting state, or an individual, or a group of individuals, or an NGO, may petition the Commission claiming a breach of the ECHR, so long as they have exhausted all available domestic remedies (e.g. court proceedings, appeal hearings, grievance procedures, administrative processes and so forth). The Commission will then rule as to whether the application is admissible, in accordance with its Rules of Procedure, under the terms of the ECHR, i.e. whether it reveals a *prima facie* breach of the Convention, and the breach is actionable under its terms. No appeal lies against this preliminary ruling by the Commission. If the Commission rules that the application is admissible, it will then investigate the allegations, and must seek to reconcile the parties. All these stages of the procedure are held in private. If conciliation does not succeed, the Commission will report its findings to the Committee of Ministers, who will decide by a two thirds majority whether a breach has occurred. Alternatively, within three months of the report being submitted to the Committee of Ministers, either the Commission or the relevant state may refer the matter to the European Court of Human Rights, for a final ruling, which will adjudicate accordingly. Individuals cannot refer cases themselves to the European Court. The Court will consist of a chamber of nine judges. Decisions of the Court are binding on the states concerned, and must be enforced. However, with the very considerable increase in the work of the Strasbourg institutions in the last fifteen years, the system has become subject to severe delays. Protocol 11, which is

---

62   See Brind v Secretary of State for the Home Department (1991) 1 AC 696.

63   The great majority of contracting states have now incorporated the Convention directly into their domestic law, which means that it can be invoked and enforced in domestic courts without reference to Strasbourg.

now open to signature, will reform the procedure. In particular the Commission is to be abolished, and replaced by an expanded Court, which will be organised into specialist sections who will deal with most aspects of each case independently.

2. The European Union

Since 1972[64] the United Kingdom has been a member state of the European Community, now constituted as the European Union. One consequence of such membership is that community law takes precedence over domestic law, and thus any legal right enshrined in the law of the European Union is enforceable in the domestic courts of each member state, including the United Kingdom, which must also provide an appropriate remedy.[65] Despite the introduction in 1974 of an initial action programme to promote the rehabilitation of disabled persons in the European Community,[66] and the adoption in 1986 of a rather weak EC recommendation on the Employment of Disabled Persons,[67] European Union law has not, to date, developed any substantive rights specific to disabled people (see Daunt 1991, and Moreton 1992). For example, the present Treaty of the European Union contains no mention of disability, which is of great significance, as it is the Treaty that transfers powers to the Community, and which specificies the fields in which the Community is competent to act' (Waddington 1995, p.9). There is now, however, some optimism that the new White Paper on Social Policy[68] might change this situation. Moreover, as the

---

64   European Communities Act 1972.

65   Some law of the European Union is 'directly effective' and therefore enforceable in the United Kingdom Courts. A law will be 'directly effective' if it is sufficiently clear and precise, is unconditional and leaves no discretion to a member state as to its implementation (Van Gend en Loos v Nederlandse Administratie der Belastingen (Case 26/62) 1963, ECR 1). Other European Union law, often in the form of *Directives*, may not directly create rights enforceable in national courts, but instead establishes goals which the governments of the Member States must achieve. Failure by a Member State to change the law in conformance with the *Directive* can result in that State having to pay damages. The European Court has ruled that three conditions attach to the right to claim damages. First, the right must confer benefits upon individuals, second, the content of such a right must be contained in the directive itself, third, there must be a causal link between the breach of the obligation and the damage suffered by the person affected (Francovich v Italy (Cases C6 and C9/90) 1993, 2 CMLR 66). For more discussion of these issues see Bowen 1995.

66   Established under Articles 128 and 235 of the treaty of Rome as Council resolution, 27.6.74: OJ C 80/30 (9 July 1974).

67   According to Daunt (1991, p.22) a recommendation (which has no legal effect) was preferred to a Directive, because at the time Europe was undergoing a period of high unemployment, and thus to insist upon special laws to oblige employers to increase their disabled workforce would be politically impossible: 'A Recommendation on the other hand would have a fair chance of being adopted within a reasonable time, its weakness of form being compensated by a relative richness of content'.

68   see infra p.55.

European Union also has no treaty, or convention relating to human rights *in general*, the European Court of Justice in Luxembourg, the supreme adjudicating body regarding the applicability of European Union law, has ruled in a series of cases that *the principles of the ECHR must be applied* when a domestic court is considering the impact of European Union law upon its decisions. In a landmark case, this principle was formulated in the following way:[69]

> Fundamental rights form an integral part of the general principles of law which the European Court of Justice enforces. (It) should not allow measures which are incompatible with the fundamental rights recognised and guaranteed by the constitutions of such states. The international treaties on protection of human rights in which member states have co-operated or to which they have adhered can also supply indications which may be taken into account within the framework of Community (Union) law.

In addition to the above important statement of general principle regarding the integration of fundamental human rights (as set out in the ECHR) into the domestic and transnational law of the European Union, there is a further highly important instrument known as the Social Charter, or European Community Charter of Fundamental Social Rights, which was adopted by 11 of the 12 Member States of the European Union (then the European Community) in December 1989. *The United Kingdom did not, however, adopt the Charter.*[70] A Charter does not have the same legal force as the main law making machinery of the European Union (the Articles of the Treaty, and the Instruments of the Commission) as it is not legally enforceable *per se*, but is nevertheless, a 'solemn proclamation of fundamental social rights' which has its own action programme set out by the Commission that seeks to encourage member states to implement its philosophy into domestic law. The crucial article of the Charter for our purposes is as follows:[71] 'Whatever the nature of the disablement, disabled persons are entitled to concrete measures to improve their social and occupational integration, especially vocational training, ergonomics, accessibility, transport and housing.'

As part of the inevitable development of the integrationalist policy of the European Union, the Social Charter was further developed and refined in the course of the discussions that led to the signing of the Maastricht Treaty in 1994. After considerable, and at times fraught debate and negotiation, it was agreed that the new version of the Social Charter should be included as part of the Social Policy Chapter of the Maastricht Treaty, but that the United Kingdom was effectively to 'opt out' of any need to comply with either the

---

69 4/73 Nold v Commissioner of EC (1974) ECR 491, p.505 CMLR 339, p.354. For further discussion of this principle see Grief (1991) and Ehlermann (1980).

70 Printed as a booklet by the Office for Official Publications of the European Communities.

71 Article 26. Charter 13 of the Social Charter sets out the implementation programme for Article 26.

letter or the spirit of this part of the Treaty.[72] As a consequence, the United
Kingdom is excluded from the decision making processes with regard to the
implementation of the Social Chapter, preferring to rely upon its national
domestic policies, and to go it alone outside the European Union, in this respect.
One of the many consequences of this 'opt out' will be that any European Court
caselaw in respect of this Chapter will not be binding upon the United Kingdom
Government. Whether this policy will continue will depend very much upon
the political complexion of the UK Government in the coming years. The
outcome of the renegotiation of the Maastricht Treaty (Maastricht Two) in 1996
following the European Union Intergovernmental Conference in Turin may also
have a significant bearing on this issue.

The European Disabled People's Parliament

The European Disabled People's Parliament is an informal network of the key
pressure groups in Europe organised by disabled people themselves who are
pushing national governments to legislate for the full integration of disabled
people into society. The parliament met for the first time on 3 December, 1993,
the European Day of Disabled Persons, in the Hemicycle of the European
Parliament Building in Brussels, at the joint invitation of the European Commission and the European Parliament. It met again exactly one year later and
again in 1995 (Secretariat of European Day of Disabled Persons 1995). The
intention is to continue this annual meeting in perpetuity in order to review
progress across a wide range of issues,[73] and in particular to monitor implementation of the Resolution of the first Disabled People's Parliament, of 1993,
which was as follows:[74]

> The EDPP (after preamble):
>
> 1. Invites the Community institutions and the Member States of the
>   European Community to take practical steps to guarantee the human
>   rights of disabled people by the adoption or adjustment of legally
>   binding instruments, and to adopt and to ensure implementation of the
>   UN Standard Rules on the Equalisation of Opportunities for Disabled
>   People.

---

72   The 'opt out' clause is contained in The Social Protocol no.14 attached to the Maastricht
     Treaty.
73   Thus, for example, the main agenda item for the 1995 European Parliament meeting was
     to discuss the report on non-discrimination prepared by a group of disabled and
     non-disabled lawyers and experts in human rights, with a view to formulating a policy on
     introducing a clause into the revised Maastricht Treaty, outlawing, within the European
     Union, discrimination on grounds of disability. The report with commentary was
     published shortly thereafter: Secratariat of European Day of Disabled Persons 1995.
74   Report of the First European Disabled People's Parliament, 9 December 93, DPI-EC,
     pp.20–21.

2. Invites the Commission of the European Communities:

    i)   to examine the status of equal opportunities within Directorate-General V and to consider renaming the Directorate General as follows: 'Employment, Industrial Relations and Equal Opportunities'. There is an urgent need to develop policy in the area of equal opportunities for all citizens of the European Community, and in particular for disabled people.

    ii)   to establish a new Directorate within DGV with the responsibility for developing policy initiatives in relation to equal opportunities legislation and to ensure that disabled people are employed at all levels within this new Directorate.

    iii)   to publish in 1994, a Green Paper, the contents of which should include the UN Standard Rules on the Equalisation of Opportunities for Disabled People, and an outline of the Commission's plans to initiate Community legislation for its adoption and implementation.

    iv)   to present at the European Parliament of Disabled People, 3 December 1994, a report on the progress of the Green Paper on the UN Standard Rules on the Equalisation of Opportunities for Disabled People, and the Commission's proposals for the introduction of Community legislation, including a comprehensive social policy initiative.

3. Invites the Community institutions and the Member States of the European Community to support studies on human rights of disabled people, and to ensure that disabled people, through their representative organisations, are involved in all stages of the planning and management of such studies, and that the results of the studies are disseminated as widely as possible.

4. Invites the Community institutions and the Member States to adopt equal opportunities instruments in the areas of employment, contract compliance and funding criteria.

5. Invites the Community institutions and Member States to ensure that at the time of revision of the Treaty on European union ('Maastricht') a general anti-discrimination provision is included.

European White Paper on Social Policy

(European Commission 1994)

In 1994 the European Commission published an important paper that set out the main lines of action with regard to European Union wide social policy development for the rest of the 20th century. The paper followed a somewhat short consultation process following the publication in 1993 of a Green Paper on Social Policy,[75] which asked the question:

---

75   COM (93) 551, 17 November 1993.

What sort of society do Europeans want?

The White Paper is based on the principle that: 'Europe needs a broadly-based, innovative and forward-looking social policy if it is successfully to meet the challenges ahead' (European Commission 1994, p.7).

The main thrust of the paper is jobs, and the need to ensure that not only is an effective jobs and training programme in place that will ensure the continuing growth and competitiveness of the European Union on the world stage, but also that a new dynamic based upon 'social protection, equal opportunities for all and public health', operates alongside such a programme. The crucial section of the White Paper for Europeans with disabilities can be found at Chapter VI, pp.22–27. This section was only incorporated into the White Paper as a result of intensive lobbying by disability rights groups, and represents a victory for a concerted campaign, running in parallel to the work of the European Disabled Peoples Parliament.

The relevant section of the White Paper is entitled *Promoting the Social Integration of Disabled People.* Having conceded that: 'As a group, people with disabilities undoubtedly face a wide range of obstacles which prevent them from achieving full economic and social integration. There is therefore a need to build the fundamental right to equal opportunities into Union policies', the White Paper spells out a number of clear policies as follows:[76]

1. The Commission will build on the European Disability Forum to ensure that needs of disabled people are taken into account in relevant legislation programmes and initiatives. This includes ensuring that to the maximum extent possible Union programmes are accessible to disabled people and that they are actively encouraged to participate in them.

2. The Commission will prepare an appropriate instrument endorsing the UN Standard Rules on the Equalisation of Opportunities for Persons with Disabilities.

3. The Commission will as part of this process to encourage model employers, prepare a code of good practice in relation to its own personnel policies and practices, and encourage discussions within the framework of the social dialogue on how such a model could be extended more widely.

4. The Commission will also examine how Union action could contribute to the key issue of improved access to means of transport and public buildings and press for the adoption of the proposed Directive on the travel conditions of workers with motor disabilities.[77]

At the time of writing, progress with regard to these measures has been slow.

---

76 European Commission 1994, para.23.
77 COM (90) 588, 28 February 1991.

CHAPTER THREE

CIVIL RIGHTS FOR PEOPLE WITH DISABILITIES
Reform Through Domestic Law

In the last chapter we looked at the powerful range of international legal tools and instruments that have been assembled over the past fifty years, primarily through the work of the United Nations, but more recently through the regional groupings within Europe, that can be used by disabled people and their representative organisations in the development of a universal framework of rights that are designed to bring about greater equality of opportunity between the disabled and the rest of society. Although international and European transnational law and policy can exert quite a considerable influence upon domestic policy it nevertheless remains a truism that ultimately the most effective way of improving the position of people with disabilities is by assertion of their civil rights within national, domestic law. As will be seen a little later in this chapter, the United Kingdom has a relatively poor record in this respect, having traditionally been wedded firmly to the 'medical model' of disability, handing out specific benefits in given circumstances, but never really accepting the 'rights model' of equality. By way both of context, and of comparative critique, we therefore devote the first part of this chapter to an exploration of alternative approaches to the issue of disability rights in various national jurisdictions, concluding the chapter with a detailed account of the current approach to the civil rights of disabled people in the United Kingdom.

The current position regarding the civil rights of people with disabilities will be considered with respect to the following countries:

A. Australia

B. Canada

C. France

D. Germany

E. Hong Kong

F. India

G. Ireland

H. Libya

I. Nepal

J. New Zealand

K. Philippines

L. Scandinavian Countries

M. Thailand

N. Uganda

O. United States of America

P. Zimbabwe

Q. United Kingdom

A. AUSTRALIA

Federal Law

According to one commentator (McDonagh 1993, p.162): 'The legislative package available to Australians with disabilities while not comprehensive does provide for basic rights for people with disabilities.'

Under Australian Federal Law, the Federal (Commonwealth) Government only has power to legislate within the Constitution, on a limited range of matters. One such power is called the external affairs power, whereby the Commonwealth Government can impose legislation upon States if they deem it necessary to ensure that Australia is complying with her obligations under international treaty law. These powers have been used for example to ensure State adherence to the International Convention on the Elimination of All Forms of Racial Discrimination,[1] the International Convention on Civil and Political Rights,[2] and most important of all, the ILO Discrimination (Employment and Occupation) Convention.[3] The culmination of this activity was the introduction in 1993 of the Disability Discrimination Act, one of the most comprehensive rights-based pieces of anti-discrimination that the world has yet seen, and a major reform in the law prohibiting discrimination against people with disabilities (McDonagh 1993, p.152).

Since 1993, the Disability Discrimination Act has been in operation throughout Australia. It is a comprehensive piece of anti-discrimination legislation covering people with all impairments or a history of impairments. By choosing to deal with disability in legislation separate from other instruments

---

1   See Chapter Two, p.35.
2   See Chapter Two, p.29.
3   See Chapter Two, p.46.

dealing with discrimination, the Act is sending out a clear message to disabled people that their situation should not necessarily be lumped into one whole, and that discrimination on the grounds of disability raises a whole set of discrete issues that are different from those associated with, for example, race or gender. The Federal Human Rights and Equal Opportunity Commission has responsibility for its operation, via the newly appointed Disability Discrimination Commissioner.[4] The burden of proof that discrimination has occurred rests, however, with the disabled person.

The functions of the Commission are considerable,[5] and include:

- To enquire into alleged infringements of the anti-discrimination provisions of the Act, and to endeavour by conciliation to effect a settlement. Complaints of this nature can be laid by a person claiming discrimination against them, by another individual on their behalf, and most significantly of all, by two or more persons on behalf of a person or persons aggrieved (i.e by a group representative of disabled people).

- To report to the Minister on matters relating to the development of disability standards, and to prepare and publish guidelines for the avoidance of discrimination on the grounds of disability.

- To undertake research and educational programmes, and other programmes, on behalf of the Commonwealth (of Australia) for the purpose of promoting the objects of the Act.

- To examine actual and proposed enactments in order to ascertain whether they might be inconsistent with the aims of the Act, and report to the Minister accordingly.

- (With leave of the Court) to intervene in any legal proceedings that involve issues of discrimination on the grounds of disability.

In defining *discrimination*, the Act describes two types of disability discrimination, *direct discrimination* and *indirect discrimination*.

Direct discrimination is said to occur when:

Because of the aggrieved person's disability, the discriminator treats or proposes to treat the aggrieved person less favourably than, in circumstances that are the same or not materially different, the discriminator treats or would treat a person without the disability.[6]

Indirect discrimination is said to occur when:

The discriminator requires the aggrieved person to comply with a requirement or condition:

---

4   Currently Ms Elizabeth Hastings.
5   Disability Discrimination Act 1992, no.135, s.67.(1).
6   DDA s.5 (1).

(A) with which a substantially higher proportion of persons without the disability comply, or are able to comply;

and (B) which is not reasonable having regard to the circumstances of the case;

and (C) with which the aggrieved person does not or is not able to comply.[7]

The Act applies in a wide variety of settings as follows:

Employment: This extends to partnerships, contract work, trade or professional bodies, trade unions and employment agencies, and covers application and interview arrangements, transfer, promotion, training and dismissal.[8]

Education: This extends to admission of students, denial of benefits, expulsion of students and subjection of the student to any detriment.[9]

Access to Premises: This includes any refusal of access to public premises or terms imposed upon access similarly to access to facilities that are available on such premises, once access is obtained.[10]

Provision of goods, services and facilities: Discrimination is prohibited with respect to refusal to provide goods, services or facilities to a disabled person.[11]

Accommodation: This includes, with relation to both residential and business accommodation, any form of discrimination for example in relation to allocation procedures, refusal of permission to make necessary alterations and adaptations, and denial of access of benefits normally associated with such accommodation.[12]

Clubs and sports: Discrimination is forbidden with regard to membership application and criteria for clubs, and to benefits provided by such clubs, similarly to access to any sporting activity, or its coaching or administration.[13]

State laws

Since the introduction of the Disability Discrimination Act, state laws regarding discrimination against disabled people have become less important. Nevertheless in a variety of ways, state law in Australia provides further layers of protection to the rights of disabled citizens, and also in some cases introduces the related concept of affirmative action programmes.

The civil rights of *physically disabled* citizens not to suffer discrimination are protected by law in four of the seven Australian States: New South Wales, Victoria, South Australia and Western Australia. With the exception of South Australia, this protection is extended to include *discrimination on grounds of intellectual impairment.* In Victoria and Western Australia, *mental disorder* is also included.

---

7   DDA s.6.
8   DDA Part 2, Division 1.
9   DDA s.22.
10   DDA s.23.
11   DDA s.24.
12   DDA s.25.
13   DDA ss.27–8.

Mention should also be made of two important pieces of legislation in the state of Victoria, the Intellectually Disabled Persons' Services Act 1986 (IDPSA) and the Disability Services Act 1991 (DSA).[14] The IDPSA sets standards regarding provision of services, and admission and treatment of the mentally disabled in residential institutions. It also establishes a code of conduct, or set of principles, based upon concepts of equity, integration, participation and civil rights. The DSA regulates the funding of disability services for both physically and mentally disabled people, based upon a set of articulated principles set out in the Act and defined as follows:

> Persons with disabilities are individuals who have the inherent right to respect for their human worth and dignity, have the same basic human rights as other members of Australian society and have the same rights to realise their individual capacities for physical, social, emotional and intellectual development, to access to services which will support their attaining a reasonable quality of life, to participate in decisions which affect their lives, to receive services in a manner which least restricts their rights and opportunities, to pursue grievances in relation to services.

Affirmative action programmes

Whilst anti-discrimination programmes can and probably will address the worst and most blatant abuses regarding people with disabilities they cannot alone address the problem of inequality. For, as Gaze and Jones have pointed out (Gaze and Jones 1990, p.431):

> Legislation based on equal opportunity cannot deal with all the systemic and structural features which contribute to the problems of disadvantaged groups, such as poor access to education, and other social resources including wealth, and consequent lack of power and societal devaluing of the characteristics and interests of the group.

In similar vein, Eisenstein has argued that: 'Equal employment opportunity can only be achieved after complaint-based legislation is supplemented with affirmative action' (Eisenstein 1985, p.73).

The Australian Federal government, whilst aware of this problem, has generally steered clear of imposing quotas through legislation, believing that quotas do not achieve their purpose and can be counter-productive, in that they breed resentment in some, and insecurity in those who benefit from them. The legislature of the State of New South Wales has, however, introduced affirmative action legislation affecting people with disabilities in the public sector.[15] The programme that has been created by the legislation is aspirational rather than

---

14 For a more detailed discussion of the first of these two statutes see Preston and Gregson 1987, and Carney 1988.

15 This is contained in the Equal Employment Opportunity Management Plan, which state authorities have since 1983 been required to prepare regarding people with disabilities, by virtue of an amendment to the New South Wales Anti-Discrimination Act 1977, Part IXA.

proscriptive. This means that numerical targets are set annually for public employers to aspire to reach, without imposition of quotas, and the legislation 'requires the appointment of the best person for the position, regardless of that person's race or sex or physical capacities, except where these are directly job related' (Eisenstein, p.74).

Under the programme, public services employers have to draw up an annual Equal Employment Opportunity (EEO) Management Plan and to submit an annual Report to the Director of the NSW Office of Equal Opportunity in Public Employment. This Report must contain detail on how the Plan is being implemented with information regarding improvements of both a statistical and a strategic kind. The Plan itself is divided into three parts, a statistical section regarding the composition of the workforce, with reference to data on (inter alia) physical and mental disability, a section reviewing personnel practices and procedures in the organisation, that seeks to be alert to any that are actually or potentially discriminatory, and a section that draws upon the data in the other two sections in order to set out a strategic plan for improvement. Thus, there is in place a system that is capable of bringing about significant improvement in the employment prospects for disabled people in the state of New South Wales. In these circumstances it remains a cause for some concern, that the senior adviser on people with a physical disability was able to report in 1990[16] that official state statistics regarding the employment of people with disabilities: 'indicate that the representation levels of people with a physical disability have not improved as a result of the government's EEO program.'

B. CANADA

Canada was the first country in the world to include a full equality clause in its constitution that unequivocally included disability in its wording.[17] The Canadian Charter of Rights and Freedoms[18] states as follows:

> Every individual is equal before and under the law and has the right to the equal protection and equal benefit of the law without discrimination and, in particular, without discrimination based on race, national or ethnic origin, colour, religion, sex, age or mental or physical disability.

It should be noted that the Charter demonstrates a highly assertive and positive approach to the problem of inequality by adding the words, equal protection

---

16 Jenkin, P. The 1990 EEO Survey Report, *Policy Directions: People with a Physical Disability*, pp.2–3. For a full history of the development of equal opportunity in employment in the Australian Public Service consult Radford 1985.

17 For a full account of the campaign that led to this outcome see Lepofsky and Bickenbach 1985, Bayefsky and Eberts 1985.

18 The Charter is the supreme law of Canada, and any statute that is inconsistent with it is invalid. Constitution Act 1982, s.52, Law Society for Upper Canada v. Skapinker, 1984, 9. D.L.R. (4th) 161.

and equal benefit' a protection that is reinforced by a further section of the Charter that seeks to protect affirmative action programmes from being outlawed as discriminatory':[19]

> Subsection 1 does not preclude any law, program or activity that has as its object the amelioration of conditions of disadvantaged individuals or groups including those that are disadvantaged because of race, national or ethnic origin, colour, religion, sex, age or mental or physical disability.

The significant limitation on the Charter provision is, however, that it only applies to federal and provincial government legislation and activity. It does not apply to discrimination by private citizens.[20] Its impact on the lives of many Canadians with disabilities has, however, been considerable:

> The introduction of the Charter has had important implications for people with disabilities. All federal and provincial legislation is now subject to Charter scrutiny, and can be challenged on the basis that it discriminates against people with disabilities. Discrimination in the provision of housing, education, conditions of employment, as well as differences of treatment in criminal and civil law can now be challenged as violating the equality guarantees. (Kimber 1993, p.192)

The Canadian Human Rights Act[21] has reinforced these sentiments in detail, and at the same time created a special Human Rights Commission for dealing with complaints about discrimination:

> Every individual has an equal opportunity with other individuals to make for himself or herself the life that he or she is able and wishes to have...without being hindered in or prevented from doing so by discriminatory practices based on race, national or ethnic origin, colour, religion, age, sex, marital status, family status, disability or conviction for an offence for which a pardon has been granted.

In addition to the above federal law provisions, which can be used to declare unconstitutional any provincial law that runs contrary to these guarantees, each of the 10 provinces have themselves enacted their own human rights protections for disabled people under provincial legislation. The first province to do so was New Brunswick, which in 1976 introduced its first human rights legislation, and specifically included disabled people within its remit. Then, in 1980 Ontario passed a law stating that every child in the province was worthy of an education appropriate to its needs, regardless of impairment. The problem with the provincial laws, as compared to the federal laws, is that they can only be enforced through individual legal action by a disabled person claiming discrimination, which severely reduces their impact quite considerably.

---

19 Charter s.15(2).

20 Charter s.32. See also Retail, Wholesale and Department Store Union v Dolphin Delivery Ltd (1986) 33. D.L.R. (4th) 174. For a critique of this narrow range of the Charter see Petter 1989.

21 R.S. 1985, c.H-6.

C. FRANCE

Since July 1990 it has been unlawful under the French Penal Code,[22] and therefore a criminal offence, to discriminate against a person on the grounds of health or impairment, where this is unjustified, in providing goods, services or employment. Furthermore, an employer cannot refuse to recruit a person, nor dismiss an employee, nor take action short of dismissal on grounds of health or disability, unless the employee's inability to continue has been certified by a doctor. Offenders can be punished by imprisonment from two to twelve months, or a fine of 2000 to 20,000 French Francs, or a combination of both.

In addition to the above penal provisions, France also operates a quota scheme across both public and private sector employment for undertakings employing at least 20 staff.[23] Since 1991 the quota has been set at 6 per cent of full-time or part-time positions (from an original figure of 3% on 1988). There are, however, a number of ways in which an employer can be exempted from these provisions, most of which have financial implications.

D. GERMANY

Germany presents a different approach to the question of civil rights protection from that in any of the above examples, and also from that which currently operates in the United Kingdom.[24] A number of rights are drafted directly into the Constitution, which is binding on all the states of Germany (known as Länder or Land (sing.). As a direct consequence, any law passed by a state that contravenes any Article of the Constitution will be without legal force and can be ruled as such either by the court structure within the Land in question (Landgericht, Oberlandgericht) by the appeal court which overarches all the Länder (the Bundesgerichthof) or by the constitutional court itself (the Bundesverfassungsgeicht).

Whilst there was no Article in the original post-war Constitution of Germany dealing *explicitly* with discrimination on grounds of disability, or the rights of the disabled, Article 1 of the Constitution is clearly relevant and has great potential as a guardian clause that can be used pro-actively on behalf of this constituency. Article 1 states (in part) as follows:

The basic rights

'The dignity of the human being is inviolable. It is the duty of all State authority to have regard to it and to protect it.'

---

22   Amendments to Articles 187 and 416 Penal Code. Law no.90.602 12 July 1990. See J. Officiel de la Republique Française, 13 July 1990 at 8272.

23   Law no.87.517 10 July 1987.

24   See generally Brooke-Ross and Zacher 1983; Brooke-Ross 1984; Jochheim 1985; Rasnic 1992; Youngs 1994.

Although in principle, the Basic Rights of the German Constitution only bind the 'organs of state' (i.e. they do not operate on transactions between private organisations and individuals) in one case in the Mannheim Court,[25] involving an attempt by a private school to expel an epileptic child from their school on the basis that other children and their parents were upset by their being in the presence of a 'fitting' child, the court held that such an act violated Article I and was therefore unenforceable.

More recently the German Constitution has been amended, with a new equal protection clause which states as follows that:

- all human beings are equal before the law

- men and women are equal

- (added to the existing clause that there shall be no discrimination based on race, language, nationality, social origin, beliefs, religious or political opinion is the phrase):

    No-one may be disadvantaged on account of his disability.[26]

Germany also has a quota system for employment similar to that operating in France. Under German employment law an employer with at least 19 employees has to employ a quota of at least 6 per cent disabled employees. Failure to comply with this requirement can lead to a cumulative financial penalty for continuing non-compliance in the civil courts, and in cases of gross abuse to a substantial fine under the criminal law.

Unlike in the United Kingdom, where the level of enforcement of quotas has been derisory to the extent that they are soon to be abolished (see Chapter Five, pp.121–3), it would appear that in Germany the system has worked. In 1983, for example, around £1m was paid by employers by way of penalty for non-compliance, which money was reinvested in state disabled employment initiatives (WHO 1990). Those who were not subject to penalties tended to employ disabled people significantly above quota. German unfair dismissal laws are also very protective of employees who are or who become disabled in the course of their employment (Doyle 1995, p.68).

E. HONG KONG

Through legislation first proposed in 1994, the Hong Kong government has expressed the desire to set up an Equal Opportunities Commission, from which inter alia disabled citizens can seek redress when they consider themselves to have been discriminated against, harassed or vilified on the grounds of their disability. Disability in this respect includes those diagnosed HIV positive or

---

25 Mannheim: Civil Code (CC) s.626 I Acceptance by a kindergarten of a child suffering from epilepsy.

26 Basic Law, Article Three, Paragraph Three.

with AIDS. The proposed new legislation bears striking similarity to that coming into effect in the United Kingdom,[27] but it is wider as it covers not only discrimination at work, and housing, but also extends to access to and use of buildings, recreation and education. Its significant opt-out clauses refer to 'unjustifiable hardships' and work with 'inherent requirements'.

F. INDIA

In May 1995, the Government of India published a draft Bill relating to the improvement of the quality of life of disabled people in India.[28] Under the Bill it is proposed to set up a Central Co-ordination Committee for the promotion of opportunities, the protection of rights, and the encouragement of full participation in society of disabled people. Under the Bill, 'disability' means[29] any of: 'Blindness, low vision, leprosy-cured, hearing impairment, locomotor disability, mental retardation, or mental illness.'

This central committee will monitor the activities of a national network of local committees, which will be charged with policy implementation over a wide range of issues including promoting the integration of disabled people, reviewing with donor agencies funding policies from the perspective of disabled people, and developing affirmative action policies in employment, vocational training, and care and protection systems. The Bill also contains a non-discrimination clause specifically aimed at disability abuse with punishment by fine or imprisonment in some cases for up to two years e.g. using a disabled person against their will for begging, or obtaining benefits meant for disabled people.[30]

It is expected that the Bill will become law in 1996. According to Disability Awareness in Action:[31]

> The new law will should (sic) make a big difference to disabled people in India. The Central Co-ordination Committee will be the national focal point on disability and help form a comprehensive policy for disabled people. The Non-Discrimination chapter, for example, means rail compartments, buses, ships and aircraft, including their toilets, must be accessible to wheelchair users.

G. IRELAND

The Irish Commission on the Status of People with Disabilities was established in December 1993 with the purpose of presenting the Irish government with proposals that would give disabled people the same opportunities to participate

---

27 See p.77 et seq.
28 Persons with Disabilities (Equal Opportunities, Protection of Rights and Full
    Participation) Bill 1995.
29 Quoted in *Disability Awareness in Action Newsletter 33*, December 1995, p.2.
30 *Disability Awareness in Action Newsletter 28*, pp.8–9.
31 *ibid.*

as all other people in Irish life. The Commission is expected to report in April 1996. Chaired by a judge, 60 per cent of its members are made up of disabled people, their advocates, or family members, the rest being drawn from statutory and voluntary agencies. The Commission has adopted a deliberately high profile, organising a series of large public meetings across the country, and receiving over 3000 pages of written submissions.[32] Amongst the many issues that it is addressing are education, housing, employment and transport needs, and the possibility of introducing comprehensive anti-discrimination measures to include disability.[33] Since 1977, Ireland has also adopted a 3 per cent employment quota although this is limited to the public sector.

H. LIBYA

Under Libyan law:[34]

> Every disabled person is entitled to housing, care services at home, prostheses and appliances, education, rehabilitation, employment, exemption from income tax, accessible public transport, buildings and resorts, and exemption from custom duties on imported appliances.

I. NEPAL

Legislation passed in Nepal in 1982,[35] as part of its commitment to the International Year of Disabled Persons[36] deals comprehensively with the political and socio-economic needs of disabled people, and as such is one of the more advanced statements of law that are in line with the general philosophy of the ICESCR.[37] The Preamble of the Act states as follows:

> To enable disabled people to participate as active and productive citizens, provisions will be made to protect their welfare through prevention of impairment, health education, training facilities and employment opportunities and by defining a fundamental right to equality.[38]

---

32 *ibid.* for short summary of some of the main concerns expressed in the submissions.

33 For more information contact the Commission on the Status of People with Disabilities, Department of Equality and Law Reform, 43–49 Mespil Road, Dublin 4, Ireland.

34 The People's General Congress Law no.3 on Disabled Persons 1981.

35 Disabled Protection and Welfare Act 1982.

36 See Chapter Two, p.39.

37 See Chapter Two, p.29.

38 For greater detail and commentary on this and other recent developments in the Asian Pacific Rim and Asia generally see ESCAP 1993.

J. NEW ZEALAND

On 1 February 1994 New Zealand passed the Human Rights Act, a piece of comprehensive legislation that renders unlawful discrimination on the grounds of race, gender and impairment, and ensures that providers of public service facilities make reasonable accommodation against discrimination. New Zealand has also created the Disabled Persons Assembly, which is a participative monitoring and development agency, involving disabled people and others in the progressing of new legal powers to clamp down on discrimination. One example of such legal powers is contained in the Employment Equity Act of 1990, which obliged the government of New Zealand to set up a working party to look at barriers which might prevent women, ethnic minorities and disabled people from taking part in employment.

K. PHILIPPINES

Since 1990 the Organisation of Disabled Persons in the Philippines has served as the primary national organisation for disabled people co-ordinating campaigns, and monitoring the enforcement of the Philippines' imaginative and progressive legislation for disabled people. The two major legal instruments that contain the guarantees of the rights of disabled people in specific situations are:

1. The Philippine Constitution 1987.
2. The Magna Carta' for Disabled Persons 1992.[39]

Philippine Constitution

The new Philippine Constitution of 1987 contains a number of clear provisions with regard to disabled people as follows (DAA 1995A, p.41):

- The right of disabled persons to vote without the assistance of other persons.
- The selection of a sectorial representative for disabled persons.
- A comprehensive approach to health development which makes available essential goods, health and other social services to all people, with priority given to the needs of the underprivileged including disabled persons.
- The right to participate in all levels of social, political and economic decision-making.
- The protection of rights of all citizens to quality education at all levels. This provides impetus to education programmes for special groups and for free public education for disabled students at elementary and secondary level.

---

39   Republic Act no.7277 24 March 1992.

- The provision for vocational skills training for disabled persons along with adults and seniors of school-aged youth.

As part of the process of securing these rights the Constitution also states: 'The State shall establish a special agency for disabled persons for their integration into the mainstream of society,' which has duly happened, with the creation of the National Commission Concerning Disabled Persons, described as 'an all encompassing consultative forum advising and co-ordinating all matters pertaining to the welfare of disabled people' (DAA 1995A, p.40).

The 'Magna Carta' for disabled persons

This was enacted as a further piece of legislation that is designed to amplify and extend the implementation of the provisions set out in the constitution. The 'Magna Carta' (Act) provides for: 'The rehabilitation, self-development and self-reliance of disabled persons and their integration into mainstream society.'

Furthermore, it states itself to be also serving as a framework for future legislation, aimed at the realisation of: 'Full participation and equalisation of opportunity.'

Contained in this Act are a number of detailed provisions including the prohibition of discrimination against disabled people in specific settings; use of public facilities, transportation services, and employment; and the setting up of rehabilitation, and self-reliance projects for disabled people.

Finally, it should be noted that the Philippine Government has recently passed further laws protecting disabled people in particular situations: for example, the Accessibility Law requires installation of special parking places, ramps on doorways and stairs, bars in public toilets, and other aids and adaptations to help disabled people. And the White Cane Act has declared that 1 August should be observed each year as White Cane Safety Day.

L. SCANDINAVIAN COUNTRIES

With their long proud tradition of advanced social welfare programmes it is not surprising that the countries of Scandinavia have a fairly advanced rights-based legislative programme designed to integrate people with disabilities into normal society. Thus, in *Sweden* organisations of disabled people receive grants, and are treated as public sector partners in the decision making process. The guiding principle throughout all these processes in one of integration, seeking to make normal society as available as possible to the disabled by a process of adaptation and access. The Social Services Act, the Act Providing for Adaptation of Public Transport to the needs of the Disabled, the New Syllabus for the Compulsory School, and the Building Code, all contain examples of the practical operation of this principle. In *Norway*, an extensive Plan of Action for Disabled People, containing over 50 measures, has been in place since 1990, and involves a highly imaginative programme of co-ordinated activities across a number of government ministries including such measures as improving access to public buildings, development grants for new technology in industry facilitating disabled employment opportunities, and a big 'books-on-tape' campaign across a number of sectors. The Norwegian activities extend beyond their national frontiers to include assisting groups of disabled individuals in developing countries.[40] *Denmark* has a long history of social legislation that includes provision on the rights of disabled persons, based upon principles of equality and participation by all who wish in public life. The implementation of these measures has largely been devolved to local authorities.

M. THAILAND

As in Nepal, the United Nations Decade and Year of the Disabled were used by the Thai Government as the catalysts for the introduction in 1992 of the Welfare and Rehabilitation Law for the Disabled. In the field of employment a system of tax incentives has been introduced to try to encourage employers to accept disabled people on their staff, together with penalties for those who do not, paid into the National Rehabilitation Fund. The incentives are real, allowing an employer to deduct from their income for tax purposes double the amount of money they pay in wages to the disabled employee. A similar incentive has been set up for the owners of buildings, vehicles or other public services who improve their facility to make it more accessible to disabled people (ESCAP 1993).

Another important development in Thailand, signalled through the 1992 Law, was the creation of the Commission for Rehabilitation of Disabled Persons, which runs a national registration scheme for disabled people that triggers entitlement to special medical and educational services, and to advice about employment, and legal advice.

N. UGANDA

On 22 September 1995, Uganda adopted a new Constitution.[41] The Constitution takes a strongly progressive line with regard to the rights of disabled people. For example:

- Society and the State shall recognise the right of persons with disabilities to respect and human dignity.[42]

---

40   A copy of the Plan of Action, which is being monitored by the Norwegian Ministry of
     Health and Social Services, can be obtained from the Publications Division, PO Box
     8196 Dept 0032 Oslo 1, Norway.
41   The Constitution was adopted by the Constituent Assembly on 22 September and
     published on 8 October.

- Persons with disabilities have a right to respect and human dignity and the State and Society shall take appropriate measures to ensure that they realise their full mental and physical potential.[43]

- Parliament shall enact laws for the protection of persons with disabilities.[44]

O. UNITED STATES OF AMERICA

The landmark legislation of the United States in the field of disability protection, the Americans with Disabilities Act (herein after referred to as the ADA), came into effect in 1990.[45] Justin Dart, Chair of the President's Committee on the Employment of People with Disabilities, described the Act in the following terms:[46]

> ADA is a landmark commandment of fundamental human morality. It will proclaim to America and to the whole world that people with disabilities are fully human; that paternalistic, discriminatory, segregationist attitudes are no longer acceptable.

Justin Dart is hereby saying that the law is not just a landmark for Americans with disabilities, it is a landmark for all Americans (see Thornburgh 1991, and Solomon 1992).[47] It is customary for landmark legislation of this nature to be

---

42 Ugandan Constitution: Social and Economic Objective XVII.

43 Ugandan Constitution: Protection and Promotion of Fundamental and Other Human Rights and Freedoms: Chapter Four, para.35 (1).

44 *ibid.* para.35 (2).

45 A great deal has been written both in this country and elsewhere about the history, impact and philosophy of this legislation. A good overview which both analyses the Act and looks at it from a British perspective is Doyle 1993. For a full and comprehensible study of the ADA see Gostin and Beyer 1993. For an assessment of the constitutional authority for such legislation see Mikochik 1991. The best source for updated information on US Disability Law is the journal *Physical and Mental Disability Law Reporter,* which is an ABA periodical publication.

46 *Worklife Commemorative Issue* p.1.

47 Notwithstanding this optimism, Justin Dart has more recently publicly expressed real anxiety about the future of the programme in a speech in Sydney, Australia, when he uttered the following warning:

> But now, on the threshold of a golden age of human rights, we are confronted by a terrifying worldwide resurgence of traditional paternalistic authoritarianism. Outspoken opponents of democracy and human rights have been elected or have seized power in many nations. We see neo-fascists attacking people with disabilities in Germany, the United Kingdom and Holland. Our new Leader of the House of Representatives in the United States Congress has spoken of eliminating national enforcement of the Americans with Disabilities Act. There is an increasing focus on the cost of keeping people with disabilities alive, and on our so-called 'right' to die.

Justin Dart, speaking at the DPI World Assembly, Sydney, 3–9 December 1994, reported in *Disability Awareness in Action Newsletter 23,* January 1995, p.3.

grounded upon Congress' stated 'findings' that led to the perceived need to introduce such legislation. In the case of the ADA the findings of Congress were significant:

- 43 million Americans were believed to be affected by disability and the historical reaction of society to such findings was described as one of isolation and segregation[48]

- the group thus affected occupied an inferior status in society and was disadvantaged socially, vocationally, economically and educationally[49]

- individuals with disabilities were a discrete and insular minority.

The ADA affects discrimination in both the private and the public sector. The Act covers four main areas: Employment, Public Accommodations, Public Transport Services, and Telecommunications. For the purposes of this Act, an individual is considered to have a *disability*, and therefore come under the protection of the Act if he or she has a physical or mental impairment that 'substantially limits' (Zappa 1991) one or more 'major life activity', and either has a record of such impairment or is regarded as having such an impairment (Feldblum 1991a). Protection also extends to those who have a known relationship or an association with such a disabled individual. The list of what constitutes a 'major life activity' is extensive and includes seeing, hearing, speaking, walking, breathing, performing manual tasks, learning, caring for oneself, and working. A further interesting feature of this protected class is that it extends to those who are seen or treated as handicapped by others, even though they are not. This is justified by the Supreme Court in the following way:[50]

> An impairment might not diminish a person's physical or mental capabilities, but could nevertheless substantially limit that person's ability to work as a result of the negative reactions of others to the impairment... Congress acknowledged that the society's accumulated fears about disability and disease are as handicapping as are the physical limitations that flow from actual impairment.

Employment

According to one expert analyst: 'The ultimate aim of (this section) is the development of a capacity for independent living as well as social integration through employment' (Quinn 1993, p.54).[51]

---

48 ADA s.2 (a) (1)-(2).
49 ADA s.2 (a) (6).
50 School Board of Nassau County, Florida v Arline, 1987 283–4. Although this case was decided prior to the introduction of the 1990 ADA, it was interpreting the same phrase which was contained in its more limited predecessor, the 1973 Federal Rehabilitation Act 1973.
51 For a detailed assessment of the philosophy of the sections of the ADA that deal with employment rights for disabled people see the following: Kemp and Bell 1991; Mayerson 1991; Powell 1991; Davenport 1992.

An employer with 15 or more employees cannot discriminate against a 'qualified individual' with a disability. A 'qualified individual' is someone who meets legitimate skill, experience, education and other requirements, and who can perform the essential functions of the job, with 'reasonable accommodation' (Cooper 1991, Murphy 1991 and Stine 1992) by the employer, for example making existing facilities accessible to disabled employees, adapting or acquiring new equipment or machinery, special training materials, readers, interpreters and so forth.[52] Essentially, what is expected by the legislation under this concept of 'reasonable accommodation' is that which is 'readily achievable' i.e. easily accomplishable and able to be carried out without too much expense or difficulty. The size and nature of the business is taken into account when deciding what should be achieved. Employers are not expected to invest in changes that would cause them 'undue hardship' (see Tucker 1992), for example if the 'accommodation' required might 'fundamentally alter the nature or operation of a business.'[53] Thus, a nightclub owner employing a visually impaired waiter could not be expected to increase the light power in the club to enable the waiter to see better, as in the long term this would act to the detriment of the employer and other employees.[54]

Note also that if outside funding is unavailable and the cost of making the job accessible to the disabled employee could cause undue hardship to the employer, the disabled individual must be allowed (though not required) to pay the proportion of the cost causing the 'undue hardship', themselves. Best practice suggests that: 'To comply with the law employers must identify and document the requirements for a position in terms of skills, experience and education, and should apply job analysis techniques to catalogue the essential functions of the post' (Doyle 1993, p.95; see also Barlow and Hane 1992; Phelan 1992).

Financial assistance is available to employers in the form of tax credits and deductions should they need to carry out any such adaptations. The relevant ADA regulation in this regard explicitly defines the process of determining reasonable accommodation as 'an informal, interactive problem-solving technique involving both the employer and the qualified individual with a disability'.[55] It is not anticipated that the cost of accommodation should be excessive.[56]

---

52 42 USC p.12111 (9) For detailed commentary on these provisions see Cooper (1991) and Weirich (1991).
53 See Alexander v Choate, 469 U.S. 287.
54 This example is taken from the EEOC Interpretive Guidance to the ADA 29 CFR 1630.2(p), App. p.414.
55 29.C.F.R. para.1630.
56 According to the Jobs Accommodation Network, a service of the President's Committee on the Employment of People with Disabilities, 31 per cent of accommodations are of no cost, 19 per cent cost between $1 and $5, 19 per cent between $50 and $500, 19 per

Preliminary research suggests that where applied, the process of making 'reasonable accommodation' is, in fact, reaping positive financial benefits for employers (Light 1995):

> For every dollar a company spends in making an 'accommodation', they get back 35 dollars in terms of increased productivity, reduced employee turnover, lowered training costs, and savings in insurance compensation costs.

Public services

No qualified individual with a disability shall by reason of such disability be excluded from participation in or be denied the benefits of the services, programmes or activities of a public entity or be subjected to discrimination by any such entity. Public services, for these purposes, include those who provide services or goods to the public, even though the service is privately run, e.g. shops, cinemas, schools, restaurants and so forth (Burgdorf 1991; Jones 1992).

The legislation deals with the question of affirmative obligations with regard to existing obligations in the following way:

> Public entities shall make reasonable modifications in policies, practices or procedures when the modifications are necessary to avoid discrimination on the basis of disability, unless the public entity can demonstrate that the modifications would fundamentally alter the nature of the service or activity.[57]

Thus, where existing physical facilities are concerned: 'A practical entity shall operate each service, program or activity, so that (such service)...when viewed in its entirety, is readily accessible to and usable by individuals with disabilities.'[58]

Alterations to existing facilities must: 'To the maximum extent feasible, be altered in such a manner that the altered portion of the facility is readily accessible to and usable by individuals with disabilities.'[59]

The exceptions to this overall provision are as follows:

- 'affirmative action that would threaten the significance of an historic property.'[60]

---

cent between $500 and $1000, 11 per cent between $1000 and $5000, and one per cent cost more than $5000, see Scott 1994, p.9–10).

Gary Moulton from Apple Computers says as follows:

> Reasonable accommodation is a moving target, but that is as it should be, it is flexible enough to take advantage of improved technology and as more becomes possible, cheaper, better and more portable so the ADA will be able to develop to include more assistive technology.

Seminar Washington Hilton, July 1993, cited in Scott 1994, p.11.

57   C.F.R. 35.130(b)(7).
58   C.F.R. 35.150(a).
59   C.F.R. 35.151(b).
60   C.F.R. 35.130(a)(2).

- 'action that the service could demonstrate would result in a fundamental alteration in the nature of the service, or in undue financial administrative burdens.'[61]

More positive, however, is the section relating to the construction of new facilities by public entities: 'Every new building must be designed and constructed in such manner that the facility is readily accessible to and usable by individuals with disabilities, if the construction was commenced after 26 January 1992.'[62]

Public transport services

The central importance of public transport was recognised by a number of speakers in the Congress debates that led to the introduction of the ADA (Dempsey 1991). This importance was well captured by Congressman Luken when he spoke as follows:

> All of us recognise the crucial role transportation plays in our lives. It is the veritable lifeline which enables all persons to enjoy the full economic and social benefits which our country offers. To be denied effective transportation is to be denied the full benefits of employment, public and private services and other basic opportunities. (Dempsey, p.310).

In framing the terms of the public transport provisions, Congress favoured the integrationist approach, i.e. the adaptation of regular transport for disabled users rather than the provision of special transport. Under the public transport provisions, all public transport services must now be guaranteed accessible to disabled passengers, although there are limited exceptions such as where it is not technically possible, or adaptation will impose upon the provider an 'undue financial burden'. The provisions are stringent and comprehensive. Thus for example, every new bus must have a wheelchair lift installed (Quinn 1993, p.91), and every second-hand bus purchased must demonstrate 'good faith efforts' to ensure that the bus is accessible to disabled people. All 'key' rail stations[63] must be readily accessible and usable by individuals with disabilities by no later than 25 July 1996.

---

61 C.F.R. 130(a) (3).

62 C.F.R. 35.151(b).

63 These are defined as those which, after public consultation, are identified by the network concerned, taking account of a number of factors including the particular importance of end stations, stations serving major activity centres, major interchange stations, and stations where passenger boardings exceed the average by more than 15 per cent: 49 C.F.R. 47–51.

Telecommunications[64]

By virtue of this section all telecommunications equipment must be altered to enable hearing and speech impaired people to use such equipment in the future within a three year period at no extra cost to the disabled user (the extra cost in reality being born by an increase in the cost of calls for all users) (Scott 1994, p.24). The aim of these changes is to attempt to reduce the sense of isolation experienced by the hearing impaired, an isolation that could be dramatically reduced by the use of technologies through telecommunication.

General issues arising from the ADA

The issue of medical screening of applicants in advance of appointment is of major importance when measuring the efficacy of the sorts of measures contained in the ADA. For, if medical and genetic screening processes are carried out on potential employees at a pre-selection stage, and disabled applicants are not placed at this stage on short lists, how will they ever be able to know if this was in fact the reason for their exclusion and seek to enforce their other rights under the ADA? The Act does, however, seek to address this issue head on by introducing elsewhere a comprehensive monitoring procedure in respect of application forms, medical questionnaires and examinations, and interview questions (Feldblum 1991b, Gordon 1992) This may go some way to alleviating the problem and closing the loophole, but the suspicion remains that such processes can never be wholly effective in eliminating discrimination at this preliminary stage.

The progress of the ADA in bringing about changes in the aspirations of disabled people, the assertion of their rights, and the perceptions of others is difficult to chart, but early indications are that it is making quite considerable impact. A major review of the impact of the Act (Light 1995) suggests that progress is being made, even though an alarming number of Americans still do not know of the existence of the Act! Much still remains to be done, however.

O. ZIMBABWE

The Zimbabwe Disabled Persons Act provides for the rehabilitation and welfare of disabled persons and has the stated aim of achieving equal opportunities for disabled people to receive all community and other services. The Act has created a National Disability Board, with a full-time Director for Disabled Persons Affairs, who works with government ministries to put the Act into practice. The high-powered Board is also charged with drawing up policies to effect equalisation of opportunities, independent living, freedom from discrimination, employment, income generation, the provision of orthopaedic appliances and improvements to the social and economic status of disabled people.

---

64   See generally on this issue Strauss and Richardson (1991).

Penalties for discrimination in breach of the Act include a fine of up to $4000, and/or a year in prison.

P. UNITED KINGDOM

In contrast with the countries above, there is little tradition in the United Kingdom of a rights-based approach to the problems encountered by citizens with mental or physical disabilities (see Campbell 1980). A number of specific statutes provide special assistance to disabled people in given situations e.g. rights to special financial benefits, to housing adaptations, to special parking facilities, access to special services and so forth, and mentally disabled people who are subject to restriction under a Mental Health Act detention order, or under arrest for questioning are given special rights and protections by law (Cooper 1994, Chapter 5). The concept of an overarching protection from discrimination on grounds of disability, either in specific settings (as in the United States) or generally (as in Canada) has to date found little favour in the United Kingdom. The recent history of attempts to introduce legislation designed to outlaw discrimination is instructive as to prevailing governmental attitudes in this respect.

Early in 1979, Mr Alf Morris, Labour MP for Manchester Wythenshawe, himself a seasoned campaigner for the rights of the disabled[65] and then Minister for Disabled People, appointed a committee of inquiry to examine the possibility of introducing an anti-discrimination law to protect disabled people, similar to that in existence for discrimination on grounds of race or gender. This Committee, known as the Committee on Restrictions Against Disabled People reported to the Government in 1982, recommending comprehensive anti-discrimination legislation, arguing that:

1. There should be legislation to make discrimination on the grounds of disability illegal.

2. The law should cover all areas where discrimination occurs.

3. There should be a regulatory body or Commission with powers to investigate, conciliate and if necessary take legal action on individual complaints of discrimination.

But by now there had been a change of government from Labour to Conservative, and no action was taken on the report. In the absence of any clear steer from government on this issue, campaigners turned their attention to the possibility of introducing a private member's bill, designed to reflect the recommendations of the Committee. Under British parliamentary procedure all prospective legislation begins its life in the form of a parliamentary bill, which

---

65 Alf Morris was, for example, the architect and introducer of the private member's bill that led to the Chronically Sick and Disabled Persons Act in 1970.

can be either a government sponsored bill, or a private member's bill.[66] In late
1991, Alf Morris won a place in the ballot for presenting private members
bills,[67] and introduced his Civil Rights (Disabled Persons) Act, which sought
to ensure that disabled people had the same rights as others with regard to
employment, housing, education, public transport and the provision of other
goods, services and facilities. The bill fell at the Second Reading, having been
'talked out' by the Conservative MP Robert Hayward. In February 1993, the
Labour MP for Tooting, Mr T.M. Cox, succeeded in carrying a motion through
the House, calling for the bill's enactment, and in June 1993, a Scottish and a
Welsh MP, (respectively Mr G. McMaster and Mr Alyn) attempted to keep
interest in the fallen bill alive, by introducing versions of the bill directed at the
inhabitants of Scotland and Wales. This bill suffered a similar fate to Alf Morris's
bill, and was blocked by government whips at its Second Reading. By now a
momentum was building in support of the bill, and another strong campaigner
for the rights of the disabled, Dr Roger Berry, Labour MP for Kingswood, won
a place in the November 1993 ballot for private members bills, and decided to
reintroduce Alf Morris's bill. Despite the previous two defeats suffered by the
bill, he took comfort from the fact that it had received extensive support in the
House of Lords, that campaigning organisations outside the Houses of Parliament had done much to raise the profile of the campaign with considerable
success, and that his early-day motion[68] backing the bill, had recently received
all party support on the floor of the house.

The Civil Rights (Disabled Persons) Bill (CRDPB) in its new form, received
its First Reading on 16 December 1993. A First Reading is a mere formality,
making the House generally aware of the nature of the proposed legislation, in
preparation for the first debate on the bill, which will occur at the Second
Reading. The Second Reading of the CRDPB took place on 11 March 1994.
At this reading, the main principles of the bill were debated, and the debate

---

66 There is also a third type of bill, known as the private bill, which is specific to an
    individual or a group, and is not relevant to our particular context.

67 Each parliamentary session all MPs can enter a ballot for a placing in the list to introduce
    a private member's bill (i.e. one that is not introduced by the Government). It is open to
    Government to adopt the bill as their own if they so wish. Normally, only one or two
    private members' bills get onto the statute book each year, as only 12 Fridays during the
    session are set aside for the stages of the bill which need to be undertaken on the floor of
    the House, and in any event Government can use a variety of tactics to kill the bill if they
    so wish (Griffith and Ryle 1989, p.385).

68 Backbench MPs have an almost unlimited right to table motions. These are formally for
    debate (at an 'early day') but in reality are never debated. This opportunity compares
    favourably with their much constricted ability to participate in debates and other
    activities on the floor of the House. Through submitting a motion a member can draw
    attention to any matter. Statements made in the motion are protected by Parliamentary
    Privilege. Other MPs can add their name to the motion. The Government will sometimes
    respond to motions which are signed by a significant number of their own supporters.
    For more detail on these procedures consult Griffith and Ryle 1989, p.379.

was followed by a vote on the 'main principles of the bill' which was passed by 235–0.

After its Second Reading a bill passes to the Committee Stage, where it is examined and debated in rigorous detail by a small parliamentary committee, whose political constitution reflects the political balance of the Commons, in proportionate numbers. It is at the Committee Stage that the Government normally makes its intentions clear, by laying down any amendments that its wishes to make to the bill. There were three sittings of the Standing Committee which examined the CRDPB with close attention on 30 March, 12 April and 13 April. A number of amendments were discussed of which most were acceptable to the sponsors. Significantly, Mr Nicholas Scott, the Minister for Social Security and Disabled People, tabled no amendments to the bill at the Committee Stage. After the Committee Stage of a bill has been completed, the amended bill returns to the House of Commons for further consideration by the full house. This is known as the Report Stage. It was at this stage that things started to go badly wrong.

The Report Stage commenced on the floor of the House of Commons on the morning of 6 May, in a highly charged atmosphere. Rising to his feet, Mr Alf Morris began as follows:

> On a point of Order, Mr Deputy Speaker. This is a deeply serious point of order of which I gave notice to the Clerk of the House on Wednesday of this week. On Tuesday evening I was informed by a highly authoritative source that a huge number of amendments for the Report stage of the bill had been drafted by the Government for tabling by Conservative Members. The following morning no fewer than 80 amendments appeared in the names of five Conservative Members, who have taken little, if any, part in the debates on the bill since I first presented it to the House nearly two and a half years ago.

In a nutshell, it seemed that the bill was yet again about to be 'talked out' by an unyielding government. Alf Morris's intervention was followed in quick succession by a series of angry statements by the other key sponsors of the bill, Mr Dafydd Wigley, Mr Alan Howarth, Dr Roger Berry, and Mr Barry Sheerman, the latter speaking with special vituperation when he stated:

> The House must be being held in contempt. The bill has had its Second Reading and has been considered in Committee – during which stage the Government tabled no amendments. If this subterfuge goes ahead today and the bill is sunk because of the Government encouraging certain kinds of backbenchers to come in at a late stage and destroy it, it must be bad for the reputation of the House. It could be cleared up if the Minister (Nicholas Scott) would say this morning, before we go on our way, that he deplores this late attempt to delay and subvert the bill. If he made that clear statement we would know where the government stand and that could save the reputation of the House.

In the course of the following debates on the Report Stage of the bill, on both 6 and 20 May, there took place some of the most acrimonious exchanges witnessed in the Commons for several years. The Minister and others were effectively accused of lying, of weakness, of filibustering, of dishonesty, and of misleading the house by speaker after speaker, collectively furious that the Government had allowed the process to reach this very late stage before applying the last rites to the bill. On 20 May the Minister, Mr Nicholas Scott, finally came clean:

> Given the considerable controversy that surrounds the bill and the proceedings in the House on 6 May (First Report Stage), I should preface my remarks on this group of amendments with a clear and unambiguous statement. The Government have and have always had reservations about the bill promoted by (Dr Berry)... The Government themselves have made clear their intention to consult and to act on five key areas that affect the quality of life of disabled people and the obstacles that are placed before them in a number of important areas... What I have never said is that the Government support the bill... The bottom line has always been that the Government cannot accept the bill because of the considerable cost implications involved.

Despite valiant attempts by the bill's sponsors to allow it to proceed, Dr Berry, even offering to accept *all 80 amendments*, to allow the bill to proceed to the House of Lords and to its Third Reading, it failed to proceed any further. The Government was, however, sufficiently embarrassed by its handling of the whole affair, to act swiftly on its promise on 6 May to engage in a process of 'wide consultation' and on 15 July, Nicholas Scott published a paper entitled *Consultation on Government Measures to Tackle Discrimination Against Disabled People*.[69] In the autumn Government reshuffle Nicholas Scott was replaced as Minister for Social Security and Disabled People by William Hague, who not long thereafter was replaced by Alistair Burt.

The Consultation Document was an upbeat attempt to regain the initiative having manifestly lost it in the previous twelve months of parliamentary shenanigans. Claiming that the Government 'gives a high priority to helping people live independently and with dignity', the paper listed a number of areas in which it had taken proactive action on behalf of disabled people, including raising spending on disability benefits from £5 billion in 1978–1979, to £17 billion in 1993–1994 and changing care and support policies to place greater emphasis on helping disabled people to live in their own homes.[70] The paper sought views on further steps to take in five key areas:

1. Employment

    Under this head the paper sought views inter alia on the 'quota' system,[71] on the introduction of a statutory right for disabled people not to be unjustifiably discriminated against in employment, on the circumstances under which discrimination might be considered fair, on the factors to

---

69   Published as DL1 July 1994, but also produced as a video, and an audio cassette.
70   DL6 July 1994, p.3.
71   See Chapter Five, p.121.

take into account, and on the appropriate categories of disability to which such a provision might be applied.

2. Building regulations

Under this head the paper sought views on strengthening the existing building regulations with regard to non-domestic buildings, to consider in particular whether there should be new requirements in the design of new buildings to take greater account of the need of disabled people.

3. Access to goods and services

This head dealt with access to a range of goods and services, including outlawing discrimination with regard to public buildings, accommodation, theatres, restaurants and public transport.

4. Financial services

Whilst not proposing legislation under this head, the paper sought views on the introduction of Statements of Good Practice for banks, building societies and insurance companies in their dealings with clients with disabilities.

5. The creation of a new advisory body on disability

The consultation period ended on 7 October 1994. Despite the shortness of the consultation period, the Government received around 1000 representations in response to the request for views.[72] Shortly thereafter, it issued a White Paper[73] that was intended to form the basis of the subsequent legislation. Although the legislation that finally arrived on the statute book[74] largely followed the original terms of the Consultation Paper, the Parliamentary process that debated the stages of the bill[75] did lead to a number of amendments that reflected at least some of the concerns of the disability lobby, the majority of whom were

---

72 Figures provided by Ian Bynoe, Research Associate at the Institute of Public Policy Research at Jordan's Disability Discrimination Seminar, London, 28 November 1995.
73 Ending Discrimination Against Disabled People, cmnd.2729. HMSO. 1995.
74 The bill finally received the Royal Assent in November 1995.
75 Although running in parallel to the parliamentary passage of the ultimately defeated Civil Rights (Disabled Persons) Bill, the bill had its own timetable as follows:
     Commons: Second Reading 24 January, Standing Committee E, first Sitting 31 January–13th Sitting 28 February, Report and Third Reading 27–28 March.
     Lords: Second Reading 22 May, Committee 13, 15, 27 June, Report 18 and 20 July, Third Reading 24 October.
     Commons: Consideration of Lords Amendments 31 October.

strong supporters of the considerably more comprehensive Civil Rights (Disabled Persons) Bill.

The unamended Disability Discrimination Bill, in its original form, made a number of proposals relating to employment discrimination, delivery of services, goods and facilities, transport, and education, described by RADARs being 'neither comprehensive, effective or enforceable'.[76] Consequently, on 24 January 1995, the day the Government's Disability Discrimination Bill was receiving its Second Reading, Labour MP Harry Barnes revived the Civil Rights (Disabled Persons) Bill yet again, successfully obtaining the right to introduce it as a private member's bill, on the grounds of its considerable difference from the Government bill. Harry Barnes' bill, like its predecessor, passed its Second Reading on 10 February without difficulty.[77] Already, however, it was becoming clear that the bill was going to suffer the same ultimate fate as its predecessor, as William Hague made it abundantly clear that the Government had no intention of allowing the Private Member's bill sufficient parliamentary time to become law. This was made all the more certain by the parallel existence of the Government's bill, which had completed the Committee Stage and was due to return to the House of Commons for the Report Stage in March.

The existence of the rival bill, and the powerful and well-organised lobby that supported its philosophy both within and without the House of Commons, was, however, a key factor in influencing the Government to make significant amendments to their own bill when it returned to the House for the Report Stage. These amendments included the introduction of new powers covering buses, trains, coaches, trams and underground systems; the extension of the scope of the bill to those with a history of disability, not merely those with a current disability; the introduction of measures against discrimination in the sale and letting of property; the inclusion of access to, and use of, information services and means of communication under 'access to services'; clarification of the kind of measures that an employer may take in relation to a disabled employer; and parallel proposals for new initiatives regarding special needs policies in schools and places of further and higher education.[78] The amended bill then passed on to its second reading in the House of Lords, which took place on 22 May. In the meantime, the Government duly killed off Harry Barnes' bill by tabling approximately 100 amendments at its committee stage, thereby effectively ensuring it ran out of parliamentary time. The bill entered the law as the Disability Discrimination Act in November 1995, to come into Force, in part about a year later.

---

76   RADAR Bulletin, no.245, February 1995, p.1.
77   175 MPs voted in favour of the Bill, and none against.
78   See Chapter Nine.

The Disability Discrimination Act 1995

One of the first commentators on the new disability legislation who had been extensively involved in lobbying during its gestation described it in the following terms:[79]

> This legislation represents a new departure in social policy terms and is being introduced by a Government which has demonstrated very great reluctance to embark on such new law. Prior to this legislation, the Government has relied on voluntary or self-regulatory approaches. It appears to be changing the law not because of a confident acceptance of the philosophy and purpose behind the legislation...but because of significant and irresistible pressure. This factor has not only shaped the law itself – thus there is no enforcement Commission, many definitions are restrictive, justifications for discrimination are broadly defined, small employers are exempted – but may also influence the regulations and guidance to follow and the make-up of the National Disability Council.

The Act, though on the statute book, is not yet in force. The likely (though still speculative) implementation timetable is set out below.[80] It will apply to England, Wales, Scotland and (in slightly modified form) Northern Ireland, and is divided into a number of discrete parts as follows:

Part I

ss.1–3. Definitions of disability and disabled person, including physical or mental impairment and persons deemed to be, or to have been, disabled.

Part II

ss.4–18. Discrimination in employment, including meaning of discrimination, general prohibition on unlawful discrimination, the defence of justification, the duty of employers to make 'reasonable adjustments', and advertisements (See Chapter Five, p.129 et seq).

Part III

ss.19–28. Discrimination in the provision of access to goods, facilities and services, including the general prohibition on unlawful discrimination, the weaning of goods, facilities and services in context, building regulations and discrimination in relation to premises.

Part IV

ss.29–31. Provisions relating to education (see Chapter Nine)

Part V

ss.32–49. Provisions relating to access to public transport

---

79   Ian Bynoe, Lecture Notes for Disability Discrimination Act 1995 Conference, Jordans. London, 28 November 1995.

80   See infra p.84.

Part VI

ss.50–52. The National Disability Council

Part VII

ss.53–59. Supplementary provisions relating inter alia to liability of employers, principals and victimisation.

Part VIII

ss.60–70. Miscellaneous further provisions

Schedules 1–8 provide a wide range of supplementary detail re. all of the above.

The proposed implementation programme for the Act is a lengthy, slow and complex one. Consultation on the Employment Code of Practice started in early 1996, together with the establishment of the National Disability Council, which will then proceed to work on the production of a further Code of Practice, with regard to Part III. In the first half of 1996 the Government is preparing the Regulations that will dictate the detailed implementation of all aspects of the legislation, through a further consultation process. The first parts of the legislation actually to be brought into force, probably at the very end of 1996, early 1997, will be Part II (Employment Rights: see Chapter Five, p.129) and those aspects of Part III that deal with the right not to be refused service (see Chapter Five, p.163). Implementation of other Parts of the Act and Schedules are likely to follow at an indeterminate later stage, unless a change of government brings about new policies. The Act will grant new legal rights to disabled people in certain situations. The detail relating to each of these situations will be dealt with wherever the context arises in the course of the book. Thus Employment, and Access to Goods and Services are dealt with in Chapter Five.

The meaning of disability and disabled person under the act

1. The status protected by the Act is a 'disabled person', defined as a person who has a disability.'[81]

2. For the purposes of the Act a person has a disability if he or she has: 'A physical or mental impairment which has a substantial and long-term adverse effect on their ability to carry out normal day-to-day activities.'[82]

---

81   DDA s.1(2).
82   DDA s.1(1).

As a result of a key amendment to the Act during the Committee Stage in the House of Lords, the definition of a disabled person includes 'a person with a history of disability' (i.e. has had a disability) even though they no longer suffer from that disability.[83] In these circumstances, the definition is applied as though the Act were in force when the person did have the disability that they argue still gives rise to the discrimination that they allege.[84]

At the time of writing, there is little further guidance on how to interpret the various words setting out the definition of a disabled person for the purposes of alleging discrimination under the Act. This guidance will emerge in the fullness of time in the form of regulations to be promulgated by the Secretary of State together with case law that will emerge as cases start to appear before courts and tribunals, along with Guidance which will emerge in parallel from various government Ministers and Departments.[85] For example, it is likely that regulations will be made prescribing conditions' that are, or are not to be treated as amounting to impairments' under the Act. Commonly accepted impairments such as sensory impairments, will certainly be included. The problem will arise with new, or controversial conditions where the level of impairment is a matter of conjecture or opinion.

Although mental impairment' is not further defined by the Act, it is stated that:[86] '*Mental impairment* does not have the same meaning as in the Mental Health Act 1983,[87] but the fact that an *impairment* would be a *mental impairment* for the purposes of that Act does not prevent it from being a mental impairment for the purposes of this Act.'

Furthermore, the Act states that the definition of mental impairment if emanating from mental illness will only be established if it is from or consisting of a mental illness that is clinically well recognised.[88] This restriction is likely to exclude from the definition not only controversial' mental disorders such as kleptomania, psychopathy, or pyromania, but also recognised' mental disorders that are still not fully established in the patient.

---

83 Lords Committee Stage 13 June 1995.
84 DDA s.2 BS Schedule 2.
85 On the relative weight to be attached to Regulations, Guidance and Advice see Chapter Four, p.90.
86 DDA s.67(1).
87 See Chapter Eight, p.216, fn.7.
88 DDA Schedule 1 para.1(1).

3. Once an impairment is established it will be deemed to affect the person's normal day-to-day activities if it affects one or more of the following:

    - mobility
    - manual dexterity
    - physical co-ordination
    - continence
    - ability to lift, carry or otherwise move everyday objects
    - speech, hearing or eyesight
    - memory or ability to concentrate, learn or understand
    - perception of the risk of danger.

    There is a special provision that allows regulations to be made that deem an impairment to come within the definition even though it is not covered by any of the above descriptions, and conversely regulations can also be made that deem an impairment not to be such even though covered by the description.[89]

4. The phrase 'substantial adverse effect' is bound to cause controversy, and is likely to generate its own case law. The only further guidance in the Act regarding its interpretation is the statement that if the effect has once been substantial, has ceased, but is likely to recur, it will be treated as continuing to have a substantial adverse effect.[90]

    In an attempt to alleviate the concern of disability groups that 'substantial means severe' the latest Minister with responsibility for the legislation, Alistair Burt, has said the following:[91]

    > There has been a lot of misunderstanding about the degree of disability covered by the bill's definitions. I am seeking to be reassuring. People think that 'substantial' means 'severe' disability. That is wrong. The word 'substantial' is used in the definition to indicate 'more than minor'. As a result, many disabled people who may think that the bill does not cover them will find that they enjoy its protection. That will become clearer once we have published guidance on the matter.

    Whilst this statement may well provide superficial reassurance to disability rights groups seeking to understand the extent of the law's reach, considerable caution is recommended in seeking to rely upon Mr Burt's enthusiastic beliefs, as a court of law may well find Mr Burt's definition to stretch the English language beyond its ordinary and natural meaning

---

89 DDA Schedule 1 para.4(1)(a).
90 DDA Schedule 1 para.2(2).
91 Alistair Burt MP, Minister for Social Security and Disabled People, Consideration of Lords Amendments, Official Report, 31 October 1995, co.174.

and would effectively, for example, exclude from the purlieu of the English language the concept of 'moderate'!

5. Not only must the adverse effect be 'substantial', it must also be 'long-term.' The Act states[92] that an adverse effect of an impairment will be deemed to be long-term (unless regulations are brought in to the contrary) if it has lasted for at least 12 months, or the period that it can reasonably be expected to last is at least 12 months, or the rest of the person's life (whichever is the shorter).

6. In addition to the above definitions the Act also includes a number of special situations, of which the following are the most significant:

A. Progressive conditions[93]

A person with a progressive condition causing an impairment that has *some but not yet substantial* adverse effect on normal day-to-day activities (sufferers from multiple sclerosis, muscular distrophy, HIV and some forms of cancer may fit this category) are nevertheless deemed to be a disabled person for the purposes of this Act, if their condition is expected to result at a later stage in substantial adverse effect. Not included in this definition are those with asymptomatic conditions, i.e. where no impairment is yet experienced, and those who are genetically predisposed to such conditions, but who have not yet acquired them.

B. Controlled or corrected conditions

A condition that is controlled or corrected, for example by medication, or the use of a prosthesis or other aid, is still deemed to be a disability for the purposes of the Act, if but for the control or correction, there would be a disability meeting all the parts of the definition set out above (p.86.). Regulations will be able to exclude certain controlled or corrected conditions from this protection. The Act itself already excludes sight impairment that is correctable by spectacles or contact lenses.[94]

---

92 DAA Schedule 1 para.2(1).
93 DAA Schedule 1 para.7.
94 DAA Schedule 1 para.6.

C. Disfigurement[95]

A person with a severe disfigurement (a term not defined in the Act, but designed to cover, for example, burn scarring, disfiguring birthmarks and so forth) is to be treated as falling within the definition of a disabled person for the purposes of this Act, although regulations are likely to put a restrictive interpretation in this definition to exclude disfigurement caused by self-mutilation, tattoos, body piercing and so forth.

D. Persons already registered as disabled

As a general rule, a person who meets a generic definition under one piece of legislation will not automatically be deemed to satisfy that definition for all other purposes, e.g. a person deemed to be self-employed under employment law will not automatically be deemed self-employed under tax law. Thus, a person who is on the local authority disabled person's register under the Chronically Sick and Disabled Persons Act 1970[96] will not automatically be deemed to be disabled for the purposes of the Disability Discrimination Act. The exception to this general rule is a person who was registered as a 'disabled person' for employment purposes on 12 January 1995, who in certain defined circumstances will be deemed to be covered by the Act. This matter is dealt with in more detail in Chapter Five.

E. Reputed Disability

Contrary to the position adopted in the United States to this issue, the Government resisted all attempts to include in the definition of disabled person somebody without an impairment who nevertheless experiences discrimination because of the stereotyped attitudes of others towards their condition. This group might have included, for example, those suffering from cerebral palsy, learning disability, and mild mental illness. The House of Lords amendment to the bill, to include this group where access to goods and services is concerned, was rejected when the bill returned to the Commons for its final reading.[97]

---

95   DAA Schedule 1 para.3.
96   See Chapter Four, p.92.
97   31 October 1995.

ENFORCING DISABILITY RIGHTS
The Statutory Framework

In the last two chapters we examined ways in which the law can be used, both in the United Kingdom, and in jurisdictions across the world, to assist disabled people to oblige their governments to provide them with support and assistance, where needed, by the development and enforcement of concepts of human and civil rights. The guiding principle in these developments is the belief that the human and civil rights of those with disabilities should be seen as identical to those without disability, and various strategies to achieve this principle were explored. In this chapter we will examine the legal duties and responsibilities that are directly imposed by law on local authorities in this country with respect to the provision specifically of support and assistance for those with disabilities in need of such services.

LEGAL DUTIES OWED BY LOCAL AUTHORITIES TOWARDS DISABLED PEOPLE

Where a statute lays down a *legal duty*, this can be considered the law with which a local authority must comply. Failure to comply with this law can lead to legal action against them, designed to enforce the law. Sometimes, however, a statute merely speaks of a *legal power* to do something, in which case the discretion rests with the local authority as to whether they do it or not. Failure to exercise a power is not normally actionable in law. Where there is a dispute or uncertainty concerning the meaning, scope or extent of a legal duty or power, the matter frequently ends up before a court of law, at which a judge is asked to rule as to what the law actually is. This is the process known as *litigation*. The decision of a judge in the case generated by the litigation becomes law, in the same way as a statute creates law. This form of law is known as *case law*.

A further complication arises from the fact that even when a statute lays down a *duty*, the local authority can retain substantial discretion as to whether that duty has come into operation in a particular case. An example of the operation of this discretion in deciding whether to exercise a duty is given below in relation to the local authority duty to make an assessment of needs.[1]

As well as the above primary sources of law, there are a number of secondary sources of law which are of great importance as they often contain the detail that primary sources do not contain. The main secondary sources of law are *statutory instruments, regulations, directions* and *approvals*. *Statutory instruments* and *regulations* are delegated sources of law, usually drawn up by the Secretary of State, or minister responsible for the enforcement of the policy area in question. They often impose further legal duties and powers on local authorities. Ministers can also issue *directions* and *approvals*, with regards to the administration of the services for which they are responsible, which also create further legal duties (directions) and powers (approvals).

Finally, on the lowest rung of influence we find *guidance*, and *guidelines*, issued in great abundance by government, as a way of indicating to local authorities how they wish their legislation to be carried out in practice. *Guidance* and *guidelines* can be in the form of *codes of practice, policy guidance, practice guidance, circulars* or simply advice. *Charters* are also becoming increasingly popular in this respect.[2] *Charters* have no legal effect, but perform a 'customer service' function that can be used to great effect or embarrassment when they are manifestly not adhered to.[3] *Guidance* frequently appears in the form of *circulars*. Because it is not law, it cannot be treated with the same authority as the primary and secondary sources of law outlined above.[4] It is, however, useful evidence of government intentions when seeking to interpret the law, as is reference to

---

1 See pp.92–3.
2 The NHS Patient's Charter is already in existence. There are also plans to introduce a Community Care Charter (see DOH 1994).
3 For a useful article regarding the legal status of charters see Barron and Scott (1992).
4 An exception to this general principle is 'policy guidance' issued under s.7 of the Local Authority Social Services Act 1970 which places a legal duty on local authorities to 'act under the general guidance of the Secretary of State'. Whether this extends to a legal duty to follow more specific guidance on matters of detail is, however, unlikely, although in the case of R v North Yorkshire CC ex parte Hargreaves 1994, CO/878/94 30 September 94 reported in *The Times* 9 November 94 and Crown Office Digest, a judge ruled that a local authority's failure to take into account people's preferences in the course of an assessment regarding respite care rendered their decision unlawful because it was in breach of (certain) paragraphs of the Policy Guidance DH 1990.

parliamentary debate on the issues which can be found in Hansard,[5] and can be particularly helpful when trying to resolve a dispute. The importance of *guidance* and its relationship with law was made explicit in the parliamentary debates on the National Health Service and Community Care Bill in 1990, when the government minister Baroness Hooper stated as follows:[6]

> My understanding is that the use of the word *guidance* is different from the use of the word *guidelines*. *Guidance* apparently has some significance in that if an authority fails to observe *guidance*, the Secretary of State can enforce the suggestion by means of *directions*. Therefore the effect of *guidance* is quite strong.

This statement on the importance of guidance was further reinforced by a Department of Health publication (DOH 1990) which stated:

> Though they are not themselves law in the way that regulations are law, guidance documents are likely to be quoted or used in court proceedings as well as in local authority policy and practice papers. They could provide the basis for a legal challenge of an authority's action or inaction, including (in extreme cases) default action by the Secretary of State.

Statutory duties

There are a number of statutes (described hereafter as 'the legislation') which lay down legal duties owed by local authorities towards disabled people. The key provisions setting out these duties are to be found in the following statutes:

1. National Assistance Act 1948 (NAA).
2. Health Service and Public Health Act 1968 (HSPHA).
3. Chronically Sick and Disabled Persons Act 1970 (CSDPA).
4. National Health Service Act 1977 (NHSA).
5. The Mental Health Act 1983 (MHA).
6. Disabled Persons (Services, Consultation and Representation) Act 1986 (DPSCRA).
7. Children Act 1989 (CA).
8. National Health Service and Community Care Act 1990 (NHSCCA).
9. Carers (Recognition and Services) Act 1995 (CRSA).

The next section outlines how people living with disabilities in the community can access local authority and other sources of care and support by virtue of these statutes.

---

5   In 1992 the House of Lords decided that it is permissible for courts to refer to Hansard where legislation is ambiguous or obscure, or leads to an absurdity; where the material relied on consists of one of more statements by a minister or other promoter of the Bill together if necessary with such other parliamentary material as is necessary to understand such statements and their effect, where the statements relied upon are unclear. Pepper v Hart 1992 3. W.L.R. 1033 (HL).

6   H85 1990.

Central to all the *legal duties* owed by local authorities are the duties laid down in the two central Acts, the NAA and CSDPA (supplemented by the NHSA). As a result of these two Acts, a local authority has the following *statutory duties*:

1. To become informed

Under the legislation, a local authority must inform itself of the number of disabled persons living in the area of its control.[7] For the purposes of this legislation, 'disabled' means: 'suffering with a permanent and substantial handicap.'

The definition clearly extends beyond physical disability to include those with learning disability so long as it is 'permanent and substantial'. A local authority will normally satisfy this duty by keeping a register of disabled people in their area. Any person who thinks they qualify as 'disabled' under the legislation should contact their local social services department and ask to be registered. Councils employ occupational therapists, occupational therapy assistants and, sometimes, social work assistants specially trained for this task. Although registration is not a precondition to receive special services it is clearly administratively useful in organising and prioritising limited resources.

2. Assessment

A local authority *must* assess the needs of each disabled person within their area for any one of the list of services contained in the legislation.[8] Local government ombudsmen (the independent body who deal with complaints about council services: see p.114) have stressed that the legislation makes no distinction between the Council's duty to make an assessment in 'urgent' or 'non urgent' cases. (Thus) any disabled person is entitled to request and to expect that the request is met within a reasonable time.[9] This duty applies as soon as the Council is made aware of the need for an assessment.[10] In December 1992, the Social Services Inspectorate issued guidance on what is meant by 'assessment' including guidance on the appropriate level of assessment, the procedures to be followed in each case, and publicity about such procedures.[11] According to the guidance the overriding consideration is 'to keep the process as simple and efficient as possible.' It follows from the above that once a local authority becomes aware of the need to assess, they enter into a quasi-legal relationship with the client which raises the possibility of consequential liabilities for any injury suffered by the client in the interim period awaiting assessment, and

---

7   CSDPA s.1.

8   See p.95 and CSDPA 1970 ss.1–2 and NAA s.29.

9   CLAE 1992, 91/A/0482.

10 CLAE 88/C/0814, p.15.

11 CI(92)34. See also Seed and Kaye 1994, which provides good practice guidance on the application of a needs-led, person-centred approach to assessment interlinking the two processes of assessment and care-management.

assistance. What happens if a disabled person suffers injury in the period between notification and assessment, or between the assessment and the provision of assistance, if that injury can be *causally linked* to the Council's failure to exercise either function, is discussed below under *Actions in Negligence.*

3. Need

If the local authority is satisfied that any disabled person in its area has a need for any of the listed services[12] and that need is not being met, the local authority must inform that person of any welfare services it provides that could satisfy that need, and if necessary, must make arrangements for the service to be provided to that person through any appropriate agency. The term 'need' is one that is hard to define, and one that is clearly capable of subjective interpretation. What is one person's need could be another's necessity and to a third a mere luxury.[13] Circular *guidance* states that when a local authority is satisfied 'that an individual is in need, they are to make arrangements which are appropriate to his or her case.'[14]

Although it has frequently been argued by disability experts and public law specialists that lack of resources on the part of the local authority cannot be a factor in determining whether there is a need for that resource, this argument received a major setback in the recent series of cases that were taken against Gloucestershire County Council who had openly told clients in need of community care services that the provision of services would have to be regulated by resources, notwithstanding any suggestion that the legislation imposed upon them an absolute duty to provide services, regardless of resources (see Schwehr 1995). The clients who challenged Gloucestershire's decision lost their case, although at the time of writing the case may well go to appeal.[15] In reply to the argument that 'once a need has been established it cannot be reduced or eliminated by virtue of a reduction in the resources available to meet it', the court expressed the view that

> such an interpretation would be impractical and unrealistic and hence one to be avoided if at all possible. In assessing need those doing so will inevitably compare the extent of the disabilities of the persons concerned in order to arrive at a view as to who needs help more. That comparative exercise is obviously related to

---

12 See p.95.

13 It is important to distinguish here between rights, merits and needs. A person may have a right to a service that they neither merit nor need. Alternatively, they may need a service that they do not merit, and to which they have no right. Finally, they may merit a service they do not need, whether or not they have a right to it.

14 DHSS 12/70, para.7.

15 The judgement of the Divisional Court in the first instance was delivered on 16 June 1995. The Appeal, if it takes place, is likely to occur in the spring of 1996.

resources… A local authority faces an impossible task unless they can have regard to the size of the cake so that they know how fairest and best to cut it.[16]

However disappointing to those campaigning for greater local authority intervention this decision may be, it has to be said that the decision merely reinforces the statement contained in a 1970 DHSS Guidance Circular on the Act, which suggested that: 'criteria of need are matters for the authorities to determine in the light of resources.'[17]

This statement was backed up by the then Minister, Barbara Castle, in 1975, when she explained:

> Of course 'need' is an imprecise concept and local authorities have discretion in determining that 'need'. Parliament did not attempt to define that need precisely, so that there is and must be an area of discretion of which local authorities will take advantage in dealing with the conflict between what they desire to do and the resources they have available.[18]

For further discussion of the importance of this case in the light of the further duties created by the NHSCCA 1990 see p.100 and Schwehr 1995, Schwehr 1995A.

4. Making arrangements to meet acknowledged need

The legislation and case law make it clear that providing the service directly is not the only way of meeting the need.[19] The local authority can employ a voluntary agency,[20] or an appropriately skilled individual, to provide all or any of these services. Its legal duty is to ensure that the needs are met. In appropriate cases, it would, for example, be sufficient for the local authority to advise the client on the adaptations to the home necessary for them to meet their needs and then to assist them in applying for grant aid to provide the adaptations,[21] although such assistance must be real and not merely token.[22] The local authority cannot use budgeting difficulties as a basis for refusing to provide the service. It seems that the local authority may charge for the services that it provides, by virtue of a 1983 statute, which gives local authorities the discretion whether to charge or not for such services.[23] This has been made quite specific

---

16 per Lord Justice McCowan in R v Gloucestershire County Council ex parte Mahfood *et al. (ibid.)* from unrevised transcript at pp.16 and 17.

17 DHSS 12/70 para.7.

18 HC 38 1975.

19 Audit Commission 1993 and CLAE 90/C/2203 at 2.

20 See PCA c.799/81 1981–1982.

21 CLAE 89/C/1114, p.5.

22 CLAE 91/C/0565.

23 There is nevertheless still a residue of controversy regarding this view. Section 17 of the Health and Social Services and Social Security Adjudications Act 1983 states that local authorities have a discretion about whether to charge or not for various services. Services provided under section 2 of the CSDPA are not included in this direction. However, *community care services* provided under the NHSCCA are included in this direction to charge, and if, which is generally thought, *community care services* now include services provided

by a local ombudsman who stated, in a 1990 decision, as follows: 'The CSDPA 1970 does not place a statutory obligation on the council to make a financial contribution. Indeed, I do not doubt that in the prudent management of a limited budget the Council would wish to assess the claimants' resources.'[24]

The charges must be reasonable. If an individual satisfies the local authority that their means are insufficient, the local authority cannot require the individual to pay more than they are practically able to pay.

5. What are the relevant services?

(a) Services attached to duties (i.e. local authority *must* make arrangements for these services to be available in its area). The relevant services are as follows:[25]

- practical help in the home, which might include the support of a home help to do cleaning and shopping
- the provision of a television or radio, and help in using the local library
- assistance towards attending educational facilities, games or outings, and, if available, council day centres, where a variety of activities might take place
- adaptations to the home such as ramps for wheelchair access, extensions, and the provision of other specialist equipment (grants may be available for this work: see Chapter Five, pp.134–137) which are designed to secure greater safety, comfort or convenience for the disabled occupant
- help towards a holiday
- meals at home, or in a day centre
- provision of a telephone, and any special equipment needed to operate it.

(b) Services attached to powers, where a local authority *may* make arrangements for the services to be available in its area, but is not obliged by law to do so. The importance of *powers* is that they give to a local authority the right to spend public money on such services items if they think fit, though they are under no legal *duty* to do so. Without legal powers they could not spend the money at all. They include the power:

---

under s.2 of the CSDPA, local authorities clearly do have the discretion to charge, or not to charge, even if prior to the introduction of the NHSCCA they possibly did not.

24 CLAE/90/B/1676, p.19.

25 This list of services is derived from s.29 National Assistance Act 1948, from s.2 Chronically Sick and Disabled Persons Act 1970, and from the National Health Service Act, 1977, Sched. 8, para.3 (1).

- to provide holiday homes
- to provide free, or subsidised travel for persons not receiving concessionary travel from some other source
- to provide assistance in finding suitable supportive lodgings
- to provide warden assistance to occupiers of private housing
- to contribute towards the cost of employing a warden, or the cost of welfare functions in a warden-assisted housing scheme
- to provide instruction for people in their own homes on ways of overcoming their disability
- to provide work for disabled people in their own homes or elsewhere
- to provide recreational facilities at a disabled person's home or elsewhere
- to provide meals-on-wheels for house bound people
- to provide remuneration.

All the services outlined above must now also be included in the local authority's community care plans, by virtue of the NHSCCA (see p.98 et seq).

The NHSA added a further list of discretionary powers[26] enabling local authorities to provide laundry facilities to people who need them because of illness, handicap or age, and to provide other services for those suffering from physical or mental illness, or in aftercare from such illness, including day centres, meals, social work support, and residential accommodation. These latter services can also be provided 'for the prevention of illness'. Many of these discretionary powers relating to residential accommodation have now been subsumed within the contracts that local authorities will have to draw up with a home that is caring for somebody placed there by them.[27]

The DPSCRA further developed the responsibilities of local authorities, and strengthened the rights of disabled people as follows:

- If a local authority fails to assess the needs of a disabled person for any of the services listed above, it can be ordered to do so by a court. This would be an action in the High Court by way of a 'judicial review', a procedure that is explained in detail on page 107 et seq.

- Where a disabled person is living at home and receiving a substantial degree of care from a carer (who is not a person employed to care for them by a statutory body), the views of this carer, and the extent of the carer's willingness and ability to continue giving such care, must now be taken into account when assessing the disabled person's future needs.

---

26   s.21 and Schedule 8, National Health Service Act 1977.
27   For further details on these contracts see DOH Circular HSG(92)50.

The principal aim of this change appears to be to promote the concept of genuine shared care between informal carers and social services, where feasible.

- The local authority must inform a disabled person, whose needs it has assessed, of all relevant welfare services of which it has knowledge, from which that person might benefit. This duty extends beyond those services provided by the local authority to include all the relevant services from the voluntary sector, of which the local authority has knowledge. Many councils produce comprehensive booklets, setting out details of such services. The onus is clearly on those who provide a specialist service for the disabled to ensure that their local authority is aware of it.

- All disabled school leavers must receive statutory assessment by their local authorities prior to leaving school.

- There is a provision in the DPSCRA which states that any disabled person, who is not able to make representations on their own behalf, can appoint their own 'authorised representative' concerning any claim they may have under the CSDPA. This provision has never been implemented, but it can be argued that the wide consultation requirements associated with the provision of community care services under the NHSCCA can effectively be used to insist that in appropriate cases, representatives of disabled people should be appointed to be consulted at every stage of an assessment and to be allowed to make representations to the local authority on the disabled person's behalf.[28]

Further legal duties imposed upon local authorities by NHSCCA 1990

Community care services

The NHSCCA has added further duties on the local authority towards adult disabled people in their area (for the new duties towards those under 18, see page 102). The underlying principle of the NHSCCA is that every local authority must now produce and publish a plan for the provision of *community care services* in their area. Social services departments have direct legal and financial responsibility for producing such a plan (see Clark and Lapsley 1995). *Community care services* include services provided by the local authority, and those which they arrange to be provided by any other appropriate body. Under funding arrangements imposed by central government, 85 per cent of the money provided by central government to local authorities for this purpose must be used to purchase *community care services* from the independent (private

---

28 For a useful summary and commentary on the DPSCAA see the *Handbook of Voluntary Organisations on the Disabled Persons (Services, Consultation and Representation) Act 1986* IVSO/GLC.

or voluntary) sector,[29] a requirement which has forced sweeping and radical changes upon the structure and organisation of social services departments across the country.

As already stated,[30] according to the Department of Health the term *community care services* also now includes services provided by virtue of the CSDPA 1970, a view which was supported by the minister Virginia Bottomley in 1990 when she stated: 'The CSDPA 1970 relates to local authority functions under s.29 of the National Assistance Act 1948, and it is therefore already covered by the definition of *community care services*.'[31]

Community care services also include residential and nursing home accommodation and welfare services provided under Part III of the National Assistance Act 1948 (normally referred to as Part III Accommodation);[32] welfare services for older people provided under the Health Service and Public Health Act 1968;[33] home help and laundry facilities provided under the National Health Service Act 1977,[34] and after care services provided to some ex-detained patients under the Mental Health Act 1983.[35] The full definition of *community care services* is to be found in s.46 (3) of the Act. Where community care needs also extend to health care services, the local authority has a duty to notify the District Health Authority that this is the case, and invite them to assist in the assessment 'to such extent as is reasonable in the circumstances.' Curiously, the Act does not however place any duty on the District Health Authority to co-operate in the assessment.

Responsibilities under NHSCCA

If it appears to the local authority that any person for whom they provide or arrange *community care services* may be in need of such services, they have a *statutory duty*:[36]

1. To carry out an assessment of that person's needs for those services AND

2. To decide whether any needs discovered by the assessment call for the provision by the local authority of any of their *community care services*.

3. If, during the course of the assessment, they decide that the person has needs which can be met by either the District Health Authority, or the

---

29 This requirement is contained in the Community Care Special Transitional Grant Allocations and Conditions for 1994/5 Circular LASSL (94) 1, issued under the Local Government Finance (England) Special Grant Report no.10 (1994).

30 supra fn.23.

31 ibid.

32 See Chapter Five, p.155.

33 s.45.

34 s.21 and Schedule 8.

35 s.117 See also Chapter Seven, p.192.

36 NHSCCA s.47 (1)(a).

local Housing Authority, they should invite them to participate in the assessment, and help meet any needs so ascertained.[37]

The purpose of the last of the above provisions is to encourage joint and multi-agency approaches to meeting the community care needs of an individual: 'All relevant agencies should be involved in the assessment process before commitments are made.'[38]

In the case of manifestly urgent need, the Act goes on to say as follows:[39]

Nothing in this section shall prevent a local authority from temporarily providing or arranging for the provision of community care services for any person without carrying out a prior assessment of his (or her) needs…if, in the opinion of the authority, the condition of that person is such that he requires those services as a matter of urgency.

Circular guidance[40] makes it clear that local authorities: 'do not have a duty to assess on request, but only when they think that the person may be in need of services they provide.'[41]

Notwithstanding this clear guidance, a Government Minister, Baroness Blatch, stated in the parliamentary debates surrounding this provision that:

The clause requires any local authority to carry out an assessment of any person for whom it appears the authority might arrange community care services. The provision was intended to be as wide-ranging as possible and not to deny anybody making a request for an assessment the opportunity to have one.[42]

Assessment under NHSCCA *(Seed and Kaye 1994)*

Policy guidance under the NHSCCA states as follows:

Assessment arrangements should normally include an initial screening process to determine the appropriate form of assessment. Some people may need advice and assistance which do not call for a formal assessment, others may require only a limited or specialist assessment of specific needs, others may have urgent needs which require an immediate response. Procedures should be sufficiently comprehensive and flexible to cope with all levels and types of need presented by different client groups.[43]

The consultation paper *Framework for Local Community Care Charters in England* (DOH 1994) recommends that people should have:

An entitlement to expect that assessments will be provided within a reasonable time, which might include specific standards for time between the response and the start of the assessment, for time for completion of each type of assessment and for time between the completion of assessment and the start of services.

---

37   s.47(3).
38   DH 1990 para.3.33.
39   NHSCCA s.47(5).
40   See p.90 as to status of such guidance.
41   CI(92)34.
42   H18 1990.
43   3.20 DH 1990.

If, following screening, no assessment for *community care services* is deemed necessary, the local authority responsibility towards that person ceases to exist, although onward referral for other purposes may be appropriate in particular cases. If assessment is deemed necessary, assessment must be carried out following an agreed set of procedures. The Social Services Inspectorate of the Department of Health published in 1991 a *Practitioner's Guide,*[44] and a *Manager's Guide*[45] in respect of care management and assessment under the NHSCCA (See also Seed and Kaye 1994). The guidance covers publishing of information, determining levels of assessment, assessing need, implementing the care plan, monitoring and reviewing of decisions. The guides stress the need for local authorities to ensure consistency of application of criteria in relation to such matters as prioritisation of response, and allocation of resources. By doing so, local authorities can minimise the risk of legal challenge to their decisions.

The Department of Health consultation paper (DOH 1994) sets out clear guidelines as to what patients leaving hospital in need of *community care services* are entitled to expect:

> An entitlement to expect that community care assessments for people being discharged from hospital will be carried out in good time and to a high standard, so that:
>
> - no-one will be discharged from NHS care until it is clinically appropriate
> - no-one will be discharged from hospital until appropriate arrangements have been put in place for their subsequent care
> - these arrangements will begin as soon as the patient is discharged
> - patients and – unless the patient objects – their families and friends, will be informed and involved at all stages, will be given sufficient time and information to make decisions, and will be told how to seek a review of any decisions made.

Whether all the above actually happens in practice is a moot point.

Need under the NHSCCA

The first point to note is that it is not 'need' itself which triggers the duty to assess, but 'appearance of need'. This includes possible future need. Thus, for example, a local authority was ordered by the courts to carry out an assessment on a prisoner who could not gain parole from the Parole Board without a prior assessment as to his likely needs on coming out of prison, an assessment that the local authority in question had declined to make.[46] Need' has been held to include psychological as well as physical need.[47] Thus, the High Court has upheld the right of a severely mentally disabled adult to have his preferences

---

44 SSISWSG 1991a.

45 SSISWSG 1991b.

46 R v Mid Glamorgan CC ex parte Miles 1993, Legal Action, January 1994, p.21. For discussion on this issue see Clements (1993, 1995).

47 R v Avon CC ex parte M 1994 2 FCR 259.

taken into account when placing him in respite care. In this case, the Court also made it clear that local authorities must follow *policy guidance* when determining need during the course of an assessment.[48]

As 'need' is not defined by the Act it is clearly a matter for concern that different authorities may define need in more or less restrictive ways, leading to inconsistency of provision. In this respect the House of Commons Health Committee has made the following observations:[49]

> Local authorities have limited access to assessments so that only those with a certain level of need will be assessed. This is done through the application of criteria which assign individuals to particular categories depending on their level of need. Very strict criteria could lead to an apparent very high level of success in meeting assessed needs, whereas if the criteria are broader and thus the gateway to assessment wider, it is less likely that the authority will appear to be meeting all the needs of those it assesses.

Despite the absence of a statutory definition of need, the Department of Health *Manager's Guide* (SSISWSG 1991b) suggests that need should be equated with: 'The requirements of individuals to enable them to achieve, maintain or restore an acceptable level of social independence or quality of life as defined by the particular care agency or authority' (Public Law Project 1994, p.11).

The point has already been made earlier in this chapter that following the court's decision in the important test case taken against Gloucestershire County Council,[50] it is probably reasonable for local authorities to establish their own criteria for prioritising assessments according to levels of 'need' and degrees of urgency, notwithstanding the fact that a number of people with expertise in this area have repeatedly expressed a contrary view, such people including senior specialist counsel in this field,[51] and local government ombudsmen, in the latter case on several occasions.[52]

The thrust of the court's decision in the Gloucestershire case was that the relevance of resources in determining need was the same, whether it be under the CSDPA 1970 or the NHSCCA 1990.[53] The judges were quite clear in their view that: 'A local authority is right to take account of resources both when assessing needs and when deciding whether it is necessary to make arrangements to meet those needs.'[54]

They did nevertheless place the following important qualification on this statement:

---

48   R v North Yorkshire CC ex parte Hargreaves, 1994, supra fn.4.

49   Health Committee (House of Commons) (1993) at vol.1 p.xxi.

50   See supra fn.16. For useful commentary on this case see Schwehr 1995.

51   Gordon (1993b) p.15.

52   See for example CLAE 92/C/1994 p.16.

53   A useful book to assist professionals in developing community care plans, including costing, budgeting, and fee charging is Clark and Lapsley (eds) 1995.

54   per Lord Justice McCowan, supra fn.16 p.18.

There will however be situations where a reasonable authority could only conclude that some arrangements were necessary to meet the needs of a particular disabled person and in which it could not reasonably conclude that a lack of resources provided an answer. Certain persons would be at severe physical risk if they were unable to have some practical assistance in their homes. In those situations (we) cannot conceive that an authority would be held to have acted reasonably if it used shortage of resources as a reason for not being satisfied that some arrangement should be made to meet those persons' needs.[55]

Level of assessment

The legislation does not specify the level of assessment that is appropriate in any particular case, but the *Practitioner's Guide* (SSISWSG 1991a, p.42) suggests a model whereby assessment can be at any one of six levels, each level being more complex than the other, thereby reflecting the complexity of need.

The six levels are as follows (brackets contain examples of possible service outcome):

- simple (bus pass, disabled car badge)
- limited assessment (low-level domiciliary support)
- multiple assessment (assistance with meals, chiropody, basic nursing)
- specialist assessment: simple (simple disability equipment)
                                              complex (home adaptation)
- complex assessment (speech therapy)
- comprehensive assessment (family therapy, substitute care, intensive domiciliary support).

Cross-reference to the procedures outlined above with respect to assessments of a disabled person 'with a permanent and substantial handicap' under the CSDPA 1970 is explicitly contained in s.47(2) of the NHSCCA. Circular guidance in this respect is as follows: 'A full scale assessment of all needs should be offered to individuals appearing to be disabled.'[56]

Additional responsibilities towards disabled children

The Children Act 1989 (CA) has added a further raft of duties that are specifically related to 'disabled children'.[57] For these purposes a 'disabled child' is one who is: 'blind, deaf or suffers from mental disorder of any kind or is substantially and permanently handicapped by illness, injury or congenital deformity or such other disability as may be prescribed.'[58]

---

55   ibid.
56   CI 92. SSI Implementing Caring for People: Assessment.
57   For further detail on this issues consult Volume 6 of the Guidance to the Children Act.
58   Children Act 1989 s.17 (11).

These duties also extend to a child whose physical or mental health is unlikely to reach a reasonable standard, or is likely to be significantly impaired, or further impaired, without the provision of special services.[59]

The duty to this group of children is to provide services designed to minimise the effect on them of their disabilities, including so far as it is consistent with that duty, to promote their upbringing *by their families* (our italics), and to give them the opportunity to lead as normal a life as possible. In addition, they must consider whether it is also appropriate to provide disabled children, who are living with their families, with any of a list of services, including advice, counselling, home helps, laundry facilities, assistance with a holiday, and assistance with travel to special day facilities. It should, however, be noted that the local authority will in most cases already have a duty to provide these services under the operation of the CSDPA.[60] For further analysis of these provisions see Chapter Nine, page 238 et seq.

Inspection procedures

There are detailed inspection procedures relating to any premises in which 'community care services' are to be provided.[61] The purpose of these procedures is to complement the complaints procedures, particularly where premises are not for some reason protected by current procedures,[62] and the power to inspect extends to:[63] 'private and voluntary services with which the local authorities have made contracts... It does not exclude smaller homes.'

Under these procedures any person authorised by the Secretary of State may at any reasonable time enter and inspect any premises in which community care services are, or are proposed to be, provided to examine a range of matters including the state and management of the premises, the facilities they provide, records relating to the premises, and may also interview in private any persons residing there.[64] These powers complement those already in place with respect to homes registered under the Registered Homes Act 1994.[65]

Commenting on the purpose of the powers in the Parliamentary debates leading to the passage of the Bill into law, Baroness Blatch said as follows:

---

59   Children Act 1989 s.17(11).

60   The full detail and extent of these responsibilities and duties is set out in the Children Act 1989 ss.17(5), 18, 20, 23 and 24.

61   For full detail consult NHSCCA 1990 s.48.

62   Two new recent publications could be of valuable assistance to those who are concerned with the principles upon which to review and/or evaluate services for disabled people under these provisions, namely Pilling and Watson (eds) 1995, and Phillips and Penhale (eds) 1996.

63   Per Baroness Hooper, Parliamentary Under-Secretary of State for the Department of Health, Hansard HL vol.519 col 37.

64   See p.162 for full details of the provisions.

65   See Chapter Five, p.162.

We would expect such inspections to form part of the investigation of serious complaints and other major irregularities. They may also be used in conjunction with monitoring of local authorities' performance. In any event we do not expect that it will be necessary to make a great deal of use of them. The main inspection and monitoring function in respect of private and voluntary facilities with which local authorities have made arrangements will fall to the authorities themselves.[66]

Commenting on who was most likely to be asked to perform these inspections when necessary, Baroness Hooper suggested:[67]

The persons authorised by the Secretary of State to carry out the inspections...will be drawn for the most part from the Social Services Inspectorate (SSI) and from other members of the staff of the Department of Health. Where such people are not doctors they are almost certain to be qualified in one or other of the caring professions – for instance nurses, social workers or therapists. Such persons will be bound by their own professional codes of conduct which place clear limits on the unauthorised disclosure of information in the course of their professional activities. Even where this might not be the case the people concerned would still be covered by the codes of conduct covering the use made by civil servants of information gained in the course of their employment.

The Carers (Recognition and Services) Act 1985 (CRSA)

An important new piece of legislation, the CRSA, comes into effect on 1 April 1996 (see generally Bates and Clements 1996). This new law explicitly brings the needs of carers into the local authority assessment procedures outlined above in this chapter. In particular, when a disabled person's needs are assessed under the CSDPA, or the NHSCCA or the CA, their carer is also entitled to an assessment, so long as they are a private carer, who is either providing, or intending to provide regular and substantial care[68] to a disabled, ill or elderly person.[69] The local authority must then include the results of this assessment when making decisions about the services that they may provide to the disabled person.

The term carer' applies to adult carers, parent carers and young carers. The legislation also covers carers in Scotland and Northern Ireland, although in Scotland parent carers will not be entitled to receive their own assessment until their own Children (Scotland) Act 1995, comes into force in April 1997.

Community Care (Direct Payments) Bill 1995

This bill received all party support at its second reading on 7 December 1995, and is therefore likely to become law in the course of 1996. The purpose of the bill is to enable local authorities to give disabled people cash rather than services with the object of enabling them to choose, within the resources

---

66   Hansard, HL vol.519, cols 41–2.
67   Hansard, HL vol.520, col 1394.
68   Not defined in Act, but more assistance may be provided by the Policy Guidance which will be forthcoming in the spring of 1996.
69   CRSA 1995 s.1.

available, how and when the services they needed will be provided. It will, however, confer a power rather than a duty, and disabled people will be able to choose whether they would prefer cash or services, or a mix of the two. The categories of disabled people to be included in the bill are to be set by regulations following a consultation process.

The Act will apply in Scotland by amendment to the Social Work (Scotland) Act 1968, and directly in England, Wales and Northern Ireland.

REDRESS FOR THOSE WHO ARE DISSATISFIED WITH THE LOCAL AUTHORITY SERVICES UNDER THE ABOVE RESPONSIBILITIES[70]

I. Internal complaints procedures[71]

The background

Section 50 of the National Health Service and Community Care Act 1990 inserts a new section 7B into the Local Authority Social Services Act 1970. Under this section the Secretary of State has ordered social services' authorities to establish their own complaints procedure for considering representations and complaints concerning the discharge, or failure to discharge any of their social services functions. Many such functions relate directly or indirectly to disabled people and extend beyond the definition of *community care services* in the Act. The complaints procedure is established by legislation. Parliament intended it to be used to resolve problems and disputes concerning the performance or non-performance of social services functions. Some or all of these functions have a significant impact on the lives of disabled people so that the nature, utility and effectiveness of complaints procedures is a matter of some concern to disabled service users and their carers.

Informal complaints

Under the legislation relating to community care, a local authority is obliged in the first instance to seek to resolve all complaints informally if at all possible. If informal resolution fails (or is inappropriate because of the nature of the complaint) the local authority must then give the complainant an explanation of the formal procedure and invite them to submit their complaint in writing within 28 days. If for some reason this is impossible, an extension is permitted for up to three months.

---

70 For reasons of space it has not been possible to deal in this book with matters relating to health authorities. Excellent material covering this field is to be found in Brazier and Lobjoit (eds) (1991) and Brazier (1992).

71 For more information on these procedures see *The Right to Complain: Practice Guidance on Complaints Procedures in Social Services Departments,* HMSO 1991; Gordon (1993A, 1993B); Mandelstam (1995, Chapter 23).

Formal complaints

The government has laid down a series of new procedures for dealing with complaints about a local authority's discharge of (or failure to discharge) its 'social services functions'. Policy guidance suggests that complaints procedures should be: 'uncomplicated, accessible to those who might wish to use them and understood by all members of staff.'[72]

All written complaints must be registered by the local authority, and responded to within 28 days. If the complainant remains dissatisfied, a review panel of three people, chaired by an 'independent person' will be set up, which will be attended by the complainant and their representative who cannot be a practising lawyer. An 'independent person' is defined as:

> a person who is neither a member nor an officer of that authority, nor, where the local authority has delegated any of its social services functions to any organisation, a person who is a member of or employed by that organisation, nor the spouse of any such person.[73]

The panel must make its own recommendations to the local authority after the hearing, within 24 hours of the end of the hearing. The local authority is not, however, bound to follow this recommendation although case law suggests that if they do not do so, a very good reason must be given.[74]

Some indication of the government's intentions regarding the scope of the complaints procedures created under the NHSCCA was given by the government Minister, Baroness Blatch, during the debates that took place during the passing of the Bill through parliament. She explained that if the authority judges that a person is not a person for whom they should provide community care services, and as a result declines to carry out an assessment, then the procedure could not be used. Instead, it would be a 'matter of law' to be decided by the court[75] and a complaints procedure would not be appropriate. On a practical level, availability of the procedure to such people could pave the way for vexatious applicants wasting authorities' time. However, she also pointed out that complaint could still lie to local councillors, members of the social services committee or in the case of maladministration to the local ombudsman (see p.114 et seq).[76]

Whether it is in any event realistic to expect hard pressed local authorities to be able to comply with the above guidelines, especially with regard to the timescales, is another matter. Two preliminary studies by the Social Services

---

72   DH 1990, para.6.14.
73   *Complaints Procedure Directions* 1990; in DH, 1990, Appendix C; made under LASSA 1990, s.7B(3).
74   See R v Avon CC ex parte M, 1994, 2FCR 259.
75   See below under breach of statutory duty p.113.
76   House of Lords, 25 June 1990, col 1396–7 commented by Mandelstam (1995, p.362)

Inspectorate in 1993 revealed that many local authorities were finding these timescales more or less impossible to meet.[77]

2. Complaints to councillors and to council committees

As an alternative to using an internal complaints procedure, dissatisfied users of council services can either complain directly to the officer involved, to the officer's line manager, or to a councillor. The elected councillors are technically the employers of the council officers, and it is they therefore who have ultimate responsibility for the council's work. Every council has an information office which should be able to provide enquirers with details of each council department, together with the name and work address of the head of that department. The head of the council-paid service is called the Chief Executive. The council information office will also provide details of the name and address of the complainant's ward councillor, and of the councillors who serve on the council committee relevant to the complaint, e.g. the social services committee. The complainant can write to any such councillor seeking support for the complaint. Councillors have wide powers to investigate the work of council officials and services, including a right of access to relevant files. The complainant also has a right of access to the files held by the council, which concern their case, by virtue of the Data Protection Act 1984 and the Access to Personal Files Act 1987. It is only in very limited circumstances that access can be legally denied, primarily where revealing the information would either prejudice the carrying out of social work by seriously harming the health or emotional condition of that client or some other person, or would lead to the identification of third parties not employed by that authority, e.g informants (Cooper 1994, p.70).[78]

3. Enforcement of duties through legal action

A. Legal action for a failure to assess

Any failure or refusal by a local authority to assess the needs of a disabled person under the CSDPA can be enforced through the courts, by virtue of the DPSCRA. This, however, is easier said than done, as the only procedure available is that of *judicial review*, which is a procedure in the High Court that

---

77 SSI, 1993, *Progress on the Rights to Complain: Monitoring Social Services Complaints Procedures, 1992–1993*. London: Department of Health; SSI, 1993, Inspection of Complaints Procedures in Local Authority Social Services Department, London: HMSO.

78 For further information on the grounds for withholding information and procedures for obtaining information see the Access to Personal Files (Social Services) Regulation 1989 SI 1989/206 and the Access to Personal Files (Housing) Regulations 1989 SI 1989/503. Where the information in question is also held on computer consult the Data Protection (Subject Access Modification) (Social Work) Order 1987 SI 1987/1903, or for more general information consult either the council's own Data Protection Officer, or the Data Protection Registrar, Wycliffe House, Water Lane, Wilmslow, Cheshire.

is both lengthy and costly. It is, however, an important procedure for challenging the way in which administrative decisions are made by public bodies.

An application for judicial review can be made on the grounds that a public body, including a local authority, has acted *ultra vires*, i.e. outside its legal powers, or has failed to exercise the legal duties with which it is charged. Allegations of unreasonable, irrational and unlawful decision-making will provide the basis for such an application. Decisions concerning social services functions and community care clearly come within the ambit of judicial review (Gordon 1993A). Such decisions could encompass not only questions concerning entitlement to assessment for such services, but also the assessment process itself, the issue of service provision and the way in which complaints are dealt with. Where an application is successful, the High Court may do any of the following:

(i) It may quash the original decision by an order of *certiorari*, i.e. quash an invalid decision or action which has been made or taken.

(ii) It may issue an order of *prohibition* to prevent an illegal, irrational or improper decision from being taken.

(iii) It may issue an order of *mandamus* to compel the performance of a statutory duty.

(iv) It may issue a *declaration* about the law, or the legal rights of the applicant.

(v) It may issue an *injunction* to prevent an illegal act or to enforce the performance of a statutory duty.

(vi) It may award damages.

Despite this wide range of options, it would appear, according to one expert, that: 'The usual remedies for allegedly unlawful assessment decisions, failure of service provision or unlawful complaints procedure decisions will be *certiorari* to quash the decision and *mandamus* to require redetermination of the user's application according to law' (Gordon 1993A).

Judicial review has a number of procedural disadvantages which limit its utility as a means of establishing 'disability law' rights. Applicants for judicial review must be given *leave* to bring their application. This may be refused by the court where there is an alternative appropriate remedy (e.g. the availability of a complaints procedure) or where the applicant does not have sufficient standing, because, for example, they do not have sufficient personal interest in the outcome of the case.[79] *Judicial review* is, however, concerned with the procedure of decision-making, not with the decision itself, so that an assessment for community care services which failed to consider the views of a carer could be quashed. A reassessment which took into account the views of the carer

---

79   On standing see generally Hough 1988. In this article Hough looks in particular at the standing of pressure groups in test cases. Since this article was written however most pressure groups have persuaded courts to give them standing.

would then be secure from *judicial review* though the conclusion of the assessment may be the same. There is normally a three month time limit on judicial review applications. The period runs from the time the applicant became aware of the matter which is the subject of the application. The remedies available are, in any event, always discretionary, and the judge is under no obligation to use them.

Despite these disadvantages judicial review is an important method of enforcing duties and establishing disability law rights (see Hough 1988). A recent example of its ambit is provided by the case of *R v North Yorkshire County Council, Ex parte Hargreaves.*[80] The council offered a respite care placement in respect of a person who suffered from 'physical and mental handicap'. In making the decision, the council failed to ascertain the wishes of the disabled person concerned assuming them to be the same as those of her brother. The application for judicial review made by the brother of the disabled person, was successful on the grounds that the council were not entitled to make such an assumption. The Times Law Report identifies the significance of the decision in the language of entitlement: 'A user of community care services was entitled to express a preference as to which establishments she wished to stay at during periods of respite care.'[81]

Notwithstanding its procedural limitations, the significance of judicial review decisions for disabled people should not be underestimated. Relief is available to individual applicants and their carers. The hearing of judicial review applications by the High Court provides a formal, legalistic and public forum for the articulation and enforcement of 'disability law' rights. Legal aid is available to support the action in appropriate cases. This is in sharp contrast to the relatively informal nature of local authority complaints procedures. Legal decision-making is important in establishing the nature and breadth of the duties and rights that are an important element of disability law.

B. Taking action for failure to follow up assessment with an appropriate plan of action

Whatever the legal duties or responsibilities of a council there will be times when they fail to carry these out. At this stage, various courses of action are available that fall short of the use of judicial review, to an individual who is suffering as a consequence of such failure.

(i) Having carried out assessment under the CDSPA, failing to ensure appropriate services are provided

The procedure available to disabled people who believe that they are not receiving the services to which they are legally entitled under the

---

80   supra fn.4.
81   *ibid.*

CSDPA, following assessment for those services,[82] is to write to the Secretary of State for Social Services requesting direct intervention on their behalf. The Court of Appeal decided, in the case of *Wyatt v. Hillingdon LBC*[83] that it is not open to a complainant to take the local authority to court for failure to carry out their statutory duties under the Act, *unless* the complainant has first gone through this written appeal procedure. This is unfortunate, as research by RADAR (RADAR 1981, 1994, 1995) suggests that not only is the procedure extremely slow, taking up to one year from complaint to resolution, it is also extremely rare for a complainant to persuade the Secretary of State that a local authority is in default.

Another factor to take into consideration before mounting a complaint to the Secretary of State is that only *individual* complaints can be considered, even if a large number of people in one area have an identical complaint. This leaves the way open for large scale non-compliance by hard pressed, or negligent, local authorities who can refuse to carry out some of their duties, in the knowledge that it is most unlikely that they will be brought to task.

The actual powers given to the Secretary of State, in the event of a finding that the local authority is in breach of their statutory duty to provide a particular service, are vague. They appear to be limited to making a declaration that the local authority is 'in default', which is clearly a serious defect in the whole system, as it effectively means that a local authority can be found in default, but the complainant may receive no relief unless they are prepared to take subsequent legal action through the courts. Throughout the early 1970s RADAR conducted an extensive research project into the level of dissatisfaction with local authority provision under the 1970 Act. Its conclusions, published in an interim report entitled *Putting Teeth Into the Act*, make depressing reading, a picture that remains unchanged in RADAR's subsequent publications (RADAR 1981, 1994, 1994A, 1995). It is quite clear that local authorities, for whatever reason, have generally failed to grasp the legal nettle and accept that work under this Act is 'statutory work', i.e. work for which they have statutory responsibility under a legal duty, in exactly the same way as under mental health and child care legislation. Commenting on the complaints procedure to the Secretary of State the first RADAR report stated as follows (RADAR 1981):

> Referral to the Secretary of State has not led to the resolution of any problem if a general issue has been involved. Even when there is a cut-and-dried individual case the procedure may mean that provision is made several months,

---

82   See p.92.
83   78 Local Government Reports 727.

or even years, after the need originally arose, when the time taken by the Secretary of State is added to the delay on the part of the local authority.

Perhaps more serious is the potential conflict of interest highlighted by the report for a Secretary of State who may be a member of a government which is forcing local authorities to cut back generally on their expenditure. When in practical terms the provisions a local authority can make are largely dependent upon Central Government decisions, the Secretary of State may be required to pass judgement on a local authority for actions for which he, or she, as a member of the Cabinet, is indirectly responsible.

(ii) Invoking default powers

The new community care legislation has added a further course of action for an individual or group dissatisfied with the inaction of social services in connection with their social services responsibilities towards disabled inhabitants, through the introduction of what are known as 'default powers'. A 'default power' is: 'an administrative device of last resort which is rarely used and which has as its object the internal efficiency of the executive machinery of the state' (Wade 1988).

Although these 'default powers' are only likely to be used in instances of extreme inaction, they do allow the Secretary of State to *order* a local authority to take a particular course of action. Where a local authority has failed, without reasonable cause to comply with their duties which are social services functions, they may be declared to be in default of a duty or duties by the Secretary of State.[84] This declaration may also direct a local authority to comply with the duty or duties within a specified time. It is, however, generally agreed that any attempt to use default powers as a remedy for an *individual* disabled person adversely affected by the performance or non-performance of a social services duty is inappropriate and is unlikely to be successful:

> (A default remedy) is suitable for dealing with a general breakdown of some public service caused by a local authority's default, but it is quite unsuitable as a remedy for defaults in individual cases... It is reasonable to suppose that the general obligations of public authorities in the areas of health education and welfare are not intended to be enforceable at the suit of individuals (Wade 1988).

The way in which these powers are likely to be used was explained in the House of Lords as follows:[85]

---

84   The NHSCCA 1990 provides social services default powers by introducing a new section into the Local Government Social Services Act 1970.

85   Quoted in Vernon 1994, p.131.

We expect the default procedures to work in the following way. The first stage will be when it comes to the Secretary of State's attention that an authority is failing to discharge its functions. This may come from a number of directions – the work of the Social Services Inspectorate, information received from organisations representing disabled people or by direct representations to the Secretary of State by users of services. The first thing the Secretary of State needs to do is to satisfy himself that the authority has failed without reasonable cause to exercise its functions. This will entail some form of further investigation or enquiry and may include using the general powers of direction to direct the authority to exercise its functions in a particular way... When these powers are used the Secretary of State first has to issue an order then, if it is not complied with, he can seek an order from the court to enforce it.

C. Private law actions for compensation

(i) Actions in Negligence

An action in negligence is a private law action in which a private individual sues another individual or organisation for the damage they have suffered as a result of that person/organisation's action (or sometimes inaction). The action is normally for compensation (called damages) or for an order (for example, an injunction) that the defendant does something that they have failed to do. To establish a claim in negligence the victim must establish first that the other party had a duty of care towards them; second that they fell below the standard of care reasonably expected of a person exercising the skills in question; third that it was that party's actions that caused the injures in question; and fourth that such injuries were a reasonably foreseeable consequence of that action. The law in question is not based in any statute, it is rather the process of evolution through common law principles of fairness and justice that have been established through the courts over the past 150 years. Thus for example, a patient may sue a doctor for failing to treat them to a standard expected of a doctor, as a result of which they have suffered some extra injury, loss or damage to themselves. Similarly, if an occupational therapist installs equipment in a client's home that is so carelessly installed that it causes the client injury, that occupational therapist can be sued for negligence, and be obliged to compensate the client for any injury so caused. In both examples the principle of *vicarious liability* will also normally apply, whereby the negligent person's employer is also normally liable for the injuries caused by the negligence of their employee, unless they are self-employed in which case they will normally remain personally liable, though hopefully protected by professional indemnity insurance (Nelson-Jones 1990).

ii) Actions for breach of statutory duty

In addition to the common law action in negligence it is also sometimes possible to sue an organisation for failing to carry our their statutory duty, for example a factory that does not comply with its safety responsibilities under the Factories Acts as a result of which an employee suffers an injury. In deciding whether or not to allow an action to succeed in this area, the court normally begins by asking the question: Was it the purpose of the Act that it should be used for a private action in damages? If not, the court will not allow such an action unless it can be shown that no alternative enforcement machinery exists with relation to that statute.[86]

Thus, the question: can a disabled individual sue a local authority for damages in a private law action for failing to carry out its statutory duties towards them under any of the above legislation, where they have suffered injury, loss or damage? The law in this area is by no means clear. To date, where actions have been attempted, they have not been very successful, but that does not mean that the law will always be so negative in this respect. In the field of child care, it has been decided that local authority clients are not the same as health service patients, as the former have had services thrust upon them.[87] Thus, any duty of care owed by local authority staff, in the context of child care, has been found by the House of Lords to be owed not to the client, but to the local authority, thereby effectively denying individuals the right to sue a local authority for injuries caused by their failure to exercise their statutory duty.

In explaining the reason for this decision their lordships stated that:

> The purpose of the child care legislation was to establish an administrative system designed to promote the social welfare of the community and within that system very difficult decisions have to be taken, often on the basis of inadequate and disputed facts, whether to split the family in order to protect the child. In that context and having regard to the fact that the discharge of the statutory duty depends on the subjective judgement of the local authority, the legislation is inconsistent with any parliamentary intention to create a private cause of action against those responsible for carrying out the difficult functions under the legislation.[88]

---

86 Lonrho Ltd v Shell Petroleum Company Ltd 1982 A.C.173.
87 X and others (minors) v Bedfordshire BC, X and M (a minor v Newham London BC, E (a minor) v Dorset CC (HL) 1995 3 All E.R.353.
88 *ibid.* at 356.

This should be contrasted with a similar case regarding duty to provide after care services to certain ex-detained mental patients, where it was held that this duty was to an individual rather than to the authority.[89]

D. Complaints to the Local Government Ombudsman (LGO)[90]

If the complainant considers that not receiving a proper service from their local authority is a result of *maladministration* by the relevant officers it is always open to them to complain to the Commissioner for Local Administration, (normally described as the Local Government Ombudsman) (LGO). The office of the LGO was established by Parliament in 1974, and enhanced by further legislation in 1989. The Office of the LGO is an independent, though government sponsored, network of trained investigators whose job it is to investigate complaints by individuals alleging maladministration against their local authority. Ombudsmen will only carry out an enquiry if satisfied that all other routes to redress have been used, and the matter remains unresolved. In other words the procedure is one of last resort, once all other procedures have been exhausted.

The main grounds on which LGOs initiate investigations are allegations of maladministration. The term *maladministration* is defined very broadly to include undue delay, bias, discrimination, failure to apply rules of procedure, general misconduct and incompetence. Although legislation does not define the term 'maladministration' it is generally accepted that it includes circumstances where local authorities (the list is not exhaustive):

- use inappropriate decision making procedures
- fail to follow an agreed policy, established rules or processes
- give wrong or misleading advice

---

89   See in particular E (a minor) v Dorset CC 1994 (CA) All E.R. 4 640; and X others (minors) v Bedfordshire BC, X and M (a minor v Newham London BC, E (a minor) v Dorset CC (HL) 1995 All.E.R. 3 353; and also T v Surrey CC 1994, where a local authority was held liable for negligent misstatement in recommending a childminder they had doubts about. The failure to deregister however was not a breach of duty of care.

90   There are currently three LGO offices in England, and one each in Wales, Scotland and Northern Ireland. Their addresses are as follows:

England:
21 Queen Anne's Gate, London SW1H 9BU
(covers Greater London, Kent, Surrey, Sussex and Southend).
The Oaks, Westwood Way, Westwood Business Park, Coventry CV4 8JB
(covers South-West, West, South, East Anglia, Central England).
Beverley House, 17 Shipton Road, York, YO3 6FZ
(covers East Midlands and North of England).
Wales:
Derwen House, Court Road, Bridgend, Mid-Glamorgan, CF31 1BN
Scotland:
23 Walker Street, Edinburgh EH3 7HX
Northern Ireland:
33 Wellington Place, Belfast BT1 6HN.

- are biased or unnecessarily slow.

The jurisdiction of the LGO does not extend to issues which can be decided by a tribunal or a court, or may be referred to a minister unless it is considered unreasonable for the complainant to do so.

Though investigations by the LGO can take a substantial period of time and recommendations cannot be enforced against a local authority, such investigations nevertheless often concern issues of importance to disabled people. LGO offices have identified a number of complaints concerning disability law. These range across a wide spectrum and include complaints concerning the way in which local authorities deal with children with special educational needs and their parents;[91] the assessment of disabled people and the failure of councils to comply with statutory duties under the CSDPA, the DPSCRA and the NHSCCA.[92] In addition to reports which provide redress to individual complainants the identification of maladministration within a local authority can lead to an improvement in the quality of administration to the benefit of whole categories of service users including disabled people.

PROCEDURE FOR MAKING A COMPLAINT

The procedure for laying a complaint is straightforward. The complainant, or their representative, writes a letter to the office of the nearest LGO, setting out the nature of the alleged maladministration. The complaint should normally be lodged within 12 months of the incident, earlier if possible. The complainant must first have brought the matter to the attention of the council in question using any available complaints procedures. The LGO cannot investigate matters where there is still an existing right of appeal to a tribunal, minister or court which has not been used, so if, for example, the default powers to write to a Minister under the CSDPA 1970. have not been used, the LGO will refer the matter back to the complainant, for them to do so. LGOs have no power to investigate matters which relate to the wider community, e.g. policy issues. Their powers are confined to the investigation of individual complaints.

Once the LGO has determined they have the power to investigate the complaint[93] they will write formally to the council in question, setting out the grounds of the complaint and inviting the relevant council officials or councillors to give their side of the story. Having received the council response, the LGO will decide whether there is a case to answer. If they think there *is* a case to answer, an investigator will be despatched to the relevant offices to interview officials, councillors, and to inspect files. The council is obliged to allow the

---

91   See Chapter Nine, p.244 et seq for further details on this issue.

92   See generally supra Chapter Four.

93   It is interesting to note that in only 12 per cent of initial complaints do LGOs find grounds to proceed. Once a formal investigation has occurred, a finding of maladministration occurs in around 60 per cent of those cases. This is from a total of between 2000 and 3000 complaints a year across the country as a whole.

LGO access to their files, unless they claim that the 'public interest' requires a particular file should remain confidential to them, in which case the LGO has the same powers as the court to compel the file to be revealed, which can at this stage be opposed only through a court action by the party seeking to withhold the document.[94] If such a claim is made, only a court can decide whether or not to order disclosure of the files. Refusals to disclose are, however, rare. They are only likely to be upheld in cases where the personal social services have been involved in highly sensitive decisions regarding an individual that it would be inappropriate to disclose to a third party.

In addition to visiting the relevant council offices, homes, etc. the LGO will also interview the complainant, together with other relevant parties, e.g their relatives. All interviews are conducted in private, and are intended to be informal in nature. After the interviews have been concluded the LGO will compile a 'statement of facts' which will then be circulated to all parties, in draft, for their agreement.

Having agreed with all parties a 'statement of facts' (if this is possible, which is not always the case), the LGO will then prepare a report which will decide whether maladministration has in fact taken place. If the decision is affirmative, the LGO will also suggest an appropriate remedy, which can include financial compensation. Whilst the LGO does not have the power to enforce the proposed remedy, in most cases the decision of the LGO is accepted, and the remedy carried out by the offending council. The final report is then made public, although individuals are not identified.

The Commission of Local Administration (CLA) has published a guide in which it sets out the 42 axioms of good administrative practice, and it is around significant failures to match up to these axioms that most of the work of LGOs revolves. The list includes such matters as ensuring that decisions are always made within a reasonable time frame, giving reason for adverse decisions, publication and communication of policies to consumers, and adequate training of staff in procedures and liabilities.[95] It does appear that complaints about social services authorities' performance on home adaptations represent a large part of the caseload of a typical LGO. These can be grouped under a number of heads, of which the most common are complaint about delay. In 1993, for example, Wirral Council on Merseyside was censured for extreme delay in no fewer than four separate cases, ranging from one in which a thalidomide victim in his early thirties had to wait five years, and in great pain, for essential adaptations to his home, to another in which a woman suffering from a heart condition, arthritis and cancer had to wait two years for the installation of a shower. In all these cases compensation ranging from £300 to £2000 was recommended by the ombudsman. It should not, however, be assumed that an

---

94   Local Government Act 1974 s.29.
95   Commission for Local Administration in England, 1993, *Good Administrative Practice.*

ombudsman will automatically deem delay to be maladministration, especially if it can be shown that the local authority was under-resourced, and had taken clear steps to prioritise cases in response to the problems caused by under-resourcing.[96] Thus, a six month delay for home adaptation assessment was not deemed maladministration by the LGO, as the local authority had installed a system of priorities which took into account the sort of factors which might be important when such time scales were involved. Within this system, the applicant's priority was relatively low. In these circumstances the ombudsman was able to conclude: 'I have considered whether the application should have been given priority…, but in my view this would have been unfair to other residents awaiting adaptations.'[97]

In another case, a 15 month delay was not deemed to constitute maladministration. The ombudsman in this case concluded that:

> The local authority has adopted a policy of priority categories for the allocation of referrals, as they are entitled to do, and my investigation has shown that the applicant's referral was dealt with properly according to the policy. Taking into account the council's particular resource and staffing difficulties the delay was not so unreasonable as to amount to maladministration in this case.[98]

Other common manifestations of maladministration are inadequate procedures for screening and prioritising cases. For example, in one case maladministration was declared by the ombudsman on the basis of poor assessment forms that did not enable an occupational therapist to make an informed decision regarding clients' needs.[99] Another common form of maladministration occurs when priority criteria are applied inconsistently by local authorities. Thus, maladministration was declared to have occurred in a local authority where an applicant for a renovation grant in one part of the borough was dealt with in weeks, whilst those in another part of the borough had to wait for years,[100] and similarly in another case in which the council was found to have misapplied priority criteria in over 10 per cent of their cases.[101]

A further common source of complaint to the ombudsman is the failure of the local authority to provide an appropriate service because of understaffing, and in particular because of a lack of qualified occupational therapists able to carry out assessments and make recommendations for subsequent provision.[102]

---

96 The question whether delay in providing services, due to under-resourcing, might also amount to a breach of statutory duty (see pp.113–4) is addressed as a separate issue in the case of R v Gloucestershire CC ex parte Mahfood supra fn.16 and accompanying text.

97 CLAE 91/A/3466, p.13.

98 CLAE 91/A/1693, p.25.

99 CLAE 92/C/O670, p.7.

100 CLAE 91/A/3911, p.18; CLAE 91/A/0482, p.20.

101 CLAE 92/A/1693.

102 This is not withstanding the fact that there are currently considerable shortages of qualified OTs in the majority of local authority settings, a matter of some concern to the profession.

Caselaw in this area suggests that ombudsmen are generally unsympathetic to such an excuse from a local authority. For example, in a case involving a three month wait for assessment of a 19-year-old woman suffering from autism and in need of day centre attendance, the ombudsman decided that staff shortages or departmental organisation can never justify a failure to respond to repeated requests of this seriousness for help.[103] In another case, the ombudsman categorically asserted that: 'Shortage of money, communication and administration problems do not absolve the Council from their statutory duty.'[104]

To put it more bluntly, if appropriately qualified staff are not available to a local authority to carry out that authority's statutory responsibilities, the authority should seek other means to ensure that people do not wait too long for an assessment, whatever those means might be.

Ironically, the main problem with the LGO investigation system itself is also delay. The average processing time for a complaint to the LGO is around 47 weeks from start to finish. In fact, in England and Wales complaints to the LGO about social services departments have been comparatively rare. In the first two years of the operation of the LGO in England and Wales, only 20 of the 466 reports issued related to social services departments.

E. Complaints to the local authority monitoring officer

All local authorities are supposed to appoint a monitoring officer whose job it is to monitor possible breaches of legislation and codes of practice by the authority in question. The position is created by statute.[105] Under the statute creating the post, the monitoring officer has a duty to report on actual or possible maladministration or injustice caused by the authority, if it: 'At any time appears to him, or her, that any proposal, decision or omission constitutes (or is likely to give rise to) a contravention of any enactment or rule of law, or of any code of practice.'

Given the nature of this officer's brief it would seem appropriate to use the officer as another possible avenue of complaint, if it appears that any of the statutory responsibilities mentioned above are not going to be exercised by the authority in question.

F. Miscellaneous duties

In addition to the above specific duties, a local authority must generally consider the needs of the disabled people in its area when designing new housing schemes. Also, under a series of statutes and associated regulations, new 'non-domestic buildings', e.g. new public buildings, offices, shops, and ground floor extensions to such buildings should include a number of features designed to assist the access and mobility of those with disabilities, including impaired

---

103 CLAE 93/C/0005.
104 CLAE/C/0670, p.7.
105 Local Government and Housing Act 1989 s.5

hearing and/or sight. These features include the construction of staircases with standardised hand rail height; the use of marked glazed panels on entrance doors; the use of platform lifts as an alternative to a ramp where there is a change of level within a building; regulations on the scale and design of special toilet provision, and so forth.[106] Although the responsibilities are to be welcomed, these new powers and duties are, however, by no means comprehensive, they generally apply only to new buildings, and no significant grant aid is available for this installation. Finally, it should be stressed that the circulars do encourage each local authority to appoint an 'access officer' to provide a clearly identified point of contact on questions of access for the disabled, from members of the public and it is important that local authorities should be pressed to make such an appointment.

---

106 For details see in particular The Building Regulations 1991; *Access for Disabled People. Approved Document M* (amended 1992) DOE/HMSO, although it should be noted that these are in a constant state of change and revision, and also the level of enforcement does vary significantly between areas. In reality this is a question of good practice, politics and benchmarking rather than strict law enforcement.

CHAPTER FIVE

EMPLOYMENT, HOUSING, GOODS AND SERVICES

EMPLOYMENT

Although 70 per cent of people with disabilities in the UKdevelop their disability after reaching working age, the rights of disabled people to special employment consideration are poor and remain largely unenforced. Both the National Audit Office and the Public Accounts Committee of the House of Commons have regularly voiced criticism of the system and called for strong action to reform the system. In recent years, largely in response to this criticism, the Government's Employment Service has reorganised its disability employment programme. The Employment Service is now the principal government agency responsible for co-ordinating and improving efforts to assist disabled people in finding employment, with its primary focus being on job centres and benefits. From this service can be obtained a host of leaflets and booklets providing further information on all of their activities. There are also a number of leaflets dealing with the specialist difficulties associated with the employment of those with mental illness or learning disability, with epilepsy, with multiple sclerosis and those who are visually or hearing impaired. The Employment Service is part of the Department of Education and Employment. At a local level much of the formal activity associated with implementing government initiatives with regard to disability and employment is devolved to local Placing, Assessment and Counselling (PACT) teams, working in Job Centres.

Whilst legislation in this area has traditionally remained outmoded, and inadequate, the 1995 Disability Discrimination Act holds out substantially greater prospects than in the past for significant advances to take place with regard to employment prospects for people with disabilities, if it is enforced in a positive way. Even without this new legislation, a lot can be done to assist disabled people to acquire, or keep employment with adequate advice and information.

The historical position

Prior to the introduction of the Disability Discrimination Act in 1995[1] there existed a *quota system*, that was supposed to achieve a limited level of 'positive discrimination' in favour of disabled people seeking employment.[2] By virtue of the *Disabled Persons (Employment) Acts* of 1944 and 1958, certain categories of employer were obliged to operate a quota system whereby a minimum of 3 per cent of their workforce was supposed to be drawn from the Register of Disabled Persons.

This Register is the general responsibility of the Employment Service, under the overall control of the Department of Education and Employment. It is a different Register from the register kept by the Social Services Department under the CSDPA 1970.[3] The definition of a disabled person for the purposes of this Register was located strongly within the 'medical model':

> A person who on account of injury, disease (including a physical or mental condition arising from imperfect development of any organ) or congenital deformity, is substantially handicapped in obtaining or keeping employment, or in undertaking work on his own account, of a kind which apart from that injury, disease or deformity would be suited to his age experience and qualifications.[4]

'Disease' was defined as 'including a physical or mental condition arising from imperfect development of any organ.'

In addition to falling within this definition the disabled person had to show themselves to be likely to remain disabled for at least 12 months and be actively looking for work, with some prospect of finding work. The prospect of finding work referred to the degree of impairment suffered by the disabled person and not to the general employment conditions in the area.

To get onto the Register, an applicant filled out a form provided by the Disability Employment Adviser (DEA, now subsumed in the local PACT team: see page 123) at their local job centre, describing the nature of their disability. If the conditions described above were clearly satisfied, the DEA immediately registered the applicant and granted them a Green Card (certificate of registration). The certificate could be granted for a period of from one to ten years, or until retirement. It could be renewed on further application. The registered

---

1   For the background to the introduction of this Act see Chapter Three, p.77 et seq.

2   See generally Leighton and Painter 1987 and Doyle 1995. This section is written largely in the past tense because it is the intention of the Disability Discrimination Act 1995 by virtue of ss.61 and 70, and Schedules 7–7, to remove the quota system (including reserved employment) at the same time as introducing the sections of the Act (Part II) relating to the new employment discrimination regime. This is currently expected to occur c. December 1996–January 1997. It is interesting to note in this context that both France and Germany have retained (and in this case of Germany expanded) such a quota system in employment: see Chapter Three, p.64.

3   See Chapter Four, p.92.

4   Disabled Persons (Employment) Act 1944 s.1.

person could apply to remove their name from the Register at any time they wished by writing to the local job centre or to the Employment Service. The Register is divided into two sections:

Section One: comprising people who seemed to be capable of 'open' employment.

Section Two: comprising those deemed only to be suitable for 'sheltered' employment (see page 127).

If there was any doubt as to the applicant's eligibility, the application went before a panel of the Committee for the Employment of People with Disabilities (CEPD). This Committee included representatives of employers and workers, doctors and people interested in the problems of disablement. The panel included a representative of each of the categories listed above. The applicant was invited to attend before the panel, and could be accompanied by a representative of their choice, e.g. a social worker, trade union representative or advice worker. The panel could require medical evidence – normally a letter from the applicant's GP. Alternatively the job centre arranged a special medical examination. Any loss of earnings or travelling expenses incurred by this medical examination were met by the job centre. The hearing was in private, after which the panel made a recommendation to the DEA. If accepted, registration took place.

Any employer with a workforce of 20 or more was subject to the Act, with the exception of the Crown and government departments. Local government departments, who by law are only allowed to make paid appointments on *merit*,[5] were specifically allowed to ignore this criterion in respect of registered disabled applicants, if the authority in question was below quota. The crucial flaw in the system, however, was the fact that it was possible for an employer to apply for a temporary permit exempting them from compliance with the quota, normally for a period of six months. Although such a permit was only supposed to be granted to the employer who had produced convincing evidence why no job suitable for a disabled employee was likely to become available within the following six months, official government figures published in 1988 stated that in 1986 only 27 per cent of employers met the 3 per cent quota while 56 per cent had obtained exemption permits (Clarke 1994, p.105). Being below quota

---

5   s 7 Local Government and Housing Act 1989. By virtue of the proposed abolition in December 1996/January 1997 of the quota: see supra fn.2, local authorities will no longer be able to practise this very helpful type of 'positive discrimination' as they will be obliged to make all paid appointments on *merit* alone. The 'reasonable adjustment' provisions of the Disability Discrimination Act 1995 will, however, make an impact in this area: see page 131, and local authorities should still be able to offer guaranteed or preferential interviewing, and special recruitment drives for disabled applicants so long as the jobs are not 'reserved' for a disabled quota. Similarly, in appropriate circumstances, e.g. the appointment of disability advisers or co-ordinators, it will remain lawful to include in the job description reference to 'experience or understanding of disability' as an essential or a desirable criterion.

has never been an offence in itself. *Being below quota when a suitable disabled person was available to do the job* was the offence, punishable on conviction in a magistrate's court by a fine not exceeding £400. If the employer was a corporate body, the maximum fine was, and still remains, £2000.

The 'quota system' was, by common consent, an abject failure. First, disabled workers have always been reluctant to register as disabled, on the grounds that they perceived (probably correctly) that being on the Register stigmatised them in the eyes of many. The evidence for this assertion is to be found in the figures which show that between 1950 and 1986 the numbers on the Register fell from 936,000 to 389,272 (Clarke 1994, p.109). Second, failure to comply with the law on quotas hardly ever led to any punishment. In the 50 years of the quota system's existence there were only ten prosecutions under the Act.[6] It is scarcely credible that this low number is explicable by a similarly low number of breaches of the Act! Third, only the Secretary of State for Employment had the power to initiate prosecutions under the Act. For political reasons this was a very poor enforcement tool. Fourth, a glance at the limited caselaw demonstrates that as an enforcement tool the legislation was, in any event, more or less worthless, given its liberal drafting:

> In 1992 a registered disabled employee who was dismissed from her job sought a judicial review of the Employment Secretary's refusal to prosecute her employer, on the ground that the Minister failed to give any reason for his decision. As a result the Minister provided the reasons. He denied that there was a policy of non-enforcement, but stated that officials would first attempt to settle any case by negotiation. If that failed, then prosecution would be considered, in the light of all the evidence, including whether the employer had a defence that the dismissal was reasonable (Clarke 1994, p.109)[7]

Not surprisingly, the Public Accounts Committee concluded in 1994 that the quota system was 'ineffective, unenforceable and out of date'. Only the most abject forms of unskilled manual work were reserved as priority work for disabled people under the 'quota scheme', namely electric lift operators and car park attendants which by law had in the first instance to be registered disabled people. Only if no such person was available for the job could it be offered to non-disabled people. The failure to add any more substantial jobs to this list was one of the serious inadequacies of the system.

The introduction of PACTS

A more promising initiative that has been developed to encourage more disabled people into the workforce is the creation in 1993 of Placing, Assessment and Counselling Teams, otherwise known as PACTS. PACTS are a positive step forward by providing local centres that focus upon good practice in the

6   Figures taken from House of Commons Select Committee 1990–1991, and cited in
     Clarke (1994).
7   The actual case is cited in IRLIB, no.457, p.16.

employment of people with disabilities. They are essentially a team of people skilled and experienced in keeping people with disabilities in work. The PACTS bring together the former work of Disablement Employment Advisers (DEAs), the Disability Advisory Service (DAS) and parts of the Employment Rehabilitation Service (DRS). PACTs also work with local disabled people on vocational training and rehabilitation (Berthoud, Lakey and McKay 1993, p.39). PACTS provide written guidance to employers in the form of the *Code of Good Practice on the Employment of Disabled People*. This Code, which was first issued in 1984 by the Manpower Services Commission (the precursor of the Employment Service), was reissued in March 1993 by the Department of Employment (now Department of Education and Employment). Research suggests that where the Code has actually been received by employers (in about 20% of the total employment force) penetration of the Code throughout levels of management is good (Morrell 1990). PACTS offer public re-enforcement of such compliance, for example the 'disability symbol' (logo) can be awarded by PACTS to employers who wish to advertise the fact that they have taken positive steps to make employment of disabled people easier, and who encourage disabled employees to work for them. The Register of Disabled Persons (so long as it remains in existence) will continue to be the responsibility of the local PACT.

Local PACTS are supported by nine regional Ability Development Centres (ADCs), who work on developing new techniques in providing employment advice 'for disabled people entering work, or for employees who have become disabled and need to adjust to new circumstances'.[8] For large employers, there is an additional good practice advisory service called Major Organisations Development Unit (MODU) that is based in London, but available nationwide. There are also a number of practical sources of help to employers that may act as an incentive to employ more disabled people.

Legal duty of companies to state their policy concerning disabled employees

Any company employing more than 250 people[9] is obliged by law[10] to include in the Director's Report a statement of the company's policy for that year concerning disabled employees, including information on such matters as the employment, training and advancement of disabled persons in that company.

---

8   For further information on ADCs contact the Employment Service Disability Services Branch, DSI, c/o Rockingham House, 123 West Street, Sheffield S1 4ER (Tel: 0114-2739190).

9   By this figure is meant companies with an average number of employees exceeding 250 within the United Kingdom in each week of the previous financial year: Companies Act 1985 Schedule 7 para.9.

10   The Companies (Directors' Reports) (Employment of Disabled Persons) Regulations 1980, SI No.1160 together with the Companies Act 1948 s.454(1) and the 1985 Companies Act s.234.

If the company has no policy, it should say so. Only the civil service, nationalised industries, health authorities and local authorities are exempted from this legal duty. Directors' Reports are available for public inspection at the Companies Registration Office. Specifically, the report must contain a statement setting out the measures they have taken in the past 12 months:

- to ensure the continuing employment of, and appropriate training for employees who became disabled during their employment with the company
- to ensure full and fair consideration has been given to job applications by disabled people, having regard to their particular aptitudes and skills
- for the training, career development and promotion of disabled employees.

This duty applies to all 'disabled workers' whether or not they appear on the Register. Failure to produce a statement is a criminal offence by the directors,[11] unless they can show they took all reasonable steps to ensure the statement was included in the Report, notwithstanding its non-appearance.[12] There is a Code of Good Practice associated with the provision, Part One of which gives guidance on implementation of policies to bring about higher levels of recruitment of disabled employees. Adherence to the practice and spirit of the provisions is, however, weak, and whether many, or indeed any prosecutions have occurred under this provision is unlikely (see Doyle 1987, p.20).

Disabled employees and dismissal

Under general employment law, an employee only acquires statutory protection from unfair dismissal once they have been in the continuous employment of their employer for at least two years. Statutory protection means that after two years of continuous employment, dismissal will only be lawful if it was 'fair', a category that is carefully defined by the relevant case law and legislation (see generally Lewis 1994, p.242). A registered disabled employee may be entitled to special consideration by an employer, including consideration of their personal difficulties, before a decision to dismiss is taken.[13] If an employer seeks to dismiss a disabled employee for incompetence, their disability must be taken into account. The dismissal is then only likely to be fair if the employee's performance is still below what can reasonably be expected of them. If the disability leads to an unacceptable level of ill-health absenteeism, the employer should follow exactly the same procedure for ill-health dismissal as for an able-bodied employee.[14] If the disability or ill-health was known to the

---

11 Companies Act 1985 s.234 (5).
12 Companies Act 1985 s.234 (6).
13 Seymour v British Airways Board 1983 ICR 148 (EAT).
14 Shook v Ealing London Borough Council 1986 ICR 314 (EAT).

employer at the time of engagement,[15] or was job-related, the employer should take especially sympathetic steps to try to avoid dismissal, or to provide more appropriate alternative employment.[16] In the case of an employee who becomes disabled during the course of their employment such that they are no longer capable of performing their job to a satisfactory level, consequential dismissal *will* however be deemed to be fair, so long as the employer has acted reasonably in all the circumstances. If evidence supports the conclusion that a disabled employee cannot continue in his or her job without being a danger to others, it would normally be permissible either to move that employee to other work (if practicable) or to dismiss.[17]

Finally it is important to stress that in all other employment respects, disabled employees enjoy the same employment rights as able-bodied employees.[18] For a more detailed account of the general rights of all employees with regard to appointment, dismissal, redundancy, maternity leave and pay, time off for trade union and public duties, consult Lewis (1994, p.215).

Financial assistance schemes

Since mid-1994, a number of previously diverse schemes for the assistance of disabled people in obtaining access to work have been grouped together by the Department of Employment (and Education) under the *Access to Work Scheme.*

Access to Work Scheme

The Scheme provides support for disabled workers and their employers. It is estimated that it helps around 9000 disabled people obtain or keep jobs every year, and thereby saves £23.5m in benefits (TUC 1995). The future direction of the scheme is, however, at the time of writing under review by the Employment Service.

At present the Scheme provides support for the following services:

- communicators for people who are deaf or have a hearing impediment, including the use of a communicator at a job interview

- a part-time reader or assistance at work for someone who is blind or visually impaired

- support workers, if person needs practical help at work, or getting to work

- equipment or adaptations to existing equipment to suit individual needs. For example, the Employment Service can loan employers special tools, or other 'high-tech' equipment such as braille typewriters, talking calculators, hoists and hearing aids in appropriate cases. A special scheme

---

15   Kerr v Atkinson Vehicles (Scotland) Ltd 1984 IRLR 36 (IT).
16   Garricks (Caterers) Ltd v Nolan 1980 IRLR 259 (EAT).
17   Harper v National Coal Board (1980) IRLR 260 (EAT).
18   See general RADAR booklet, *Employment Rights: a Guide for Disabled People.*

also exists to help self-employed people with the start-up costs of installing appropriate technology in the home

- alterations to premises or a working environment so that an employee with a disability can work there. For example, grant aid is available to adapt premises to accommodate the particular needs of disabled employees, to install such items as access ramps, special toilets, rails or other adaptations

- adaptations to a car, or taxi fares or other transport costs to enable a disabled employee to get to work.

Up to £21,000 can be made available in respect of a disabled individual (employed, unemployed or self-employed) over a five year period, which can be spread over more than one job in that period. Exceptionally, the Employment Service can authorise payment over this amount. Priority is given to helping those who are currently unemployed. Employers do not have to make any financial contribution.

Under the Scheme the DEA can also advise employers on how to recruit disabled people, on ways of retaining an employee who becomes disabled, on workplace adaptations, and on the provision of a follow-up service, once the disabled person has been in place for a period of time.[19]

Job Introduction Scheme

Under the *Job Introduction Scheme* the Employment Service can make a grant to an employer towards the cost of the employment of a disabled applicant[20] for a six week trial period so long as the position is expected to last for at least six months after the trial period. In addition, under this scheme the employer can pay the employee a small amount to cover travel, midday meal, and out of pocket expenses, which can be claimed back from the Employment Service.

Sheltered Placement Schemes

There are special alternative work schemes offered by many local authorities in conjunction with their local DEA known as the *Sheltered Placement Scheme*. Under this scheme, certain disabled people (normally those who are able to do a particular job but at a very slow pace) are employed as if they can work at normal speed, and paid a normal wage from the employer, then the employer claims a subsidy from the Employment Service to cover the lost productivity. Thus, in practice the employer will simply pay the employee for the work done, and their salary will then be 'topped up' by the Employment Service. Further

---

19 For full details consult Employment Service Leaflet PGP 10.

20 Defined for these purposes as a disabled person (who need not be registered as disabled) who in the opinion of the DEA or Employment Adviser requires a period of adjustment in the proposed job to help them demonstrate their capabilities to the new employer.

information on all the above schemes can be obtained from the Employment Service Disability Services Branch,[21] or the local PACT.

Training for Work Scheme

Finally, note should be taken of the *Training and Enterprise Councils (TECs)*, which have devolved regional responsibility to undertake a broad range of training and job development initiatives on behalf of central government. Of particular importance here is the *Training for Work Scheme*, which is specifically focussed on groups of disadvantaged unemployed people seeking employment, including those who are unemployed and disabled, or unemployed and in receipt of invalidity benefit or severe disability allowance. For more details contact the local TEC.

Health and Safety

The Health and Safety at Work Act of 1974, as supplemented by a host of statutory instruments, European Law directives, common law, and other guidance sets out the framework governing the duties of employers to provide a safe workplace for employees. Once an employee with a known disability has been engaged by an employer, that employer has a common law duty of care to ensure that any reasonable adjustments are made to the workplace to ensure that the employee is reasonably safe from injury or accident, taking into account the particular nature of the employee's disability.[22]

Groups that can help

The Employers Forum on Disability[23] is a national employers' organisation which aims to provide enhanced job prospects for people with disabilities and to help employers to recruit, retain and develop disabled employees. It provides practical support and advice to members wishing to improve employment practice, and works with government and voluntary agencies to improve policies of job and training prospects. It publishes a quarterly newsletter, and a series of booklets on such matters as *Disability Etiquette, Welcoming Disabled Customers, Employer's Agenda on Disability, Employers Action File on Disability* and a variety of other leaflets and information packs.

In addition to the above a number of excellent books and articles have been written in recent years setting out good practice for managing disability at work (Kettle and Massie 1986; Smith, Povall and Floyd 1991), for promoting further recruitment of those with physical and mental disabilities (Wansborough and Cooper 1979; Bolderson 1980; Kulkarni 1981; Cornes 1982; Floyd, Gregory, Murray and Welchman 1983; Doyle 1987a), and demonstrating the capacities

---

21   For full address see fn.8.
22   Qualcast (Wolverhampton) Ltd v Haynes (1959) AC 743 (HL); Paris v Stepney Borough Council (1951) AC 367 (HL).
23   Nutmeg House, 60 Gainsford St, London SE1 2NY (Tel: 0171-403 3020).

for self-employment for disabled people, in particular in the developing countries of Africa and Asia (Harper and Momm 1989). Two international overviews are also available (Habeck, Galvin, Frey, Chadderton, Tate 1985 and Lunt and Thornton 1993).

The Disability Discrimination Act 1995

Reporting in 1986 on the current state of legislative support for the greater deployment of disabled people in the workforce, the National Advisory Council on the Employment of Disabled People commented as follows:[24] 'Legislation properly designed and applied is an essential tool, particularly when supported by persuasive action, for helping the employment prospects of disabled people.'

The *Disability Discrimination Act 1995 (the DDA)*, is the first real fruit of that stated policy (Doyle 1996).

DDA Part II

Part II of the DDA is the Part of the Act that deals with discrimination in connection with employment'. Discrimination in connection with employment covers recruitment, selection, treatment whilst in employment, and dismissal. This is to be the first Part of the Act to come into force.[25] In many ways it follows the parallel provisions of the Sex Discrimination Act 1975 and the Race Relations Act 1976, with regard to discrimination on the grounds of gender or race with the very important difference, that unlike in those two cases there is to be no Commission charged with the enforcement and implementation of the DDA, a source of considerable criticism amongst disability groups.

The general purpose of Part II is to render unlawful certain types of discrimination against actual or potential employees or service providers if that discrimination is based upon their disability. It only applies to employment within Great Britain[26] or Northern Ireland.[27] It does not cover discrimination in partnerships, although it does cover discrimination by partners with regard to employees of that partnership. As much of the detail of the DDA is to be developed in the course of 1996 through the publication of detailed regulations and a Code (s) of Practice, not to mention the interpretative case law that will inevitable develop, once Part II has come fully into force in 1997, this section of the chapter can only provide an outline commentary on the structure and likely impact of Part II. It should also be read in conjunction with Chapter Three,[28] which set out the broad definitions of disability that are used in the

---

24 *Report of National Advisory Council on the Employment of Disabled People,* para.6.6.
25 At the time of writing this is expected to be between early December 1996 and late January 1997.
26 DDA s.68
27 DDA s.70(6) and Schedule 8.
28 In particular see pp.84–8.

DDA. There is already a good detailed analysis commentary on the DDA available by Brian Doyle (Doyle 1996). Others will surely follow.

Employment excluded from the protection of the DDA

The following groups are exempted from the provisions of the Act:

- small businesses with less than 20 employees.[29] It is not clear from the Act how numbers will be determined in cases of associated employers or corporate groups. This will be dealt with in policy guidance and/or the Code of Practice.

- statutory office holders e.g. the police force, prison officers, armed forces, and fire fighters, though not non-statutory employers carrying out any of these tasks e.g. Group 4 acting as custody officers.

If employers are providing special supported employment to disabled people under the Disabled Persons (Employment) Act 1944,[30] or some other charitable authority, they will not be bound by the terms of the Act, where they discriminate on behalf of one disabled group against another disabled group.[31]

WHEN WILL DISCRIMINATION OCCUR?

Discrimination in any of the above employment settings (unless in an exempted category) will be unlawful, and therefore actionable through an application to an industrial tribunal if it can be shown:

1. that the employer has *for a reason related to the person's disability* (our italics) treated that person less favourably than the employer treats, or would treat, others to whom that reason does not apply, and

2. that the employer cannot show the treatment in question is justified.[32]

1. Treated less favourably
   this process requires the adoption of the comparative approach, whereby the individual alleging discrimination produces an example (real or hypothetical, hence the use of the phrase 'treats, or would treat'), of another individual *without* their disability being treated *more* favourably than themselves in the employment related situation, so long as they can relate their less favourable treatment to their disability (e.g. refusal to employ a wheelchair user because of inconvenience of a wheelchair in office, or blind person because of dislike of guide dogs, etc.).

---

29 Although this does not appear a very large figure its significance is drawn out by the realisation that 96 per cent of UK companies employ fewer than 20 employees! The DDS s.7 does, however, make provision for this figure to be adjusted downward by the Secretary of State at some indeterminate date in the future.

30 See pp.127–8. This is separate from the employment of disabled people under the quota system, which will disappear from 1997.

31 DDA s.10.

32 DDA s.5.

This provision has to be read alongside the very important further provision contained in this Part of the DDA which places a statutory duty on employers (unless excluded) to make *reasonable adjustments* to work arrangements[33] and the working environment so as to accommodate disabled employees.[34] This duty to make *reasonable adjustments* will arise whenever any physical features of premises, or any arrangements made by or on behalf of an employer, place the disabled person concerned at a substantial disadvantage in comparison with persons who are not disabled. In these circumstances the employer (or potential employer) must take such steps as can be considered *reasonable in all the circumstances* of the case in order to prevent those features or arrangements having that effect.[35]

Detailed advice on what sorts of steps employers might be expected to take by way of reasonable adjustments to avoid charges of discrimination will emerge through guidance and case law. The DDA does, however, provide some illustrations (though non-exhaustive) of typical steps as follows:[36]

- making adjustments to premises. Note that there are special provisions[37] covering the situation where an employer occupies premises under a lease and the landlord unreasonably withholds consent to allow the employer to make alterations to the premises, as *reasonable adjustments*. In these circumstances, the landlord can be joined to any legal proceedings and even forced to compensate the disabled complainant.
- allocating some duties to another employee
- being flexible as to working hours
- being flexible as to place of work
- being flexible as to absence from work for rehabilitation, treatment and assessment
- giving or arranging special training
- acquiring or modifying equipment
- modifying procedures or reference manuals

---

33 DDA s.6(2) (a) (b) defines *arrangements* in this context as arrangements for determining to whom employment should be offered, and any term, condition or other arrangements on which employment, promotion, transfer, training or any other benefit is offered or afforded.
34 DDA s.6.
35 DDA s.6(1).
36 DDA s.6(3).
37 DDA s.16 and Schedule 4.

- modifying procedures for testing or assessment
- providing a reader or interpreter
- providing supervision.

The Act also provides guidance on what factors should be taken into account in deciding whether a particular proposed *adjustment* is, or is not, *reasonable in all the circumstances.* The factors it lists are the following:[38]

- consider the preventative effect of the action (i.e. will it achieve its goal)
- is the proposed adjustment practicable?
- weigh up the financial and other costs that it would incur
- consider any disruption to the employer's activities
- consider the employer's financial and other resources
- consider the availability of financial or other assistance.

Note, however, that it seems likely that employers faced with expensive adaptation bills to carry out reasonable adjustments will have access to the government sponsored Access to Work Scheme whereby they can receive a grant of up to £21,000 towards the cost of reasonable adjustments to premises over a five year period.[39]

2. Discriminatory treatment justified

    Once a discriminatory act has been shown to exist the employer can only avoid a finding of unlawful discrimination if it can be established that the discriminatory act was *justified.* To do this the employer must show that the reason for such discrimination was both 'material to the circumstances of the particular case and substantial'.[40]

Enforcement provisions

Under the DDA Part II, any individual alleging discrimination under the above provisions can apply to an Industrial Tribunal, alleging discrimination, so long as they do so within three months of the alleged discriminatory act. As there is no statutory enforcement agency to which they can turn for assistance, and legal aid is not available for representation at Industrial Tribunals (although free or subsided legal advice and assistance short of representation *is* available),[41] it is likely that disabled people's action groups (see generally Chapter Ten) will have an important role to play in this activity, at least in the early stages. Applicants will be assisted by a requirement in the Act that employees can *insist*

---

38   DDA s.6(4).
39   See pp.126–7 but note that at the time of writing this scheme is under review.
40   DDA s.5(3).
41   See generally Cooper (1994, Chapter One).

that the defendant employer fill out a detailed 'statutory questionnaire' in response to the allegation.

If the matter does not settle and goes to a hearing, the Industrial Tribunal has the following options, in the event of a finding in favour of the applicant:

- a declaration that discrimination occurred *and*

- recommendations to ensure that there is no future recurrence of such discrimination *and*

- power to award to the applicant unlimited compensation', plus interest, such compensation to include, where appropriate, a category of compensation for injury to feelings'.[42]

HOUSING FOR DISABLED PEOPLE

For a disabled person a home can be a prison. Whilst some disabilities do not affect the mobility of a person, the majority do, and consequently the internal arrangements for comfort and mobility within a home take on a special significance. If the home of a disabled person is unsuitable in some way for their particular needs, there are two possible ways of coping with the problem. The first is to carry out adaptations to their home to render it more suitable and comfortable for them. The second is to enable them to move to more suitable accommodation. What part do legal rights play in these two alternative courses of action?

Adapting the existing accommodation

If a local authority is satisfied that the home of a disabled person is in some way failing to meet the special needs arising from their disability (e.g. no access for a wheelchair, inaccessibility of toilet and bathing facilities) it is under a statutory duty by virtue of the CSDPA 1970[43] to ensure that those needs are met, by arranging for any necessary adaptations to be made. Any person on the local authority Register of Disabled People can apply for assistance of this nature. Although it is not strictly necessary to be on the Register to receive help with housing adaptations it is advisable, as it is possible to obtain other benefits as a result of registration, e.g. travel passes. Applications to go on the Register are usually processed by social services departments and occasionally by the area health authority.

DOE Circular 59/78[44] set out in detail the sorts of housing adaptations that could be possible under the above legislation. In particular, Appendix I to the circular listed a large number of structural changes to property that might

42 In race and sex discrimination cases, compensation under the category of 'injury to feelings' has led in recent cases to four and five figure awards.

43 See Chapter Four, p.93.

44 Although this Circular is now obsolete it still contains some very useful guidance.

be made for the benefit of a disabled occupant, which would also now be eligible for inclusion in an application for a *Disabled Facilities Grant* when proposed for a disabled person in private sector housing.[45] The list includes building extensions, widening access areas and doors, constructing handrails, installing stair lifts, refixing water and electricity sources, acoustic insulation, kitchen conversion, and the installation of special baths and toilets.

Detailed technical advice on such adaptations may be obtained from the occupational therapist who is working through the social services department and is also usually appointed to assess need and make recommendations as to the work to be carried out. Further ideas, particularly on up to date equipment and access methods, from a host of publications and reports can be obtained from the Centre for Accessible Environments.[46]

A new system for the renovation, repair and improvement of houses in England and Wales was introduced in 1990.[47] Scotland retains a separate grant system.[48] The most important grant concerning adaptations to a home to make it suitable for a disabled occupant is the *Disabled Facilities Grant* (DFG).

Disabled Facilities Grants

The DFG is provided by the local authority, although the money comes ultimately from central government. The DFG is means tested, and is either *mandatory* or *discretionary*. The maximum limit for a *mandatory* grant is £20,000, but the government is proposing that in future local authorities can also give a further *discretionary* grant where the proposed works would attract a mandatory grant but for the fact that their cost would exceed the grant limit.[49] Local

---

45 See below.

46 Nutmeg House, 60 Gainsford Street, London SE1 2NY (Tel: 0171-357 8182).

47 Largely contained in the Local Government and Housing Act 1989 Part VIII. The relevant government circulars, which provide detail on each of these grants, are 6/90 (Code of Guidance for dealing with unfit housing); 10/90 House adaptations for people with disabilities; 12/90 House renovation grants; 5/91 Changes relating to house renovation grants and other advice; 1/89 Repairs notices; 8/94 Grant limits, resources, services supplied to, and drainage from, premises. For a more detailed account of all these provisions up until the proposed changes consult an excellent article by Bourne (1995). The proposed changes (see p.138) are at the time of writing contained in the Housing Grants, Construction and Regeneration Bill.

48 Details of the Scottish system can be found in a pamphlet entitled *Improve your home with a grant* available from the Scottish Development Department, St Andrew's House, Edinburgh EH1 3DD.

49 See the *Government Housing White Paper, Our Future Homes: Opportunity, Choice, Responsibility,* published 27 June 1995, which led to the Housing Grants, Construction and Regeneration Bill, which was published on 3 February 1996, and if all goes well should receive the Royal Assent in July, and come into effect in October 1996. The proposals for change in this regard are relatively minor, but will nevertheless have some impact on the financing of alteration in certain circumstances, in particular with regard to Home Repair Assistance: see p.138.

authorities are under a statutory to determine all DFG applications within six months of the date on which they are received. The government is proposing that a condition could be attached to the grant that claims for payment may not be made until 12 months after the date of the application which should enable local authorities to prioritise according to the availability of resources.[50]

An application for a DFG is made by, or on behalf of, the *disabled occupant* of a dwelling. The *disabled occupant* is defined as 'the disabled person for whose benefit it is proposed to carry out any of the relevant works'. The word 'disabled' here means a person who is on the social services disability register (see p.92), or would qualify to be on the register if they chose to apply. The *disabled occupant* must normally live in the dwelling in question, but need not have a legal interest in the dwelling, i.e. as a tenant or an owner. The dwelling does not have to be privately owned, e.g. it can be a council dwelling, or belong to a housing association. If the applicant is a private tenant they must get the landlord's consent to the adaptation before the local authority can approve the application. The applicant must provide a *certificate of future occupancy*, stating as follows:[51]

> (owner) that they or a member of their family intend to live in the dwelling as their only or main residence for at least a year after the works are completed. If the property is disposed of within a three year period after the completion of the works, the owner may be ordered to repay all, or some of the grant. Advice should be sought from the local authority on the details of this provision before an application is submitted.

> (tenant) that they intend to live in the dwelling as their only or main residence

> (landlord) that they intend to let the dwelling as a residence (not for a long lease, nor a holiday home, nor to a member of their family) for at least five years after completion of the works.

There are two types of DFG, the first is *mandatory*, the second is *discretionary*.

1. The Mandatory DFG

    Mandatory DFGs are available under the scheme, if the proposed work is 'necessary and appropriate to meet the needs of the disabled occupant' and if it is 'reasonable and practical to carry out the works taking into account the age and condition of the dwelling'. These phrases have been explained in government circulars in the following ways:

    > The assessment of whether the works are 'necessary and appropriate' must involve consideration of whether the proposed adaptation or improvement is needed in order to enable any care plan to be implemented, and to enable the disabled occupant to remain in his or her home, retaining or regaining as great a degree of independence as can reasonably be achieved. It is neither appropriate nor practical to impose strict boundaries on what works may be regarded as 'necessary and appropriate' to meet the assessed needs: much will

---

50 *ibid.*
51 DOE Circular 10/90 supra fn.46.

depend on the circumstances of each individual case and on the judgement of the professional advisers concerned.[52]

Subject to the above paragraph, Mandatory DFGs will be available for adaptation work that assists the *disabled occupant* in any of the following purposes:

- facilitates access to and from the dwelling or the building in which the dwelling, or flat, is situated
- facilitates access to a room used as the principal family room, or to a room used or usable for sleeping, or providing such a sleeping room
- facilitates access to a room in which there is a lavatory, bath, shower, or washhand basin, or helps them to use such facilities, or provides the facilities if they are not already there
- preparing and cooking food
- improves any heating system, or providing a new system to meet their particular needs
- helps them use existing sources of power, light or heat, e.g. moving switches, adding levers etc.
- facilitates access around the dwelling to help them care for another resident of the dwelling in need of such care.

2. The Discretionary DFG

Discretionary DFGs are hard to get, but they are available for any other type of work that makes the dwelling or building 'suitable for the accommodation, welfare or employment of the disabled person'. This vague, catch-all phrase covers inter alia changes to the home that would improve the quality of life of the occupant, but for which there is no statutory responsibility to provide under the CSDPA or the community care legislation.[53]

Whether the DFG is *mandatory* or *discretionary*, the beneficiaries' of the proposed work will always be means tested. Currently, the means test for both the *mandatory* and the *discretionary* DFG is applied not only to the *disabled* occupant, but to each other relevant person, which means any other person living or intending to live in the dwelling who has an interest in the dwelling (as an owner or a tenant). It is, however, being proposed by the government[54] that in the future the means test for the *mandatory* DFG will be applied only to the collective means of the disabled applicant, their spouse and partner (if any) (and to their parents

---

52 *ibid.*
53 For more detail on the implementation of this legislation see Chapter Four, p.39 et seq.
54 See fn.49 supra.

in the case of those under 18), and will no longer take into account the means of other occupants. The criteria for applying the means test for discretionary grants will, however, remain the same.

The actual means test is fairly complex, but is broadly similar to the means test for *housing benefit* (see p.140). There is no set capital or income point above which no grant is payable.[55]

Discretionary Minor Work Grants[56]

In italics because of likely replacement in 1996 with Home Repair Assistance

At the time of writing, in addition to the above grants, an owner occupier or a private sector tenant can apply to their local authority for a minor work grant, up to a statutory maximum of a little over £1000 (Bourne 1995, p.21). Repeat applications are also possible, with a ceiling of around £3500 over a three year period. The grant is discretionary and means tested. It is likely to be replaced at some later date by the Home Repair Grant.[57] To be eligible, the applicant must be in receipt of at least one of the following:

- *family credit*
- *disability working allowance*
- *council tax benefit*
- *housing benefit*
- *income support.*

Application is on a simple application form to the local authority. The grants cover very broadly, the following types of work:

1. *Thermal insulation grants*
   These would include the insulation of lofts, tanks and pipes and draught proofing, but do not extend to improving heating or fixing a dampness problem (see below at 'patch and mend').

2. *'Patch and Mend' grants*
   These are to ensure that dwellings in areas scheduled for clearance are wind and weatherproof.

3. *'Staying Put' grants*
   These are for householders aged 60 or over whose dwelling is reasonably sound, but in need of some repair work, adaptation, improvement or basic security installation, and to carry out major work would be too disruptive to the occupant(s).

---

55 For a detailed account of the working of the means test, see *Disability Rights Handbook* 20th Edition.

56 For more information on Minor Works Grants see DOE Circular 4/90 Assistance with Minor Works in Dwellings.

57 These changes are also contained in the legislation referred to above at fn.49.

4. *'Elderly Residents Adaptation' grants*
    These grants finance small adaptations like an extra toilet, more cooking facilities,
    a new shower unit and so forth, to enable a person of 60 or over who is not an
    owner occupier or a tenant, to live in the dwelling.

Home Repair Assistance

This new type of financial assistance is to be available,[58] at the local authority's discretion, to owner occupiers, private tenants, most licensees and certain other occupiers who have a power to carry out works but who do not satisfy current ownership criteria, e.g. mobile home or houseboat owners. Applicants must be 18 or over and in a 'priority group', which means *either* that they are 60 or over, *or* they are infirm *or* they are in receipt of an income-related benefit. This discretionary assistance is most likely to be forthcoming for help in the carrying out of repairs or improvements to a domestic property that will either allow the applicant to continue in residence, or will allow an elderly or disabled person to move into the house to be cared for. It could also be available to provide help with insulation, replacement of lead pipes and radon associated work. The maximum assistance proposed in the legislation currently being considered by Parliament is £2000 per application up to a maximum of £4000 over a three year period. It could cover up to 100 per cent of the cost, either by money financial assistance or the provision of materials.

Top-up grants

It should be noted that in cases of grave hardship or other exceptional circumstances, local authority social services departments and a range of charities *may* be willing to cover all or part of the difference between the grant and the total cost of the work, so that the applicant pays nothing at all.[59]

Housing-based costs and benefits

Costs

COUNCIL TAX

Council tax came into effect on 1 April 1993 to replace the community charge. Each property has one council tax attached to it, regardless of how many people live there, and regardless of whether it is rented, owned, squatted or empty. The amount of the tax is linked to the estimated value of the property on 1 April 1991. Each property is placed in a Band, from A (lowest) to H (highest). The tax is divided into two parts:

---

58 At the time of writing it is unlikely that any changes to the current position could be effected before, at the earliest, the autumn of 1996, so this section must remain speculative only. There is 'many a slip twixt cup and lip...'

59 For a list of relevant charities consult the Charities Digest available from the Family Welfare Association, 501–505 Kingsland Road, Dalston, London E8 4AU (Tel: 0171-254 6251).

1. A 50 per cent *property tax*.

2. A 50 per cent *personal tax*.

The 50 per cent *personal tax* can be reduced to 25 per cent if there is only one person living in the property, and by up to 50 per cent, if there are 'invisible' adults living there. An 'invisible' adult is one who is deemed not to count for the purposes of council tax, i.e. they are not included as living in the property for the purpose of the *personal tax*. This means that if no 'visible' adults live in the property, a 50 per cent discount of the personal tax is permitted, and if there is one 'visible' adult, a 25 per cent discount is permitted. The reductions are known as *status discounts*.

The categories of invisible status' that may be relevant to disabled people are as follows:

- a person who is severely mentally impaired, and in receipt of a qualifying benefit[60]
- a patient in hospital, where the property is their sole or main residence
- a person in a nursing home or residential care home or hostel where care is provided
- a carer[61] or live-in care worker.[62]

(The list also includes young people, students, student nurses, youth trainees, apprentices and certain others).

There are also a number of reductions available in the *property tax* (though not the *personal tax*), if one or more people with disabilities live in the home, the effect of which will be to place the property down a Band.[63] Disability reductions are available against this tax if anybody resident in the dwelling is 'substantially and permanently disabled' and because of that disability the dwelling contains *either* a second bathroom or kitchen or some other room which is predominantly used to meet that person's special needs *or* sufficient floorspace to enable a wheelchair to be used within the dwelling *and* the local authority is satisfied that the above are necessary because of the disability. Application for council tax relief is by letter to the local authority setting out

---

60 For example, invalidity benefit, severe disablement allowance, attendance allowance, disability living allowance, (high/middle care component), disability working allowance, or income support which includes a disability premium on grounds of incapacity for work.

61 To be eligible the carer must be caring for a disabled person for at least 35 hours a week and that disabled person must be in receipt of higher rate attendance allowance, higher rate component of disability living allowance, or constant attendance allowance.

62 To be eligible the live-in carer must be providing care via a charity organisation, earning less than £30 a week, and providing care for at least 24 hours a day.

63 For a detailed stage by stage description of the tax, and how it works, see a series of articles in *Legal Action*, 1992–1993 by Alan Murdie, and Zebedee 1993–1994.

the case for reduction. If a reduction is not allowed the applicant can appeal to a local valuation tribunal.

Benefits
HOUSING BENEFIT TO ASSIST IN PAYING RENT

For those who have difficulty meeting their housing costs, it is always worth considering the possibility of applying for Housing Benefit (HB).[64] The benefit is available both to council and to private tenants, to offset the cost of the rent. The benefit is means-tested.[65] It is a government scheme that is administered by local councils. It is claimed by filling out a detailed form that is supplied by the local authority DSS (for all claimants in receipt of *income support*; see Chapter Six, pp.179–80) or otherwise by the local authority HB section. Whatever a person's source of income, the same formula will be used for calculating whether or not they are entitled to receive any HB. The process appears complex, but if the stages set out below are followed, the claimant or their adviser can quickly gain a clear idea of their level of entitlement.

Stage One: If the claimant is in receipt of income support, they will be entitled to receive the maximum level of HB, which will be 100 per cent *eligible rent*.[66] They must, however, claim their HB separately from the IS (i.e. there is no automatic payment to an income support claimant). If the claimant is **not** in receipt of income support proceed to Stage Two.

Stage Two: calculate the claimant's capital. Any capital below £3000 will be disregarded. If the claimant has between £3000 and £16,000, this capital will be deemed to generate £1 weekly income for every £250 (or part of £250) in excess of £3000. Thus, a claimant with capital of £4400 will be deemed to generate income of £6 per week from their capital.[67] *Capital* includes money in bank and building society deposits, premium bonds, unit trusts, stocks and shares, lump sum redundancy belonging to the claimant (but above a certain capital level the child cannot be included as a dependent). There are special rules on charitable payments. Some items of capital are entirely disregarded. These are the same items that are disregarded for the purposes of a claim for *income support*. Any claimant with capital in excess of £16,000 will be ineligible for HB.

---

64 See generally Housing Benefit (General) Regulations 1995.

65 For more detailed information consult one of a number of guides as follows (CPAG 1995; Ward and Zebedee 1995–1996). The DSS also produces a *Fact Sheet on HB; DSS Leaflets RRI Guide to Housing Benefits; DSS Leaflet RRI Help with Housing Costs*. Both leaflets are available from local councils and RRI can also be obtained from post offices. The detailed manual that DSS officers themselves use when assessing HB is *The Housing Benefits Guidance Manual* (DSS).

66 See p.141 for definition of *eligible rent*.

67 On the distinction between capital and income see Child Poverty Action Group 1995.

Stage Three: calculate the claimant's *applicable amount*. The formula for this calculation is exactly the same as for calculating eligibility for *income support* (see Chapter Six, pp.179–80), but for the purposes of HB it is of course being applied to those who (for whatever reason) are *not* in receipt of income support. The amount will vary considerably according to the age and level of disability (if any) of the claimant and any dependants.

Stage Four: calculate the claimant's *income*. The formula for this calculation is again the same as for calculating eligibility for *income support*.[68]

Stage Five: calculate the claimant's *eligible rent*. i.e. amount of rent against which they may claim benefit. Some parts of rent charges are not eligible for HB; i.e. they must be deducted by the claimant from their rent before filling out the form. The following charges are all ineligible: water and sewerage charges, charges for meals, laundry, leisure facilities, cleaning (except for common areas), transport, medical and nursing care, and alarm systems (except on accommodation for sick and elderly or disabled people). Service charges are eligible for HB, i.e. they can be included on the form, so long as they are reasonable and have to be paid as part of the tenancy. They would include such things as contributions towards the upkeep of lifts, common refuse chutes, and play areas. There are further complex rules regarding rent which includes fuel charges, some of which will not be included in the eligible rent according to a scale that can be found in all the handbooks.

Stage Six: If there is a non-dependant living in the claimant's home, deduct a fixed sum from the *eligible rent* to reflect the amount they are deemed to contribute. A non-dependant is someone who lives in the claimant's home and is not dependent on them, e.g. an adult relative (unless they are dependent), a child for whom the claimant does not receive Child Benefit, a friend or a lodger. Where there is a non-dependant living in the claimant's home there will be an automatic deduction from the HB otherwise payable, according to a set scale. This deduction is intended to reflect the amount of contribution that the non-dependant makes to the housing costs, regardless of whether they do make any such payment.

Stage Seven: compare income with applicable amount.

- If *income* is less than *applicable amount*, maximum HB is payable, i.e. 100 per cent *eligible rent*.
- If income is higher than *applicable amount* the following formula is applied:
  1. Work out *excess of income* over *applicable amount to* = X

68   On *income support* see Chapter Six, pp.179–80.

2. Deduct 65 per cent of X from maximum *eligible rent* and the resulting figures will be the HB payable. (No HB will be paid if the figure is less than 50 pence per week.)

WHAT HAPPENS IF THE LOCAL AUTHORITY CONSIDERS THAT THE RENT IS TOO HIGH?
Parliamentary Regulations set out the grounds on which *eligible rent* can be restricted by a local authority for HB purposes.[69] These Regulations have been further amended in a way that effectively passes back to rent officers a significant role in determining rent levels, as it states that in certain defined situations, a rent officer will be asked to determine whether a rent is reasonable for the purposes of housing benefit subsidy.[70] Leaving aside this additional rent officer function, details of which can be obtained from the local housing benefit section, the law allows councils to restrict the 'eligible rent' on which they will pay housing benefit where they feel either that the dwelling is larger than reasonably required by the occupants or the rent is unreasonably high in comparison with similar accommodation elsewhere. They cannot, however, do this if the household includes any of the following:

• someone aged 60 or over;

• a sick or disabled person;

• a child or young person;

The protection of these special categories will not, however, apply to new or renewal applicants from January 1996.[71]

In extreme circumstances, such as where the council believe that rents are being set deliberately high to take advantage of the housing benefit scheme, they can withdraw HB completely, or until the rent is reduced to reasonable levels.[72] As if all the above potential restrictions were not enough, it should also be noted that local authorities widely operate a policy of '*rent stop*', whereby they will not pay HB on any sum in excess of the subsidy threshold laid down by the DSS for their area. Central government will pay 97 per cent of all HB

---

69 Whilst these rules remain in force for all applicants prior to January 1996, all new or renewed claims after that date are subject to new regulations contained in the Housing Benefit (General) Amendments Regs. 1995 SI 1229.

70 The Rent Officers (Additional Functions) Order 1990. The rules to be applied will differ according to the date of application with the new rules applying to all new or renewal applications post-January 1996; see fn.69. Under the new regulations rent officers will be asked in the deregulated private sector to set 'local reference rents' calculated at the mid-point of a range of rents for similar accommodation in the locality, excluding local authority, housing association or regulated rents. This will be matched against the 'property specific rent'. If the latter is lower than the 'local reference rent' housing benefit will reflect the lower amount. If it is more, housing benefit will meet half the difference.

71 See fn.70 and Griffith 1995.

72 For more detail on the complex developments in this area of law read East (1992) and for a study of the impact of these changes on rent levels see Sharp (1991).

paid out by local authorities, if it is below the threshold, but only 25 per cent of HB paid out above the threshold. As a result of this policy, many, if not most, local authorities, strapped for cash, are refusing to pay HB above the threshold, except in very extreme cases.[73]

Finally, a person may also be denied HB if their tenancy is too informal, i.e. they are renting on a non-commercial basis from a friend, or from a close relative or partner.

The maximum benefit period is 60 weeks, though local authorities have a discretion to make the payments for a shorter period. Once the period has expired the claimant must resubmit their claim. Local authorities have the power to backdate HB for up to 52 weeks. They can also recover overpayments in certain circumstances. It is likely that they will have some incentive to claw back overpayments (unless they were themselves grossly negligent in the initial payment) and also not to backdate unless absolutely necessary as they will get a lower subsidy on any such payments.

PAYMENT OF HB DIRECT TO A LANDLORD

HB will normally be paid direct to the landlord in the following circumstances:

- where the claimant or their partner is receiving IS and the DSS decide to pay part of the benefit to the landlord to cover arrears
- where the claimant has rent arrears of eight weeks or more.

In addition, the local authority may agree to pay the HB direct to the landlord if the claimant has so requested or if the local authority decides it is in the best interests of the claimant's family. In all of these circumstances both the landlord and the tenant must be notified of the decision. The claimant can request a review of an unfavourable decision.

APPEALS

A procedure exists enabling a claimant to appeal (known as a review) against any decision regarding their claim. There is no independent tribunal appeal system but there is a two-stage review procedure consisting of an internal review and an application to a review board. (The latter can only be requested after an internal review has been carried out.) The request for an internal review must be in writing – a letter will suffice – and it must arrive at the local authority no later than six weeks from the date that the letter of notification of the decision was posted. A request for a further hearing before a review board (which will consist of local councillors) must be made within four weeks of the posting of the notification of the decision of the internal review.

---

73 This discretionary power to pay 'over the limits' remains under the new regulations (see above at fn.70) but only where this is the 'only practical way' to prevent 'exceptional hardship'.

Council Tax Benefit for disabled tenants or owner occupiers who need financial assistance in paying their council tax

There are two types of council tax benefit available, *main council tax benefit* (CTB) and *alternative maximum council tax benefit* (AMTCB).

1. CTB
    This can be claimed by anybody aged 18 or over, who is liable to pay the council tax on their home, and who is resident in that home. The procedure for claiming CTB is exactly the same as for Housing Benefit, and it is normal to claim both benefits together. The only difference in the two procedures comes at Stage Five (where the eligible council tax is the full council tax payable) and at Stage Seven, where the percentage applied to X for purposes of the final calculation is 20 per cent and not 65 per cent.

2. AMCTB
    This benefit can be claimed even if the applicant's personal income and capital make them ineligible for CTB. It is commonly known as 'second adult rebate' and is designed to compensate council tax payers who share their homes with other adults who do not contribute anything towards the tax, and who cannot afford to do so. An applicant must be liable (or jointly liable) to pay council tax, and a person who would have got a 25 per cent status discount if they had been living alone, or with 'invisible' people (see p.139) Although AMCTB is claimed by the person liable to pay council tax, it is in fact calculated upon the income of a 'second adult' of 18 or over living on a non-commercial basis with the claimant such as grown up sons and daughters still living at home. The logic of the benefit is that the claimant would have expected the 'second adult' to contribute to the council tax, had they the money to do so. The rebate can apply even if there is more than one extra adult, in which case it is calculated on their combined incomes. Finally, note that there is no minimum amount of council tax benefit payable. For a more detailed explanation of how the system works see Zebedee (1993–1994).

Moving to other accommodation

All councils have a stock of housing which they must make available to those who most need it. In order to inform the public of the availability of such stock they must by law publish a summary of the rules and procedures they adopt in allocating their housing stock to tenants. This summary will normally be in the form of a short pamphlet available in housing offices and the Town Hall. It must be free of charge. It will describe the system that the council uses in establishing its priorities but it does not have to state how long an applicant will normally have to wait before being offered a home. A more detailed description of the rules and procedures must also be made available to anybody on request, normally for a small charge. In addition, anybody who has actually applied for council accommodation (e.g. by putting their name on the waiting list) is entitled to a free copy of their application form, in order to check that the details are correct.

There are very few legal constraints on the type of allocations policy that a council must adopt. In practice, a council is likely to adopt one of three different types of allocations policy: a date order scheme whereby tenancies are allocated to the person who is top of the waiting list on a 'first come first served' basis; a merit scheme whereby tenancies are allocated according to the views of councillors as to the merit of each particular case; or a points scheme whereby points are allocated to each applicant on a complicated scale of need and tenancies are granted to those who achieve the highest number of points. The points scheme has become the most widely used in recent years, but the factors for which points are awarded vary considerably between councils. They may include such factors as length of time on the waiting list, existing housing conditions, age, number of children, overcrowding in current accommodation and health factors. They should also normally include additional points gained by virtue of certain disabilities experienced by members of the applying household, although in any event these will also normally be caught by the community care and other statutory duties set out in Chapter Four.

In addition to the points system or other allocations procedures, a council must by law consider the needs of disabled people in any new housing scheme it designs, and also in any new public building.[74] The commonest way in which this duty is satisfied is in the form of Wheelchair Housing Projects or Mobility Housing Projects. Wheelchair Housing Projects are designed principally for those confined to a wheelchair, to enable them the maximum mobility within their home. Mobility Housing Projects are principally for those who are ambulant, but have mobility problems. Whilst it lies entirely within the local authority's discretion how much housing of this nature they provide, it is clear that if they provide nothing at all, they are failing to fulfil their statutory obligations. In these circumstances legal advice should be sought from a solicitor to investigate whether the local authority could be taken to court for failure to carry out its statutory obligations.

Finally, it should be noted that more and more housing associations specialise in providing accommodation adapted for disabled people, and direct application to these associations should always be encouraged. Local authorities frequently work closely with such associations in the allocation of this specialist accommodation.

There are two circumstances where a council *must* provide a person with accommodation regardless of their own procedures:

---

74 Although now obsolete, the DOE Circular 59/78 still provides useful guidelines on ways in which the former duty may be satisfied. See also Part M of the *Building Regulations on Access and Facilities for Disabled People*.

1. Forced displacement

If a person(s) is displaced from their existing home by virtue of a compulsory purchase order, a closing order, a development, clearance or demolition order, or the service of an improvement notice under the Housing Act 1985 their local authority must normally provide them not only with alternative accommodation, but also in some circumstances with financial compensation. The financial compensation may be in the form of a *Home Loss Payment* or *Disturbance Payment*.

(A) HOME LOSS PAYMENT

Any person who is displaced from their home in any of the following circumstances may (in addition to being rehoused) be entitled to financial compensation in the form of a Home Loss Payment. A Home Loss Payment is paid by the local authority (or if appropriate the Housing Association) to any occupier of a home in the relevant premises who had a legal right to be there, and had lived there continuously as their main or only home for a period of at least five years at the date of the displacement. The claimant may be the tenant, or a person living with the tenant. If the claim is by joint tenants the payment will be split equally between them. If the claimant has lived in a series of dwellings within the same building, for example in a succession of bedsits, during the five-year period they will still be eligible. If the claim is under the first head the claimant does not have to remain in occupation until required by the local authority to leave, so long as they are in occupation on the date that the local authority are given permission to buy the property. The amount of the home loss payment will vary according to the date of the displacement, and the figures should be carefully checked with an independent housing adviser. All claims must be made within six years of the displacement on a special form provided by a local authority. The form can also be obtained from a local Citizens' Advice Bureau, a Housing Aid or Action Centre or a local law centre.

(B) DISTURBANCE PAYMENT

A person who is entitled to claim a *Home Loss Payment* is also entitled to claim a Disturbance Payment. This is a sum of money to cover the reasonable expenses they have incurred as a result of their displacement and settlement in another home. It can thus cover not only removal expenses, but also the costs of setting up a new home, which may be substantial. Even if a person is not entitled to a *Home Loss Payment*, e.g. because they have not lived in the premises for at least five years, the local authority still has a discretion to make them a disturbance payment.

An appeal lies to the Lands Tribunal, regarding the above payments. This is one of the few tribunals for which legal aid is available.[75]

---

75 For further information see 'How to Use the Lands Tribunal' 40 *Community Action 33*.

2. Homeless

In some carefully defined circumstances, a local authority will also have a duty to provide accommodation to a homeless person under the *homelessness legislation*, which should also be seen alongside other statutory responsibilities to those in need of *community care services* under the NHSCCA 1990.[76]

Note also that a council cannot discriminate either directly or indirectly against an applicant on the grounds of their colour, race, nationality, sex or ethnic origins. This means that any policy to encourage a reasonable black/white balance on council estates is unlawful, whatever the merits of its intentions. As will be seen below, the Disability Discrimination Act 1995 will eventually make it unlawful to discriminate on grounds of disability in relation to accommodation services, and in relation to any service provider by a public authority.

WHAT DUTIES DO COUNCILS HAVE TO PROVIDE ACCOMMODATION TO HOMELESS PERSONS?

The answer to this question is to be found in Part III of the Housing Act 1985. This Act is supplemented by a Code of Guidance, and a Local Authority Agreement. All Homeless Persons Units attached to councils in England and Wales are supposed to operate strictly according to the terms of the Act. The Act has been much scrutinized and modified by a number of important cases. The basic position under this legislation is that a council has a legal duty to provide permanent accommodation to certain categories of people who are either homeless or threatened with homelessness and to provide temporary accommodation or advice and assistance to certain other categories. As would be expected, each one of these words has been exhaustively analysed and defined by the courts. In addition, official reports demonstrate that the ways in which local authorities in practice interpret their responsibilities differ widely.

WHAT DOES HOMELESS MEAN?

The law considers a person to be homeless if they have 'no accommodation' in England, Wales or Scotland.[77] 'They' extends to any person who might normally be expected to live with the homeless person as a member of their family, for example a carer, if the person is disabled, a caring relative, a child or a spouse.[78] The phrase 'no accommodation' is a legal term and means something different from a 'roof over your head'. It means — accommodation that the occupier has a legal right to occupy, i.e. which they own, rent, occupy under a trust, have a licence to occupy, or which they have a special legal right to occupy, for example as a result of a post-divorce settlement or pending a

---

76 See Chapter Four, p.98. In 1995 the Government issued a draft circular on *Community Care, Housing and Homelessness*. The consultation period ended on 27 October 1995, and a circular based on the draft is likely to appear in early 1996.

77 Housing Act 1985 Part III s.58(1). Hereafter cited as HA 1985.

78 HA 1985 s.58(2).

court possession order hearing. The decision as to 'homeless' should be made according to these strict criteria, as set out in the Act and the Code and Practice, and should not be 'tainted' by the subjective opinions of the housing officer.[79] The accommodation must also be more than temporary.[80] The definition also includes under the head of 'no accommodation', accommodation that is legally available to the homeless person to occupy but which they are prevented from occupying through fear of domestic violence or because the landlord has illegally locked them out.[81] The accommodation must be 'available' to live in, and it must be accommodation which it is reasonable to expect them to continue to occupy.[82] But in deciding what is 'reasonable', a council can take into account the general standard of accommodation in their area, i.e. if housing is generally bad in the area, the standard of the accommodation need be no better than the prevailing standard.

A person is 'threatened with homelessness', if they are likely to become homeless within 28 days.[83] Thus, a person who has received a possession order, or a person in temporary hostel accommodation with a maximum stay period of less than 28 days is 'threatened with homelessness'.

---

79 R v Tower Hamlets London BC ex parte Hoque, [1993] *The Times* 20 July 1993 QBD. Another case illustrating this facet of the decision-making process involved an applicant who needed a full-time live-in carer to help with looking after her sick daughter. The case reinforces the fact that objective criteria must be applied in distinguishing between a *need* for a carer (which might render the current accommodation unsuitable), and a *wish* for a carer, which would *not* be a relevant consideration: R v Royal Borough of Kensington and Chelsea, ex part Kassam [1993] QBD, reported in *Legal Action*, March 1994, p.14.

80 The answer to the question, what is temporary for the purposes of the legislation, will depend on how 'temporary' the accommodation is. A woman given temporary accommodation in a women's refuge is, for example, certainly homeless: R v LB Ealing ex parte Sidhu [1982] 2 HLR 45, QBD. Similarly, a person given temporary accommodation in a night shelter is homeless; R v Waveney DC ex parte Bowers [1980] *The Times*, May, HC. If the legal rights of the occupant are slightly more strong, e.g. they have a temporary license to be there, they will not be homeless, but they may well be 'threatened with homelessness' if the notice period necessary to remove them is less than 28 days. The fact that an applicant in temporary accommodation in the United Kingdom may have accommodation in another country is not a relevant consideration in deciding whether they are homeless although it may be a relevant factor in deciding if they are intentionally homeless which will enable the local authority to refuse to house them. This factor is of particular importance to new immigrants and refugees. Some particularly hard pressed local authorities have refused to house applicants precisely because they have accommodation in another country, that in the view of the council they should not have left.

81 HA 1985 s.58(3).

82 HA 1985 s.58 2A.

83 HA 1985 s.58(4).

Any person who considers themselves homeless can present themselves as such to any council homeless person's unit. They must, however, have sufficient mental capacity to understand the concept of being offered accommodation, which means that adults without mental capacity cannot apply for accommodation in their own right.[84] Similarly, dependant children cannot apply in their own right. The adults on whom both the above categories depend must apply on their collective behalf. Subject to the above, a council has a legal responsibility towards any person who presents themselves to the council as 'homeless' or 'threatened with homelessness' to make any necessary enquiries to establish whether this is true, sufficient to come to a rapid and fair decision.[85] Furthermore, if at the time of application the applicant appears to be in *priority need*, the council must provide the applicant(s) with temporary accommodation pending the outcome of their enquiries.[86] In hard pressed inner city areas this will normally be 'bed and breakfast' accommodation.

If after initial enquiries the council accepts that the applicant is homeless the council officers must then carry out a number of further enquiries to establish the following:

1. Does the applicant have a priority need?

2. Did the applicant become homeless intentionally?

3. Does the applicant have a local connection with another housing authority in England, Wales or Scotland? (They will only make this third enquiry if the applicant appears to have no local connection with them, and even then, they are not obliged to follow this third procedure.)

I. PRIORITY NEED

The law defines *priority need*[87] as a person in any one or more of the following categories:

- a pregnant woman, or a person with dependant children either living with them or who ought reasonably to be living with them, e.g. the children are in voluntary care because the parents are unable to accommodate them. Grandchildren, foster children and adopted children all come in this category, but dependency is normally deemed to end at 16 (19 if child is in full-time education or training and not otherwise able to support his or herself)

---

84   R v Tower Hamlets London BC ex parte Begum [1995] 2 All E.R. 65 (HL). It is up to the local authority to determine if the applicant has mental capacity or not.

85   HA 1985 s.62(1).

86   HA 1985 s.63 (1).

87   HA 1985 s.59 (1).

- anybody who ought reasonably to be living with the above people, e.g. spouse, cohabitee or dependant children
- a person who is homeless through flood, fire or other disaster
- a person who is *vulnerable* either as a result of old age (near or over normal retirement age) or for some other special reason such as physical or mental disability (including illness).

It is clearly the last of these categories that is the most likely to be relevant in the case where an applicant, or a person reasonably expected to be living with the applicant, has a disability. It is thus important to understand how the word *vulnerable* has to be interpreted. The Code of Guidance accompanying the Act states as follows:[88]

A person has *priority need* (inter alia) if he is, or if his household includes one or more members who are, vulnerable for one of the following reasons.

(i) Old age. Authorities should treat as vulnerable those above normal retirement age and any others approaching normal retirement age who are particularly frail or in poor health or vulnerable for any other reason.

(ii) Mental illness or handicap or physical disability. This includes those who are blind, deaf, dumb or otherwise substantially disabled mentally or physically. Authorities are asked to take a wide and flexible view of what constitutes substantial disability, recognising that this will depend on individual circumstances. The help of the area health authority and the social services authority will be appropriate in assessing a number of these cases.

Councils are not normally willing to include what they term self-imposed disabilities, e.g. alcoholism and drug addiction, unless other disabilities are also manifested. For applicants who are disabled this is the key provision.

Caselaw has added further interpretive assistance. In one case,[89] it was held that vulnerability means being: 'less able to fend for oneself so that injury or detriment will result where a less vulnerable man (or woman) will be able to cope without harmful effects.'

It has further been held that vulnerability in this respect means vulnerability in 'housing terms'[90] which would include not only less ability to fend for oneself when homeless, but also in finding and keeping accommodation.[91] This criterion is, however, interpreted fairly strictly as in one case in which it was held that an epileptic applicant was not vulnerable within the Act, as there was no evidence he had difficulty in finding or maintaining housing.[92] The question

---

88   Code of Guidance to Act 2 2.12 (c).
89   R v Waveney DC ex parte Bowers [1983] QB 238.
90   R v Bath CC ex parte Sangermano [1984] 17 HLR 94, QBD.
91   R v LB Lambeth ex parte Carroll [1987] 20 HLR 142, QBD.
92   R v Reigate and Banstead BC ex parte Di Domenico [1987] 20 HLR 153, QBD.

of whether epilepsy constitutes vulnerability has therefore to be decided on the facts of the particular case, and will depend primarily upon the regularity and intensity of attacks.[93] Finally, the courts have made a clear distinction between mental illness and mental handicap, and in the latter case in particular have stressed that there is no automatic association with vulnerability.[94] Nor are they willing to accept that what they term 'self-imposed disabilities' such as addiction to drugs or alcohol, can render an applicant *vulnerable*, in the absence of other collateral disability being manifest.[95]

2. INTENTIONAL HOMELESSNESS

This is the part of the legislation that has caused the most difficulty and controversy. The idea behind this part of the legislation is to disqualify from eligibility for immediate accommodation anybody who has deliberately given up their existing accommodation. Regrettably, many councils have exploited this loophole in the legislation as a way of avoiding responsibility to house people who are often in a desperate plight. Case law has tended to come out on the side of councils in this area and a line of restrictive decisions has resulted in many homeless people never getting beyond this hurdle.

In claiming 'intentional homelessness' and thereby avoiding the need to provide permanent accommodation, councils may rely upon either the applicant's deliberate acts or the applicant's failure to do something. Thus, not only is an applicant intentionally homeless if they deliberately give up accommodation they have a right to occupy, they are also intentionally homeless if they fail to do whatever is necessary to keep their existing accommodation, e.g. wilfully refuse to pay rent, fail to keep their family or lodgers under control or illegally sublet, resulting in their own eviction. It is also possible that giving up of the most temporary and unhappy accommodation, for example short life accommodation, might subsequently taint the applicant with 'intentional homelessness'.[96]

The case law in this area is prolific, and legal advice from an expert should always be sought if there is any suggestion by the council of 'intentional homelessness'. The Code of Guidance to the Act is also very important because although it is not legally binding it should not be departed from unless it has first been considered and a reason for departure from it has been given.[97] The Code emphasises the fact that the disqualifying conduct of the applicant, whether by an act or a failure to act, must be shown to have been in bad faith

---

93 R v Wandsworth BC ex parte Banbury [1986] 19 HLR 76, QBD.
94 See supra fn.90.
95 See supra fn.89.
96 See R v London Borough of Brent ex parte Awua [1995] 3 WLR 215 (HL) and the interesting discussion on this case between Arden 1995 and Gellner and Gallivan 1995.
97 See for example, De Falco, Silvestri v Crawley BC [1980] QB 460, CA; In Re Betts [1983] 2 AC 613.

and not just the result of a genuine lack of understanding. Thus non-payment of rent in ignorance of the availability of housing benefit or the acceptance of temporary accommodation in the belief it was permanent would be examples of behaviour that may lead to homelessness, but would be unlikely to give rise to a successful allegation of 'intentional homelessness'.

The giving up of accommodation that cannot accommodate those with whom the applicant reasonably expects to share the accommodation, e.g. his or her children, or if a disabled person, with his or her carer, does not amount to 'intentional homelessness' even though the accommodation may remain available to the applicant if living alone. Councils may, however, look beyond the immediate cause of the applicant's homelessness for an earlier act that amounted to 'intentional homelessness' and thereby avoid any liability to provide accommodation. This is called the 'chain of causation'. Once a person has been 'tainted' with an act of 'intentional homelessness' it is very difficult for them to break the causation chain. It can only be done if they manage to secure for themselves some 'settled accommodation' in which they spend a period of time. This will have the effect of breaking the chain so that if they have the misfortune to become homeless at some date in the future the council will no longer be able to refer back to the earlier act of 'intentional homelessness'. 'Settled accommodation' means accommodation in which the occupant has a 'reasonable degree of security' and will not therefore be established by a period in temporary hostel accommodation, or a holiday let.

3. LOCAL CONNECTION WITH ANOTHER HOUSING AUTHORITY

In some circumstances the local authority will also inquire whether the applicant has a 'local connection' with another housing authority in England, Wales or Scotland, in order to pass the responsibility to house the applicant to that authority. But this can only be done in very limited circumstances.[98] The local authority can only invoke this line of enquiry if neither the applicant, nor anybody who might reasonably be expected to live with them, has any 'local connection' with them. By 'local connection' is meant a connection with the local authority because of one or more factors: employment in the area; past or present voluntary residence in the area; family associations in the area or for any other special reason. Thus, if a person gets off a train in London and presents themselves as 'homeless' and they have no 'local connection' with that authority it is legitimate for that local authority to contact an area with which they do have a 'local connection', providing one exists. There is a Local Authority Agreement which states that a period of residence of less than six months in the 12 months immediately prior to the application will not normally be sufficient to establish a 'local connection'. This Agreement is *policy*, however, and not law and if an applicant has established a 'local connection' after a shorter

---

98   HA 1985 s.67.

period the policy need not be applied, particularly where a local connection is argued also on the basis of, say, family associations.[99]

If a local authority does use the 'local connection' provision they must provide the applicant with temporary accommodation whilst the matter is being determined. If that other authority accepts responsibility for the applicant the first authority must then continue to provide them with temporary accommodation whilst their transport back to the other authority is being negotiated.[100] It follows from the above that if the applicant has no 'local connection' with any other authority in England, Wales or Scotland, e.g. they are a political refugee from another country, or they have just got off a boat from Belfast or Dublin, the provisions are of no relevance. (But note the alternative possibility of an argument of 'intentional homelessness', see p.151).

The 'local connection' provisions will also not apply if the applicant runs the risk of domestic violence should they be returned to the housing authority with which they have a 'local connection' and which area they have presumably left because of this risk.

WHAT ARE THE COUNCIL'S DUTIES ONCE IT HAS CARRIED OUT ALL THE ABOVE ENQUIRIES?

The enquiries may take anything from a few days to many weeks, depending on their complexity. The applicant should co-operate with the council as far as they are able (also note that giving false information is a criminal offence)[101] but should also seek the help and support of an experienced adviser, particularly before signing any forms or statements. The help of a social worker could be very significant at this stage. The applicant should be given copies of any forms that they sign. Once a decision has been taken it must be communicated to the applicant in writing. It has already been stated that if the applicant is homeless and in priority need the council must provide them with temporary accommodation pending the completion of any other enquiries. The following is a list of the council's duties to the homeless applicant once the enquiries are completed:

1. If it finds that the applicant is *homeless* but without *priority need* the council's duty is limited to providing 'such advice and assistance as the council considers appropriate'. This may in practice mean no more than a list of accommodation agencies, hostels and bed and breakfast hotels.

2. If it finds that the applicant is *homeless*, has *priority need* but is *intentionally homeless*, its duty is to provide the applicant with temporary accommodation for a reasonable period to enable them to find accommodation of their own. There is no fixed period, and it will

---

99   In Re Betts [1983] 2 AC 613.
100   HA 1985 s.68.
101   HA 1985 s.74.

depend upon the facts of the individual case, but the applicant cannot expect to be allowed more than a few weeks as a maximum.

3. If it finds that the applicant is *homeless*, has *priority need* and is *not intentionally homeless*, it has a duty to ensure that the applicant, together with those reasonably expected to live with the applicant, are provided with 'suitable accommodation'. Failure to make available such accommodation may be challenged by judicial review, and an action in damages for negligence may also be possible.[102] This can be provided by themselves or somebody else, for example housing associations. The deliberate insertion of the word 'suitable' is an explicit recognition by Parliament that the particular needs of the applicant, and if necessary their family unit, must be taken into account. Thus, for example, the courts have held that such matters as the particular psychological need of an applicant to be housed near a parent, and the likelihood of racial harassment occurring to a black applicant in a particular area, are the types of factor that a local authority *cannot* ignore, in deciding whether particular accommodation is suitable.

If the applicant is disabled, the word 'suitable' is clearly one that is of particular importance, and a person in this position would be well advised to make a simultaneous application to be assessed for housing needs and adaptations, by the local authority social services department, as is their statutory right under the CSDPA and NHSCCA.[103]

THREATENED WITH HOMELESSNESS

If the applicant is not homeless, but is *threatened with homelessness* the duties of the council officers are more straightforward. First, they must establish whether the applicant and/or their dependants are in priority need. If they are not in priority need the council's duty rests at 1 above. If, on the other hand, the applicant and/or their dependants are in priority need the council has a duty to take steps to try to prevent the threatened homelessness coming about. This could mean, for example, advising the person on their rights to obtain housing benefit and other welfare rights if the homelessness is threatened as a result of rent arrears. Or it could mean taking action against a landlord who is threatening illegal action to evict a tenant.

RIGHTS TO COUNCIL ACCOMMODATION IF NOT HOMELESS

There are few legal obligations on local authorities to provide accommodation to disabled people. If a disabled person is actually homeless, their homelessness is not 'intentional', and they are considered to be 'vulnerable', the local authority will have a duty to house them. Once such accommodation has been provided,

---

102 See 'Offers of Accommodation to the Homeless', *Legal Action* May 1993, p.19, and R v Lambeth LBC ex parte Barnes, 25 HLR 140, QBD.
103 See Chapter Four, pp.91–100.

the disabled person will be able to apply to the council for any necessary adaptations to the new home, following the procedures set out above. Otherwise, the provision of alternative accommodation to a disabled person who already has accommodation, however unsatisfactory, is entirely a matter for the council's discretion, subject, of course, to the range of other statutory duties and responsibilities towards disabled people with respect to housing already explained in Chapter Four.[104]

Residential accommodation

We shall define the accommodation that is provided for those who do not live in their own homes as *residential accommodation*. This is distinct from, for example, hotel accommodation in that the term *residential accommodation* includes both board and personal care for persons in need of personal care and attention which is not otherwise available to them, by reason of age, illness, disability, or any other circumstances.[105] *Residential accommodation* for disabled people is provided from three different sectors, local authorities, voluntary (non-profit-making) organisations and the private sector. Although the sources of funding of each category of home will clearly differ, there is considerable overlap in practice between the three sectors, with each sector being subject to statutory regulation, and many disabled people being placed by local authorities in one of the other two sectors, either because there is no available space in any local authority home, or because the home in question is more suitable to the needs and wishes of the disabled person. In fact, since 1 April 1993, local authorities are obliged to ensure that 85 per cent of the total residential accommodation budget at their disposal is spent in the independent sector, which could be either residential or domiciliary care.

Which department in the local authority should be approached for assistance in finding residential accommodation for disabled people?

If the person is *homeless* or *threatened with homelessness* the local *housing department* should be contacted. Most housing departments have special units to deal with applications from homeless people. In all other cases, responsibility rests with the *social services* department.

In general, a local authority cannot be *forced* to find or provide residential accommodation for a non disabled older person who requests it: In other words the provision of residential accommodation for non disabled older people is a *power* and not a *duty*. But the whole issue has also to be looked at in the context of the community care legislation, introduced in 1993, and the duties and

---

104 *ibid.*
105 Definition taken from s.21(1) (a) of Part III of the National Assistance Act 1948 as amended by the National Health Service and Community Care Act 1990.

responsibilities that this legislation has placed upon local authorities towards older people.[106]

Are there any circumstances in which an older person can be forced into residential accommodation (including a hospital) against their will?

There are three circumstances in which action may be taken to compel an older person to enter residential accommodation (which can include a hospital) without their consent:[107]

1. Where the older person is deemed to be suffering from a mental disability or disorder under the Mental Health Act 1983, and one of the procedures for committing a mentally disabled person to a mental institution is followed (see Chapter Seven).

2. Where an older person is considered by a local authority to be in the above category, but the alternative of Guardianship Proceedings is chosen, and the local authority as guardian wishes to place the older person in a particular home. This procedure is currently rarely used (less than 200 cases per year) but may become a more attractive option if the current emphasis on 'community care' is strengthened by further allocation of resources.

3. There is a procedure under section 47 of the National Assistance Act 1948 (used in practice in only about 200 cases per year) whereby a magistrate can make an order to remove an older person to a residential home (or hospital) for up to three months at a time if s/he is satisfied, on the evidence of the District Community Physician, that the older person is:

    • suffering from grave chronic illness

    and

---

106 Under the National Health Service and Community Care Act 1990 if it appears to a local authority that a person for whom they provide, or arrange for the provision of *community care services* (e.g. older residents of their area), may be in need of such services, they must:
  1. carry out an assessment of that person's needs for those services, *and*
  2. decide whether these needs should be met by such services, in the light of the assessment.

  The provision of *residential accommodation* for older people, under Part III of the National Assistance Act 1948 is now incorporated within the definition of *community care services*, and it therefore follows that local authorities have clear statutory responsibilities to ensure that accommodation requirements of needy older people in their area are met, either through direct provision, or more likely through referral to the voluntary and private sectors. (See further above Chapter Four, p.91–100.)

107 For an interesting study of the wider philosophical and legal issues surrounding the restraint of elderly or incapacitated adults, unable to care for themselves, see Parkin 1995.

- living in insanitary conditions

and

- not receiving proper care and attention

and

- it is in the interests of that person to be detained either for their own good, or because they are a serious nuisance to other people.

Seven days' notice of the application must be given either to the older person direct or to some person in charge of them, unless the District Community Physician and one other doctor certify that removal of the person without delay is necessary, in their own interests, in which case written notice is not required. If written notice is not given, however, an order can only be made with a maximum duration of three weeks, although it is open to the local authority to apply, on notice, to extend that order to three months during that period. In addition, the person managing the premises to which it is intended to remove the older person must be given seven days' notice of the hearing to give them the opportunity to explain their position to the magistrate and express any objections that they may have to receiving the person – objections which may influence the decision. After the three months have expired the local authority can apply to extend the detention for further three month periods, and further periods thereafter, for a seemingly indefinite number of times. Legal aid is not available to a person who wishes to contest the application. The section does not permit compulsory medical treatment of any person thus removed. Use of the section remains controversial and there is wide regional variation in its use: some local authorities never use the section as a matter of policy. Only 15 per cent of those admitted under Section 47 ever return to their homes, and the average survival rate once admitted is only two years.

The British Geriatric Society (BGS)[108] and the British Association of Social Workers (BASW)[109] have produced guidelines for the use of Section 47 applications which can be obtained from either organisation. BASW, for example, recommends that any decision under this section should only be made following a case conference, and the authority must be satisfied that the physical, emotional and psychological well-being of the person would be improved by compulsory removal from their home, given the distress this involves.

Local authority residential care homes

The circumstances in which a local authority might offer their own residential accommodation to those in need of it are broadly set out in Part III of the

---

108 British Geriatric Society, 1 St Andrew's Place, London NW1 4LB Tel: 0171-935 4004.
109 British Association of Social Workers, 16 Kent St, Birmingham B5 6RD Tel: 0121-622 3911.

National Assistance Act 1948 (NAA). The primary test is one of *need*. The NAA states that 'Part III accommodation' may be provided to those who are 'in need of care or attention by reason of age, infirmity or any other circumstances and for whom such care or attention is not otherwise available'. It is thus not strictly necessary for the applicant to have reached retirement age. There is continuing controversy over the adequacy of current assessment procedures prior to the acceptance of older people into Part III accommodation. There are no standard procedures, although there is a basic approach that the Government believes should be universal and which is described in a document produced by the DSS.[110] The new procedures being introduced at local levels to ensure the proper implementation of community care packages are likely to converge to standard models as time progresses, but at present there is little uniformity of approach.

If following assessment the local authority decides to offer residential accommodation to the applicant they will normally offer a particular home, or choice of homes. However, if the applicant does not like the home offered, or wishes to be given a place in an alternative home, they have a right to request such an alternative, which the local authority must provide, so long as the accommodation is suitable to the person's assessed needs, a place is available, the accommodation in question is willing to enter into a contract on the authority's usual terms and conditions, and the accommodation does not cost more than the authority would usually expect to pay for someone with similar needs. The High Court has stressed the importance of this provision, stating that where the needs assessment is clear about the type of home necessary to meet the applicant's particular needs, it is not open to the local authority to offer accommodation that does not meet the fully assessed needs, simply on the grounds that it is cheaper. If a third party is willing to pay the additional costs of a more expensive home, the local authority is obliged to accept this offer and to arrange a place in the more expensive home, recouping the difference from the third party.[111]

Applicants must satisfy certain residence requirements before the local authority will consider the application, as follows. They must fall within *one* of the following categories:

> They must be *either* ordinarily resident in the area of the local authority *or* be in that area with no settled residence anywhere *or* be ordinarily resident elsewhere but nevertheless in the area at the time of application and in urgent need of residential care. In addition, the local authority can offer accommodation to any other persons provided that the local authority in whose area they normally reside

---

110 Social Services Inspectorate Development Group (1985) *Assessment Procedures for Elderly People Referred for Local Authority Residential Care (DSS)*.

111 For further information on this issue see *National Assistance Act 1948 (Choice of Accommodation) Directions 1992—Local Authority Circular (LAC) (92) 27*.

consents (it seems unlikely that many local authorities would be likely to refuse such an offer...).

If the local authority decides to offer the applicant residential accommodation, it does not have to be in one of its own homes. It may be in a home run by the local authority in its own area, or in another area. It may be in a home run by a voluntary organisation but under the general management responsibility of the local authority, or it may be in the fully voluntary sector, or in the private sector. Under the NHSCCA 1990,[112] it is the responsibility of the local authority 'care manager' to 'purchase' whatever services are necessary to meet the needs of the applicant, under the care package. This may include 'purchasing' a place for the applicant in a private residential home. Indeed, local authorities are obliged by government policy to spend at least 85 per cent of their allocated community care budget on 'purchasing' private sector accommodation for applicants in need of *residential accommodation*. The mechanics of the word 'purchase' are explored in more detail below.

Who pays for the accommodation?

Anybody entering *residential accommodation* since 1 April 1993 is subject to a new charging regime, in the light of the community care legislation. The new regime also applies *to those placed in homes by a local authority (mostly Part III accommodation) prior to 1 April 1993*. Those already in place in *registered care homes* (private sector) on that date are not affected by these changes and will have had their existing charging and social security benefit regime 'preserved'.[113] Under the new system if, following a *community care assessment*,[114] a local authority agrees to arrange a place for the applicant in *residential accommodation*, the local authority will be responsible for paying the full fee to the home. The local authority will then be able to recoup all, or some of the fees from the applicant under the *charging assessment procedures*. This procedure applies regardless of the type of accommodation (i.e. council, voluntary or private).

THE CHARGING ASSESSMENT PROCEDURES

The *charging assessment procedure* is carried out according to national rules,[115] roughly similar to the rules for determining *Income Support*.[116] First, the local authority must set a 'standard rate' for the accommodation, which in the case of their own accommodation is the full cost of providing a place, and in the case of other homes is the gross cost of paying for the accommodation under

---

112 See generally Chapter Four, p.97.
113 For further information on 'preserved rights' to social security benefits see *DSS Leaflet SSCCI.*
114 See Chapter Four, p.99.
115 National Assistance (Assessment of Resources) Regulations 192, as amended, and explained in LAC (92) 19 and in the *Charging for Residential Accommodation Guide (CRAG).*
116 See Chapter Six, p.179.

the contract with the home. An applicant with more than £8000 in savings[117] will pay the full 'standard rate' until their capital falls below that £8000. If the applicant owns their own home, this will be treated as capital, unless to do so would cause hardship to somebody with whom they had previously been sharing the home on a long-term basis. Those with capital below £8000 are means tested, and a check is also made to ensure they are receiving all the state benefits to which they are entitled. Applicants in private or voluntary homes are entitled to receive Income Support, plus a Residential Allowance, towards the costs of their care and accommodation, together with a small weekly personal allowance. Applicants in local authority homes cannot claim Income Support or Residential Allowance, unless their income is below the Basic Pension.[118]

Can an applicant transfer their assets to their family prior to moving into residential accommodation?

It is not possible for a person who anticipates going into residential accommodation to avoid this charge on their capital by transferring the house to another person shortly before moving into the residential accommodation. In these circumstances, the law will allow the local authority to recover payment from anyone to whom a person in residential accommodation has transferred assets (including a house) less than six months before entering the home if they did so 'knowingly and with the intention of avoiding charges for the residential accommodation'. If the transfer was blatantly to avoid payment, recovery can in fact be enforced even if the transfer was more than six months prior to entering accommodation.

Whilst a local authority cannot force a person to sell their home in order to meet the charge that is levied by the local authority to cover the cost of the residential accommodation, it can protect its interest by insisting that a legal charge is placed on the property. This legal charge will enable it to recover any unpaid fees at a later date, when the property is transferred either by will, or on intestacy or sale. This factor is one of great importance to consider, if an older person wishes to leave their home to a relative, as a long, accumulating debt expressed as a charge on that property will substantially reduce the value of the legacy to the relative. Most residents will also be in receipt of some form of social security assistance from the state to help them with their costs.

In addition to placing a charge on the resident's house to protect its financial position in the event of non-payment of the fees, a local authority can also issue

---

117 Note, however, that some items of capital are ignored for these purposes, e.g. most personal possessions, unless acquired for the primary purpose of reducing capital, and a home that the applicant intends to return to, that is still available, or that is to be sold to purchase another home for the applicant.

118 For full details of the scheme, which is complex, see Age Concern England *Factsheet 10: Local Authority Charging Procedures for Residential and Nursing Home Care* or *Disability Rights Handbook 18th Edition Chapter 35*.

proceedings in any court for the recovery of any outstanding debts, or proceedings against the resident's spouse, but not against any other member of their family.

Can a resident ever be evicted from the residential home in which they are living?
PART III ACCOMMODATION

There are a number of safeguards to the security of tenure of a Part III resident:

1. The resident will have the status of a *secure tenant* even though they only hold a licence to occupy. In these circumstances they can only be evicted if the managers of the home can establish grounds for possession.

2. The *National Assistance Act 1948* allows the Secretary of State to intervene in any situation where s/he thinks fit to do so, if satisfied that the local authority has failed to carry out its responsibilities to provide Part III accommodation. Whilst this power is rarely used, it is a useful fallback position for a dissatisfied person to adopt, if they feel they have been wrongfully deprived of their residential accommodation. Even if this formal power is not used, a complaint to the DSS can always be considered in cases of serious concern about the conduct in question. The right to complain to the DSS has the effect, however, of precluding any right to complain to the courts. Finally, once the new inspection and complaints procedures set out in the NHSCCA[119] are in place, a further tier of monitoring and scrutiny will be available.

3. The Local Government Ombudsman can always be brought in where maladministration or bias is suspected.[120]

PRIVATE SECTOR ACCOMMODATION

As the status of the resident will almost invariably be that of a licensee and not a tenant, it will always be legally possible for the owners or managers of the home to evict the resident, although it will be necessary to do so through court proceedings.

What controls operate on residential accommodation to ensure that they are properly run?
PART III ACCOMMODATION

Part III residential accommodation is the responsibility of the local authority social services department and thus any controls that operate on these homes are those which the local authority itself imposes. This also means that all the complaints procedures outlined in Chapter Four are available in connection with Part III accommodation. If the complaint amounts, however, to an allegation by a member of staff about patient care, and the home is part of the National Health Service, there is a procedure available that has been devised by

---

119 Chapter Four, p.104 et seq.
120 See generally Chapter Four, p.114 et seq.

the National Association of Health Authorities (NAHA).[121] Since April 1993 local authorities have started to put in place a system of monitoring and inspection of their homes, together with a mechanism for making complaints about homes. The government wishes free standing inspection units to be set up in local authorities that will eventually take responsibility for the inspection and monitoring of voluntary, private and public sector homes.[122]

PRIVATE SECTOR ACCOMMODATION

Most of these homes are regulated by the *Registered Homes Act 1984* which is a long, complex, but comprehensive piece of legislation.[123] Anybody who is engaged in social work in this area would be well advised to familiarise themselves with its general provisions. In summary, the Act provides a system of registration for a whole range of residential homes, including any home providing 'residential accommodation with both board and personal care for persons in need of personal care by reason of old age'. If the residential home also provides either physical or mental nursing care, it will be subject to a further set of detailed regulations governing the conduct of the institution, and the services and facilities they provide. Local authorities are required to inspect the home at least twice a year, and one of the visits should be unannounced.

Any home covered by the Act cannot operate unless it has been registered. Operating a residential home covered by the Act without registration is a criminal offence. Applications for registration are considered by the social services department of the local authority in which the home is situated. An application may be refused, accepted, or accepted with conditions. There is a right of appeal to a registered homes tribunal.[124] The registers of a registration authority must be made available to the public for inspection at all reasonable times, and members of the public are entitled to take copies of entries on payment of an appropriate fee. Any complaints about a particular home should be addressed in the first instance to the registration authority, and if the complainant alleges maladministration by the registration authority in its registration, then the Local Government Ombudsman.[125]

---

121 Contained in a 1985 publication called *Protecting Patients: Guidelines for Handling Staff Complaints about Patients' Care.*

122 For further information see also *Inspecting for Quality: Social Services Inspectorate Guidance on Practice for Inspection Units in Social Services Departments and Older Agencies* (SSI).

123 Guidance on the Act is provided by DHSS Circulars Nos. LAC(84)15, HC(84)21 LAC(86)6 and HC(86)5. LAC(90)13. See also supra fn.63

124 Detailed information regarding registration can be found in *Home Life: Code of Practice for Residential Care*, 1986, Centre for Policy on Ageing. Registration officers should also consult the BASW Practice *Notes for Social Workers and Residential Officers Working with the Private and Voluntary Residential Sector.*

125 See generally Chapter Four, p.114 et seq.

Finally, for detail on Residential Care and Mobility Payments consult Ashton (1993).

DISCRIMINATION IN RESPECT OF GOODS AND SERVICES

A more long-term goal of the DDA 1995 is to provide protection from unlawful discrimination in the provision of goods (any personal or moveable property), services and facilities and in relation to the management and disposal of premises. The Act provides an illustrative, though not exhaustive list of what services are to be caught by the legislation, which includes access to, and use of, any place which the public are permitted to enter; access to and use of means of communication or of information services; accommodation in hotels, boarding houses and so forth; banking and insurance facilities, grants, loans, credit or finance; facilities for entertainment, recreation or refreshment; services of a profession, trade and a local or public authority. All these provisions are largely contained in Part III of the DDA. There is also provision for a right of access linked to a new duty on the providers of services, goods and facilities, and the duty to provide auxiliary aids and services, if reasonable, to facilitate such access. Such steps will not be required, however, if they would fundamentally affect the nature of the service or business. However, with the exception of certain provisions relating to the right not to be refused service, the detail regarding the provisions, together with proposed implementation dates seem to be at present some way in the future.[126] The Government has, however, been talking of the creation of a National Telephone Hotline to offer some sort of limited advice, and even conciliation service. This is to be welcomed, if it happens, as the potential complexity of this part of the legislation is awesome. Complaint lies not to the Industrial Tribunal but to the County Court, where Legal Aid is available in appropriate cases, although complainants will not be entitled to a response to a statutory questionnaire as for employment discrimination cases, and therefore the collection of evidence is likely to prove especially problematic.

It is clear, therefore, that with regard to discrimination against disabled people in these areas there is considerable uncertainty at present as to what benefits, if any, are likely to accrue from this new legislation.

---

126 Consultation over the Part III Code of Practice is to await the creation in 1996 of the National Disability Council.

CHAPTER SIX

DISABILITY AND THE SOCIAL SECURITY SYSTEM

DISABILITY, POVERTY AND SOCIAL SECURITY

The link between poverty and disability has been established and acknowledged for some time. In 1984 the DHSS commissioned the Office of Population Censuses and Surveys to undertake research into the number of disabled people in Great Britain and into their circumstances. The research was undertaken by survey and the results published as a series of reports. Report 2, *The financial circumstances of disabled adults living in private households* (OPCS 1988), identified the particular aims and objectives of the survey as:

(i)   to examine the extent to which disability affects people's income;

(ii) to establish whether extra expenditure is incurred as a result of disability and to estimate the magnitude of that expenditure;

(iii) to evaluate the overall impact of disability on the standard of living and financial circumstances of disabled adults and their families (OPCS 1988, p.1).

By identifying these aims, two important consequences of disability were acknowledged. First, potential or actual loss of income, and second, the possibility of extra expenditure being incurred as a result of disability.

Survey evidence confirmed the existence and consequence of both of these features as characteristics of the experience of disability. The Report concluded that disabled adults are less likely than the population as a whole to earn income from employment, and where they are in paid employment they are likely to earn less than other adults in work. Extra expenditure as a consequence of disability is incurred by the majority of disabled adults, and the level of this extra expenditure reflects the nature and severity of the disability: 'Overall disabled adults are likely to experience some financial problems and to have lower standards of living than the population as a whole as a result of having lower average incomes' (OPCS 1988, p.xviii).

In such circumstances income derived through social security benefits assumes a central significance for the financial security of disabled people and their families. The absence of employment, or the loss or reduction of income resulting from disability, and the extra costs incurred, give rise to claims on the state through the social security system. It should also be recognised that the level of benefits paid may not provide an income adequate to meet the actual costs of disability.

Though the benefit system distinguishes between disability-related income maintenance benefits and disability costs benefits, the OPCS Report established that even where both types of benefits are in payment, disabled adults and their families had significantly lower income levels than families in the general population, and 24 per cent of disabled adults thought they needed to spend more because of their disability than they could afford to spend.

Despite being criticised for underestimating the costs of disability, the conclusions of the report have been of considerable significance (Abberley 1993, p.169). The Disability Income Group were particularly concerned about the figures produced by the OPCS, arguing that the costs associated with disability were considerably higher than those identified in the report. They argued that the under-estimation was so significant that the OPCS report should not be used as the basis for policy-making (Disability Alliance 1988, p.29). Despite this criticism, and because the surveys were commissioned to provide information for the reform of benefits, it was inevitable that the general conclusions of the report would be influential particularly as they confirm the extra financial costs of disability.

At the same time that the surveys were being conducted and the report written, the Disability Alliance was developing policy in the same area. The central plank of their policy was the call for a comprehensive disability income scheme designed to counter the negative impact of the financial consequences of disability. The Alliance argued that the poverty associated with disability, and the social security provision for disabled people, is both discriminatory and restricts full participation in society.

> Current social security provision for people with disabilities is both inadequate and discriminatory. Even taking account of the available benefits, people with disabilities are still more likely to suffer from poverty than non-disabled people. Also, people who are equally severely disabled can receive widely differing amounts of money according to the cause or origin of their disability, their national insurance contribution record, their age, or their marital status.

> It is a fundamental principle that people with disabilities should have equal rights to participation in customarily accepted activities, roles and relationships in society. There are many areas in which changes need to be made to the way that society is organised, in order to ensure that these rights can be fully exercised. Access to adequate levels of income, although not sufficient alone, is one essential element (Disability Alliance 1987, p.1).

Their proposal for a comprehensive disability income scheme was designed to address these issues by providing an income benefit based on the severity of disablement regardless of factors such as the cause of disablement, age, and national insurance record. Additionally, the benefit would address important issues of equity as between people with disabilities and non-disabled people, among people with disabilities and between degrees of disability.

The benefit proposed by the Disability Alliance consisted of a disablement allowance based on the severity of disability and a pension payable to disabled people unable to work or who have a restricted capacity for work. They also proposed that there should be adequate financial provision for carers.

Similar proposals were made by the Social Security Advisory Committee in their report, *Benefits for Disabled People: A Strategy for Change*, which proposed a unified benefit with elements to provide for income replacement and the extra costs associated with disablement (Social Security Advisory Committee 1988).

Despite the weight of these arguments the government's response to the OPCS surveys, published in a White Paper, *The Way Ahead: Benefits for the Disabled*, rejected the concept of a unified or comprehensive benefit in favour of incremental reform, based on changes to the existing structure of benefits (DSS 1990). The proposals contained in the White Paper were said by government to reflect four principles:

1. A wish to shift the balance of disability benefits to those who were unable to work and to those disabled from birth or disabled early in life.

2. To provide help with the costs of disability experienced by those of working age and below.

3. To help disabled people to enter and remain in the labour market.

4. To avoid duplication with other sources of help.

The central feature of the proposals was the rationalisation of care and mobility-based benefits into a new disability allowance, and the introduction of an allowance to encourage disabled people into employment and to support the low incomes of disabled people in work. These two allowances were legislated for in the Disability Living Allowance and Disability Working Allowance Act and were introduced in April 1992.

The inevitable consequence of introducing two new benefits into a system of disability benefits which remained largely unaltered was to reproduce, and possibly increase, the complexity and 'ad hocery' which had been a depressing feature of the system prior to 1992. The current system is therefore characterised by the large number of individual benefits, some of which are designed to provide income replacement whilst others are directed to care and mobility needs. The different benefits are themselves subject to the more familiar distinctions of the social security system between contributory and non-contributory benefits, between means and non-means tested benefits and between industrial and non-industrial benefits. The result is that a disabled person who has to claim benefit to meet some or all of the financial consequences of their disability, is faced with a confusing and complex system of individual benefits. Establishing entitlement within such a system may seem unnecessarily difficult to the claimant faced with the reality and financial consequences of disability.

A brief survey of current benefits illustrates this complexity. Income replacement is the primary objective of incapacity benefit, statutory sick pay, disability working allowance and severe disablement allowance. Invalid care allowance provides some income replacement for those who are unable to work full-time because they have taken on the role of the primary carer of a disabled person. Within this group of benefits disability working allowance utilises an element of means testing, incapacity benefit is a non-means tested contributory benefit, severe disability allowance is non-means tested and non-contributory, and statutory sick pay is available to those in employment.

Benefits designed to compensate for some of the costs associated with disablement include disability living allowance and attendance allowance. Though there has been significant rationalisation there are still differences between benefits paid to claimants who have suffered an industrial injury or contracted an industrial disease and those available to claimants whose disability has no industrial base.

Income support is the means tested benefit paid to those whose resources fail to meet their requirements (set at subsistence level by government). Consequently a significant number of disabled people claim income support to provide a basic level of income, their basic entitlement being supplemented by a number of weekly premiums which are paid in recognition of some of the extra costs associated with disability. The weekly income of many disabled people is thus provided through a complex equation of entitlement criteria and individual benefit systems.

INCOME MAINTENANCE BENEFITS

The category of income maintenance benefits for claimants with a disability incorporates both short-term and long-term benefits.

Statutory sick pay

Short-term illness and disability which interrupts a person's employment may result in a claim for *statutory sick pay*, a benefit which provides entitlement to a minimum level of income maintenance.[1] Statutory sick pay is paid and administered by employers in circumstances where there is no occupational sick pay

---

1   The statutory basis for the statutory sick pay scheme is contained in the Social Security Contributions and Benefits Act 1992. Other details of the scheme, principally those concerning the administrative structure and financing of the benefit, are set out in the Statutory Sick Pay 1994.

scheme in place or sick pay does not reach the minimum level of statutory sick pay fixed by law, including a figure which is now out of date in a hostage fortune and up-rated annually by regulation. Where occupational sick pay is paid at a level below this figure, statutory sick pay will be paid at a figure that establishes the claimant's level of income at the statutory figure.

The privatised character of this benefit raises a number of issues of concern for people with a short-term sickness or disability, and for those who have a chronic complaint which has an impact on their employment health record. Within the law employers are able to design and enforce their own notification of sickness procedures with the result that such procedures may take on a disciplinary character with a disproportionate effect on employees with poor health or a continuing disability. Disputes concerning entitlement to statutory sick pay can be referred to an adjudication officer,[2] and questions concerning the incapacity of an employee may be referred to the Benefits Agency Medical Service with the consent of the employee.

There is little doubt that since responsibility for the administration and payment of statutory sick pay has been devolved to employers they are likely to take an increasingly rigorous attitude to the incapacity of their employees. It is also likely that employers will consider the health record of potential employees to be a matter of considerable importance with the result that disabled people may be discriminated against in the labour market. The indirect protection offered by an unfair dismissal action is only available after two years' employment with an employer so that dismissal for reasons of illness or disability before this period cannot be challenged in an industrial tribunal. Once again the experience of disability is characterised by discrimination.

Incapacity benefit

Incapacity benefit, which was introduced in April 1995 to succeed the contributory schemes of sickness benefit and invalidity benefit, is the major long-term benefit for those who are unemployed and not able to work because of a physical or mental incapacity. Like its predecessors, it is a contributory benefit so that claimants must have paid or been credited with sufficient national insurance contributions; incapacity benefit is non-means tested.

The argument for the introduction of incapacity benefit was established through government concern about increased expenditure in the social security system. The number of claimants receiving invalidity benefit had increased from 600,000 in 1978–1979 to approximately 1.5 million in 1992–1993 with a doubling of cost since 1982–1983 (DSS 1993). It was argued by government that this growth in numbers and costs, at a time when it was said that the health of the nation was improving, could only be explained by the incorrect

---

2   An adjudication officer is an officer of the Benefits Agency or the Employment Service whose task is to make decisions on matters relating to entitlement to benefit.

application of entitlement criteria or absenteeism from work and fraud. One particular criticism was that the test for *incapacity for work* had been developed, through case law decided by the Social Security Commissioners, to a criteria where incapacity had only to relate to work which the claimant could reasonably be expected to undertake. This, it was claimed, meant that too much concern was being directed to non-medical criteria. Though these concerns have been criticised[3] as unfounded or exaggerated, they established a sufficient rationale for government to legislate for reform, and incapacity benefit was introduced by the Social Security (Incapacity for Work) Act 1994.

Incapacity benefit is paid to claimants who are incapable of work. Claimants who have exhausted entitlement to statutory sick pay, but whose incapacity for work continues, are transferred to incapacity benefit. Claimants who are not employed but who have a sufficient national insurance contribution record are able to claim incapacity benefit from the onset of their incapacity.

Incapacity is established by one of two tests, the 'own occupation' test and the 'all work' test. The 'own occupation' test is used to establish the incapacity for work of the claimant in employment and those who have recently been forced to give up their job because of their illness or disability. The test relates to the claimant's ability to undertake work within their employment that they could reasonably be expected to do. After 28 weeks of incapacity such claimants will be subjected to the 'all work' test. The 'all work' test also applies, from the outset of incapacity, to all claimants without regular employment.

The 'own occupation' test is, in essence, the test used in invalidity benefit, the predecessor of incapacity benefit. The day to day application of this test had been the subject of much government criticism[4] targeted at scroungers, and on doctors for being too ready to provide medical certification of incapacity. Nonetheless, it seems that for the first 28 weeks of an incapacity benefit claim from those with a regular occupation, reliance will continue to be placed on medical certification from a claimant's general practitioner.

The very different, and supposedly more rigorous, 'all work' test is reserved for those with no regular occupation and for those claimants with a regular occupation who are still on benefit after 28 weeks and have therefore become a long-term claimant. The 'all work' test requires a claimant to test their functional ability against a number of physical and mental criteria. The resultant 'scoring' of ability to undertake such functions as walking, climbing stairs, sitting, standing, bending, kneeling, manual dexterity, lifting, carrying, speech,

---

3   See Ogus, Barendt and Wikeley 1995, p.168.
4   See reports of the parliamentary debates on the Social Security (Incapacity for Work) Bill, for example Hansard, H.C. cols 35–136 (24 January 1994).

hearing, comprehension and mental health, determines the issue of entitlement to benefit.[5]

The use of these functional criteria is said to establish the 'medical' assessment of incapacity, thereby limiting or excluding other extraneous factors.[6]

A claimant's self-assessment will be subject to confirmation, or contradiction, by reference to their GP's diagnosis and a decision on entitlement by a Benefits Agency adjudication officer. In practice this latter decision will only be taken after advice from a Benefits Agency Medical Service doctor who is able to examine the claimant.[7]

A number of people with a severe disability or illness are exempted from the 'all work' test. These include those receiving severe disablement allowance or the highest rate of the care component of disability living allowance, and claimants who are terminally ill or registered blind. Other exempting conditions are tetraplegia, paraplegia, dementia, persistent vegetative state, severe learning disability, a severe and progressive neurological or muscle wasting disease, progressive inflammatory polyarthritis, progressive impairment of cardio-respiratory function which severely and persistently limits effort tolerance, a severe and progressive immune deficiency state characterised by the occurrence of severe constitutional disease, opportunistic infections or tumour formation (e.g. AIDS), or a severe mental illness.

Despite the identification of exempting conditions the new assessment of incapacity established by the 'all work' test is a rather crude tool for measuring the very complex interaction of factors which go to establish a physical and mental impairment which renders a person incapable of work. The choice of this functional and 'medical' test is probably best explained by the desire of government to reverse the increase in spending in this area of benefit entitlement.

> There was never any secret that the primary aim of the reform was to control the rapidly increasing level of spending on invalidity benefit. In that light, the reform will be successful; it is expected to produce an annual saving of £1 billion in three years time. During 1995 and 1996, 200,000 people who had already been receiving invalidity benefit, perhaps for many years, will be reassessed, and lose entitlement to incapacity benefit because they score less than 15 points. In future, it is estimated that 55,000 other people will be assessed as capable of work every year after receiving six months' benefit (at the lower rate) on the basis of their doctor's sick note (Berthoud 1995, pp.81–82).

---

5 These functional tests are specified by the Schedule to the Social Security (Incapacity for Work) (General) Regulations 1995.

6 For a detailed discussion of the assessment of incapacity used in establishing entitlement to invalidity benefit and incapacity benefit see Berthoud 1995, pp.61–85.

7 For a detailed discussion of the new test see Bonner 1995, pp.86–112.

The impact of more rigorous criteria for establishing incapacity is one element of the objective of reducing expenditure in this area of benefit. The structure of incapacity benefit also means that access to long-term higher rates of benefit are delayed for longer than under invalidity benefit, and access to child dependency increases is also delayed. The impact of these restrictions will be to reduce expenditure on incapacity benefit and consequently to force more claimants to claim means tested income support.

It is too soon to assess the full impact of incapacity benefit but it is likely that the introduction of functional testing against a threshold score for entitlement will produce a significant number of difficulties, particularly in the interpretation of individual tests such as the inability to 'walk up and down a flight of 12 stairs without holding on and taking a rest'; or 'cannot pick up and pour from a full saucepan or kettle of 1.7 litre capacity with either hand'; or 'cannot hear well enough to understand someone talking in a normal voice on a busy street'; or 'needs encouragement to get up and dress'.[8] The desire to replace the discretion inherent in the use of non-medical factors to determine incapacity may in time be seen to have resulted in the creation of excessively detailed tests which are difficult to define comprehensively because in practice they are themselves imprecise. What is a busy street; how long does a pause in climbing stairs have to be before the pause constitutes a rest?

Severe disablement allowance

Incapacity benefit is a non-means tested and a contributory benefit. Its non-contributory equivalent is severe disablement allowance. This benefit is designed for claimants with a long-term incapacity for work who do not have a sufficient national insurance contribution record to qualify for incapacity benefit. Additionally, the long-term entitlement criteria of 196 consecutive days' incapacity for work must have begun before the claimant's 20th birthday. Alternatively, the claimant must be disabled to the extent of 80 per cent and have been so disabled for 196 consecutive days.[9]

For many claimants the 80 per cent disablement test is satisfied by their receipt of the care component of disability living allowance at the higher or middle rate, the higher rate of the mobility component or attendance allowance.

---

8   Taken from the Schedule to the Social Security (Incapacity for Work) (General) Regulations 1995.

9   These and other detailed entitlement criteria are set out in section 61 Social Security Administration Act 1992 and in the Social Security (Incapacity Benefit) (General) Regulations 1995. Incapacity is established by the application of the tests set out in these regulations though claimants getting severe disablement allowance on 12 April 1995 will be exempt from the new test for incapacity so long as they remain incapable of work. New claimants will be required to satisfy the 'all work' test unless they are exempt by reason of their entitlement to the highest rate of the care component of disability living allowance or because they have any one of a number of specified conditions. (See Poynter and Martin 1995.)

Percentage disablement can also be established by reference to the rates of disablement set out for the industrial injuries scheme. Decisions on the level of disablement are taken by an adjudicating medical authority with an appeal to a Medical Appeal Tribunal. Severe disablement allowance is a non-means tested and non-contributory benefit.

Disability working allowance

Disability working allowance was introduced in 1992 as part of the government's reform of disability benefits provided for in their White Paper, The Way Ahead: Benefits for Disabled People (DSS 1990). The rationale for this benefit was based on a recognition of the reduced earning levels of disabled people and on the government's argument in favour of providing incentives to work for people with a partial rather than full incapacity for work. The benefit, which is closely modelled on Family Credit, is means tested and is designed to supplement the low income of those in full-time work (defined as 16 hours or over in a week) who have a physical or mental disability which puts them at a disadvantage in getting a job. This test is satisfied where the claimant is receiving the higher or middle rate care component or the higher rate mobility component of disability living allowance, or attendance allowance. The test may also be satisfied where the claimant is unable to perform one of a number of functional tests.[10]

The Social Security Advisory Committee had argued for just such a benefit in their report, *Benefits for Disabled People: a Strategy for Change* (Social Security Advisory Committee 1988) and had welcomed the benefit when it was introduced. However, its record since introduction has been disappointing. By March 1994 there were only 3680 current awards. Research by the Policy Studies Institute has commented that low take-up and the lack of eligible non-recipients are major factors for the small number of successful claims (Rowlingson and Berthoud 1994). Arguing for reforms to increase the number of those receiving the benefit, the editors of the Journal of Social Security Law have suggested a reduction in the threshold in the number of hours worked to qualify for benefit (currently 16) on the grounds that a third of all claims currently fail this test (Harris and Wikeley 1995).

Invalid care allowance

Invalid care allowance, which is paid to the carer of a disabled person, is by character an income replacement benefit. The allowance is paid to claimants who are regularly and substantially caring for a disabled person.[11] This is further defined as involving such care for 35 hours or more a week. The disability of the person being cared for is established only by their receipt of specified benefits: higher or middle rate care component of disability living

---

10   These tests are set out in the Disability Working Allowance (General) Regulations 1991.
11   Social Security (Invalid Care Allowance) Regulations 1976.

allowance, attendance allowance or its industrial equivalent, constant attendance allowance. The carer cannot qualify for benefit if they are in gainful employment (defined by a higher earnings limit) or are receiving full-time education.

Invalid care allowance is a non-means tested, non-contributory benefit paid to claimants between the ages of 16 and 65. The cost of caring for a disabled person is considerable and the availability of benefit to provide some level of income replacement for those who spend the equivalent of a working week to look after relatives and other disabled people is important for carers and makes sound economic sense for the state. This is particularly the case when the absence of such a carer would necessarily involve the provision of expensive community care services or personal or nursing care in a residential or nursing home. However, the level of benefit paid (currently £35.25 plus dependency increases) is likely to impose a life of poverty on many full-time carers who have no other source of income. Where such carers are single men or women they may well be forced to claim income support to raise their level of income to what is probably no more than subsistence level. This problem is most likely to affect women who constitute the majority of such carers. Where such women are married the employment and income of their partner may preclude any claim for income support, with the result that the state is in effect paying for the care of often severely disabled people at the weekly rate of £35.25p at current rates.

BENEFITS FOR CARE AND ASSISTANCE

Benefits paid to disabled people in respect of their care and assistance are administered within the structure of disability living allowance and attendance allowance.

The care component of *disability living allowance* and *attendance allowance* are important benefits for a significant number of people whose disability establishes a need for care and assistance. The allowance was introduced by the Disability Living Allowance and Disability Working Allowance Act 1991 and is available at three levels to people who, because of their severe mental or physical disablement, require care and attention from another person.

The current legislation contains six disability tests. The *lower rate* is paid to claimants who satisfy what is known as the part-time day care test. The claimant must be:

(a) so severely disabled physically or mentally that –

    (i) he requires in connection with his bodily functions attention from another person for a significant portion of the day (whether during a single period or a number of periods); or

      (ii)   he cannot prepare a cooked main meal for himself if he has the ingredients.[12]

The *middle rate* is paid to claimants who satisfy either one of the two day time conditions or either one of the two night time conditions.

  (b) is so severely disabled physically or mentally that, by day, he requires from another person -

      (i)   frequent attention throughout the day in connection with his bodily functions, or

      (ii) continual supervision throughout the day in order to avoid substantial danger to himself or others.[13]

    is so severely disabled physically or mentally that, at night, –

      (i)   he requires, from another person prolonged or repeated attention in connection with his bodily functions, or

      (ii) in order to avoid substantial danger to himself or others he requires another person to be awake for a prolonged period or at frequent intervals for the purpose of watching over him.[14]

The *highest rate* of benefit is paid to those claimants who satisfy both or either of the two day time tests and both or either of the two night time tests.

    The different conditions contain a number of concepts that have required interpretation by the Social Security Commissioners and the courts. The criteria that attention or supervision should be required from another person has been interpreted to mean *reasonably required* rather than *medically required*.[15] The House of Lords has recently decided that a blind person reasonably required help and attention in walking outside in unfamiliar situations and in reading letters.[16]

    Attention has been defined as involving an active provision of services[17] in contrast to supervision which is said to be passive.[18] The attention that is required is attention in connection with bodily functions. These have been defined as including: 'breathing, hearing, seeing, eating, drinking, walking, sleeping, getting in and out of bed, dressing and undressing, eliminating waste products, and the like, all of which an ordinary person, who is not suffering from any disability, does for himself.'[19]

    Where attention is required 'for a significant portion of the day,' it is generally accepted that this involves about an hour a day. *Frequent attention* is

---

12   Section 72(1)(a) Social Security Contributions and Benefits Act 1992.

13   Section 72 (1)(b).

14   Section 72(1)(c)

15   R(A) 3/86.

16   Mallinson v Secretary of State [1994] 2 All E.R.295.

17   R(A) 3/74.

18   R(A) 2/75.

19   R v National Insurance Commissioners, ex parte Secretary of State for Social Services [1981] All E.R.738.

said to mean 'several times not once or twice'.[20] *Prolonged attention* is taken to mean 20 minutes of attention whilst repeated attention means twice or more.

Continual supervision in order to avoid substantial danger has been considered by the Commissioners and is said to include four elements:[21]

i) There must be a substantial danger to the disabled person or to someone else as a result of the disabled person's condition.

ii) The danger must be one against which it is reasonable to guard.

iii) There must be a need for the supervision.

iv) The supervision must be continual (Poynter and Martin 1995, pp.139–140).

For the purposes of 'watching over', the person so doing must be awake for a prolonged period or at frequent intervals. This is thought to mean being awake for 20 minutes or more, whilst 'frequent intervals' means more than twice (Poynter and Martin 1995, pp.140–141).

Disability living allowance is a non-means tested and non-contributory benefit payable to disabled people who satisfy the entitlement criteria outlined above and have done so continuously for three months prior to their claim and are likely to continue to satisfy the criteria for six months after the claim. These 'backwards' and 'forwards' tests do not need to be satisfied by a claimant who is terminally ill.[22] There is no lower age limit for the care component though children under 16 cannot qualify for the lower rate by purporting to satisfy the 'cooking' test.[23] The upper age limit for claiming disability living allowance is 65 though a claim made up to a claimant's 66th birthday will be accepted as long as the conditions were met on the day prior to their 65th birthday.

Attendance allowance is an equivalent benefit to the care component of disability living allowance but is only available for claimants over the age of 65. Attendance allowance is paid at two rates which correspond to the higher and middle rate care component of disability living allowance, with the same disability conditions to establish entitlement.

Disability living allowance also provides a mobility component for people whose disability has consequences for their ability to walk. Benefit is paid at

---

20   *ibid.* p.741.

21   R(A) 1/83.

22   Section 66(2) Social Security Contributions and Benefits Act 1992 provides that a person is suffering from a terminal illness and he or she can reasonably be expected to die of their progressive disease within six months.

23   A child under 16 can qualify for the care component providing they satisfy additional conditions set out in section 72(6) Social Security Contributions and Benefits Act 1992:
     s/he has attention or supervision requirements 'substantially in excess of the normal requirements of a person of his age'; or
     s/he had substantial attention or supervision requirements 'which younger persons in normal physical and mental health may also have but which persons of his age and in normal physical and mental health would not have' (Poynter and Martin 1995, p.132).

two rates and entitlement is established by reference to a number of disability conditions set out in section 73 *Social Security Contributions and Benefits Act 1992*.

For a claimant to be entitled to the higher rate they must have a physical disability which renders them unable or virtually unable to walk; or they are both blind and deaf; or they were born without feet or they are a double amputee. An alternative qualification can be established where the claimant is severely mentally impaired with severe behavioural problems and is entitled to the higher rate of the care component.

Entitlement to the lower rate of mobility component is established by showing that as a consequence of severe mental or physical disability the claimant is unable, ignoring familiar routes, to take advantage of their ability to walk without guidance or supervision from another person most of the time.

A number of the concepts contained in the statutory tests are further explained by regulation.[24] Virtual inability to walk is defined in the following terms:

> his ability to walk out of doors is so limited, as regards the distance over which or the speed at which or the length of time for which or the manner in which he can make progress on foot without severe discomfort, that he is virtually unable to walk; or the exertion required to walk would constitute a danger to his life or would be likely to lead to a serious deterioration in his health (Regulation 12(10)(a).

The severe behavioural problems which might lead to qualification for the higher rate are further defined by Regulation 12:

> he exhibits disruptive behaviour which is extreme; and

> he regularly requires someone else to intervene and physically restrain them in order to prevent them causing injury to themselves or others, or damage to property; and

> he is so unpredictable that another person has to be present and watching over them whenever they are awake

Claimants below the age of five are not entitled to the mobility component of disability living allowance and first claims must be made before the age of 66 so long as the claimant was disabled enough to have qualified on the day prior to their 65th birthday. The consequence of this upper age limit is that many people who develop limitations to their mobility when they are over 65 are excluded from entitlement. This deliberate exclusion reflects the fact that the benefit is designed for people with a particular disability rather than for the much larger category of people whose mobility decreases as they get older. However, the arbitrary age limit causes a number of decisions which must seem harsh to a person over 66 who has lost their mobility, or a substantial element of it relatively close to retirement age.

---

24 Social Security (Disability Living Allowance) Regulations 1991.

Claimants with a mental or psychological condition which causes them mobility problems may have considerable difficulty in establishing entitlement. The higher rate is only available to those with a physical disablement unless the claimant is severely mentally impaired and has severe behavioural problems. Consequently agoraphobics will not qualify for the higher rate and others with psychological problems which affect their mobility may have to establish a physical cause to qualify. Such claimants and those who suffer from panic attacks, fits or blackouts will be limited to claiming the lower rate and will have to establish that they need supervision to an extent that constitutes more than reassurance.

BENEFITS FOR INDUSTRIAL INJURIES AND DISEASES

Where illness or disability is work-related, claimants may be able to claim industrial injuries benefits. A distinct system of industrial injuries benefits was an important element of the social security structure established by legislation after the Second World War though such benefits have a history that can be traced back to the Workmen's Compensation Act 1897. Traditionally, industrial injuries benefits have incorporated an 'industrial preference', that is: 'the more favourable treatment given to the victims of industrial accidents and diseases over those disabled by other causes' (Ogus, Barendt and Wikeley 1995, p.297),

Though this preference has gradually been reduced by the incremental rationalisation of industrial and non-industrial 'disability' benefits it still has an important basis in the availability of disablement benefit which seeks to compensate for disablement resulting from loss of faculty arising from an industrial injury or industrial disease.[25]

Claims for disablement benefit must satisfy the criteria that the 'employed earner suffers personal injury caused by accident arising out of and in the course of his employment.'[26] This legislative test, and its predecessors, has generated a substantial amount of case law, much of which has been directed to interpretation of the criteria 'arising out of and in the course of his employment' and to distinguishing between an accident, for which benefit is payable, and injury resulting from the effects of a long-term industrial process, which does not

---

25   Loss of faculty is the damage to a particular part of your body or mind caused by an accident or disease, while disability is the inability to do things that is caused by that damage (Poynter and Martin 1995, p.169).
26   Section 94(1) Social Security Contributions and Benefits Act 1992.

satisfy the criteria for benefit under this section, though it may amount to an industrial disease.[27]

Where an employed earner has contracted an illness which is employment related they may be able to found a claim for disablement benefit if the disease is a 'prescribed disease'. A number of diseases are prescribed in relation to particular employment on the basis that they are a special risk of that employment. If a claimant can show that he or she is suffering loss of faculty from a prescribed disease and that they are or were employed at the relevant time in an employment prescribed for that disease, then, with the benefit of a statutory presumption, they can establish entitlement to disablement benefit.

Benefit is only available for percentages of disablement over 14 per cent,[28] though any assessment between 14 per cent and 19 per cent is treated as a 20 per cent disablement. Benefit is paid as a weekly pension and at a level which reflects the level of disablement up to 100 per cent.[29] Two additions may be payable:

- *constant attendance allowance* is payable where the claimant's disablement is assessed at 100 per cent and he or she needs constant attendance as a result of the relevant loss of faculty. This addition is payable at a higher or lower rate;

- where the higher rate is in payment the claimant may also be entitled to *exceptionally severe disablement allowance.*

The continued legitimacy of the industrial preference may seem to conflict with the argument for a unified and comprehensive disability benefit. However, this seeming paradox may be explained by the recent history of industrial injuries benefits which is one of cuts in the coverage of the scheme and cuts in the level of benefit imposed through rationalisation with the non-industrial scheme.[30] Within such an experience it is important to argue for the retention of whatever preference remains.

Within the industrial diseases system there are two issues which cause continuing critical comment. First, the list of prescribed diseases is limited and

---

27 For a detailed discussion of the industrial injuries system and of this test in particular see Ogus, Barendt and Wikeley 1995, Chapter 7.

28 Exceptionally three lung diseases, byssinosis, diffuse mesothelioma and pneumoconiosis, may be assessed for benefit payment at between one per cent and 13 per cent.

29 The Social Security Act 1986 abolished a gratuity payment for percentage disablement assessment of below 20 per cent. By doing so the government was able to eliminate 90 per cent of all new awards of disablement benefit.

30 The abolition of reduced earnings allowance for accidents or disease occurring after September 1990 is just such an example. This benefit compensated for loss of earning capacity resulting from industrial injury or industrial disease, and though pre-1990 entitlement is continued, its abolition was an important development in the rationalisation of the industrial and non-industrial benefit structure, as well as being a clear limitation of the industrial preference and a continuing cut in expenditure.

the process of prescription, which is largely the responsibility of the Industrial Injuries Advisory Council, is slow and cumbersome (Ogus, Barendt and Wikeley 1995, p.325). This criticism is of particular concern in an era when hazards to health arising from the speed and nature of technological development in industry may outstrip increased concern about and regulation of health issues in employment.

The second, and related issue, concerns the limitations of the prescription system itself. Though the system provides entitlement to benefit where the claimant's illness is prescribed in relation to his or her employment it provides no entitlement to benefit for illness which is employment related but falls outside the prescription system either because it is itself not prescribed or because it is not prescribed in respect of the claimant's employment. One way of extending the industrial injuries benefits scheme to all employment-related illnesses would be to introduce what has been termed an 'open or individual proof' system within which entitlement could be established where a causal link between employment and illness can be proved. The Industrial Injuries Advisory Council considered such proposals in its *Report on Industrial Diseases 1981* (IIAC 1981), and though broadly in favour of the idea concluded that such a system would need to be limited by the inclusion of an exempt list of diseases including lung cancer, stroke, heart disease and mental disorder, where entitlement could not be established by individual proof.

Entitlement to industrial injuries benefits does not preclude a person injured at work, or a person who contracted a prescribed disease, also taking an action in negligence for damages. However, under a recoupment scheme introduced by the *Social Security Act 1989*, the state may recover from those paying damages a sum equivalent to specified benefit payments paid to the injured person.

INCOME SUPPORT

A substantial number of disabled people will have to claim income support as their sole means of income or as a top-up benefit in addition to their entitlement to specific disability benefits. Income support is the safety net benefit for those whose income, from all sources, does not meet their everyday requirements. The basic scheme is set out in the *Social Security Contributions and Benefits Act 1992* and the details are provided in a number of complex sets of regulations.

Entitlement to income support is calculated by reference to two figures, a claimant's 'applicable amount', and their income. The applicable amount includes a basic level of subsistence income, known as the personal allowance, weekly premium payments and some housing costs. Premiums are paid to reflect the regular increased costs faced by particular groups of people.

These different elements are aggregated together to establish the claimant's applicable amount. A claimant's income, earned income and some benefit payments are deducted from their applicable amount and the gap between the two figures is met by the payment of income support. The applicable amount and income are aggregated figures which take account of the resources and requirements of the claimant and his or her family unit.

The extra costs associated with disability are recognised, though certainly not compensated for in full, by a number of income support premiums. There are four premiums which address the extra costs associated with disability directly:

- disability premium
- severe disability premium
- the disabled child premium
- the carer premium.

Disability premium is paid to claimants under the age of 60 who are receiving a qualifying benefit: attendance allowance, disability living allowance, disability working allowance, incapacity benefit at the long-term rate, severe disablement allowance or mobility supplement; or to claimants who are incapable of work (for the purposes of incapacity benefit) and have been so for 365 days.[31]

Entitlement to *severe disability premium* is established by reference to three conditions: receipt of a qualifying benefit, attendance allowance or the middle or higher rate care component of disability living allowance; the requirement that no non-dependent aged 18 or over is living with the claimant; and no one is receiving invalid care allowance for looking after the claimant.[32]

The *disabled child premium* is paid in respect of each child in the claimant's family who is receiving disability living allowance or is blind.

The *carer premium* is paid where the claimant or their partner is receiving or is entitled to invalid care allowance. The premium can be paid twice where both the claimant and their partner satisfy the conditions.[33]

Higher pensioner premium is paid where the claimant or their partner is over 60 and either of them satisfy the conditions for entitlement to the disability premium; or the claimant was entitled to income support, including the disability premium just before their 60th birthday and has continued to be entitled to income support since they reached the age of 60.

Income, for the purposes of income support calculation, is comprised of earnings, other income and capital. Where the claimant or their partner are employed for 16 hours or more a week there is no entitlement to income

---

31 For a detailed discussion of the rules of entitlement see *Child Poverty Action Group* 1995, and subsequent annual editions; or the *Disability Alliance/ERA* 1995, and subsequent annual editions.

32 The criteria for entitlement to the severe disability premium have been amended on a number of occasions and are now recognised as being very restrictive.

33 Receipt of invalid care allowance may jeopardise entitlement to the severe disability premium. See: Child Poverty Action Group 1995, p.297–298.

support, though for the disabled claimant there may be entitlement to disability working allowance. Net earnings are used for the purposes of income support calculation and claimants or their partner receiving a disability-based premium are entitled to have £15 of their earnings disregarded in the calculation of income.

The general rule is that benefit income is counted in full for the calculation of income support. However, payment of a number of disability benefits are ignored; these include:

- attendance allowance (or constant attendance allowance, exceptionally severe disablement allowance)
- the care and mobility components of disability living allowance.

Capital of £8000 or more belonging to a claimant and their partner will disqualify a claim for income support. Capital between £3000 and £8000 will be taken to produce an income of £1 a week for every unit of £250 above £3000.

SOCIAL SECURITY BENEFITS FOR PEOPLE IN RESIDENTIAL CARE

The rules relating to social security benefits for people living in residential care homes and nursing homes are extremely complex.[34] The general rule is that attendance allowance and disability living allowance care component will stop being paid after four weeks in an independent sector home unless the resident is paying the full cost of care themselves. These benefits are not payable to residents in local authority residential accommodation. Disability living allowance care component and attendance allowance are both payable to terminally ill residents in a voluntary sector hospice.

Income support is payable, subject to the usual rules of entitlement and to the capital cut off of £8000, to residents in independent sector care or nursing homes, and local authority homes though at a different rate, and will include any premiums that relate to the disability of the resident.

All other social security benefits can be claimed by people living in residential care homes and nursing homes, subject to the usual rules of entitlement.

CLAIMING AND COLLECTING BENEFITS

Where physical disability prevents a claimant being able to collect benefits he or she may appoint an agent to do so on their behalf. Regulations provide for

---

34   For a detailed discussion see Disability Alliance ERA 1995 and subsequent annual editions.

an application to be made to the Secretary of State for the applicant to be made an appointee to act on behalf of a person with a mental disorder or learning disability which prevents them acting for themselves.[35] The appointee is responsible for all issues relating to benefit claims and payments. Where the Court of Protection has appointed a receiver in relation to the financial affairs of a person with a mental disorder under the provisions of the Mental Health Act 1983, the receiver will have full authority to act on behalf of that person in respect of all social security matters.

DISABILITY AND THE SOCIAL FUND

The introduction of the Social Fund represented a major shift in social security policy. Hitherto social security benefits had been subject to demand-led funding so that expenditure increased as more claimants were able to establish entitlement to particular benefits. Demand-led funding is the corollary of legal rights to benefit. Though the Social Fund adopted a different structure for the major part of its coverage, claims for payments from the 'statutory social fund', that is maternity payments, funeral payments and cold weather payments, are subject to rules of entitlement and demand-led funding. Rules of entitlement to the statutory social fund are set out in regulations. Claims are decided by a Benefits Agency Adjudication Officer and are subject to an appeal to a Social Security Appeal Tribunal. Benefits paid under this part of the Social Fund are means-tested and non-contributory.

The more important 'discretionary Social Fund' is constituted by community care grants, budgeting loans and crisis loans; they are subject to discretionary decision-making and a cash-limited budget. The discretionary social fund, and in particular the availability of community care grants, are of interest to disabled people because of their specific link with the policy of care in the community: 'Community care grants are intended to promote community care by helping people to move out of, or stay out of, institutional or residential care and by assisting families under exceptional pressure' (Child Poverty Action Group 1995, p.375.)

The discretionary Social Fund is cash-limited and consequently there is no legal entitlement to the grants or loans that are subject to discretionary decision-making by Social Fund officers. Social Fund officers are bound by a series of Directions issued by the Secretary of State and they are also required to take account of Guidance also issued by the Secretary of State. The impact of cash-limited funding is evidenced in the fixing of priorities though these do not determine decisions on individual claims. Social Fund payments can be made by way of loans or grants; unsurprisingly, the budget for loans is much larger than that for grants.

---

35   Regulation 33 Social Security (Claims and Payments) Regulations 1987.

Budgeting loans are available to people who have been receiving income support for at least six months and who are unable to budget for a particular expense. Crisis loans are for expenses caused by an emergency or a disaster and they must be the only way in which serious damage or serious risk to the health or safety of the claimant or his or her family can be averted. The loans are interest free but cannot exceed £1000 at any one time. Loans will not be made if the Social Fund officer concludes that they cannot be repaid.

Community care grants are intended to help income support claimants who are facing difficulties arising from their special circumstances, and in particular to support the policy of care in the community. The Social Fund Guide identifies a number of priority groups, including people with all types of disabilities, those who are chronically sick, and families under stress. An indication of the purpose of these grants is given by examples of the needs for which grants will be given so long as funds are available in the budget: setting up home after leaving hospital or residential care; clothing and shoes on leaving institutional care, or where they are needed because of rapid weight loss or gain; bedding which is needed because someone is bedridden or incontinent; and a washing machine, spin dryer and tumble dryer where a family member is incontinent and the existing facilities are unsuitable or inadequate.

Decisions concerning Social Fund loans and grants are discretionary in nature and will depend on a number of factors including the provisions of the Directions and the Guidance, established priorities, the level of the office budget and the ability of the claimant to be able to repay a loan. There is therefore no entitlement to such payments, many of which used to be available under the old supplementary benefit scheme within a structure of regulations which created rights to benefit for claimants whose circumstances brought them within the rules of entitlement. The shift to discretionary decision-making within a system which is cash-limited has withdrawn any right to payments for the expenses covered by the Social Fund. This shift from rights to discretion is significant for those people, many of whom will be disabled, whose financial circumstances necessitate applications for grants and loans. This disadvantageous position is compounded by the absence of any right of appeal against the decision of a Social Fund officer to an independent social security appeal tribunal; instead, the decisions of Social Fund officers are subject to a system of internal review by a different Social Fund officer and ultimately to review by a Social Fund inspector.

NON-STATUTORY SCHEMES FOR SEVERE DISABLEMENT

Within the social security system disabled claimants may have to rely on a number of distinct claims to different benefit systems to establish a basic weekly income. Those with a severe disability may also receive help from one of the extra-statutory schemes which originated with the Independent Living Fund, set up by government in 1988 as a discretionary trust fund. The original fund was established to make payments to severely disabled people in respect of their needs for personal care and domestic support required to live an independent life within the community. The fund was wound up in 1993 when the care in the community system was established by the implementation of the community care aspects of the *National Health Service and Community Care Act 1990* in April 1993,[36] though the Independent Living (Extension) Fund continues the support to approximately 22,000 claimants assisted by the original fund.

More limited help is provided by the Independent Living (1993) Fund. This assistance is provided in conjunction with local authorities so that joint care packages incorporating community care services and cash from the fund are available for severely disabled people.

CONCLUSION

This discussion of the structure of statutory-based disability benefits, their individual rules of entitlement, and of the Social Fund and the Independent Living Funds, is in no respect a comprehensive account. However, even this simplified account should provide sufficient evidence of the complexity of the structure of benefits, the legal basis of entitlement to individual benefits and the discretionary character of the Social Fund.

This complexity is compounded by the different adjudication and appeal systems that confront any claimant to disability benefits. The basic adjudication structure involves initial decision-making by a Benefits Agency adjudication officer with a right of appeal to a Social Security Appeal Tribunal and a further appeal on a point of law to the Social Security Commissioners. Some medical or disablement questions relating to disablement benefit and severe disablement allowance are decided by an adjudicating medical authority, normally a single medical practitioner. Appeals from these decisions are heard by Medical Appeal Tribunals. Appeals from the decision of an adjudication officer concerning disability living allowance or attendance allowance are heard by a Disability Appeal Tribunal. A further appeal on a point of law lies from both to the Social Security Commissioners.

The difficulties inherent in dealing with this complex law and legal system are similarly compounded by the fact that the legal aid system does not extend to pay for legal representation before Social Security Appeal Tribunals, Disability Appeal Tribunals, Medical Appeal Tribunals, or the Social Security Commissioners though it may be possible to obtain preliminary legal advice and assistance under the Green Form scheme.

The disadvantage represented by these features of social security law and its legal system may have a disproportionately negative impact on disabled people

---

36   See generally Chapter Four.

and particularly on those with learning disability or other form of limited intellectual capacity. Their ability to deal with the mechanics of claiming benefit such as form filling, time limits for claiming and understanding the consequences of disclosing or not disclosing particular information, may be significantly reduced; the impact of a mistake could be substantial. Dealing with the appeal system raises similar concerns; when and if to appeal against the decision of an adjudication officer, preparing for an appeal and the ability to adequately represent their position and interests, are all decisions which may have important consequences for the disabled claimant. This is particularly so when the disabled person relies heavily on social security benefits for their basic income.

Despite the evidence of the OPCS surveys and reports and the subsequent introduction of Disability Living Allowance and Disability Working Allowance, poverty is still one of the defining characteristics and experiences of disability.

> Disability inevitably leads to extra costs. It is far more difficult for a disabled person to manage on the same income as someone of the same age who is not disabled. Yet the average disabled person has a much lower income than the average non-disabled person. And, despite the range of benefits and other help available to people with disabilities, not all people manage to work their way through the jungle and claim their full legal entitlements. The weekly loss can be substantial.

> Even among people who have claimed all they are entitled to there are still anomalies. People who are equally severely disabled can be entitled to different amounts of non-means tested income. How old you were when you became disabled; how you became disabled; the effects of your disability; how long you have lived in the UK; and whether you worked and paid the right national insurance contributions at the right time; all can make a difference to the total amount you may be entitled to (Disability Alliance ERA 1995, p.1).

Unhappily there seems little prospect of real improvement in this depressing picture.

CHAPTER SEVEN

MENTAL HEALTH AND DISABILITY

INTRODUCTION

Mental health law seeks to balance a number of potentially conflicting principles: the individual rights of patients, *and* society's responsibility to protect them
and to protect other people from the harm which mental disorder can cause
(Department of Health 1993A). The law attempts to provide for the proper
recognition of individual rights to self-determination and choice whilst also
allowing for the exercise of paternalistic power to protect patients from harming
themselves, and also to recognise the need for protection of the public. The
current legal structure of mental health law is established through numerous
statutes, regulations and case law, but is principally set out in the *Mental Health
Act 1983* and increasingly within the broad framework of community care law.

The 1983 Act is the latest in a long legislative history in the field of mental
health, a history which has been characterised as: 'A pendulum swinging
between two opposing schools of thought – legalism and professional discretion' (Gostin 1983, p.47).

Here 'legalism' is understood to reflect a felt need to restrict the discretionary
power of psychiatrists by imposing control through law whilst 'professional or
medical discretion' seeks to free psychiatry from unnecessary legal controls.

The recent history of mental health law provides clear evidence of this
swinging pendulum. The Mental Health Act 1959 is often understood as being
characterised by 'medicalism' or psychiatric discretionary power. Gostin ex-
plains why it was that legislation in 1959 should invest power in the psychiatric
profession.

Medicine was perceived as making great advances in the search for the aetiology
and treatment of schizophrenia. This was the time of the discovery of the major
tranquillisers and it was to be the beginning of an era where patients were to leave
institutions to be cared for in the community. It was within this social context that
medicine was perceived as manifestly humane, whereas the law was seen as
subordinating the individual's welfare to the collective good. The assumption was

that psychiatrists could reliably and validly diagnose particular forms of mental disorder, that they have an ability to predict future behaviour in cases where the layman could not and that treatments with established benefits exist (Gostin 1983, p.55).

Experience of the mental health system under the legal framework of the 1959 Act did not bear out this level of optimism. Psychiatry became associated with the use and abuse of power. Szasz has argued that:

> Mental illness is a metaphor. More particularly, as this term is used in mental hygiene legislation, mental illness is not the name of a medical disease or disorder, but is a quasi-medical label whose purpose is to conceal conflict as illness and to justify coercion as treatment (Szasz 1974, p.xi.)

Szasz further argued that the power of psychiatry is frequently exercised within the therapeutic relationship between patient and psychiatrist so that the treatment of psychiatric patients and their containment within the psychiatric health care system become aspects of the power of the (therapeutic) state.

Reaction to the character and reality of the psychiatric health care system provided under the legislative framework of the 1959 Act gained momentum during the 1970s and early 80s. There was little desire to return the pendulum to the formal legalism of the earlier Lunacy Laws. The blueprint for reform presented by MIND, the National Association for Mental Health, advocated a 'new legalism' based on the ideology of entitlement. It was directed toward the provision of mental health services, to setting limits on measures such as compulsory hospital admission and treatment and to ensuring the civil status of patients with a mental disorder.

This ideology of entitlement, with its rights-based strategy, was subjected to criticism from commentators such as Rose who argued that a rights-based discourse in the field of mental health is subject to significant limitations: 'The essence of Rose's critique is that the 'legalisation' of psychiatry does not alter the nature of the decisions which are made, and does not provide effective monitoring and constraining of psychiatric discretion' (Fennell 1986, p.39).

Indeed Gostin, the author of MIND's reform proposals, writing after the implementation of the *Mental Health (Amendment) Act 1982*, acknowledges that an ideology of entitlement: 'appears to be an ill-conceived philosophy upon which to promote the interests of any socially impoverished group of people' (Gostin 1983, p.66).

Whilst acknowledging the limits of the ideology of entitlement Fennell reasserts the value of rights within the mental health system.

> We have seen how mental patients are more often the objects than the subjects of legal relations and hence their rights are public law, due process, rights; not rights to deal, but entitlements that certain procedural and substantive limits will be adhered to in the way they are dealt with. Yet neither the origins nor the character of these rights should allow us to lose sight of their intrinsic value. Whilst they may not often affect substantive outcomes, they do open up areas of the psychiatric system to scrutiny which might otherwise remain hidden, and they require those

who operate the system to reflect on and justify what they are doing (Fennell 1986, pp.58–59).

It is arguable that changes in the mental health care system render the metaphor of the swinging pendulum between legalism as medicalism as no longer sufficient properly to understand the character of mental health law. Indeed, recognition of the impact of change has established a locus for reform of the 1983 Act. The closure of a significant number of the long stay psychiatric hospitals and the consequent reduction in the number of patients living and being treated in such establishments and the further advance of the principle of care in the community consequent upon the implementation of the National Health Service and Community Care Act 1990[1] are important elements in the re-siting of much mental health treatment and care. The 1983 Act, with its concentration on provisions relating to compulsory admission, treatment and discharge, and the civil rights of detained patients is often recognised as a piece of legislation dominated by provisions concerned with institutionally-based care and treatment.

Reform of the 1983 Act, the need for which is now largely accepted, will have to take account of the fundamental shift away from a hospital-based system of mental health care to a system which has substantially shifted to the provision of care and treatment in the community.

> The incremental distancing of mental health services from those which pertained in the 1970s, and for which Parliament was appropriately legislating in the early 1980s, is such as to call for legislation, to match the substantially changed environment of mental health services, in the facilities for care and treatment, psychiatric practices and public expectation of the services for the mentally disordered (Mental Health Act Commission 1993, p.106).

The force of this argument is reflected in part by recent debates concerning treatment in the community and in the provision for supervised discharge orders contained in the Mental Health (Patients in the Community) Act 1995.

The re-siting of the mental health care system and the need to reform the law to take account of this, is one element of the discussion concerning the nature and character of mental health law. Another element is characterised by the call for a recognition of the principles of a 'therapeutic jurisprudence': 'This basically simple idea, that law ought – provided that basic legal and procedural rights have been protected – to encourage, or at least not discourage, therapeutic rather than anti-therapeutic outcomes' (Carson and Wexler 1994, p.83).

The concept is commended by the Mental Health Act Commission:

> Therapeutic jurisprudence...with its emphasis on an essentially inter-disciplinary and co-operative approach and its concern to see that services are effective in the community as well as in institutions provides an important new dimension to the

---

1   See generally Chapter Four.

theoretical framework which at the very least is worth considering. (Mental Health Act Commission 1993, p.102)

Carson and Wexler conclude by claiming that: 'Therapeutic jurisprudence involves opening up more choices for more people to take; it need not be a case of law or psychiatry, but rather one of law and psychiatry' (Carson and Wexler 1994, p.92).

THE MENTAL HEALTH ACT 1983

The 1983 Act is said to be a: 'careful balance…between the individual rights of patients and society's responsibility to protect them and other people from the harm which mental disorder can cause' (Department of Health 1993A, p.iii.)

This attempt to balance the principles of self-determination and paternalism is reflected in the substance of the Act which is principally concerned with the provision of psychiatric health care services in institutional settings for compulsorily (formally) detained patients. It is, of course, important that the exercise of compulsory powers are regulated by Parliament, however such an emphasis reflects neither the fact that the vast majority of hospital patients are voluntary (informally admitted) patients, nor the development of the care and treatment of patients in the community entirely outside the compulsory regulation of the Act.

Whilst the Act provides for the exercise of compulsory powers and legislates, both expressly and by implication, for patients' rights, the Code of Practice, issued under section 118 of the Act, is concerned to emphasise the importance of self-determination and the provision of psychiatric health care services that reflect individual needs and circumstances:

> individuals should be as fully involved as practicable, consistent with their needs and wishes, in the formulation and delivery of their care and treatment,… It means that patients should have their legal rights drawn to their attention, consistent with their capacity to understand them. Finally it means that, when treatment or care is provided in conditions of security, patients should be subject only to the level of security appropriate to their individual needs and only for so long as is required (Department of Health 1993A, p.2).

Consistent with this attempt at balancing self-determination and paternalism the Act provides for the informal admission of patients and the Code of Practice advocates the use of informal admissions where the patient is willing.

> Nothing in this Act shall be construed as preventing a patient who requires treatment for mental disorder from being admitted to any hospital or mental nursing home in pursuance of arrangements made in that behalf and without any application, order or direction rendering him liable to be detained under this Act, or from remaining in any hospital or mental nursing home in pursuance of such arrangements after he has ceased to be so liable to be detained.[2]

---

2   Mental Health Act 1983 s.131.

Where admission to hospital is considered necessary and the patient is willing to be admitted informally this should in general be arranged. Compulsory admission should, however, be considered where the patient's current medical state, together with reliable evidence of past experience, indicates a strong likelihood that he will change his mind about informal admission prior to his actual admission to hospital with a resulting risk to his health or safety or to the safety of others (Department of Health 1993A, p.5).

Assessment

The Act requires all patients to be assessed prior to any application for admission to ascertain whether formal admission to hospital is both appropriate and necessary, whether alternative arrangements can be made for care and treatment in the community or whether such admission should be informal. The Code of Practice identifies a number of broad principles that should underpin the assessment process which again reflect attempts at balancing the principle of self-determination and paternalism:

> That people being assessed for possible admission under the Act...should:
>
> - receive respect for and consideration of their individual qualities and diverse backgrounds – social, cultural, ethnic and religious;
> - have their needs taken fully into account though it is recognised that, within available resources, it may not always be practicable to meet them;
> - be delivered any necessary treatment or care in the least controlled and segregated facilities practicable;
> - be treated or cared for in such a way that promotes to the greatest practicable degree, their self-determination and personal responsibility consistent with their needs and wishes;
> - be discharged from any order under the Act to which they are subject immediately it is no longer necessary (Department of Health 1993A, p.1–2).

Section 13(2) requires approved social workers[3] to be satisfied that: 'detention in a hospital is in all the circumstances of the case the most appropriate way of providing the care and medical treatment of which the patient stands in need.'

Behind this statutory duty is the important principle that an approved social worker will have an independent professional view on whether an application for formal admission is necessary.[4] This view will reflect a number of factors

---

3   Section 114 provides for the appointment of approved social workers by local social services authorities. The authority may only appoint those whom they approve as 'having appropriate competence in dealing with persons who are suffering from mental disorder.' s.114(2). Approved social workers exercise important powers under the Act, principally in relation to assessment and admission to hospital.

4   The application for formal admission to hospital is the responsibility of the approved social worker or nearest relative but must be supported by a medical recommendation.

which include the personal circumstances of the patient and whether there are alternative community-based treatment facilities available. The Act reflects the principle that compulsory admission to hospital is a last resort but may be necessary where the patient is suffering from a mental disorder and admission is in the interests of the patient's own health or safety or is necessary for the protection of other people.[5]

The assessment process is the responsibility of the approved social worker and should involve consultation with other professionals involved with the care of the patient and with the patient's family and the nearest relative.[6] The Act requires the approved social worker to interview the patient in a suitable manner. This duty is clarified by the Code of Practice which recognises that the patient's illness may have an impact on the nature of any interview and the fact that gaining access to the patient may be necessary before any interview can take place. Consequently, where access to the patient is a problem section 135 of the Act provides powers for an approved social worker to apply to a magistrate for a warrant which allows the police, together with a doctor and the approved social worker to enter private premises and remove a person to a place of safety for assessment and possible admission to hospital.[7]

Medical examination is a vital element of the assessment process. The doctor carrying out the examination has a responsibility to decide whether the patient is suffering from a mental disorder as defined by the Act and whether the patient's admission is necessary in the interests of their own health or safety or for the protection of others. It is the doctor who provides the necessary medical recommendation for admission where the statutory criteria are satisfied and ensures that a hospital bed is available for the patient's admission. Applications for admission, other than in an emergency, require medical recommendations, one of which must be made by a doctor approved under the provisions of section 12(2) by the Secretary of State as having special experience in the diagnosis or treatment of mental disorder.[8] In the event of an application in an emergency

---

5   Chapter 2 of the Code of Practice provides further guidance on the criteria to be considered during assessment.

6   The nearest relative is defined in order by section 26: spouse, son or daughter, father or mother, brother or sister, grandparent, grandchild, uncle or aunt, nephew or niece, non-related house/flat sharer with whom they have shared for at least five years.

7   The applicant must establish that they have reasonable cause to believe that the person is suffering from a mental disorder and 'has been, or is being, ill-treated, neglected or kept otherwise than under proper control, or is living alone and is unable to care for himself.' MHA 1983 s.135. The patient can be removed to a place of safety for up to 72 hours so that the necessary examinations and interviews can take place and appropriate arrangements made.

8   This power has been delegated to health authorities.

the Act requires one medical recommendation and specifies that this must be provided by a doctor who has previous knowledge of the patient.

Compulsory (formal) admission

Formal admission to hospital requires a diagnosis of *mental disorder*. As defined by the Act the term *mental disorder* encompasses mental illness, severe mental impairment, psychopathic disorder and mental impairment.[9]

A deliberate consequence of the terms of these definitions is that patients with learning disability[10] (mental handicap) are not subject to compulsory admission to, and detention in, hospital *unless* they exhibit seriously irresponsible or abnormally aggressive behaviour. If a patient with learning disability is additionally suffering from a mental illness within the terms of the Act then they will be subject to the formal admission criteria.

Section 1(3) provides that a patient cannot be defined, for the purposes of the Act, as suffering from *mental disorder* by reason only of: 'promiscuity or other immoral conduct, sexual deviancy or dependence on alcohol or drugs.'

Medical diagnosis is an important element of the assessment and admissions process but is not the sole criteria for compulsory admission. The health and safety of the patient and the need to protect others are equally important conditions that must be satisfied for such admissions.

The Act provides for formal admissions in three circumstances, for treatment, for assessment and in an emergency. The provisions for admission, the maximum length of detention and the rights of patients vary in each circumstance. The more significant and lengthy the admission the greater the protections provided for the patient and the more significant the conditions which must be satisfied for admission.

An application for admission for the purposes of assessment is made under section 2 by an approved social worker or the nearest relative and must be supported, in the terms required by section 2(2)(a) and (b), by the medical recommendations of two doctors, one of whom is approved under section

---

9   Mental Health Act 1983 s.1. Severe mental impairment means a state of arrested or incomplete development of mind which includes severe impairment of intelligence and social functioning and is associated with abnormally aggressive or seriously irresponsible conduct on the part of the person concerned.

'Psychopathic disorder' means a persistent disorder or disability of mind (whether or not including significant impairment of intelligence) which results in abnormally aggressive or seriously irresponsible conduct on the part of the person concerned.

'Mental impairment' means a state of arrested or incomplete development of mind (not amounting to 'severe mental impairment') which includes significant impairment of intelligence and social functioning and is associated with abnormally aggressive or seriously irresponsible conduct on the part of the person concerned.

10   On this see generally Chapter Eight.

12(2).[11] Patients admitted for assessment may be treated for their mental disorder under the provisions of Part IV of the Act. Section 2 provides for detention for a period not exceeding 28 days.

Applications, under section 3, for admission for the purposes of treatment are made by the approved social worker or the nearest relative.[12] Where the approved social worker makes the application they must obtain the agreement of the nearest relative; if this is refused the approved social worker may make an application to the County Court for the nearest relative to be displaced on the grounds that their agreement is being unreasonably withheld.

The application for admission to hospital must be supported by two medical recommendations, one of which is from a doctor who is approved under section 12(2). Detention under section 3 may be for up to six months.

There are powers under section 20 to renew detention for treatment for a further six months and then for periods of one year at a time. Such renewals require the responsible medical officer to report to the hospital managers that the original diagnosis for admission still exists and that treatment is likely to alleviate or prevent a deterioration of the patient's condition and it is necessary for the health or safety of the patient or for the protection of other persons that he should receive such treatment and that it cannot be provided unless he continues to be detained. Where a patient is suffering from mental illness or severe mental impairment and cannot be treated they may nonetheless continue to be detained where they are unlikely to be able to care for themselves or to obtain the care they need, or to guard themselves against serious exploitation.

Applications for emergency admissions are made under section 4 and must be supported by the medical recommendation of a doctor who has previous

---

11   '(2) An application for admission for assessment may be made in respect of a patient on the grounds that –
   (a) he is suffering from mental disorder of a nature or degree which warrants the detention of the patient in a hospital for assessment (or for assessment followed by medical treatment) for at least a limited period; and
   (b) he ought to be so detained in the interests of his own health or safety or with a view to the protection of other persons'.

12   An application for admission for treatment may be made in respect of a patient on the grounds that –
   (a) he is suffering from mental illness, severe mental impairment, psychopathic disorder or mental impairment and his mental disorder is of a nature or degree which makes it appropriate for him to receive medical treatment in a hospital; and
   (b) in the case of psychopathic disorder or mental impairment, such treatment is likely to alleviate or prevent a deterioration of his conditions; and
   (c) it is necessary for the health or safety of the patient or for the protection of other persons that he should receive such treatment and it cannot be provided unless he is detained under this section.

knowledge of the patient.[13] The medical recommendation must certify that the criteria for admission under section 2 are met and that there is an urgent necessity for admission and detention but that there is not enough time to obtain the second medical recommendation required for an admission for assessment under section 2. The maximum period of detention under section 4 is 72 hours.

The Code of Practice emphasises that applications under section 4 should only be made in an emergency which must be evidenced by there being a significant risk of mental or physical harm to the patient or others, danger of serious harm to property, or the need for the patient to be physically restrained.

Sections 2, 3 and 4 establish not only the power compulsorily to admit a patient but also the power compulsorily to detain that patient in hospital possibly until the time limit for their section expires. These are significant powers the exercise of which may, in extreme circumstances, involve the use of physical and/or 'chemical' restraint and day to day restrictions on the freedom of movement and choice of patients. The provisions of the legislation concerning compulsory admission and detention are strict and significant and reflect the principle that the use of compulsion in this aspect of psychiatric health care is very much a last resort and may only take place in highly regulated circumstances.

The Code of Practice identifies a number of broad principles which underpin the legislation and professional care and practice within its provisions:

> Individuals should be as fully involved as practicable, consistent with their needs and wishes, in the formulation and delivery of their care and treatment. Where linguistic and sensory difficulties impede such involvement reasonable steps should be taken to attempt to overcome them. It means that patients should have their legal rights drawn to their attention, consistent with their capacity to understand them. Finally it means that, when treatment or care is provided in conditions of security, patients should be subject only to the level of security appropriate to their needs and only for so long as it is required (Department of Health 1993A, p.2).

Compulsory holding powers for informal in-patients

The powers identified in sections 2, 3 and 4 provide for the authority to admit and detain a patient. Section 5 of the Act provides for the situation where an informal patient identifies and seeks to exercise their right to leave hospital in circumstances where the professionals involved in their care consider it necessary to admit them as a formal patient. Section 5(2) authorises the detention of the patient for up to 72 hours and requires the doctor in charge of the patient's treatment to furnish a report to the hospital managers that an application should

---

13   (2) An emergency application may be made either by an approved social worker or by the nearest relative of the patient; and every such application shall include a statement that it is of urgent necessity for the patient to be admitted and detained under section 2 above, and that compliance with the provisions of this Part of the Act relating to applications under that section would involve undesirable delay.

be made for formal admission. The power to detain under the section can only be used where the doctor has personally examined the patient.

Section 5(4) provides registered mental nurses with an emergency holding power which allows them to detain an informal in-patient receiving treatment and prevent them from leaving the hospital. This power can only be exercised in an emergency where the doctor with the power to use section 5(2) is not available. The power to detain expires after 6 hours or until the doctor with the power to use section 5(2) arrives, whichever is the earlier. Nurses using this power are entitled to use the minimum force necessary to prevent the patient from leaving hospital.

Guardianship

Placing a patient under the guardianship of a local social services authority may be an appropriate alternative to compulsory admission to hospital. The patient must be: 'Suffering from mental disorder, being mental illness, severe mental impairment, psychopathic disorder or mental impairment and his mental disorder is of a nature or degree which warrants his reception into guardianship under this section.'[14]

The reception into guardianship must also be: 'necessary in the interests of the welfare of the patient or for the protection of other persons.'[15]

The application must be founded on two medical recommendations and must state the age of the patient or at least that the patient is believed to be 16 years of age.

Section 8 specifies the limited powers of a guardian. They are to require a patient:

- to live at a particular place;

- to attend for medical treatment, occupation, education or training and,

- the power to require that access be given to the patient for a doctor or approved social worker. Though the Code of Practice identifies the purpose of guardianship as: 'enabling patients to receive community care where it cannot be provided without the use of compulsory powers' (Department of Health 1993A, p.43).

It is acknowledged that the order does not provide for treatment to be administered to a patient living in the community without their consent. Consequently very few guardianship orders are made.

---

14   Section 7(2)(a).
15   Section 7(2)(b).

Discharging formal patients from hospital

Powers to discharge patients who have been formally admitted are provided for in the Act and are variously given to the Secretary of State, health authorities, nearest relatives and Mental Health Review Tribunals.

Hospital managers

Section 23 provides for discharge of a formally admitted patient by order of the Secretary of State and by the appropriate health authority. In practice this power is exercised by hospital managers. There are no statutory criteria for the exercise of this power.

Nearest relatives[16]

The power of a nearest relative to order the discharge of a patient admitted and detained under sections 2 and 3 is established within the provisions of section 24 and 25. Nearest relatives are required to give 72 hours written notice to the hospital managers of the order to discharge. During this period the discharge can be prevented by the responsible medical officer reporting to the managers of the hospital that in his or her opinion if the patient were to be discharged they would be likely to act in a manner dangerous to themselves or other persons. The making of such a report blocks the discharge order from the nearest relative and prevents them from making another during a period of six months. In the event of the nearest relative being prevented from discharging the patient section 66 gives the nearest relative the right to apply to a Mental Health Review Tribunal for the patient's discharge.

The Mental Health (Patients in the Community) Act 1995 creates a supervised discharge order which provides for a detained patient to be discharged into the community but be subject to after-care under supervision. Under the terms of the legislation the health and social services authorities have powers to determine where a patient should live, order attendance for medical treatment, occupation, education or training. Where the patient neglects or refuses to comply with the terms of their supervision re-admission would be considered.

Mental health review tribunals

Part V of the Act provides for the constitution, jurisdiction and powers of these tribunals.[17] Applications are heard by a 'three person' tribunal with a lawyer chairperson appointed by the Lord Chancellor. The tribunal has a medical member, normally a consultant psychiatrist, and a lay member who is required

---

16   For definition see fn.6.
17   Mental Health Review Tribunals also have important powers concerning the discharge of patients detained under Part III of the Act, that is patients concerned in criminal proceedings or under sentence. These are considered further in the section on The Criminal Justice System and Mentally Disordered Offenders.

to have appropriate knowledge and experience. Patients may be legally repre-sented and legal aid is available under the 'assistance by way of representation' (ABWOR) provisions of the Legal Aid Act 1988.

Section 66 sets out the various circumstances in which patients and nearest relatives may apply to the tribunal for discharge, including the right to a tribunal hearing for patients admitted for assessment under section 2. Section 68 imposes a duty on hospital managers to refer to a tribunal patients admitted for treatment who do not make an application within the first period of their detention and for another hearing after three years where no other application has been made.

Powers of the tribunal to discharge patients

The powers of the tribunal are established by section 72. They include a discretionary power to discharge any patient detained under the Act (section 72(1)) and a number of mandatory duties to discharge patients if certain criteria are established.

In relation to patients detained for assessment under section 2 the tribunal must discharge the patient if they are satisfied:

(i)   that he is not then suffering from mental disorder or from mental disorder of a nature or degree which warrants his detention in a hospital for assessment (or for assessment followed by medical treatment) for at least a limited period; or

(ii) that his detention as aforesaid is not justified in the interests of his own health or safety or with a view to the protection of other persons.[18]

In relation to patients detained under other sections of the Act the tribunal again shall discharge if they are satisfied:

(i)   that he is not then suffering from mental illness, psychopathic disorder, severe mental impairment or mental impairment or from any of those forms of disorder of a nature or degree which makes it appropriate for him to be liable to be detained in a hospital for medical treatment; or

(ii) that it is not necessary for the health or safety of the patient or for the protection of other persons that he should receive such treatment; or

(iii) in the case of an application by virtue of paragraph (g) of section 66(1) above, that the patient, if released, would not be likely to act in a manner dangerous to other persons or to himself.[19]

The tribunal has equivalent powers in relation to patients subject to guardian-ship.

---

18   Section 72(1)(a).

19   The subsection applies to applications made to a tribunal by a nearest relative after their order to discharge has been blocked by the responsible medical officer under the powers in section 25.

The tribunal may direct discharge at a future date and, with a view to facilitating discharge in the future, grant a patient leave of absence or order a transfer to another hospital or into guardianship.

Hospital managers are responsible for preparation of a social circumstances report concerning the planned after-care of all patients applying to the tribunal and for its presentation to the tribunal.

Mental Health Review Tribunals are independent judicial bodies established by statute. Their jurisdiction and the range of powers and duties vested in them provide important safeguards for patients and their nearest relatives. The number of applications to the tribunal have increased significantly since the introduction of the 1983 Act, from 3445 in 1984 to 10,243 in 1993 with an increase in hearings from 2133 in 1984 to 5831 in 1993.[20] These figures should be read in relation to an estimated current detained population of between 7 and 8000 patients.[21]

Though the Mental Health Review Tribunal is an independent body with duties to discharge in certain circumstances, its decisions may be undermined by the ability of hospital authorities, responsible medical officers and approved social workers to make arrangements for and to secure the readmission of patients very recently discharged by tribunals. Though such practices may be necessary where a patient's condition has deteriorated almost immediately after discharge the High Court has ruled that an admission a day after discharge by a tribunal was lawful even where there had been no change in the health of the patient.[22] Such decisions might be seen to dilute the rights accorded to patients through their ability to apply to an independent tribunal for discharge.

Treatment for mental disorder

Medical treatment for the purposes of the Act is defined in section 145 to include nursing, care habitation and rehabilitation under medical supervision.

Principles of English common law protect bodily integrity by requiring consent to any bodily interference. Consequently all medical treatment for mental disorder, whether administered to a formal or an informal patient, requires the patient's valid consent if it is not to constitute assault and/or battery.[23]

---

20 see *Department of Health* (1993B).

21 It is likely that the number of applications will increase to reflect the new rights to make an application to the tribunal which is included in the Mental Health (Patients in the Community) Act 1995 which introduces supervised discharge orders.

22 R v Managers of South Western Hospital and Another ex parte M (*The Times*, 27 January 1993). Discussed in Gibbons (1993).

23 It is clear, therefore, that English law allows an individual to make what might be termed irrational health care decisions even to the extent that such a decision, for example, to refuse treatment for a physical illness or injury, may result in their death.

This basic common law rule does not apply in two important circumstances. First, the administration of treatment to a patient without capacity where the treatment is in the patient's best interest, for example where it is necessary to save life or prevent a deterioration or ensure an improvement in the patient's physical or mental health;[24] and secondly where statute authorises treatment in the absence of consent. Part IV of the Mental Health Act 1983 provides limited circumstances in which treatment for mental disorder can be administered without the consent of the patient.

In common law a valid consent requires a number of elements:

1. a voluntary and continuing permission that relates to a particular treatment

2. the permission is based on adequate knowledge and understanding of the purpose of the treatment, of its nature, likely effects and of the risks of the treatment including the likelihood of success and adequate knowledge of any alternatives

3. permission must not be given under any unfair or undue pressure or duress.

The satisfaction of these elements presupposes that the patient has sufficient capacity to make a decision about treatment. Currently English law places the responsibility for assessing and deciding whether a patient has such capacity on the medical profession. The Code of Practice identifies a number of basic principles which inform this decision:

An individual in order to have capacity must be able to:

- understand what medical treatment is and that somebody has said that he needs it and why the treatment is being proposed;
- understand in broad terms the nature of the proposed treatment;
- understand its principal benefits and risks;
- understand what will be the consequences of not receiving the proposed treatment;
- possess the capacity to make a choice (Department of Health 1993A, pp.54–55).

The Code also emphasises that assessment of capacity must be specific to a proposed treatment and that capacity can vary over time and should therefore be assessed at the time the treatment is proposed.

It is important to recognise that patients with a mental disorder may nevertheless have capacity to make decisions concerning their own treatment. This important principle has been confirmed by the High Court in the case of *Re C*. A patient in Broadmoor, diagnosed as a chronic schizophrenic, was suffering from gangrene in a foot and was recommended amputation. He refused his consent to the proposed operation and sought an injunction in the High Court to prevent the amputation taking place without his consent. The

---

24   Re F (Mental Patient: Sterilisation) [1990] 2 AC 1. Also see generally Chapter Eight.

injunction was granted on the basis that a diagnosis of mental disorder was not in itself conclusive on the issue of the patient's ability to consent to proposed medical treatment. Consequently an individual assessment of capacity was necessary. In this case the High Court decided that C had capacity to refuse consent.[25]

Part IV of the Act applies to treatments for mental disorder only. Patients with a mental disorder, whether detained or not, who require treatment for physical illness and disability are therefore subject to the common law on consent outlined earlier. If they have appropriate capacity they may give or refuse consent; if they lack capacity to consent treatment may only be given if it is in the patient's best interests to do so.[26]

In relation to treatment for a mental disorder the Act makes a distinction between two categories of treatment, those which require consent and a second opinion (section 57), and those which require consent or a second opinion (section 58).

Section 57 treatments

Section 57 concerns psychosurgery, that is: 'any surgical operation for destroying brain tissue or for destroying the functioning of brain tissue' and, because the treatment has been specified by the Secretary of State, the surgical implantation of hormones for the reduction of male sexual drive. These treatments may have serious long-term effects and they raise significant ethical issues, consequently the law has established important procedural safeguards before such treatments may be administered. The valid consent of the patient must be obtained. The validity of the consent has to be confirmed in writing by a doctor appointed by the Mental Health Act Commission and known as the second opinion appointed doctor (SOAD) who is also responsible for providing a written certification that:

> Having regard to the likelihood of the treatment alleviating or preventing a deterioration of the patient's condition, the treatment should be given s.57(2)(b).

Before giving this written certification concerning the efficacy of the proposed treatment the second opinion appointed doctor is required to consult with two other people who have been professionally involved with the patient's treatment 'and of those persons one shall be a nurse and the other shall be neither a nurse nor a registered medical practitioner.[27]

The Mental Health Act Commission is responsible for the appointments and administration of this elaborate section 57 second opinion procedure. Their 5th Biennial Report covering the period July 1991 to the end of June 1993 reports that 46 referrals were made to the Commission and all related to psychosurgery

---

25   Re C (Adult: Refusal of Treatment) [1994] 1 WLR 290.

26   Re F (Mental Patient: Sterilisation) [1990] 2 AC 1.

27   s.57(3).

(Mental Health Act Commission 1993). Issues concerning hormone implants for reducing the male sex drive are rarely referred to the Commission and there is some concern over whether such treatments are treatments for mental disorder.[28] Section 1 of the Act specifies that a person should not be defined as suffering from a mental disorder by reason only of sexual deviancy.[29]

Section 58 treatments

These treatments are electro-convulsive therapy (ECT) and the administration of medication. In relation to ECT the Act requires the patient's valid consent to treatment and the responsible medical officer or another doctor to certify in writing that the patient is capable of understanding the nature, purpose and likely effects of the treatment and has consented to the treatment. Alternatively, under subsection (3)(b), ECT may be administered where an appointed (SOAD) doctor (not the responsible medical officer) certifies that the patient has not consented or that the patient is not capable of understanding the nature, purpose and likely effects of the treatment but that, having regard to the likelihood of the treatment alleviating or preventing the deterioration of the patient's condition, the treatment should be given. Before providing this certification the doctor must consult two people who have been professionally concerned with the patient's treatment, one must be a nurse and the other must be neither a nurse nor a doctor.

In relation to treatment for mental disorder by medication, these provisions only apply after three months from the first occasion when medication was given during that period of detention. Consequently, section 58 permits the administration of medication for mental disorder for up to three months without consent though the Code of Practice makes it clear that no such treatment should be given without an attempt to obtain a valid consent.

Section 60 provides for the withdrawal of consent by patients. If treatment is to continue the patient will have to provide a fresh valid consent or the provisions of section 58 will have to be complied with.

Section 62 makes it clear that the provisions of sections 57 and 58 do not apply to the administration of urgent treatment which is immediately necessary to save the patient's life; or which (not being irreversible) is immediately necessary to prevent a serious deterioration of his condition; or which (not being irreversible or hazardous) is immediately necessary to alleviate serious suffering by the patient; or which (not being irreversible or hazardous) is immediately necessary and represents the minimum interference necessary to prevent the patient from behaving violently or being a danger to himself or others.

---

28   For a full discussion of the issues surrounding such treatments see Fennell 1988.

29   See R v Mental Health Act Commission, ex parte W 1988 (*The Times*, 27 May 1988) in which the Commission's refusal to give a certificate covering treatment by a drug designed to reduce testosterone to castrate levels was challenged by the patient, a convicted paedophile.

Section 63 specifies that treatments for mental disorder which are not covered by sections 57 and 58, such as psychological and social therapies, do not require the patient's consent so long as they are given by the responsible medical officer or under his direction. Again the Code of Practice directs that consent should always be sought for all treatments.

The Mental Health Act Commission is responsible, under section 61, for reviewing all treatments under section 57 and section 58(3)(b). These treatments must be reported to the Commission by the responsible medical officer. The Commission has the power to cancel the treatment certificate.

Treatment and care in the community

The programme of hospital closures which began before the implementation of the National Health Service and Community Care Act 1990 and is continuing, has meant that a significant number of mentally disordered patients are now living in the community. Section 117 imposes a duty on district health authorities and local social services authorities to provide after-care services for patients who have been discharged from hospital having been detained for treatment under section 3, or mentally disordered offenders detained for treatment under section 37 or transferred to hospital from prison under sections 47 or 48.

The Code of Practice identifies that when the decision to discharge or grant leave of absence to such a patient is made the responsible medical officer should take a lead in the establishment of a care plan. The Code identifies the following possible elements of after-care: 'Day care arrangements, appropriate accommodation, out-patient treatment, counselling, personal support, assistance in welfare rights, assistance in managing finances, and, if necessary, in claiming benefits' (Department of Health 1993A, p.108).

Section 117 requires the provision of after-care until it is established that the patient no longer needs such services. Importantly, section 117 is identified by section 46 *National Health Service and Community Care Act 1990* as a community care service so that the duty to assess those people who may need community care services will include consideration of the need for after-care services under section 117.

The duty to provide after-care under section 117 only applies to a very limited number of patients who have been detained for treatment. The *care programme approach* should provide an equivalent service for other patients discharged from hospital including informal patients and those detained for assessment.[30] Under the *care programme approach* health authorities are required to assess patients leaving hospital and those being taken on by the specialist psychiatric health care services and to produce a care plan for the patient to be supervised by a psychiatrist acting as the key worker. Early evaluation of the

---

30   The care programme approach is detailed in Circular H.C.(90)23/LASSL(90)11.

care programme approach has shown its implementation to be patchy,[31] and the Audit Commission Report, published in 1994,[32] expresses a continuing concern about the provision of community mental health care services.

The Mental Health Act Commission has expressed some concern about the implementation of after-care, commenting specifically on the timing of section 117 meetings in hospital just before discharge or even after discharge; the lack of appropriate procedures for reviewing after-care; the practice of granting leave of absence without a section 117 plan being in place and the fact that planning meetings often exclude the patient, formal and informal carers and staff who will provide care and services in the community (Mental Health Act Commission 1993).

Concern about the treatment of patients in the community is an enduring and continuing matter of concern. Section 17 of the *Mental Health Act 1983* allows detained patients to be granted leave of absence by their responsible medical officer subject to conditions which the psychiatrist may consider necessary in the interests of the patient or for the protection of others. In the early years of the Act a practice developed within which patients detained for treatment under section 3 were granted leave of absence so that their treatment could be supervised in the community. If such patients stopped taking their medication or their condition gave cause for concern they were recalled to hospital and their section was renewed. This practice was challenged in the case of R v Hallstrom ex parte W[33] and declared illegal by the High Court who decided that the power to detain a patient in hospital could not be used as a means to attach conditions to a leave of absence. The decision effectively frustrated attempts to establish some form of compulsory community treatment and supervision.

This lacuna in the law once again became a matter of public concern and debate following the publicity associated with cases such as those involving the injury to Ben Silcock at London Zoo[34] and the murder of Jonathan Zito by Christopher Clunis, a schizophrenic discharged from hospital and living in the community. Much of this debate has centred on proposals for compulsory treatment in the community.

In 1987 the Royal College of Psychiatrists had published a discussion document, Community Treatment Orders, and though this had received little support the debate was given a fresh focus by the Ben Silcock incident. In January 1993 the Royal College published a report proposing a community

---

31 See Fifth Report of the House of Commons Health Committee (1993).

32 see Audit Commission (1994).

33 [1986] 2 All E.R.306.

34 Ben Silcock, a schizophrenic, climbed into the lions' enclosure at London Zoo on New Year's Eve 1992. He was severely injured by one of the lions and the incident, which had been recorded on video, was shown on national TV.

supervision order with the objective of keeping mentally ill people as safely as possible in the community: 'This is to be achieved by enabling the compulsory supervision in the community of patients previously compulsorily detained in hospital so that their condition does not deteriorate and necessitate a further admission to hospital' (Health Committee 1993, p.vii).

In the same month the Secretary of State for Health announced a departmental review to consider:

> Whether new legal powers are needed to ensure that mentally ill people in the community get the care they need; and

> whether the present legal powers in the Mental Health Act 1983 are being used as effectively as they can be, and what action could be taken in advance of any new legislation to ensure that they are. (Health Committee 1993, p.v)

These questions were subsequently reformulated to: 'Whether or not there is some better way between either total loss of freedom in an institution or being in the community with precious few ways of ensuring compliance or co-operation with a treatment programme' (Health Committee 1993, p.vi).

The House of Commons Health Committee also set up its own inquiry into the proposals from the Royal College. Having taken evidence the Committee concluded against the proposal arguing that it did not provide a satisfactory answer to the question posed by the Secretary of State as to whether there is a middle way between compulsory detention and being at liberty in the community.

The government agreed with the Health Committee and endorsed the recommendation of the Department of Health internal inquiry to legislate for supervised discharge from hospital.[35]

The proposal for supervised discharge was further endorsed by the Christopher Clunis Report which recommended, among other things, that any such order should provide for an agreed care plan and the recall of the patient to hospital if their health is deteriorating.[36] The report also called for the establishment of a special supervision group for patients who are seriously mentally ill and: 'are at risk of falling through the net of care' (Ritchie 1994, p.115).

This recommendation would cover only a small group of patients identified by two of four criteria defined by the Report:

(a) patients who have been detained in hospital under the Mental Health Act 1983 on more than one occasion;

(b) patients who have a history of violence or of persistent offending;

---

35   For further details and discussion see: Department of Health (1993A).

36   See *The Report of the Inquiry into the Care and Treatment of Christopher Clunis*. HMSO 1994 (Ritchie 1994).

(c) patients who have failed to respond to treatment from the general psychiatric services;

(d) patients who are homeless (Ritchie 1994, p.116).

The *Mental Health (Patients in the Community) Act 1995* introduces new powers to establish a category of patients who, having been discharged from hospital, will be subject to compulsory after-care in the community. The patient's responsible medical officer would apply to the health authority for an order in respect of a patient who is suffering from a mental disorder and there is a substantial risk of serious harm to the health or safety of the patient or others, or of the patient being seriously exploited if he or she were not to receive after-care under supervision. The application would need to be supported by a social worker and a second medical recommendation. The order would empower the health and social services authorities to require the patient to live at a specified place and to attend for medical treatment, occupation, education or training. The after-care would be kept under review and where the patient neglects or refuses to comply with the arrangements made for him or her the authorities would be required to consider whether the patient should be admitted to hospital. The only right of appeal that a patient will have is against the fulfillment of criteria for making the order.

The Act has attracted criticism from the National Association for Mental Health (MIND) on a number of grounds.[37] It is argued that some of the provisions in the Act conflict with the European Convention on Human Rights, that it fails to adequately provide for patient consultation and involvement, there are no provisions for patient advocacy, the grounds for access to the Mental Health Review Tribunal are limited, that the quality of community care is unlikely to be improved by the legislation and that relationships of trust necessary for proper community care are likely to be endangered. MIND's criticisms also make the point that supervised after-care will centre on the use of drugs and concludes that: 'The right to determine what shall be done to your own body is a fundamental principle which implies the right to refuse medication. The case for further eroding this right has not been made' (Harrison 1995, p.277).

Community care services

A significant number of patients will be treated and cared for in the community without reference to section 117 after-care duties, the care programme approach or supervised discharge. Services for such patients will be provided by local health authorities and through arrangements made by local social services authorities. It is likely that the majority of patients with a mental disorder or learning disability will fall within the assessment duty imposed on local

---

37   See Harrison (1995).

authorities under the *National Health Service and Community Care Act 1990.*[38]
Assessment is for the purpose of establishing need for community care services
which are defined by section 46 of the Act. A number of the services so defined
are of particular significance for people with a mental disorder or learning
disability.

The duty to make arrangements for the provision of residential accommodation under section 21(1) of the *National Assistance Act 1948* is specifically
defined to encompass people who have been suffering from mental disorder
and to include the provision of accommodation to prevent mental disorder.[39]

Under section 29(1) of the same Act local authorities are required to provide
welfare services for a defined category of people which includes 'those who
suffer from mental disorder of any description.'[40]

The *National Health Service Act 1977* establishes a number of powers and
duties for the provision of home helps and laundry facilities, for the prevention
of illness and the care of people who are or have been ill. Of particular
significance for people suffering from mental disorder are the duties under
schedule 8 of the Act. These extend to arrangements for day centres and training
centres, the appointment of sufficient approved social workers, the exercise
guardianship functions under Parts 2 and 3 of the Mental Health Act 1983;
and to the provision of: 'Social work and related services to help in the
identification, diagnosis, assessment and social treatment of mental disorder and
to provide social work support and other domiciliary and care services to people
living in their homes and elsewhere' (Mandelstam 1995, p.42.)

The Mental Health Act Commission has reviewed the implementation of
services in the community for people with a mental disorder under the 1990
Act and has raised a number of concerns in its 5th Biennial Report. In particular
the Commission has commented on difficulties in incorporating statutory duties
in care planning arrangements and on difficulties consequent upon the split in
the assumption of responsibilities by health authorities and local social services
authorities. Specific problems have been identified in relation to the provision
of after care duties under section 117 including the timing and arrangements
for meetings to plan for the discharge of individual patients and the Commission notes: 'An insufficient range of services available in the community to meet
all the needs of mentally ill people' (Mental Health Act Commission 1993,
p.53).

---

38 Section 47(1)(a): 'where it appears to a local authority that any person for whom they
    may provide or arrange for the provision of community care services may be in need of
    such services, the authority – (a) shall carry out an assessment of his needs for those
    services.'
39 Circular LAC(93)10.
40 For the full range of powers and duties under this section see Mandlestam 1995,
    pp.41–42.

More positively the Commission identifies the sensitivity of community-based mental health services to the needs of minority ethnic communities and the quality and multi disciplinary work of community support teams set up jointly by health authorities and social services departments (Mental Health Act Commission 1993).

The concern of the Mental Health Act Commission about the provision of services in the community is reflected in other reports and inquiries. The Christopher Clunis Report comments on the inadequate services available to patients who are suffering from schizophrenia and who may pose a threat to themselves and to others (Ritchie 1994).

The House of Commons Health Committee in their first report for the 1993–1994 parliamentary session considered the care of people who are seriously mentally ill in the community. The report highlights, among other things, significant public concern centring on the perceived threat posed by a number of people who are seriously ill, the need for the proper resourcing of the care programme approach and other community based services, the pressures faced by providers and the incidence of homelessness among this group of patients (Health Committee 1994).

Any assessment of the impact of the policy of care in the community for people who are mentally ill must take into account the range and substance of the powers and duties set out in statute and elaborated on in guidance. It is also clear, however, that a number of factors influence the practical provision of services. Issues surrounding the provision of resources to social services authorities and to health authorities and the difficulties inherent in the dual responsibilities of these authorities are overlaid by pressures on government arising from public concern. The interaction of all these factors (and more) serve to make community care for people who are mentally ill an issue of continuing concern and controversy.

Defendants and offenders who are mentally ill

There appears to be general endorsement of government policy to divert mentally disordered offenders away from the criminal justice system and into the psychiatric health care system, at least where the offence is considered to be minor and the public interest would not be served by a prosecution. This policy is set out in the Home Office *Circular on Provision for Mentally Disordered Offenders* [41] directed to the police and the Crown Prosecution Service. Though the principle might be applauded its practice is often problematic.

> There are very few agencies involved in diverting people away from the criminal courts and into therapeutic treatment. The treatment available is itself being restricted. As hospital psychiatric wings are closing, resources for community care

41 no.66/90.

are being drastically reduced through underfunding (O'May and Biggs 1993, p.11).

Where diversion means formal (compulsory) admission to hospital the consequences may be entirely disproportionate to the seriousness of the criminal offence.

> In some cases, a diversion away from custody to the mental health system may condemn the person to incarceration for a far longer period than if s/he had been given a prison sentence. S/he also becomes subject to treatment often against his/her will. The initial relief at avoiding prison is often replaced by frustration at the restrictions imposed on detainees in psychiatric hospitals and at the difficulty in returning to the community (O'May and Biggs 1993, p.11).

The report of the inquiry into the Christopher Clunis case raises another equally important problem associated with the practice of the diversion principle. It highlights the fact that the police sometimes will not charge a mentally ill person who has committed a potentially serious offence 'for the most humane of reasons' (Ritchie 1994, p.124). This practice may occur where the offence has not caused serious damage or injury or where it is considered that the offender can be bound over to keep the peace. The result is that a mentally ill person who may need care and treatment does not come to the attention of either the psychiatric health service or the local social services authority.

Both mental health law and the criminal law make provision for mentally ill suspects, defendants and offenders though there is concern about the operation of particular aspects of the law:[42] 'Section 136 of the Mental Health Act 1983 gives the police significant powers to intervene to protect the safety of a mentally ill person or to protect the public.[43] There has been considerable concern about the day to day operation of this section' (Rogers and Faulkner 1987).

The Mental Health Act Commission has been concerned with the role of the police in 'psychiatric emergencies' (MHAC 1993, p.45) and the Reed Committee, among others, has commented upon the fact that black people are more likely to be removed by the police under section 136 than white people (Department of Health, Home Office 1994).

Detention in a place of safety under section 136 is also an arrest for the purposes of the Police and Criminal Evidence Act 1984. Consequently the general rights and protections available to arrested suspects under the Act are

---

42 For a detailed description and analysis of the law reference may be made to Hoggett 1990, at Chapter 5. For an analysis from a legal practitioner's perspective see O'May and Biggs 1993.

43 Under section 136 a constable has the power to remove to a place of safety any person found in a place to which the public have access who appears to be suffering from mental disorder and who appears to be in need of care and control. The person may be detained in a place of safety for up to 72 hours for the purpose of examination and assessment to establish whether an application for admission to hospital is necessary.

also available to a person detained under section 136. Additionally Code C of the Codes of Practice for the *Police and Criminal Evidence Act 1994* applies to the detention and questioning of suspects who are mentally disordered, mentally handicapped or mentally incapable of understanding the significance of questions put to them. The Code requires the provision of medical attention, the attendance of an appropriate adult and the right to a lawyer.[44]

The Mental Health Act provides the criminal courts with a number of what are essentially diversion powers. Section 35 provides for the remand of an accused person to hospital for psychiatric reports and section 36 allows the Crown Court to remand an accused person to hospital for treatment for their mental disorder.[45] Remands to hospital under sections 35 and 36 facilitate decisions concerning the fitness of a defendant to plead to the charges against them and the appropriateness of raising the defence of insanity.[46]

The Act also provides an equivalent range of powers which allow convicted offenders to be diverted to hospital as an alternative to the imposition of a criminal justice sentence. Section 37 allows the criminal courts to impose a hospital order on an offender who has committed an imprisonable offence.[47]

Section 37(3) allows the magistrates' courts to make a hospital order without conviction if they are satisfied that the defendant committed an imprisonable offence and is suffering from a mental disorder which warrants detention in hospital for treatment.

Where a hospital order has been made under section 37 the offender is detained for treatment and is subject to the provisions concerning treatment in Part IV of the Act; they may be discharged by the hospital managers. Patients detained under section 37 may not apply to a Mental Health Review Tribunal until six months after their detention.

---

44   For mental health practitioner guidance on work under section 136 see Chapter 10 of *Code of Practice Mental Health Act 1983*. Department of Health and Welsh Office. 1993 (HMSO). For criticism of the operation of the appropriate adult scheme see Fennell 1993.

45   There is some concern that, despite the availability of the power to remand defendants to hospital for assessment, it is rarely used. A substantial number of defendants with a mental disorder are being remanded into custody with the hope that the prison psychiatric service will be able to assess their health and provide the courts with a psychiatric report. See Fennell 1991.

46   *The Criminal Procedure (Insanity and Unfitness to Plead) Act 1991* provides for the imposition of a number of possible orders where a court finds that a defendant is unfit to plead or is not guilty by reason of insanity: a hospital order with or without restrictions; a guardianship order, a supervision and treatment order, an absolute discharge. See O'May and Biggs 1993.

47   The court must have medical evidence that the offender is suffering from a mental illness, psychopathic disorder, severe mental impairment or mental impairment at the time of sentence and that it must be of a degree which makes it appropriate for detention in hospital for treatment.

The Crown Court has the power to impose restrictions on a hospital order under section 41 where: 'it appears to the court, having regard to the nature of the offence, the antecedents of the offender and the risk of his committing further offences if set at large, that it is necessary for the protection of the public from serious harm.'

Such an order may be imposed with or without time limit and allows the Home Office to supervise the detention of the offender and influence any decision concerning discharge. Many offenders subject to hospital orders with restriction are detained in the Special Hospitals such as Broadmoor and Rampton.

The principle of diversion is also facilitated by sections 47 and 48 which allow prisoners on remand and serving prisoners, who are suffering from a mental disorder which warrants detention in hospital for treatment, to be transferred to hospital.

> The current level of public concern surrounding the provision of appropriate care in the community for patients with a mental disorder is heightened when a serious criminal offence is committed by a person who is suffering from a mental disorder. Responses to this, sometimes disproportionate level of concern, may result in further restrictions being imposed on the civil liberties of those who are living in the community and in an increased reluctance on the part of hospital managers and Mental Health Review Tribunals to grant leave of absence to patients or to make a discharge order. (Parkin 1991)

Any such reluctance should not be allowed to jeopardise the development of adequate and appropriate services for care and treatment in the community. With the continued closure and restriction of secure and non-secure psychiatric hospital places the policy of diversion from the criminal justice system into the psychiatric health care system will increasingly mean that defendants and offenders with a mental disorder are being cared for and treated in the community.

Patients' rights
(see generally Cooper 1994, Chapter Five)

The rights of patients are established both expressly and implicitly by legislation, regulation and case law. For example, the treatment provisions in sections 57 and 58 of the Mental Health Act can be understood to establish limited, but nonetheless important rights to a safeguarding second opinion procedure regulated by the Mental Health Act Commission. It may also be possible to understand a notion of rights outside a strict definition of the law. Though there is no legal duty to comply with the Code of Practice to the Mental Health Act its guidance is important in establishing norms of good practice; though these norms do not equate to legally enforceable rights, they articulate important principles which are directed to the protection of patients' 'rights'; the right to information is such an example.

There are distinctions between the level and the substance of rights enjoyed by voluntary and compulsorily detained patients. The extent of the right to refuse treatment is a clear example of a different 'rights' status accorded to these two categories of in-patient with voluntary patients enjoying a more extensive right to refuse. For patients living in the community we might wish to talk about 'rights' to care and treatment under the National Health Service and Community Care Act 1990 and related pieces of legislation. Any such discussion will need to consider the ability of patients to enforce their 'rights' through recourse to the law and to other quasi-legal procedures.[48]

It is also clear that legislation restricts patients' rights (Cooper 1994, Chapter Five). Formal patients are subject to statutory limitations to their personal and civil rights; hospital managers have limited rights to interfere with and censor mail and a patient's right to vote may be restricted (Hoggett 1990). It has also been established how the provisions of Part IV of the Act concerning treatment for mental disorder provides for the administration of some treatments without consent and specifically against the wishes of the patient. Significant parts of the 1983 Act are concerned with the right to detain patients and to restrict their discharge from detention. In addition, the rights of a detained patient to pursue a civil action or a criminal prosecution against a person acting in accordance with the provisions of the Act are restricted by the terms of section 139. A patient wishing to take a civil action is required to obtain the leave of the High Court by establishing that there are reasonable grounds for the patient's allegation that the person concerned acted in bad faith or without reasonable care. The permission of the Director of Public Prosecutions is required before the initiation of criminal proceedings. These restrictions do not apply to applications for judicial review.

The Mental Health Act Commission which was established by the 1983 Act has an important role in the establishment and promotion of the rights of formal patients. The Commission has a number of statutory functions including the appointment of doctors and others to provide second opinions for treatment under the Act and a general duty to review the exercise of powers and duties in relation to patients who are detained or are liable to be detained. The Commission seeks to visit and interview all detained patients and may also investigate complaints on behalf of such patients. The Fifth Biennial Report of the Commission comments adversely on the lack of sanctions available to the Commission to deal with bad practice and indicates that it wishes to see its investigatory powers extended to encompass what it calls 'de facto' detained patients.

The experience of black and minority ethnic patients is a matter of continuing concern and comment. MIND reports on research findings which have established that black people are more likely than white people to be removed

---

48 See the discussion of these and other related issues in Chapter Four.

by the police to a place of safety under section 136; detained in hospital under section 2, 3 and 4; detained in locked wards; given higher doses of medication; and to be diagnosed as suffering from schizophrenia or another form of psychotic illness (MIND 1993). This picture of discrimination is reproduced by the Reed Report in 1994,[49] which reports on the fact that black mentally disordered offenders are more likely than their white counterparts to be remanded in custody for psychiatric reports; subject to restriction orders; detained in higher degrees of security for longer; and be referred from prison to medium secure units or special hospitals.

This depressing evidence of racism in the mental health service is commented upon by the Mental Health Act Commission which concludes that the resolution of the problem 'may require fundamental change in a psychiatric profession which reflects white, middle-class and eurocentric values' (Mental Health Act Commission 1993).

It is becoming increasingly clear that in relation to personal rights, the diagnosis of mental disorder is less important than decisions concerning a person's legal and personal capacity.[50] Consequently, it is now recognised that detained patients may have capacity to refuse treatment for a physical illness or injury.[51] The *Mental Health Act 1983* makes provision for the Court of Protection to administer the financial and property affairs of patients with a mental disorder and without capacity. Where a patient retains capacity to manage their own affairs the Court would have no power to take over their administration.

Emphasis on, and the recognition of, the importance of the issue of capacity and its impact on the rights of a patient has given rise to a number of difficulties. English law recognises different standards of capacity, so that, for example, capacity to marry is different from capacity to make a will. Beyond this difficulty is the absence of a legally established forum for deciding whether an individual has capacity or not. In practice decisions concerning whether a patient has capacity to consent to medical treatment are made by the doctor responsible for a patient's treatment. The substantial difficulties raised by these and related problems have recently been considered by the Law Commission.[52] The recommendations of their report, the government's response and the implications of both of these factors for the rights of patients with a mental disorder will be considered in the chapter on mental incapacity and learning disability.[53]

---

49   see Reed (1994).

50   This matter is discussed in detail in Chapter Eight.

51   Re C (Adult: Refusal of Treatment) [1994] WLR 290.

52   Law Commission Report no.231. Mental Incapacity. 1995.

53   Chapter Eight.

MENTAL INCAPACITY AND LEARNING DISABILITY

INTRODUCTION

One of the major disabling consequences of mental incapacity is the inability or limited ability to make legally effective decisions. A legitimate expectation of the law is that it should establish a structure within which appropriate autonomy and self-determination is recognised and protected, and which also provides appropriate substitute or proxy decision-making structures, and any necessary protection from abuse, neglect and exploitation. In many respects English law is inadequate if measured against these expectations. In addition, the existing legal structure is both complex and confusing, and less than comprehensive:

> It is widely recognised that, in this area the law as it now stands is unsystematic and full of glaring gaps. It does not rest on clear or modern foundations of principle. It has failed to keep up with social and demographic changes. It has also failed to keep up with developments in our understanding of the rights and needs of those with mental disability. (Law Commission 1995, p.1)

English law currently utilises a number of different definitions of capacity and incapacity in the sense that different legal transactions require different levels of capacity.[1]

> Thus a person may have capacity to do some things but not others. For example, a person may have the capacity to make a will but not to manage his/her financial affairs, or a person may have the capacity to manage a small amount of income but not a huge amount of capital. (Roberts 1991)

Recognition of these legal problems, and their practical consequences, and of other problems such as the risk of abuse experienced by vulnerable people, became heightened in the late 1980s. In 1989 a case concerning the health

---

1   A detailed discussion is provided in *Assessment of Mental Capacity, Guidance for Doctors and Lawyers*. British Medical Association and the Law Society. Part III. 1995. London: BMA.

care of a woman with learning disability was decided in the House of Lords,[2] the Law Society published its discussion document *Decision Making and Mental Incapacity* (Law Society 1989), and the Law Commission identified the need for reform in its *Fourth Programme of Law Reform* (Law Commission 1989).

In 1991 the Law Commission published a consultation paper (Law Commission 1991) which identified problems in both private and public law, and the clear need for reform.

> The most obvious deficiencies in private law were the lack of any effective procedures for resolving disputes between individuals about the care of people without capacity, or generally for legitimating and regulating the substitute decision-making which in practice regularly takes place. Concern about public law concentrated on the absence of acceptable powers for protecting incapacitated or vulnerable people from abuse and neglect. (Law Commission 1995, p.3)

In 1993 the Law Commission published a series of three further consultation papers concerning decision making by mentally incapacitated adults: *A New Jurisdiction; Medical Treatment and Research; and Public Law Protection* (Law Commission 1993, A, B and C). In 1995 the Commission's final report and draft bill was published:

> This report is concerned with the ways in which decisions may lawfully be made on behalf of those who are unable to make decisions for themselves. It covers issues of both substantive law and procedure, and the decisions under consideration may relate to personal, financial or medical affairs. (Law Commission 1995, p.1)

This chapter will utilise the distinctions made by the Law Commission between three categories of issues that impact upon the everyday life experience of people with mental incapacity, namely property and financial affairs, health care and personal welfare. Within these categories we will provide a summary of the existing law and identify some of the major problems associated with its structure and operation. Reference will be made to these categories in an outline of the Law Commission's proposals for reform before a concluding comment is made on the reform proposals in the light of the Government's decision not to legislate on the basis of the report.

CAPACITY AND INCAPACITY

Underpinning all these issues are the important problems associated with the assessment and definition of mental capacity and incapacity. Whilst the consequences of any decision on capacity are legal, the power of assessment lies with the medical profession.

> Generally, there is a presumption that the person is capable until proved otherwise, and capacity is judged in relation to the particular decision, transaction or activity

---

2   Re F (Mental Patient: Sterilisation) [1990] 2 AC 1.

involved. There is also a basic common law test of capacity, to the effect that the person concerned must at the relevant time understand in broad terms what he is doing and the likely effects of his action. Thus, in principle, legal capacity depends upon understanding rather than wisdom: the quality of the decision is irrelevant as long as the person understands what he is deciding. (Law Commission 1991)

In relation to consent to medical treatment the consequences of using this essentially functional test of capacity are detailed by the Code of Practice issued under the Mental Health Act 1983:

An individual in order to have capacity must be able to:

- understand what medical treatment is and that somebody has said that he needs it and why the treatment is being proposed;
- understand in broad terms the nature of the proposed treatment;
- understand its principal benefits and risks;
- understand what will be the consequences of not receiving the proposed treatment;
- possess the capacity to make a choice. (Department of Health and the Welsh Office 1993, pp.55–56)

The Law Commission, in its proposals for reform, adopted a functional test of capacity which would apply to all transactions with legal consequences. The test includes a 'diagnostic threshold' (Law Commission 1995, p.34) of mental disability largely to exclude from definitions of incapacity, people who make what might be seen as irrational decisions.

We recommend that legislation should provide that a person is without capacity if at the material time he or she is:

(1)   unable by reason of mental disability to make a decision on the matter in question, or

(2)   unable to communicate a decision on that matter because he or she is unconscious or for any other reason (Law Commission 1995, p.37).

We recommend that the expression "mental disability" in the new legislation should mean any disability or disorder of the mind or brain, whether permanent or temporary, which results in an impairment or disturbance of mental functioning. (Law Commission 1995, p.36)

The use of the phrase 'mental disability' marks out the proposed test as distinct from the 'mental disorder' test of the Mental Health Act 1983 and would therefore encompass all those who lack capacity because of the disabling effect of their mental disability.[3]

The phrase 'unable to make a decision' in the recommended test of capacity is clarified by the Law Commission within further definitions of the concepts

---

3   For a full discussion of the reasons for rejecting 'mental disorder' as the threshold diagnostic test see the Law Commission 1995, p.34–36, paras.3.8 to 3.13.

involved.[4] Essentially they argue that capacity involves, among other things, the ability to understand information and the ability to utilise that information in exercising choice. Reference is made to the analysis of the stages of decision-making capacity offered by Thorpe J. in *Re C (Adult: Refusal of Treatment)*:[5] the ability to understand and retain information, believing the information, and balancing that information to make a choice.[6]

The real power in the assessment of capacity will continue to lie with the medical profession; doctors will continue to make such decisions as part of their day-to-day medical practice. Even where decisions concerning capacity or the consequences of a finding of capacity or incapacity are made by the court they will almost invariably be made on the basis of medical evidence. It is important that such decisions reflect the important principles that information must be communicated to the person concerned in an appropriate form and at an appropriate level and that they are given adequate opportunities to display their highest level of mental functioning. It is equally important that decisions which appear to be irrational to the assessor are not assumed to be evidence of incapacity merely because of their perceived irrationality. Recommendations to ensure these operational principles are included in the Law Commission's proposals.[7]

PROPERTY AND FINANCIAL AFFAIRS

There is a considerable body of current law to regulate issues concerning the property and financial affairs of a person with mental incapacity. In relation to contracts, these will be binding on a person with mental incapacity unless he or she can establish that the other party to the contract knew of his or her incapacity. The level of required contractual capacity is whether the person was capable of understanding the general nature of what he was doing. Case law has established that this level of understanding will vary from a low degree where the contractual transaction is trivial in nature and value to a high level of understanding where the subject matter of the contract constitutes the

4   Law Commission 1995, pp.38–39.
5   [1994] 1 WLR 290.
6   Law Commission 1995, p.37
7   The Disability Discrimination Act 1995 uses the concept of *mental impairment* to include a
    particular category of people within its definition of disabled person. Schedule 1 of the
    Act provides that *mental impairment* includes 'an impairment resulting from or consisting of
    a mental illness only if the illness is a clinically well-recognised illness.' *Impairment* is
    defined to cover the carrying out of a range of day to day activities including memory or
    the ability to concentrate, learn or understand; or the perception of the risk of physical
    danger.

person's main or only asset of value.[8] Capacity to make a will is set at a higher level: 'a testator must be of sound mind, memory and understanding.'[9]

In relation to social security benefits, the Secretary of State is able to appoint another person to act on behalf of a person claiming benefits who is unable to act for themselves because of their mental incapacity.[10] This appointee system, which goes beyond the collection of benefits to encompass all matters relating to entitlement to benefit, has been subject to a number of criticisms particularly concerning the inability of the system to appropriately regulate the quality of appointees, and a failure to properly monitor the operation of the system (Lavery and Lundy 1994; Cooper 1994, p.313).

Any person with capacity is free to make an enduring power of attorney under the provisions of the Enduring Power of Attorney Act 1985. The attorney should register the power with the Court of Protection when the donee, by reason of mental disorder, is losing or has lost capacity to manage their own affairs. Registration is subject to notice to the donor and their nearest relatives and to their objection. Upon registration only the attorney has power to manage the property and financial affairs of the donee, and is therefore able to act independently of the Court of Protection.

Where a person is suffering from a mental disorder, as defined by the Mental Health Act 1983, their property and financial affairs may be administered by the Court of Protection. The Court, which operates under Part VII of the Mental Health Act 1983, has jurisdiction to supervise the administration of the property and financial affairs of a person who is incapable of doing so for themselves because they are suffering from a mental disorder. The jurisdiction of the Court is usually triggered by an application from the nearest or other relative, by a friend or by an appropriate person such as a social worker or solicitor. The Court has the power to appoint the Public Trustee as receiver if there is no other suitable person willing to take on the task. The powers of the court are wide[11] and may be administered by a receiver, often a close relative or friend, appointed by the Court. Where there is no need for a receiver a Short

---

8   In re Beaney [1978] 1 W.L.R. 770.

9   For a fuller discussion of testamentary capacity and of the rules concerning capacity for other legal transaction see Law Commission (1991) or British Medical Association and the Law Society 1995.

10   Social Security (Claims and Payments) Regulations 1987.

11   Section 95 provides that the Court may 'with respect to the property and affairs of a patient, do or secure the doing of all such things as appear necessary or expedient (a) for the maintenance or other benefit of the patient, (b) for the maintenance or other benefit of the patient's family, (c) for making provision for other persons or purposes for whom or which the patient might be expected to provide if he were not mentally disordered, or (d) otherwise for administering the patient's affairs.'

Procedure Order allows the Court to give instructions for particular transactions. The Court currently looks after the affairs of over 30,000 patients.[12]

The National Audit office has reported that the work of the Public Trust Office, which administers the capital assets of Court of Protection patients, could be improved (National Audit Office 1994). The Law Commission is critical of a number of aspects of the jurisdiction and work of the Court:

> It is also a matter of concern that the jurisdiction is premised on an assumption that capacity is an all-or-nothing status. No provision is made for a partial intervention in a person's affairs, limited in scope because the person has partial or fluctuating capacity. It can be difficult for a patient to obtain a discharge,... Nor does the Court permit a patient to execute an enduring power of attorney over any of his or her property, since this would conflict with the global approach it takes to each case... Those to whom receivership powers are delegated must usually give security and submit detailed yearly accounts. The costs of this highly protective system are charged to the patients. (Law Commission 1995, p.10)

This criticism of the Court of Protection identifies one of the major problems of the current law concerning incapacity, that is the often very significant consequences of a determination of incapacity. Though, as has already been shown, current English law recognises that different levels of capacity are required for different legal transactions, the Court of Protection assumes total responsibility upon determination of incapacity consequent upon mental disorder. There are other concerns about the process and criteria of the diagnosis of mental disorder and the decision concerning incapacity to manage property and financial affairs.[13]

HEALTH CARE

English law reflects the primacy of the principle of bodily autonomy. Any intentional bodily interference involving physical touching or force without the consent of the person concerned is technically a trespass to the person and a battery and assault. Consequently, medical treatment involving physical interference with a patient's body normally requires that person's consent. The three elements of a valid consent are:

1. the provision of sufficient information about the nature and purpose of the treatment including any side effects;

2. the patient must be able to understand what s/he has been told about the treatment;

3. their consent must be given voluntarily.

---

12 A detailed discussion of the Court of Protection is provided by Whitehorn, Heywood and Massey (1991)

13 See British Medical Association and The Law Society 1995, pp.25–30.

This principle raises a number of complex problems when the patient or person concerned does not have the necessary mental capacity to give a valid consent to treatment. Before the case of *Re F (Mental Patient: Sterilisation)*[14] was finally decided by the House of Lords in 1989 there were very limited circumstances in which medical treatment could be administered without the consent of the person concerned. In this case a 36-year-old woman with severe learning disability resided in a psychiatric hospital. There was evidence that pregnancy was a risk of a relationship she had formed with a male resident. Her doctors and her mother concluded that her best interests determined that she should be sterilised. It was clear that she did not have the necessary capacity to give a valid consent to the proposed treatment; without such a consent the operation would have been unlawful. An application was made to the High Court for a declaration that the operation would not be unlawful despite the absence of the patient's consent. The declaration was granted and the High Court's decision was upheld by the Court of Appeal and the House of Lords. The basis of the House of Lords decision was articulated by Lord Brandon:[15]

> A doctor can lawfully operate on, or give treatment to, adult persons who are incapable...of consenting to his doing so, provided that the operation or other treatment concerned is in the best interests of such patients. The operation or other treatment will be in the best interests if, but only if, it is carried out in order either to save lives or to ensure improvement or prevent deterioration in their physical or mental health.

Prior to this decision, English law provided no procedure whereby any other person or a court could take such a decision on behalf of an adult person without capacity to consent. The law of wardship did not extend to adults; the treatment provisions of the Mental Health Act 1983 applied only to treatment for a mental disorder; the powers of a guardian appointed under the Mental Health Act did not extend to giving consent for medical treatment; and the jurisdiction of the Court of Protection and the powers of an attorney appointed under the Enduring Powers of Attorney Act covered only financial and property matters, and did not extend to health care decisions.

Currently then, medical treatment can only be given to a person without the necessary mental capacity to consent in the very limited situations specified by statute and the common law. These are:

- where the person is unconscious and in need of urgent treatment to preserve life, health or well-being provided there is no unequivocal evidence of the person's valid refusal of treatment in such circumstances
- where treatment for mental disorder is to be administered under the provisions of Part IV of the Mental Health Act;

---

14 [1990] 2 AC 1

15 Re f.

- where the person is suffering from a mental disorder and their behaviour is an immediate serious danger to themselves or to others and the treatment is the minimum necessary to avert that danger
- where the person's best interests require medical treatment but he or she does not have the capacity to consent.

Though the development of the common law has been concerned with medical treatment it is likely that the same principles apply to any form of personal care which involves the physical touching of another. Consequently, the best interests principle encompasses the personal care of persons with learning disability who consequently are unable to give their consent to the physical interference necessarily involved in their personal care.

In practice doctors will continue to determine whether and when a person lacks sufficient capacity to consent to treatment and personal care and what constitutes the best interests of the person concerned. In exercising these judgements doctors will be subject to the standard of care established in the case of *Bolam v Friern Hospital Management Committee*,[16] that is, the doctor must act in accordance with a practice accepted as proper by a reasonable and competent body of relevant professional opinion.

In *Re F*[17] the House of Lords determined that where a sterilisation operation is planned, or any other fundamental or irreversible intervention is envisaged, that those responsible should apply to the High Court for a declaration. In other circumstances, such as those faced daily by staff and carers in residential care homes, in nursing homes, in psychiatric hospitals and by friends and relatives providing care at home, intervention will be allowed or condoned without the requirement of consent so long as, in practice, it is in the best interests of the person concerned. This leaves open the question as to who has the legal authority to define the best interests of the person with mental incapacity and thereby trigger the physical interventions which are part of personal care. This continuing doubt is discussed by the Law Commission who recommend the establishment of a 'general authority to act reasonably'. They recognise a principle of necessity from the judgement of Lord Goff in *Re F*, who argued that such a principle governed treatment without consent where: 'not only (1) must there be a necessity to act when it is not practicable to communicate with the assisted person, but also (2) the action taken must be such as a reasonable person would in all the circumstances take, acting in the best interests of the assisted person.'[18]

It also appears from the judgements that the principle covers personal care:

---

16   [1957] 1 WLR 582.
17   See fn.2.
18   [1990] 2 AC 1, p.75.

action properly taken to preserve the life, health or well-being of the assisted person [which] may well transcend such measures as surgical operations or substantial medical treatment and may extend to include such humdrum matters as routine medical or dental treatment, even simple care such as dressing and undressing and putting to bed.[19]

The Law Commission have adopted this principle in their desire to: 'Dispel doubts and confusion and set firm and appropriate limits to informal action.' (Law Commission 1995, p.49).

Their formal recommendation is framed in the following terms:

We recommend that it should be lawful to do anything for the personal welfare or health care of a person who is, or is reasonably believed to be, without capacity in relation to the matter in question, if it is in all the circumstances reasonable for it to be done by the person who does it. (Law Commission 1995, pp.50–51)

One other aspect of the current law on health care for people with mental incapacity concerns so called *advance directives* or *living wills*. The terms have no precise or accepted legal definition in English law though the objective behind the use of such documents is clear.

It generally refers to a document in which competent adults record instructions or wishes regarding medical treatment should they subsequently become incapable of decision making. Commonly, they are concerned with the provision, or withholding, of medical treatment at the end of life. (Holt and Viinikka 1994)

Such documents seek to establish preferences for future health care or appoint a health care proxy to make or participate in health care decisions on behalf of the patient. Case law has considered the effect of advance refusals of treatment and in *Re T*[20] Lord Donaldson set out three criteria for a legally binding advance refusal of treatment; the full capacity of the patient at the time their decision was made; the absence of any undue influence; and evidence that the patient had foreseen the situation which had arisen and the consequences of their decision. The decision in *Re T* has more recently been approved in the case of *Re C*[21] where a patient refused his consent to the amputation of his foot and directed that his refusal should have effect in the future should he lose his mental capacity. The court found that the three criteria were satisfied and confirmed the validity of his advance refusal.

The legal validity of the appointment of health care proxies has not yet been tested in the courts. The Law Commission has accepted the argument for extending the powers of an attorney beyond the property and financial affairs of a person with mental incapacity currently available under an enduring power of attorney to encompass health care and personal welfare decisions. The Commission's recommendations also extend to the establishment of a new

---

19 Quoted from the judgement in British Medical Association and The Law Society 1995, p.69.
20 [1992] 3 WLR 782.
21 [1994] 1 FLR 32.

Court of Protection with extended jurisdiction over health care and personal welfare decisions including the ability to appoint a health care proxy for a person with mental incapacity.[22]

It is also necessary to make some mention of the position of children with mental incapacity and their medical care and treatment. The decision of the House of Lords in the Gillick case established that a minor of any age who has achieved sufficient maturity, in the sense that they fully understand what is proposed, has sufficient capacity to consent to medical treatment without reference to his or her parents or to any other person.[23] The Family Law Reform Act 1969 provides that a minor of 16 or 17 years of age who has mental capacity may consent to medical treatment on their own behalf. The scope of this provision has recently been limited by the courts who have decided that a refusal of medical treatment by a minor can be overruled by the courts even where there is no doubt that the minor has sufficient maturity and capacity to make their own decision.[24]

It is generally thought that where a child does not have appropriate mental capacity, either because of their age or because they have a learning disability, decisions concerning medical treatment and care are to be taken by their parents or guardian or by those with parental responsibility, who would be required to make the decision in the best interests of the child. Any such decision would be subject to an application to the High Court for wardship or to an application to the Family Proceedings court for an order under section 8 of the Children Act 1989 where there was a dispute concerning medical treatment or possibly concerning the issue of the child's capacity.[25] Any decision made by the High Court in such circumstances would be determined by the 'best interests' principle established in Re F. Where an application was made under the Children Act the court will be required to make such a decision by reference to the welfare of the child. In practice the principles are probably the same.

The doctrine of necessity should apply to the medical care and treatment of minors without capacity in the same way that it applies to adults without capacity.

PERSONAL WELFARE

Vulnerable people and those with mental incapacity are entitled to be protected against abuse, neglect and exploitation, and to be empowered where this is possible and appropriate. This protection and empowerment should extend

---

22 See Parts V, VII and VIII of Law Commission 1995.
23 Gillick v West Norfolk and Wisbech Area Health Authority [1985] 3 All E.R.402 HL.
24 Re W (A Minor) (Medical Treatment: Court's Jurisdiction) [1993] Fam 64 and Re R (A Minor) (Wardship: Consent to Treatment) [1992] Fam 11.
25 For a fuller discussion see Brazier 1992, Chapter 15.

beyond the consequence of emergency intervention under the law so that these rights and interests should also underpin the long-term care of those who have a mental incapacity and those who are vulnerable.

The ability of current English law to protect and promote these rights and interests is both partial and haphazard. The Court of Protection offers some protection in relation to property and financial affairs but personal welfare is specifically protected only by the place of safety provisions, sections 135 and 136, of the Mental Health Act, by section 47 of the National Assistance Act and the guardianship system established under the Mental Health Act.

Section 135 of the Mental Health Act provides for a person to be removed from private premises to a place of safety where he or she: '(a) has been, or is being ill-treated, neglected or kept otherwise than under proper control…, or (b) being unable to care for himself, is living alone.'

Section 136 provides for people with a mental disorder who are found in a public place to be taken to a place of safety if, among other things, it is necessary to do so in the interests of that person.

Section 47 of the National Assistance Act 1948 provides for Magistrates Courts, on the application of the local medical officer of health, to order that a person is removed from where they are to suitable premises (usually local authority accommodation), where the person concerned is: '(a)…suffering from grave chronic disease or, being aged, infirm or physically incapacitated, are living in insanitary conditions; and (b) are unable to devote to themselves, and are not receiving from other persons, proper care and attention.'

These provisions offer what is essentially emergency protection. Sections 135 and 136, place of safety powers, expire after 72 hours, and section 47 orders are for three months though they may extended by court order. Longer term protection may be available under Section 7 of the Mental Health Act 1983 which sets out the circumstances in which a person over the age of 16 may be received into guardianship:

(a) he is suffering from mental disorder, being mental illness, severe mental impairment, psychopathic disorder or mental impairment and his mental disorder is of a nature or degree which warrants his reception into guardianship under this section; and

(b) it is necessary in the interests of the welfare of the patient or for the protection of other persons that the patient should be so received.

There is a mental disorder threshold for the exercise of both section 135 and 136 powers and the earlier Law Commission working paper concluded that they are of little help for mentally incapacitated or vulnerable people who need long-term care. (Law Commission 1991). If this is the case the compulsory powers of detention and treatment in the Act may have to be used. This may not be desirable because of the express interference with autonomy involved and, in any case, would not be possible unless a person with mental incapacity is also suffering from a mental illness or is psychopathic, or they are displaying abnormally aggressive or seriously irresponsible conduct. The same comments apply to guardianship under section 7 of the 1983 Act, so that the mental disorder threshold may well exclude a significant number of people with mental incapacity from being received into guardianship. Consequently it is rarely used.

Though mental incapacity is not a criterion for the use of powers under section 47 of the National Assistance Act 1948, their utility for protecting the interests of those with mental incapacity is limited by the short-term nature of the removal power and by the general conclusion that the section is inflexible and stigmatising (Law Commission 1993c, p.15). It seems that few such orders are made each year.

The limitations and the shortcomings of this legal structure were exposed by the case involving Beverley Lewis, a young adult with profound mental and physical handicaps. She became fatally ill and emaciated at home after her mother, who lived with her and provided her only care, and who suffered from schizophrenia, refused attempts by the local social services and health authority to visit and monitor Beverley's condition (Fennell 1989).

The criminal law operates to punish those guilty of abuse, largely through prosecutions under the Offences Against the Person Act 1861, the Sexual Offences Acts and the Theft Act 1968, and though it cannot offer real protection against such offences victims may apply to the courts or to the Criminal Injuries Compensation Board for compensation where this is appropriate. Arrest, remands in custody and custodial sentences offer some, possibly short-term respite from abuse or threats of abuse, though many victims fail to report such offences for fear of exacerbating the situation, or of reprisal.

The current legal structure also fails to properly draw a balance between paternalism and autonomy in the sense that the compulsory powers in the law, which are designed to provide protection from abuse and neglect, pay little or no attention to the individual rights of people who are subject to their use, but who wish, and have the capacity, to decline protection. The principle of autonomy should be reflected in the right of vulnerable people with capacity to decline protection; for people without capacity protection from abuse and neglect reflects the other important principle of legitimate paternalism.

Other shortcomings in the law have been well illustrated by the growing concern about, and documentation of, the abuse of elderly people. Such abuse has been defined in the following terms: 'The systematic maltreatment, physical, emotional or financial of an elderly person…this may take the form of physical assault, threatening behaviour, neglect and abandonment or sexual assault' (Eastman 1984, p.23).

Unsurprisingly, given such a wide definition, there is no specific legal provision designed to deal with incidences of elder abuse. In addition to the legal provisions already identified in this discussion of personal welfare, the criminal law is undoubtedly available to deal with assaults and theft. Increased concern amongst the public and professionals has been reflected in the issue of

Practice Guidelines by the Social Services Inspectorate: 'This document sets out the issues for agencies to consider when formulating policy and practice guidelines for work with older people in domestic settings, where abuse is suspected, alleged or confirmed' (Social Services Inspectorate Department of Health 1993, p.1).

Concern about the nature and operation of emergency powers to offer protection from abuse or neglect and their inability to properly respect the autonomy of vulnerable people has led the Law Commission to recommend a new system of public law protection for vulnerable people at risk, a system which will also provide appropriate protection for people with mental incapacity.

THE NEED FOR REFORM OF THE LAW AND THE LEGAL STRUCTURE

A number of other developments, which may be understood as strictly external to the law on mental incapacity, are imposing their own imperatives for reform of the law. They render the law on mental incapacity outdated, in addition to being already haphazard and partial.

> Particular attention is drawn in the report to the continuing increase in the proportion of very old people in the population; the fact that many people who previously lived in an institutional setting are now living in the community where greatly increased opportunities for substitute decision-making arise; how advances in medical science now enable people to live longer than was previously the case often with their mental capacity impaired. These demographic, social and medical changes have taken place at the same time as a recognition by the courts that there is now no person or court in England and Wales who can lawfully take personal welfare or medical decisions on behalf of adults who lack capacity to take decisions for themselves. (Law Commission 1995b, p.1.1)

Four particular factors can be identified. First, the programme of hospital closures and the emphasis on care in the community; second, demographic changes arising from an ageing population; third, the ability of medical science to prolong physical life in circumstances where the person concerned has no mental capacity; and finally a recognition of the rights of people with a disability generally, particularly the right not to be discriminated against, and the right to appropriate protection and the right to empowerment through the recognition of civil rights and rights to services.

Care in the community is not a new policy. For example, it is entirely legitimate to think of the 1970 Chronically Sick and Disabled Persons Act as a statutory recognition of the policy of promoting the ability of people with disability to live an independent life in the community. For many people with a mental incapacity the particular impact of the policy of community care has been caused by the related policy of the closure of psychiatric hospitals with the resulting loss of many long stay beds. As a consequence significant numbers of people with a mental incapacity, who had been living in institutions, have been discharged into the community with an expectation (or hope) on the part of government, that structures for community care would be able to provide them with the necessary care and services, largely under the terms of the National Health Service and Community Care Act 1990.[26]

There is little doubt that a number of people with mental incapacity were, prior to the introduction of this Act, unnecessarily detained, either under legal powers or in practice, in institutions where they were robbed of their autonomy and a right to an independent life even to the extent that their capacity would allow. Equally the policy of community care, which is underpinned by principles of autonomy and self-determination for service users and carers, has greatly enhanced the lives of many people with mental incapacity. Nonetheless, there are two related concerns about the impact upon individual people, first, of an ill-prepared and sometimes hasty discharge from hospital, and second, their ability to survive in an unfamiliar environment where community care resources may be inadequate.

Concerns about community care also have a relevance for a society, such as the United Kingdom, which has an ageing population.[27] In 1971 2.3 per cent of the population were over 80, by 1991 this figure has risen to 3.7 per cent. The rise is predicted to reach 4.7 per cent by 2011 and 6.9 per cent in 2031. Of particular significance for our discussion is the fact that the incidence of mental incapacity is higher in this age group largely because a significant number of people over 80 have limited mental capacity largely caused by the onset and development of dementia. This places greater calls on community care resources and requires substitute or proxy decision-making in relation to property, finances, personal welfare and health care.

Advances in medical technology and health care practice have also identified new problems for a legal structure already in need of reform. In addition to the fact that medicine can keep people alive for longer it is now possible for the victims of catastrophic injuries to have their lives sustained by artificial support such as that offered by life support machines and intravenous feeding and hydration. In many cases the person concerned has very limited or no mental capacity and may be in, what is now called, a persistent vegetative state. Some of the legal consequences of these developments have recently been litigated in the case involving Anthony Bland, a victim of the Hillsborough football disaster. The House of Lords held that the best interests of the patient, who was in a persistent vegetative state and therefore had no mental capacity, would be served by the disconnection and removal of feeding and hydration tubes thus allowing him to die.[28] All the judges involved in the case identified the

---

26 See Chapter Four, pp.97–104.
27 The Law Commission (1995) quotes figures from Social Trends 24 (1994) Table 1.4.
28 Airedale NHS Trust v Bland [1993] AC 789.

important moral, social and legal consequences of their decision and a number identified the need for legislation to provide a structure for decision-making on behalf of those who are unconscious and without mental capacity.

Underlying all these developments, and the concerns they raise, is a recognition of the rights of people with mental incapacity and an acknowledgement that the current law and legal structure provides insufficient identification, recognition and protection of these rights. Evidence of the force of this 'rights agenda' is cited by the Law Commission (Law Commission 1995, pp.23–25):

- the UN Declaration of 1971 on the Rights of Mentally Retarded Persons[29]
- the civil rights arguments in the reform debate which led to the Mental Health Act 1983[30]
- the Government sponsored charter movement
- the principle of consultation with service users and carers which underpins the community care provisions of the National Health Service and Community Care Act 1990[31]
- the increased acceptance and influence of the principle of patient autonomy
- the concern around the incidence of elder abuse and the abuse of young people with learning difficulties
- the growth of advocacy movements.

All these factors affecting people with mental incapacity are also evidence of the increasing awareness of the life experience of disabled people, of the discrimination that has characterised this and of the need to combat the negative impact of mental incapacity. It is no coincidence that the work of the Law Commission, and its framing of legislative proposals in the draft Mental Incapacity Bill, should be published in the same year, and just ahead of the Disability Discrimination Act which received the Royal Assent in October 1995.[32]

REFORMING THE LAW ON MENTAL INCAPACITY – THE LAW COMMISSION PROPOSALS

The Law Commission's report, *Mental Incapacity*, was published in February 1995. Attached to the report is its draft legislation, the Mental Incapacity Bill.

---

29 Chapter Two, p.37.
30 ref. Chapter Seven, pp.186–189.
31 See Chapter Four, pp.97–102.
32 For history of this legislation see Chapter Three, p.77–82.

The Bill seeks to give effect to the proposals made by the Law Commission; in turn these proposals reflect a long research and consultation process initiated by the publication of *Fourth Programme of Law Reform in 1989* (Law Commission 1989).

The report provides a comprehensive analysis of the need for law reform and, despite the fact that the Government has recently decided not to legislate on the basis of the proposals, of the likely model to be adopted in future legislation, if only in part. The substantive description and comment that follows is provided on the basis that it facilitates an understanding of how the law could provide for the legitimate interests and rights of people with mental incapacity.

Three objectives run through the report: first, the encouragement of people with mental incapacity to take decisions which they are able to take; second, where it is in the interests of the person with mental incapacity or for the protection of others, to provide for decisions to be taken on their behalf by another person so long as that intervention is as limited as appropriate and the decision reflects what the person would have wanted, so far as this is identifiable; and finally, that appropriate protection should be provided against exploitation and neglect, and against physical, sexual or psychological abuse.[33]

The Bill contains what the Law Commission refers to as a unified approach which: 'Creates a coherent statutory scheme to which recourse can be had when any decision (whether personal, medical or financial in nature) needs to be made for a person aged 16 or over who lacks capacity' (Law Commission 1995, p.29).

The proposed legislation contains six major recommendations to facilitate this approach:

1. A definition of capacity/incapacity.

2. A single trigger criteria for the taking of decisions on behalf of a person who lacks sufficient capacity.

3. Clarification of the law concerning informal actions on behalf of a person without capacity.

4. The reformulation of powers of attorney so that they provide for all aspects of mental incapacity, i.e. covering property and financial affairs, health care decisions and personal welfare.

5. The appointment of a person to make decisions on behalf of the person without capacity or to allow such decisions to be made by a new Court of Protection.

6. A new system of emergency protection for people with mental incapacity or those who are otherwise vulnerable.

---

33   For a discussion of these principles see Law Commission 1995, pp.26–27.

Underpinning all these provisions are two basic concepts, 'mental capacity' and 'best interests'. The Commission's proposed definition of mental incapacity and the related concept of mental disability is quoted and discussed above[34] and it is only necessary here to repeat the earlier identification of the inclusion of a mental disability threshold for one of the two definitions of incapacity, and the fact that capacity and incapacity are to be defined in relation to the particular decision to be taken at the 'material' time. The draft legislation therefore utilises a generic definition of capacity and incapacity which allows for the fact that different decisions require differing levels of mental capacity.

The 'best interests' criteria is given central significance within the Law Commission's proposals: 'We recommend that anything done for, and any decision made on behalf of, a person without capacity should be done or made in the best interests of that person' (Law Commission 1995, p.42).

Consequently this standard will apply to all decisions concerning the property and financial affairs of a person without mental capacity, their health care and their personal welfare.[35]

INFORMAL DAY-TO-DAY CARE AND DECISION-MAKING

This chapter has already identified the fact that much of the day-to-day care of people with mental incapacity and the decisions involved in providing for that care, takes place within a context of legal ambiguity in the sense that there is no formal legal authority for the actions and decisions involved. Consequently the Commission recommends a statutory authority to act reasonably: 'We recommend that it should be lawful to do anything for the personal welfare or health care of a person who is, or is reasonably believed to be, without capacity in relation to the matter in question if it is in all the circumstances reasonable for it to be done by the person who does it' (Law Commission 1995, pp.50–51)

Individual recommendations make it clear that day to day informal decisions concerning financial matters are also included in this general authority. Other

---

34 see pp.214–216.
35 'We recommend that in deciding what is in a person's best interests regard should be had to:–
   (1) the ascertainable past and present wishes and feelings of the person concerned, and the factors that person would consider if able to do so;
   (2) the need to permit and encourage the person to participate, or to improve his or her ability to participate, as fully as possible in anything done for and any decision affecting him or her;
   (3) the views of other people whom it is appropriate and practicable to consult about the person's wishes and feelings and what would be in his or her best interests;
   (4) whether the purpose for which any action or decision is required can be effectively achieved in a manner less restrictive of the person's freedom of action.' (Law Commission 1995, p.45)

decisions concerning the property and financial affairs of a person with mental incapacity will be subject to specific legal authority and may therefore be made under a proposed continuing power of attorney or by the newly constituted Court of Protection.

ADVANCE DIRECTIVES FOR HEALTH CARE DECISIONS

The Commission makes a number of recommendations to provide for the statutory recognition of advance directives made by people who, at the material time for decision-making, do not have the necessary capacity to make that decision. In order to be valid and operative any advance directive must be clearly established and applicable in the circumstances. So long as these criteria are fulfilled an advance directive which seeks to refuse medical treatment, including the provision of life sustaining treatment, will be operative and enforceable. The provisions of the draft Bill do, however, provide for the provision of basic care, notwithstanding anything in the advance directive, and for medical treatment to maintain a patient's 'status quo' pending a decision on the validity, applicability or status of the directive.

The recommendations seek to define the consequences of the legal force of advance directives for those who are involved in the health care of that person. Consequently an advance refusal of treatment should have precedence over the general authority to act reasonably, but would not preclude the provision of basic care which is defined as: 'Care to maintain bodily cleanliness and to alleviate severe pain, as well as the provision of direct oral nutrition and hydration' (Law Commission 1995, p.79).

SUPERVISION OF SOME MEDICAL PROCEDURES

The Commission recognises that, because of their nature, some proposed medical interventions require independent authority either to establish that they are in the best interests of the person without capacity or that the best interests standard is not appropriate. These treatments are therefore outside the general authority to act reasonably although any decision concerning their administration will be subject to the terms of a valid advance directive.

The Commission identifies a number of procedures which, it is argued, would need the approval of the court or the consent of an attorney appointed by the person without capacity to make the decision, or the approval of a manager appointed by the court. The procedures identified are sterilisation to render, or which might render a person permanently infertile, unless it is to treat a disease of the reproductive organs or relieve the existing detrimental effects of menstruation; and the donation of tissue or bone marrow. Other treatments are identified as requiring a second confirming doctor's opinion or the consent of the person's appointed attorney or a court-appointed manager, including abortion, and treatments for mental disorder. An advance directive to refuse treatment for mental disorder made by a person who has been detained for treatment under the Mental Health Act will not operate so as to prevent such treatment.

In relation to people such as the late Anthony Bland, in persistent vegetative state with no prospect of recovery (because there is no activity in the cerebral cortex) being artificially fed and hydrated, the Law Commission recommends that treatment could be discontinued subject to independent verification and supervision of that decision.

CONTINUING POWERS OF ATTORNEY

In their desire to establish substitute decision-making structures which are comprehensive in the sense that they cover property and financial affairs, as well as health care and personal welfare, the Law Commission proposes the replacement of enduring powers of attorney by continuing powers of attorney.

An attorney appointed under the terms of the draft Bill would be under a statutory duty to act in the best interests of the donor and have regard to the best interests checklist. The proposed legislation contains a number of restrictions on the powers of the attorney. They may not consent or refuse medical treatment unless the donor is, or the attorney reasonably believes them to be, without capacity to make that decision themselves; or consent to admission to hospital for assessment or treatment for mental disorder where such admission is against the will of the donor. Attorneys will be under a duty not to confine or coerce, or to withhold or refuse basic care for the donor. The attorney will be subject to the terms of a valid advance refusal of treatment made by the donor, and they will not be permitted to consent to those treatments requiring independent supervision unless authorised to do so by the continuing power of attorney. These provisions permit the donor to allow the attorney to displace the need for independent supervision if, for example, a sterilisation is proposed. The attorney should not be able to refuse life sustaining treatment on behalf of the donor unless the continuing power of attorney makes express provision for the attorney to have this authority.

The Commission recommends that a continuing power of attorney must be registered before the donee can exercise any of the powers established in it. Registration will be undertaken by an authority to be established subject to prior notification by the donee to the donor of their intention to register. If the donor objects the registration should not take place. There will be provision for the termination of continuing powers of attorney including by disclaimer of the donee to the donor and the registration authority, and by the donor with capacity.

The Commission's proposed bill establishes a supervisory role over continuing powers of attorney for the Court of Protection. This role will include the right, subject to any expressed intention in the document, to appoint a new or additional attorney and extend or modify the scope of the donee's authority to act so long as the donor is without capacity and the Court thinks that it desirable to do so. The Court would also have the power to revoke a continuing power of attorney where the donee is, or is proposing to, behave in a way which is outside their powers or against the best interests of the donor.

A NEW COURT OF PROTECTION

The analysis of the weaknesses and gaps in existing law and the reforms proposed by the Law Commission identified the need for a new judicial forum with a last resort jurisdiction to hear and resolve the many problems and disputes which may arise because a person does not have sufficient capacity to make all or some of their own decisions.

> This jurisdiction will have a number of new and distinctive features. It will provide a single integrated framework for the making of personal welfare decisions, health care decisions and financial decisions. It will provide for both 'one-off' orders or, where necessary, for the appointment of a 'manager' with continuing powers. We also propose that it should be operated by a range of judges within the normal judicial hierarchy, according to the seriousness and complexity of the issues in any case. (Law Commission 1995, p.132)

The 'last resort' jurisdiction of the new Court of Protection would be available if discussion and agreement, and the general authority to act, were not sufficient to settle the matter. In such cases the Court would be able to make appropriate declarations and orders and would be able to appoint a manager for the person without capacity. The governing principles for the Court would be that the exercise of any of its powers would reflect the nature and extent of the person's decision-making capacity and that decisions would be taken in the best interests of the person concerned.

Declarations would be available to determine issues concerning the capacity of a person and the validity or applicability of an advance refusal of treatment. The Commission also proposes that the Court should have a jurisdiction to make orders in relation to personal welfare, health care, property and financial affairs where necessary and appropriate.

In relation to personal welfare, which is largely concerned with protecting vulnerable people and those with mental incapacity from abuse, neglect and exploitation, the Court would have the power to make orders concerning where the person was to live and with whom they should have contact. There would also be power to make appropriate 'third party' orders: 'Restraining a person from having contact with or molesting the person without capacity' (Law Commission 1995, p.138).

For health care matters the Court would be able to make orders approving or refusing approval for particular health care or treatment. The Court, however, would not have power to consent to the withholding of basic care or to consent to any treatment refused by the terms of a valid advance refusal of treatment. This exclusion of particular powers will also apply to a manager appointed by the Court.

It is also proposed that the Court should be able to order that a person without appropriate capacity should be admitted to hospital for assessment and/or treatment for a mental disorder. The criteria for admission under section 2 or 3 of the Act should be satisfied and though the best interests criteria will not apply, the Court should nonetheless have regard to the best interests factors defined in the draft Bill.

PROTECTING VULNERABLE PEOPLE FROM ABUSE, NEGLECT OR EXPLOITATION

The Commission recommends an entirely new structure to provide protection for vulnerable people which in many respects resembles the system for emergency child protection established in the Children Act 1989. Because the proposal is for a new structure the Commission argues that it should replace existing provisions contained in the National Assistance Act 1948 and the Mental Health Act 1983.

The draft Bill uses the category of vulnerable people to define the group offered and subject to the protection provisions: 'A "vulnerable person" should mean any person of 16 or over who (1) is or may be in need of community care services by reason of mental or other disability, age or illness and who (2) is or may be unable to take care of himself or herself, or unable to protect himself or herself against significant harm or serious exploitation' (Law Commission 1995, p.159).

A consequent definition of 'harm' is proposed: '"harm" should be defined to mean ill-treatment (including sexual abuse, and forms of ill-treatment that are not physical); the impairment of, or an avoidable deterioration in, physical or mental health; and the impairment of physical, intellectual, emotional, social or behavioural development' (Law Commission 1995, p.160).

The protection of vulnerable people raises a number of tensions between the principles of autonomy and legitimate paternalism. In an attempt to resolve these tensions the Commission argues that a person with a mental disability should not be able to refuse short term intervention designed to protect them and allow their circumstances to be assessed. In contrast it is proposed to allow a vulnerable person, who is not suffering from a mental disability, and objects to intervention, to refuse the protection offered by these provisions.[36]

The new structure would create a duty on local authorities to investigate and assess with the ability to provide temporary protection if needed.

> Where a local authority have reason to believe that a vulnerable person in their area is suffering or likely to suffer significant harm or serious exploitation they shall make such enquiries as they consider necessary to enable them to decide:
>
> (1) whether the person is in fact suffering or likely to suffer such harm or exploitation and
>
> (2) if so, whether community care services should be provided or arranged or other action taken to protect the person from such harm or exploitation. (Law Commission 1995, pp.163–164)

The duty to investigate is backed up by rights, invested in an authorised officer of a local authority, to enter premises and interview a vulnerable person who is thought to be vulnerable and at risk. These rights are subject to the 'veto' of a vulnerable but capable person. Where the proper exercise of these rights is being frustrated, the Law Commission proposes that entry warrants be available. Again, the application for such warrants would not be possible where the applicant, the authorised officer, knows that the vulnerable person with capacity would object. There are also proposals for the creation of assessment orders to facilitate the assessment of a vulnerable person at risk, subject to their objection. Such an order might include the ability to remove the vulnerable person at risk from their home to facilitate an assessment.

Following the model of child protection legislation established by the Children Act 1969, the Law Commission recommends the creation and granting of a temporary protection order where:

(1) a vulnerable person is likely to be 'at risk' unless removed to or kept in protective accommodation for a short period, and

(2) (unless there is reasonable cause to believe that the person is or may be suffering from mental disability) the applicant does not know or believe

---

36   The proposals in this part of the Report use the term mental disability rather than mental incapacity. Clause 2(2) of the Draft Bill offers the following definition of mental disability:

> 'For the purpose of this Part of this Act a person is at the material time unable to make a decision by reason of mental disability if the disability is such that at the time when the decision needs to be made –
>
> (a) he is unable to understand or retain the information relevant to the decision, including information about reasonably foreseeable consequences of deciding one way or another or of failing to make the decision; or
>
> (b) he is unable to make the decision based on that information,
>
> and in this Act 'mental disability' means a disability or disorder of the mind or brain, whether permanent or temporary, which results in an impairment or disturbance of mental functioning.'

the person object or would object to the order. (Law Commission 1995, p.170)

The removal would be for a maximum of eight days.

Whilst these powers are designed to provide emergency protection, long-term solutions will remain necessary for many vulnerable people at risk. The Law Commission identifies the possibility of the person with capacity agreeing to accept community care services, to a residential placement, or the creation of an enduring power of attorney. The competency of the person determines the validity of their decision; such a decision may mean they return to an abusing or exploitative environment.

It may be necessary to trigger the use of the compulsory powers of the Mental Health Act to detain and treat the person if they have a mental disorder as defined by the Act. The Commission does not recommend any major change to the guardianship provisions of the Act except to propose an extension of the guardian's rights so that they shall have the power to convey the person concerned to a residence chosen by the guardian. This would supplement the existing power to require residence at a particular place.

CONCLUSIONS ON THE LAW COMMISSION'S RECOMMENDATIONS

The proposals made by the Commission reflect a carefully researched analysis of the current law and legal structure and a significant period of consultation. There is almost universal agreement, particularly within the legal and medical professions and amongst carers, about the need for reform of the law so that those without capacity to make some or all of their own legally significant decisions can have their rights and interests recognised, protected and enhanced. This objective has much force, partly as a manifestation of the disability rights movement, but also as recognition of the particular consequences of mental incapacity.

Reaction to the Commission's proposals has been very positive. Writing about mental incapacity and medical treatment, one reviewer, writing in the *Solicitors Journal*, comments:

> The proposals, produced after extensive consultation, strike a balance between respecting patients' autonomy, facilitating such decision-making as is possible, and protecting them, where they are unable to make their own decisions, by giving others statutory powers to make decisions on their behalf. Such legislation would provide the necessary clarification much needed by doctors and carers who have to take practical decisions with very little guidance. (Stone 1995)

Despite a recognition of the need for reform the Government has announced that it will not legislate on the basis of the report.

> The Government has decided not to legislate on the basis of the Law Commission's proposals in their current form and has also concluded that it would be inappropriate to make any proposals to Parliament in the absence of full public

consultation. The government proposes to issue a consultation paper on mental incapacity in due course. (Lord Chancellor's Department 1996)

Whilst the promise of a government consultation paper is welcome, the implication that the proposals reflect something less than a proper consultation process is both insulting to the Law Commission and factually erroneous. It is possible to speculate about the underlying reasons for this profoundly depressing decision. The government is coming to the end of its term of office with the requirement of a general election by 1997. It is entirely possible that there is a fear of the moral and ethical issues, and the media and public reaction to them, which would be an inevitable part of the parliamentary debate surrounding a government sponsored Mental Incapacity Bill. The process of consultation promised by the Lord Chancellor's Department is likely to take us beyond the election and might thereby absolve this government of the responsibility of bringing forward controversial legislation. The government might also be unwilling to fund the costs of reform, for example the establishment of a new Court of Protection, which would be likely to be more expensive, and more controversial than the incumbent model. The new system of public protection for vulnerable people which would mirror, in many respects, the child protection system established by the Children Act 1989, might be politically difficult because it would involve the grant of new and additional powers to social workers.

Of greater and related concern is the possibility that legislation on behalf of people with mental incapacity is seen as unimportant and not worth the political and expenditure costs identified above. This would be deeply offensive to people with mental incapacity and to their carers and their families, and would extend the problems faced by the professions, doctors and lawyers in particular, who seek to provide for their rights to legal services and health care. However, within the history of the disability rights movement it would not be surprising, indeed it would reflect the reality of the politics of disability in which the rights and interests of people with disability are subject to both political expediency and cost considerations. It is to be hoped that the parliamentary treatment of the Civil Rights (Disabled Persons) Bill[37] and its succession by a much emasculated Disability Discrimination Act are not a model for the draft Mental Incapacity Bill.

---

37   For a detailed account of the history of this legislation, see Chapter Three, pp.77–82.

CHAPTER NINE

CHILDREN WITH DISABILITY

The legal structure within which services are provided for children with disability is both complex and confusing. The Children Act 1989 establishes local authority social services departments as the lead agency responsible for co-ordinating social services, education and health care services from a number of different providers according to the assessed needs of a disabled child. The provision of services for a child with special educational needs takes place under the terms of the Education Act 1993; health care services are provided under a number of statutory structures including the National Health Service Act 1977 and the National Health Service and Community Care 1990. Social services for a disabled child are organised under the Children Act but may be provided under a number of statutory provisions such as the Chronically Sick and Disabled Persons Act 1970, the Disabled Persons (Services, Consultation and Representation) Act 1986 and the Children Act itself. The Children Act 1989 brought together most public and private law relating to children; for children with disability, the Act establishes a principle of service integration so that work with disabled children inevitably involves working within this complex legal structure, much of which was in existence before the Act was implemented.

The statutory responsibility imposed by the Children Act on local authorities to integrate services provided by social services departments (SSDs), education authorities (LEAs) and the health service, encompasses not only the children they are looking after, whether they are in care or being accommodated, but also families who have a disabled child living with them.[1]

Behind this complex legislative structure the day to day provision of services for disabled children reflects a tension between views of the child as an individual with developing claims to autonomy and self-determination on the

---

1   Local authorities have a duty under the Children Act to provide accommodation for any child in need who requires accommodation because there is no one with parental responsibility for them, or where the child has been lost or abandoned, or where the person who has been caring for them is no longer able to provide accommodation or care.

one hand, and of the family and state as necessary decision-makers, providers and protectors on the other.

In ordinary health care this tension is played out within a complex mix of statute, common law, and the inherent jurisdiction of the High Court exercised through wardship. On a day to day basis most health care decisions for children, and for children with disabilities, will be made by parents unless and until a child establishes a level of maturity (in the Gillick sense) that means they are able, and should be enabled, to make their own independent decisions.[2] This principle, and the provisions of the Family Law Reform Act 1969, which provides for minors who are 16 and 17 to consent to surgical, medical and dental treatment on their own behalf, is now, it seems, subject to the overarching jurisdiction of the High Court operating through its inherent wardship powers, and to applications under section 8 of the Children Act.[3]

In relation to psychiatric health care minors are subject to the provisions of the Mental Health Act 1983, though it is rare for the compulsory powers of the Act to be used 'against' a minor. Again, there is a current confusion over what appears to be the overlapping jurisdictions of the Children Act and the Mental Health Act, and over the status of parental rights to decide on psychiatric health care for their children, the rights of a Gillick competent child, and the availability of wardship.[4] These confusions, although they are most frequently discussed over the issue of compulsory treatment, would also apply to voluntary admissions to hospital for psychiatric care and treatment. In relation to voluntary intervention the availability of a court order under section 8 of the Children Act and the inherent wardship jurisdiction of the High Court are avenues for the determination of inevitably difficult disputes.[5]

THE CHILDREN ACT 1989

Although services for disabled children are provided by the health service, education authorities and local authority social services, the Children Act establishes local authority social services departments as the lead and responsible authority.

---

2   The House of Lords decision in Gillick v West Norfolk and Wisbech Area Health Authority [1986] AC 112 established that children should be enabled to make those decisions which are appropriate to their maturity and experience. This principle should extend to decisions concerning health care.

3   For a detailed discussion of the complex relationship see Murphy 1992. Under section 8 of the Children Act the family proceedings court can make 'specific' orders concerning a child which could determine the provision of health care for that child.

4   See Bates 1994.

5   The situation in relation to health care decisions for a child without capacity has been identified in Chapter Eight, p.222.

Section 17(1) sets out the duty of every local authority:

a) to safeguard and promote the welfare of children within their area who are in need; and

b) so far as is consistent with that duty, to promote the upbringing of such children by their families,

by providing a range and level of services appropriate to those children's needs.

Section 17(10) identifies the circumstances in which a child shall be taken to be in need to include a disabled child and subsection 11 provides a definition of disability:

> (11) For the purposes of this Part, a child is disabled if he is blind, deaf or dumb or suffers from mental disorder of any kind or is substantially and permanently handicapped by illness, injury or congenital deformity or such other disability as may be prescribed: and in this Part –
>
> 'development' means physical, intellectual, emotional, social or behavioural development; and
>
> 'health' means physical or mental health.

These rather bald statutory duties are further defined by schedule 2 of the Act which sets out a number of specific responsibilities for local authorities which are designed to ensure that disabled children get the services they need. These include the maintenance of a register of disabled children;[6] and the power to undertake a comprehensive assessment of needs, including those under the Chronically Sick and Disabled Persons Act 1970, the Education Act 1993, and the Disabled Persons (Services, Consultation and Representation) Act 1986.[7] The schedule also specifies a duty to provide services for disabled children with the objective of minimising the impact of their disability and to provide them with the opportunity to lead lives which are as normal as possible.[8]

Underpinning these specific powers and duties is a general duty to:

> provide an appropriate range and level of services to safeguard and promote the welfare of children in need and 'so far as is consistent with that duty to promote the upbringing of such children by their families'. This general duty is supported by other specific duties and powers such as facilitation of 'the provision by others, including in particular voluntary organisations of services' (section 17(5) and Schedule 2). These provisions encourage SSDs to provide day and domicillary services, guidance and counselling, respite care and a range of other services as a means of supporting children in need (including children with disabilities) within their families. (Department of Health 1991, p.5)

Though local authority social services departments are required to take the lead responsibility, the co-ordination of services from other statutory providers is an important and often difficult task. Section 27 of the Act places a duty on other

---

6   Schedule 2, para.2.
7   Schedule 2, para.3.
8   Schedule 2, para.6.

authorities to comply with a request from a local authority consequent upon their discharge of duties to disabled children under the Act. These authorities include any other local authority, local education authorities, housing and health authorities. However, an inspection of four local authorities by the Social Services Inspectorate in 1993 identified little progress toward multi-agency work for disabled children; their report concluded that: 'There was considerable further scope for multi-agency planning, co-ordination, training and joint funding of services' (Social Services Inspectorate 1994, p.2).

The assessment and planning of services for disabled children will take place under the legislation identified above. When a child reaches the age of eighteen any need for community care services will be established by an assessment under the National Health Service and Community Care Act 1990. The expectation is that a disabled child with a continuing need for services into adulthood will have been assessed to take account of this transition on their majority so that appropriate services are in place and are not disrupted.

> The SSD's provision of services to children with disabilities should involve an initial assessment of need, a continuing process of reassessment and review of the plan for the child. Continuity should not be broken for reasons which concern organisational or administrative convenience rather than the welfare of the child or young person. A smooth transition, when the young person reaches 18 and comes within the provisions of the NHS and Community Care Act 1990 should be the objective. (Department of Health 1991, p.9)

The Children Act Guidance emphasises that the care management model of assessment and service provision which is identified for work under the NHS and Community Care Act 1990, should be adopted for work with and for disabled children. A definition is taken from guidance issued for the Act which emphasises a process of three elements:

- assessment of the user's circumstances
- design of a 'care package' in agreement with users' carers and relevant agencies to meet the identified needs within the care resources available, including help from willing and able carers
- implementation and monitoring of the agreed package: review of the outcomes for users and carers; and any necessary revision of service provision. (Department of Health 1991, p.10)

The planning and provision of services for disabled children is to be understood as being within ordinary child care services; as such planning in partnership with parents and children is an important principle underpinning practice. This principle should also inform decision making and practice concerning disabled children who are being looked after by a local authority. The views of the disabled child should be given due consideration taking into account their maturity, experience and knowledge. The Guidance acknowledges the challenges this principle might provide where a child has complex needs or communication difficulties.

Decisions may be made incorrectly about children with disabilities because of ignorance about the true implications of the disability and the child's potential for growth and development. Children with disabilities have the same rights as other children and adults to have access to information held about them in social services and health service records. Their ability to give consent or refusal to any action including examination, assessment or treatment is only limited by the general conditions regarding sufficient understanding which apply to other children under the Children Act. However, sufficient understanding may be misunderstood. Even children with severe learning disabilities or very limited expressive language can communicate preferences if they are asked in the right way by people who understand their needs and have the relevant skills to listen to them. No assumptions should be made about 'categories' of children with disabilities who cannot share in decision-making or give consent to or refuse examination, assessment or treatment.[9] (Department of Health 1991, pp.14–15)

It is inevitable that some children with disabilities will not be able, for any number of reasons, to live at home with their family. They may be accommodated by the local authority or be in care. Consequently they may be placed with a foster family or live in residential accommodation. Because disabled children are children in need under the Children Act, local authority social services authorities are required to plan and review decisions concerning their accommodation and placement in the same way as they are for other children in need.

Decisions made about placement must take account of the wishes and feelings of the child, the parents and others with parental responsibility and any other relevant people. Such decisions must have regard to the child's religion, racial origin, culture and language. Responsible authorities should endeavour to place children with parents, relatives or friends, near their homes and with brothers and sisters. (Department of Health 1991, p.30)

Supplementing this duty, which is owed to all children in need, is the duty in section 23(8) to secure, as far as is reasonably possible, that accommodation for a disabled child is not unsuitable to his or her particular needs, and the schedule 2 duty to provide services which are designed to minimise the impact of their disabilities. There is also the duty to promote contact between a (disabled) child and his or her parents, relatives, friends and other contacts.[10] The fulfilment of this contact duty may be particularly difficult where the nature of a child's disability means that they are placed in a particular residential establishment far from their own home and family.

The importance of short-term and respite care is recognised by the Guidance which argues that such care should be flexible, appropriate for the child's needs and to the child's background, culture, racial origin, religion and language, and is integrated into the planned provision of services for the disabled child.

---

9   This extract from the guidance should now be read subject to the discussion concerning decisions relating to children's health care at pp.237–238.

10   Schedule 2, para.15.

The continuation of services for a disabled child upon their transition into adulthood is an important matter. Though duties to assess need for community care services and for their provision under section 47 of the National Health Service and Community Care only apply to those over 18, the integrated assessment duties under the Children Act should provide, where necessary, for a long-term perspective which enables the transition from the statutory framework of the Children Act to the community care duties under the 1990 Act. The statutory powers and duties of the Chronically Sick and Disabled Persons Act and the Disabled Persons (Services, Consultation and Representation) Act span the transition from childhood to adulthood. Section 24(1) of the Children Act makes special provision for children who have been looked after by local authorities; the authority is required to advise, assist and befriend such children with a view to promoting their welfare when they cease to be looked after by the authority.

The aim of these provisions is to promote independent living for young adults, including those with a disability. This may not be possible where the nature of a person's disability is complex or where their family is unable to offer continued care.

> Residential care should not be regarded as a failure but as a positive option where parents, families and friends have a continuing role. With the cessation of admissions to long-stay hospitals for residential care, SSDs should consider as a matter of urgency how they can work in partnership with their health and education counterparts to develop new patterns of residential services which provide good quality care in the local community. Such care may be provided through SSDs, DHAs, voluntary or independent agencies or by combinations and consortia according to local provision. Wherever the young person is placed, SSDs, DHAs and LEAs will have a continuing role and every effort should be made to ensure that any placement encourages development and offers opportunities for continuing education. (Department of Health 1991, p.51)

Disputes and representations concerning children's services, including the assessment, planning and service provision for disabled children and their families will be subject, in the first instance, to the complaints procedures established by local authorities under the Children Act 1989. Complaints under this structure will be limited to matters concerning the actions of social services departments, so that, for example, complaints concerning the assessment and provision of services for children with special educational needs may be subject to an appeal to the Special Educational Needs Tribunals established by the Education Act 1993.

The Children Act complaints procedure is established by the Representations Procedure (Children) Regulations 1991. This requires that the procedure must have an independent element at both the first and final stage of the procedure. Complaints which cannot be satisfactorily resolved at the first stage are referred to a panel with an independent element. The findings of complaints procedures are not binding on local authorities, though they are required to give them due consideration.[11] There must be concern about the difficulties in identifying and utilising the right complaints procedure that are an inevitable consequence of the fact that services for disabled children may be provided by a number of different agencies and authorities.

It is important to understand that the Guidance on children with disabilities is not only a statement of good practice under the Children Act but is also an articulation of those principles of practice as a set of attainable objectives. To this extent it is likely that local authorities will be working toward establishing and promoting these principles over a time scale of a number of years. Their universal and comprehensive attainment in the short term is unlikely, particularly in an environment where historically services for disabled children have been significantly underdeveloped.

Despite such a caveat, the 1994 report of the Social Services Inspectorate on services for disabled children and their families raises some cause for concern.[12] In relation to policy and planning for services for disabled children the report identifies a number of factors which have hampered development.

> These included slim management structures, managers also heavily committed to implementing Community Care arrangements, lack of clear management lead for this area of service, and pressing demands from other parts of the child care service, particularly child care protection. This lack of progress was the more significant since the needs of, and services for, disabled children have historically had a generally low profile. (SSI 1994a, p.3)

Partnership with parents was patchy and though all the authorities inspected were committed to the principle of consultation with disabled children there was little evidence of direct work with such children. Only one of the authorities had developed a multi-agency structure and the Inspectorate found no evidence of effective co-ordinated assessments of disabled children under the different legislation already identified. It seems that little information had been produced for disabled children and their families and though all the authorities were intending to provide services designed to minimise the impact of disability upon disabled children, achievement was limited by: 'the sizeable mis-match between the resources provided and the demand for services. Many parents were unable to get access to the support they required in order to continue caring for their child, until they reached crisis point.' (SSI 1994a, p.5)

Serious deficiencies were identified in relation to assessment, care planning, reviews and registers of disabled children.

> In three SSDs there were no assessment procedures geared to establishing the needs of disabled children. Not all case files had evidence of assessments, but those

---

11 Adverse comments made about a similar feature of the complaints procedures established under the National Health Service and Community Care Act 1990 in Chapter 3, pp.105–107 may also be made here.

12 The inspections for the report were undertaken between March and June in 1993 (18 months after implementation of the Act) on four local authorities.

that were seen were of an uneven quality. It was rare to see evidence of inter-agency assessments. In one SSD only three out of twelve case files contained written assessments. In another SSD, ten out of eleven cases contained an assessment, although only half of those contained details of the education or health background.

It was sometimes unclear who had responsibility for implementing and reviewing plans, and there was a need for a clear model of care management to be adopted.

None of the authorities inspected were operating an effective register of disabled children. One authority was at the point of establishing a register and had developed some good practice in inter-agency working and parental participation in setting it up. However, at the time of the Inspection the lack of a register, or alternative comprehensive up to date lists, had resulted in there being no reliable current information on the numbers, nature and distribution of disabled children in those authorities. (SSI 1994a, p.6)

These rather depressing findings by the Social Services Inspectorate should be read in the light of other, more positive findings. All of the authorities were committed to the location of services for disabled children within mainstream children's services. This is a fundamental principle of the Children Act and is designed to ensure that disabled children are seen as children first and then as having a disability. Other positive findings included the likelihood of integrated planning and service provision being encouraged by the location of responsibility for disabled children in children and family sections of social services departments; the significant impact of specialist appointments on work with disabled children and their families; and a commitment from parental participation and inter-agency liaison to the introduction of a register of disabled children as an effective planning tool.

Surveys of Disability in Great Britain, the Report of the Office of Population, Censuses and Surveys published in 1988 (OPCS 1988) estimated there to be 360,000 disabled children living in the United Kingdom and highlighted the lack of support services available for such children and their families. The Children Act, and the guidance published to support it, has provided an important statutory framework and model of good practice within which this negative experience can be challenged and transformed. Unfortunately the Social Services Inspectorate Report suggests that improvements are patchy and slow. It is to be hoped that the historically low profile and importance of services for disabled children will not impede further progress for and on behalf of this important group of children.

SPECIAL EDUCATIONAL NEEDS

The law on the special educational needs of children is currently contained in the Education Act 1993. The policy behind the legislation goes back to the Warnock Report published in 1978 (DES 1978) which argued for a recognition that children with learning difficulties were not a distinct group separate from other school children, but should be seen as a part of a continuum of ability which ranged from children with severe and permanent difficulties to those with learning difficulties which were temporary or minor: 'We believe that the basis for decisions about the type of educational provision which is required should not be a single label "handicapped" but rather a detailed description of special educational need' (DES 1978, p.43 para.3.25).

The recommendations of the Committee utilised this continuum of ability and a principle of educational integration within which it was assumed that the majority of children with special educational needs would be educated in mainstream schools. The assessment of children with such needs would identify those who required a statement of special educational needs and of the special provision needed to meet those needs, whether in a mainstream school or in a special school, and a different category of children whose needs were such that they did not require a statement of their needs to be prepared. The needs of this latter category of children were to be provided within the ordinary structure of mainstream education.

The principles of the Warnock report formed the basis of the Education Act 1981, which established duties on local education authorities (LEAs) to secure provision of special education within their area and to assess children with special educational needs. These duties were to be fulfilled by the assessment of children and by the drawing up of a statement of a child's special educational needs. Provision for children with special educational needs under the 1981 Act led, in time, to substantial criticism primarily centred on the use of imprecise definitions in the Act, delays in the assessment and statementing procedures, and on the operation of the appeal processes established under the Act.

The 1981 Act used the concepts of 'learning difficulty' and 'special educational provision'. A child had special educational needs if he or she had: 'a learning difficulty which calls for special educational provision to be made for him.' (s.1(1))

In turn the phrase 'learning difficulty' was defined by section 1(2) as

a significantly greater difficulty in learning than the majority of children of his age; and

a disability which either prevents or hinders him from making use of the educational facilities of a kind generally provided in schools, within the area of the [LEA] concerned, for children of his age.

'Special educational provision' was defined by section 1(3) of the Act, in relation to children aged two and over, as: 'educational provision which is additional to, or otherwise different from, the educational provision made generally for children of his age in schools maintained by the [LEA] concerned.'

The impact of these definitions has been criticised on the grounds that their imprecision leaves too much room for interpretation and establishes a focus on the availability of provision within a local education authority rather than on the needs of the child.

The combined effect of these provisions is that the question of whether or not a child has special educational needs depends not so much on the child's specific needs considered in isolation, but rather on the appropriateness or otherwise of existing provision. (Harris 1992, p.105)

Similar criticisms are made by the Audit Commission in their report Getting in on the Act:

> As the 1981 Act does not define its client group it is very difficult for LEAs to implement it consistently. LEAs lack a definition of special educational needs and the threshold for issuing statements of special educational needs has not been established. Consequently the proportion of pupils with a statement varies from 0.8 per cent to 3.3 per cent of the pupil population in the LEAs studied. (Audit Commission 1992, p.1)

Guidance issued by the Department of Education and Science in 1989 envisaged that the assessment and issuing of a draft statement should not take longer than six months. (DES 1989.) The expectations raised by this guidance were continually frustrated by the reality of practice and by the fact that the guidance did not have the force of law and was therefore unenforceable as a time limit. The Audit Commission identified the median time to complete the process as 12 months.

> In many cases, LEAs had taken no action to reduce delays... The situation is exacerbated by the in-built financial incentive to delay the completion of statements.

> The lack of a positive incentive for LEAs to complete the process to time and of a structure for calling the LEA to account to parents for its work in this area means that there is no counter to the inherent delay, and some LEAs are likely to continue to regard the issuing of statements as an administrative task which does not warrant management attention, instead of seeing it as the cornerstone of the rights of parents and children. (Audit Commission 1992, p.19)

An additional problem with the 1981 Act was the operation of the appeal process established by the legislation. Where a local education authority assessed a child but refused to issue a statement of special educational need parents could appeal to the Secretary of State. Parents could also appeal against the statement made by the local education authority to a local appeal committee which could confirm the special educational provision specified in a statement or require the LEA to reconsider the statement in the light of the committee's comments. If the original statement was confirmed by the committee, or the LEA, upon referral of their original statement, reached a further decision which was itself unacceptable to a child's parents, then the parents had a right of written appeal to the Secretary of State who could, after consulting the local education authority, confirm or amend the statement or direct the LEA to cease to maintain the statement.

> Over a period of time it became apparent that this system of appeals was seriously flawed. Justice was not seen to be done at either of the two stages. When an appeal

committee remitted the case to the LEA for reconsideration, the LEA (albeit following quite properly the statutory procedure) were effectively judge in their own cause when adhering to their original decision, to the frustration not only of the parents of the child but also to members of the committee whose observations appeared to carry insufficient weight. (Robinson 1994, p.5)

There was also criticism of the second stage appeal structure to the Secretary of State on the grounds that the procedure adopted was unfair because the appellants did not have access to the advice which was given to the Secretary of State (Chasty and Friel 1992, p.136).

Though the number of appeals, both local and to the Secretary of State, were small, there was a clear upward trend. The Audit Commission claimed that: 'parents of children with special educational needs are becoming more litigious' (Audit Commission 1992, p.22).

In addition to these specific criticisms Baroness Warnock, who had chaired the committee whose report and recommendations formed the basis of the 1981 Act, voiced fundamental concerns about the major tenet of the original report.

> There is evidence now that the system never worked as we hoped – and that it could not have done so. The idea of a continuum of ability and disability, with only those at the very end identified by a 'statement' was too vague. It was all very well as an ideal; indeed, it may have made children with disabilities seem less of a race apart. But as a basis for legislation, especially at a time when LEAs were increasingly short of money, it was disastrous.

> The whole concept of 'statementing' for only a few children, with the rest supposedly having needs met according to what individual schools can provide, must be radically rethought. And this is the more urgent as schools become increasingly competitive over examination results and have to mange their own finances. (Warnock 1992, p.3)

The case for reform of the system was considerable; in their report the Audit Commission had concluded:

> However, there are some serious deficiencies in the way in which children with special needs are identified and provided for. These deficiencies are caused by three key problems:
>
> - lack of clarity both about what constitutes special educational needs and about the respective responsibilities of the school and the LEA
> - lack of clear accountability by schools and LEAs for the progress made by pupils, and accountability by schools to the LEA for the resources they receive
> - lack of incentives for LEAs to implement the 1981 Act. (Audit Commission 1992, p.1)

In 1992 the Department for Education (DFE) issued a consultation paper which sought to tackle some of the problems which had become apparent in the operation of the system under the 1981 Act. Particular objectives were identified: reducing the time taken by LEAs to make assessments and issue statements; improving and extending parents' appeal rights; establishing an independent Tribunal to replace the jurisdiction of appeal committees and the Secretary of State. (DFE 1992 Special Educational Needs: Access to the System.)

The consultation paper was followed by a White Paper which confirmed that legislation would be introduced to achieve the objectives identified in the consultation paper and that the government remained committed to the general principles of the 1981 Act. (DFE 1992a) Criticism from those who were now opposed to the principle analysis of the 1981 Act continued after the publication of the White Paper.

> The Government has proposals to amend the 1981 Act to give parents better access to the processes of statementing and increased rights of appeal, to new style tribunals. But the drawback with such amendments is that they will be introduced against the background of the old ill-drawn line between those who do and those who do not merit statements. What happens to those whose needs still exist, but for whom the education authority has no statutory duty, remains untouched. The suspicion must be that these children will be increasingly pushed to one side. (Warnock 1992, p.3)

The Education Act 1993 has replaced the main sections of the 1981 Act and provision for special educational needs is now organised under the 1993 Act.

Section 156 defines the fundamental concepts of the system in the same terminology as the 1981 Act. Learning difficulty is defined as:

(a) a significantly greater difficulty in learning than the majority of children of his age,

(b) a disability which either prevents or hinders him from making use of educational facilities of a kind generally provided for children of his age in schools within the area of the local authority, or

(c) he is under the age of five years and is, or would be if special educational provision were not made for him, likely to fall within paragraphs (a) or (b).

The principle of integration is restated in section 160(1) subject to a parental veto of a proposal that their child shall be educated in a mainstream school.

Section 165 establishes a duty on local education authorities to identify from among the children they are responsible for, those children who have special educational needs and the special educational provision which their learning difficulty calls for.

The procedures for making assessments under the 1981 Act are broadly re-enacted under section 167 and schedule 9. However, there are new duties to make assessments within time limits specified by regulation, and where LEAs decide not to carry out an assessment they must give parents a written notice of their decision. Ultimately parents have a right of appeal, against such a refusal, to the new Special Educational Needs Tribunal which may dismiss the appeal or order the LEA to make an assessment.

Section 168 and schedule 10 determine the procedures for making statements. The statement must contain

1. details of the assessment of the child's special educational needs,

2. the special educational provision which is to be made to meet those needs,

3. the type of school or other institution which the LEA is suggesting as appropriate, and

4. any other special educational provision, provided otherwise than in a school, which the LEA consider should be included in the statement.

Under the provisions of the section, where a LEA maintains a statement they are under a duty to arrange the provision identified in the first three heads identified above. Parents now have a right to express a preference for the school they wish their child to be educated at, but only after they have received the statement from the LEA.

The Secretary of State is required by the Act to publish a Code of Practice with the objective of giving practical guidance to those who have responsibilities under the Act or are involved in special educational needs. Five fundamental principles are identified by the Code:

> the needs of all pupils who may have special educational needs either throughout, or at any time during, their school careers must be addressed; the Code recognises that there is a continuum of needs and a continuum of provision, which may be made in a wide variety of different forms
>
> children with special educational needs require the greatest possible access to a broad and balanced education, including the national curriculum
>
> the needs of most pupils will be met in the mainstream, and without a statutory assessment or statement or special educational needs. Children with special educational needs, including children with statements of special educational needs, should, where appropriate and taking into account the wishes of their parents, be educated alongside their peers in mainstream schools
>
> even before he or she reaches compulsory school age a child may have special educational needs requiring the intervention of the LEA as well as the health services
>
> the knowledge, views and experience of parents are vital. Effective assessment and provision will be secured where there is the greatest possible degree of partnership between parents and their children and schools, LEAs and other agencies. (DFE 1994, p.2)

Though the publication and substance of the Code of Practice has been generally welcomed there is some disquiet about the ability of schools and teachers to meet the challenges its implementation makes, particularly in the context of a refusal by government to provide additional resources.

The Code confirms the importance of a continuum of special educational needs provision in which special schools have an important role.

The clear stance of the Code on the need for a continuum of SEN provision, effectively counters the widely espoused myth that a major aim of the Warnock Report (DES 1978) was to greatly increase levels of integration in mainstream schools and to close special schools (Warnock 1992; Hornby 1995, p.116).

Hornby is also complementary about the Code's focus on those children with special educational needs who do not have a statement thus identifying the range of special needs which are apparent in approximately 20 per cent of the school population; the requirement of an annual review of the statement and the child's progress, and of parental involvement in the assessment of their children. The recognition of specific learning difficulties and emotional and behavioural difficulties as being within definitions of special educational needs is also seen as important. (Hornby 1995, p.117)

Others[13] have commented on the importance of the identification of a five stage process of assessment and service provision in the Code of Practice.[14]

> In effect, schools in their stages responses to children's special needs will now need to employ clear procedures to identify and to register children whose academic and physical, social or emotional development is giving cause for concern. The development, monitoring, reviewing and recording of any action will ensure that parents can genuinely feel part of a process of action on behalf of their child. The matching of resourcing levels to schools should (in theory) be more effective because the levels of needs within individual schools should be more transparent as a consequence of the new approaches to school-based action and accountability. Above all else, the LEA should be able to initiate statutory assessment with greater confidence about the quality and coherence of information available on a particular child and in the awareness that there has been a sustained and systematic approach to resolving any difficulties at an earlier stage. (Russell 1994, p.49)

The 1993 Act also establishes a new appeal structure and a new Special Educational Needs Tribunal. The Tribunal has jurisdiction to hear a number of different appeals from parents.

1. against a LEA's refusal to make a statement. In such an appeal the tribunal may dismiss the appeal; order the LEA to make or maintain a statement;

---

13 See Russell (1994) p.48.

14 Stage 1: class or subject teachers identify or register a child's special educational needs and, consulting the school's SEN co-ordinator, take initial action
Stage 2: the school's SEN co-ordinator takes lead responsibility for gathering information and co-ordinating the child's special educational provision, working with the child's teachers
Stage 3: teachers and the SEN co-ordinator are supported by specialists from outside the school
Stage 4: the LEA considers the need for a statutory assessment and, if appropriate, makes a multidisciplinary assessment
Stage 5: the LEA considers the need for a statement of special educational needs and, if appropriate, makes a statement and arrange, monitor and review provision. (DFE 1994, p.3).

or remit the case to the LEA for reconsideration in the light of the tribunal's comments.

2. against the assessment by an LEA, the provision specified in the statement, or the fact that no school is named in the statement. In such an appeal the tribunal may dismiss the appeal, order the LEA to amend the statement, or order the LEA to cease to maintain the statement.

3. against the refusal of the LEA to make an assessment following such a request from the child's parents. In such an appeal the tribunal may dismiss the appeal, or order the LEA to arrange an assessment.

4. against the refusal of an LEA to reassess a child who has a statement. The tribunal may dismiss the appeal, or order a reassessment.

5. against the decision of an LEA to cease to maintain a statement. The tribunal may dismiss the appeal, or order the LEA to maintain the statement in its current form or with amendments.

6. against the LEAs decision not to change the name of the school specified in the statement. The tribunal may dismiss the appeal, or order the LEA to specify the parents choice of school or other institution.

The tribunal system operates under a presidential structure and individual tribunals are constituted by a legally qualified chairperson and two lay members, one with experience of special educational needs and the other with experience of local government. It is generally agreed that the new appeal structure and the tribunals are an improvement on the old system. Writing before its introduction, Robinson claims:

> Three conspicuous improvements will be the establishment of a single (rather than two-stage) process of appeal to the Tribunal, its demonstrable independence and its power to make final binding orders, subject only to an appeal on a point of law. Furthermore, the Tribunal will be able to consider the manner in which the case has been handled by the LEA in the light of the code of practice as well as the merits of the LEA's decision. (Robinson 1994, p.10)

Despite concern that the structure and principles of the 1981 Act have led to the making of statements for very few of the number of children with special educational needs, they have been retained by the 1993 Act. It is to be hoped that the impact of the widely welcomed Code of Practice and the new appeal structure with enhanced appeal rights, will remedy the manifold problems of the system as it operated under the previous Act. The decision not to make further resources available to LEAs for the improved and enhanced system recommended by the Code of Practice is an inauspicious indication of commitment by government.

SOCIAL SECURITY BENEFITS[15]

There is little doubt that entitlement to social security benefits will be a major issue for a significant number of families with a disabled child. Disability living allowance is the most important benefit for those children with care and mobility needs arising from their disability; invalid care allowance provides some income replacement for those who care for a disabled child, and the basic means tested income support benefit may be able to be supplemented with a weekly premium paid on behalf of a disabled child.

Disability living allowance has two components, care and mobility. Subject to particular rules concerning the age of the claimant, both are available to children who fulfil the conditions of entitlement. Disability living allowance is a non-means tested benefit and is paid in addition to income support; consequently, a successful claim on behalf of a disabled child will have a significant impact on the weekly income of a family relying wholly or partly on benefit income.

Subject to satisfying the ordinary conditions of entitlement[16] a child over the age of five can claim the mobility component, subject to the restriction that where they are claiming the lower rate of benefit they must, in addition to the ordinary conditions of entitlement, show either: 'that they require substantially more guidance or supervision than persons of their age in normal physical and mental health would; or that persons of their age in normal physical and mental health would not require such guidance or supervision' (CPAG 1995, p.125).

---

15   Chapter Six deals with the entitlement of disabled people to social security benefits. This short section identifies those benefits which might be of particular relevance for disabled children and their families.

16   For the higher rate of the mobility component the claimant must be suffering from a physical disability such that:
   • they are unable to walk,
   • or are virtually unable to walk,
   • or are both deaf and blind; or
   • were both without feet or are a double amputee; or
   • are severely mentally impaired and have severe behavioural problems, and qualify for the highest rate of the care component.
   For the lower rate the claimant must show that although they are able to walk they are so severely disabled, physically or mentally, that, ignoring any familiar routes, they are unable to take advantage of their walking abilities outdoors without guidance or supervision from another person most of the time.
   The claimant must have satisfied one of these conditions for at least the past three months and be likely to satisfy the condition for the next six months. (See CPAG 1995, pp.124–131)

There is no lower age limit for claims for the care component of disability living allowance though a child under 16 cannot establish an entitlement to the lower rate of benefit by satisfying what is known as the 'cooking test'.[17] There are additional tests for children under the age of 16.

s/he has attention or supervision requirements 'substantially in excess of the normal requirements of a person of his age; or

s/he has substantial attention or supervision requirements 'which younger persons in normal physical and mental health may also have but which persons of his age and in normal physical and mental health would not have' (CPAG 1995, p.132).

In the context of this chapter invalid care allowance is payable to those who are caring for a disabled child who is receiving either the higher or middle rate of the care component of disability living allowance. The care being given must be regular and substantial, a condition which is satisfied where the care is for 35 hours or more a week.

Where income support is being paid for a family with a disabled child there will be an entitlement to a disabled child premium where the child is receiving disability living allowance.

It will be seen from this brief and partial survey of the social security benefits available in respect of a disabled child, that entitlement to disability living allowance is an important threshold for passporting to other benefits. Claims

---

17 The care component disability tests are that:
- the claimant must be so severely disabled physically or mentally that he or she requires from another person:
during the day:
  i) frequent attention throughout the day in connection with bodily functions; or
  ii) continual supervision throughout the day in order to avoid substantial danger to themselves or others at night
  iii) prolonged or repeated attention in connection with bodily functions, or
  iv) in order to avoid substantial danger to themselves or to others the claimant requires another person to be awake for a prolonged period or at frequent intervals for the purpose of watching over themselves
- part-time day care
  v) the claimant requires in connection with bodily functions attention from anther person for a significant portion of the day (whether during a single period or a number of periods); or
  vi) the claimant cannot prepare a cooked meal for themselves if they have the ingredients.
The higher rate of care component is paid to claimants who satisfy:
- either or both i) and ii) *and*
- either or both iii) and iv).
The middle rate is paid to claimants who satisfy:
- either or both i) and ii) *or*
- either or both iii) and iv).
The lower rate is paid to claimants who satisfy:
- either or both v) and vi).

should be properly made and supported by necessary documentation and medical evidence if appropriate.

CONCLUSION

The payment of social security benefits is the cash element of the package of support and services needed by and for disabled children. Other elements of this package have already been identified and described, they are social services, health services and education services. Despite the implementation of the Children Act the legal structure within which these services and benefits are administered is undoubtedly confusing. The rationale underpinning the law should be the protection and promotion of the rights and interests of all children with disability.

The Gillick decision and the Children Act 1989 are important landmarks in the development of a concept and a code of children's rights. These developments were taking place at about the same time as the movement for disability rights was achieving public recognition and legitimacy. Despite a history in which disabled people, including children, suffered from a lack of support services, the rights and interests of disabled children are now becoming established as a focus for development. This chapter has considered the lead role of local authority social services departments in the organisation of service provision and identified the concerns raised by the Social Services Inspectorate about the slow start made to integrated service provision required by the Guidance published under the Children Act. However, the objectives of the Act and the Guidance are clear: the integrated and comprehensive provision of services for disabled children as a category of children in need. If this important legislative initiative is considered together with the new Education Act 1993 and its Code of Practice, and the Disability Discrimination Act 1995, then there is now in place a legislative framework within which the rights and interests of disabled children can be improved. Whether this improvement can be achieved, and whether it can be substantial, remains to be seen. The availability of resources is crucial, not least for the funding of appropriate levels of social services and social security benefits. The commitment of government to promoting the position of disabled people, including disabled children, is difficult to assess; it is to be hoped that the new legislative structure can be instrumental in achieving these objectives and is therefore seen in practice to be more than mere symbolic law reform.

CHAPTER TEN

AN OVERVIEW OF ORGANISATIONS, PRESSURE GROUPS AND CHARITIES WORKING STRATEGICALLY ON BEHALF OF THE DISABLED

In this final chapter we provide basic information on a wide range of organisations that provide some sort of service or assistance to people with disabilities, their families and carers. We have divided the chapter into the following sections:[1]

1. Sources of advice and assistance with regard to welfare benefits.

   This section provides information on the main government agencies, and independent charitable agencies that can offer advice and assistance in relation to a wide range of financial matters that affect disabled people, and those who care for them. In addition to providing the details of central government offices it also provides addresses of the principal Disability Benefits Centres in the United Kingdom and of the main Specialist Benefit Agencies.

2. National pressure groups and organisations working on specific areas of disability.[2]

   This section contains basic information on the leading organisations in England, Northern Ireland, Scotland and Wales working on a wide range of disability issues. It is subdivided in the following way:

---

1   We are indebted to Irene Clark and Dawn Black for their assistance in compiling this.

2   For a study of the use of litigation in this context see Cooper and Bharan 1986, Day, Balen and McCool 1995A, 1995B.

(a) Generic campaigning, advice and assistance organisations (UK wide).

(b) National centres working with particular disabilities.

    (i) England

    (ii) Northern Ireland

    (iii) Scotland

    (iv) Wales

3. Pressure groups working with an identifiable ethnic group.

I. SOURCES OF ADVICE AND ASSISTANCE WITH REGARD TO WELFARE BENEFIT

The vast majority of financial benefits that are available to disabled people come through central government sources. On major *policy* matters, it is advisable to write to the Chief Executive at the relevant central office as follows:

Department of Social Security, The Adelphi, 1–11 John Adam St, London WC2N 6HT (0171-962 8000).

Benefits Agency, Chief Executive's Office, Room 4C06, Quarry House, Quarry Hill, Leeds LS2 7UA (0113-232 4000).

For general advice on social security benefits that is confidential and free of charge, ring Freephone 0800-666 555 (in England, Scotland, Wales) or 0800-616 757 (in Northern Ireland). For advice in Urdu ring 0800-289188, in Punjabi ring 0800-521360, in Welsh ring 0800-289011, and in Cantonese ring 0800-252451. Also the Benefits Enquiry Line (BEL) on 0800-882200 (or in Northern Ireland on 0800-220674) specialises in giving advice on benefits to people with disabilities.

Specialist free benefits advice for older people is available on 0800-289404. It might also be helpful to contact the following service, for advice on specific debt issues:

Debtline, National 0121-359 8501/2/3. Telephone advice service in England for people in trouble with mortgage, rent, arrears and other debt problems. Information pack available.

Disability benefits centres

For matters related to regional organisation, or specific benefit queries, it is better to contact the relevant regional Disability Benefits Centre (DBC) benefits centre, which will be found in one of the following locations:

A) England

London North, Olympic House, Olympic Way, Wembley HA9 0DL (0181-795 8400). Deals with claims from N Thames E1–E18, N1–N27, NW1–NW11, W2–W5, W7, W9–W13, Bucks, Beds, Cambs, Essex, Herts, Middx (except Hounslow and Twickenham), Oxon, Suffolk, Norfolk.

Five Ways Tower, Frederick Road, Edgbaston, Birmingham B15 1ST (0121–626 2000). Deals with claims from Birmingham, The Midlands, Shropshire, Hereford and Worcs, Northamptonshire, Derby, Notts, Lincolnshire.

Government Buildings, Otley Road, Lawnswood, Leeds LS16 5PU (0113-230 9000). Deals with claims from Cleveland, Yorks, Humberside.

Regent Centre, Gosforth, Newcastle-Upon-Tyne NE3 3JN (0191–223 3000). Deals with claims from Tyne and Wear, Durham, Northumberland.

St Martins House, Stanley Precinct, Bootle, Merseyside L69 9BN (0151-934 6000). Deals with claims from Merseyside, Central and North West Lancs, Cumbria, North and West Cheshire.

Albert Bridge House East, Bridge Street, Manchester M60 9DA (0161-835 2000). Deals with claims from Greater Manchester, East Lancashire, Derbyshire (High Peak), East and South Cheshire.

Sutherland House, 29–37 Brighton Road, Sutton, Surrey SM2 5AN (0181-652 6000). Deals with claims from London postal districts WC1 and WC2, EC1–EC4, SE1–SE28, SW1–SW20, W1, W8 and W14, Hounslow, Twickenham, Berks, Hants, Surrey, Kent, Isle of Wight.

Government Buildings, Flowers Hill, Bristol BS4 5LA (0117-971 8311). Deals with claims from Cornwall, Devon, Avon, Glos, Wiltshire, Somerset, Dorset.

B) Northern Ireland
Northern Ireland Disability Benefits Administration Centre, Castlecourt, Royal Avenue, Belfast BT1 1DF (01232-336000). Deals with claims from all over Ireland.

C) Scotland
Edinburgh Disability Benefits Centre, Argyle House, 3 Lady Lawson St, Edinburgh EH3 9SHY (0131-229 9191). Deals with claims from all over Scotland.

Glasgow Disability Benefits Centre, 29 Cadogan Street, Glasgow G2 7RD (0141-249 73500). Deals with claims from Strathclyde (Postcodes G, KA, ML, PA).

D) Wales
Government Buildings, St Agnes Road, Gabalfa, Cardiff CF4 4YJ (01222-586002). Deals with claims from all over Wales.

Specialist benefit agencies
In addition to the above benefits agencies there exist a number of central units that deal with matters relating to a particular benefit, such as general administration, policy and appeals, as follows:

Attendance Allowance Unit, Room 901a, Norcross, Blackpool FY5 3TA (01253-856123). Only for those people already in receipt of attendance allowance. For initial claims, contact DBCs above or for general advice contact **Fylde Line** 01253-856123.

Child Benefit Centre, PO Box 1, Newcastle-Upon-Tyne, NE88 1AA (0191-417 9999).

Disability Living Allowance Unit, Warbreck House, Blackpool FY2 0UE (01253-856123). Handles all DLA claims (except initial claim which is processed by regional DBC centres (see above).

DLA Central Telephone Answering Unit, 01345-123456. For claimants with an enquiry on their DLA claim.

Disability Working Allowance Unit, Freepost PR1211, Preston PR2 2TF (01253-8561230). Processes all DWA claims.

DWA Central Telephone Answering Unit, 01772-883300. For claimants with an enquiry on their DWA claim. **DWA Response Line,** on 0800-100123, provides information and leaflets but not advice.

Family Credit Unit, Palatine House, Lancaster Road, Preston, Lancashire PR1 1BR (01253-856123). Deals with all family credit claims, or for advice contact **Family Credit Helpline** (01253-500050).

Independent Review Service for the Social Fund, 4th Floor, City Centre Podium, 5 Hill Street, Birmingham B5 4UB (0121-606 2100).

Invalid Care Allowance Unit, Palatine House, Lancaster Road, Preston PR1 1BR (01253-856123). Deals with all invalid care allowance claims.

Independent Tribunal Service, Office of the President of the, City Gate House, 39–45 Finsbury Square, London EC2A 1UU. Deals with Disability Appeal Tribunals, Social Security Appeal Tribunals, Medical Appeal Tribunals, Child Support and Vaccine Damage Tribunals in England, Wales and Scotland.

Independent Tribunal Service Northern Ireland, 6th Floor Cleaver House, 3 Donegal Square North, Belfast BTI 5GA.

Social Security Commissioners, Office of the,

> **England and Wales:** Harp House, 83 Farringdon St, London EC4A 4DH.

> **Northern Ireland:** 5 Linenhall St, Belfast BT2 8AA.

> **Scotland:** 23 Melville St, Edinburgh EH3 7PW.

2. NATIONAL PRESSURE GROUPS AND ORGANISATIONS WORKING ON SPECIFIC AREAS OF DISABILITY

Generic campaigning, advice and assistance organisations

Age Concern England, Astral House, 1268 London Road, London SW16 4ER (0181-679 8000).

Ageing, Centre for Policy on, 2531 lronmonger Row, London ECIV 3QP (0171-253 1787). Policy formulation and analysis.

Child Poverty Action Group (CPAG), 1–5 Bath St, London EC1V 9PY (0171-253 3406). National campaigning organisation concerned with the alleviation of poverty. Produces the annual CPAG Handbook, generally considered the most authoritative source on social security law.

Children's Legal Centre (CLC), 20 Compton Terrace, London N1 2UN (0171-359 6251). Advice on matters concerning legal rights of children by telephone and letter only.

Citizens Advice Bureaux, National Association of (NACAB), Myddleton House, 115–123 Pentonville Rd, London N1 9LZ (0171-833 2181). National network of advice agencies providing free advice to all on a wide range of issues.

Consumers' Association (CA), 2 Marylebone Rd, London NW1 4DF. Research and campaigning body on consumer affairs funded by and representative of consumers. Produces *Which?* magazine.

Consumer Council, National (NCC), 20 Grosvenor Gdns, London SW1W 0DH (0171-730 3469). Research and campaigning body on consumer affairs. Funded indirectly by government.

DIAL UK, St Catherine's Hospital, Tickhill Road, Balby, Doncaster DN4 8QN (01302-310123). DIAL supports 100 local disability information and advice services.

Disability Alliance ERA, 1st Floor East, Universal House, 88–94 Wentworth Street, London E1 7SA (0171-247 8776, or rights advice line 0171-247 8763). Provides information and undertakes research to promote a wider understanding of the needs of disabled people, particularly in relation to income and social security. Produces booklets including the important *Disability Rights Annual Handbook.*

Disability Awareness in Action (DAA), 11 Belgrave Road, London SW1V 1RB (0171-834 0477). Collaborative project between a number of international organisations that disseminates and co-ordinates information about disability rights movement in international arena. Produces important monthly newsletter.

Disability Law Service, Room 241, 49–51 Bedford Row, London WC1R 4LR (0171-831 8031). Free legal advice and information service for disabled people.

Disabled Living Centres Council (DLCC), Winchester House, 11 Cranmer Road, London SW9 6EJ (0171-820 0567). The lead co-ordinating body for the 37 participating Disabled Living Centres in the UK, the DLCC disseminates information, and promotes training and research regarding the development of property and equipment for disabled people.

Disabled Living Foundation (DLF), 380–384 Harrow Rd, London W9 2HU (0171-289 6111). Advice on daily living equipment, including publications and training.

Disablement Income Group, The (DIG), Unit 5, Archway Business Centre, 19–23 Wedmore St, London N19 4RZ (0171-263 3981). Registered charity. Promotes financial welfare of disabled people through advice, advocacy, fieldwork, information, publications, research and training.

Family Rights Group, The Print House, 18 Ashwin St, London E8 3DL (0171-249 0008). Advice service on matters of family and child law.

Help the Aged, St James's Walk, London EC1R 0BE (0171-253 0253). Freephone advice line (0800-289404). Range of free advice leaflets.

Legal Action Group, 242–244 Pentonville Rd, London N1 9UN (0171-833 2931). Does not advise individuals. Disseminates information and promotes legal reform in field of social welfare and underprivilege, through campaigns, conferences, seminars, and publications including its house journal *Legal Action.*

LIBERTY (formally the National Council for Civil Liberties), 21 Tabard Street, London SE1 4LA (0171-403 3888). Principal UK agency concerned with the defence of civil rights in the UK. Produces publications and offers advice and sometimes legal representation.

Mental Health Foundation, 37 Mortimer Street, London W1N 7RJ (0171-580 0145). Grant making charity promoting and financing research and community care projects.

Mentally Handicapped Children and Adults, Royal Society for (MENCAP), 123 Golden Lane, London EC1Y 0RT (0171-454 0454).

National Association for Mental Health (MIND), Granta House, 15–19 The Broadway, Stratford, London E15 4BQ (0181-519 2122). Works for a better life for people diagnosed mentally ill.

Royal Association for Disability and Rehabilitation (RADAR), 12 City Forum, 250 City Road, London EC1V 8AF (0171-250 3222). National disability campaigning and information service.

National centres working with particular disabilities[3]
A) England
Access Committee for England, 12 City Forum, 250. City Road, London EC1V 8AF (0171-250 0008). National focal point on access to the built environment.

Achondroplasia Group – see Turner Syndrome Society.

ACROSS Trust, Bridge House, 70/72 Bridge Road, East Molesey, Surrey KT8 9HF (0181-783 1355). Provides accompanied holidays for disabled people.

Acupuncture Association and Register, The British, 34 Alderney St, London SW1V 4EU (0171-834 1012). Produces inter alia a handbook with directory of practitioners in UK and abroad.

---

3   We are grateful to the Disability Alliance ERA which provided much of the information.

AFASIC, Overcoming Speech Impairments, 347 Central Markets, London EC1A 9NH (0171-236 3632).

AIDS Helpline, National: 0800-56723. Confidential advice by trained advisers.

Aids Ahead, 17 Macon Court, Herald Drive, Crewe, Cheshire (01270-250736, minicom 01270-250743). Information for deaf people on HIV and AIDS.

Alzheimer's Disease Society, Gordon House, 10 Greencoat Place, London SW1P 1PH (0171-306 0606). Offers advice and support to those coping with the problems of dementia.

Amnesia – See Headway.

Ankylosing Spondylitis Society, National, 5 Grosvenor Cres, London SW1X 7ER (0171-235 9585).

Ann's Neurological Trust Society (ANTS), 1 Abbey Drive, Little Heywood, Stafford ST18 0QQ. Self-help groups, helps funding into research.

Apert Syndrome Support Group, Mrs Walker, Fullers Barn, The Green, Loughton, Milton Keynes, Bucks (01908-608557). Provides emotional and practical support, information and contacts.

Arachnoiditis Trust, The Secretary, PO Box 3, North Taunton, Devon EX20 2YU. Information and self-help groups.

Arthritic Association, 1st Floor Suite, 2 Hyde Gardens, Eastbourne, BN21 4PN. Provides mutual support and self-help for those with arthritis.

Arthritis, Horder Centre for, St John's Road, Crowborough, East Sussex, TN6 1XP (01892-665577). Rehabilitation, long/short-term nursing and orthopaedic surgery for joint replacement.

Arthritis Care, 18 Stephenson Way, London NW1 2HD (0171 916 1500), Freephone Helpline (0800-289170). Advice and practical help for people with arthritis. 570 local branches UK wide.

Arthritis Care (Young), 18 Stephenson Way, London NW1 2HD (0171-916 1500).

Arthritis and Rheumatism Council, Copeman House, St Mary's Court, St Mary's Gate, Chesterfield, Derbyshire S41 7TD (01246-558033). Raises money for research and publishes range of information leaflets.

Arthrogryposis Group (TAG), Mrs D Piercy, 1 The Oaks, Common Mead Lane, Gillingham, Dorset SP8 4SW (01747-822655). Support and contact for parents and affected adults, information and research.

ASBAH (Association for Spina Bifida and Hydrocephalus), Asbah House, 42 Park Road, Peterborough PE1 2UQ (01733-555988).

Asbestosis and Industrial Diseases, Society for the Prevention of (SPAID), 38 Drapers Road, Enfield, Middlesex (01707-873025). Information and advice to people who become ill because of their work.

Asthma Campaign, National, Providence House, Providence Place, London N1 0NT (Admin 0171-226 2260, Helpline 0345-010203). Research and Information.

Ataxia (formally Friedreich's Ataxia Group), Copse Edge, Thursley Road, Elstead, Godalming, Surrey GU8 6DJ (01252-702864).

Autistic Society, National, 276 Willesden Lane, London NW2 5RB (0181-451 1114). Provides information, advice and support to families and carers as well as a range of educational and support services.

Back Pain Association, National, 31–33 Park Road, Teddington, Middx TW11 0AB (0181-977 5474). Information service.

Blind People, Action for, 14–16 Verney Road, London SE16 3DZ (0171-732 8771). Provides employment and training, holiday hotels and residential care, grants and welfare benefits advice including mobile service.

Blind, General Welfare of the, 37–55 Ashburton Grove, Holloway, London N7 7DW (0171-609 0206).

Blind, Guide Dogs for the, Hillfields, Burghfield, Reading RG7 3YG (01734-835555). Trains visually impaired people to use guide dogs, at virtually no cost to owner. Also other services/facilities/mobility training.

Blind, National Federation of the, Unity House, Smyth Street, Wakefield, W Yorks WF1 1ER (01924-291313). Pressure and campaigning group, open to all blind people.

Blind, National Library for the, Cromwell Road, Bredbury, Stockport SK6 2SG (0161-494 0217). Post-free lending service, Braille and Moon, large print available through public libraries.

Blind, Royal National Institute for the, 224 Great Portland St, London W1N 6AA (0171-388 1266, Parents Helpline 01284-753565). UK's largest organisation for blind and partially sighted people offering over 60 services including advice, information and equipment.

Blind and Disabled, National League of the, 2 Tenterden Road, Tottenham, London N17 8BE (0181-808 6030). Registered trades union of blind and disabled people campaigning on all issues affecting our lives.

BlissLink/Nippers, 17–21 Emerald Street, London WC1N 3QL (0171-831 9393). Support for parents of babies on life support systems and premature babies.

Body Positive, 51B Philbeach Gardens, London SW5 9EB (0171-835 1045). Drop-In Centre (11.00am – 5.00pm) and daily telephone helpline (7pm–10pm: 0171-373 9124). A self-help group for people affected by HIV/Aids.

Break, 20 Hooks Hill Road, Sheringham, Norfolk NR26 8NL (01263-823170). Holiday or respite care for children and adults with learning difficulties/mental handicap.

Breakthrough, Deaf-Hearing Integration, Birmingham Centre, Charles W Gillett Centre, 998 Bristol Road, Birmingham B29 6LE (0121-472 6447 voice, 0121-471 1001 minicom). Integration between deaf and hearing people through projects and training.

Breast Cancer Care (Formally Breast Care and Mastectomy Association of Great Britain), 15–19 Brittan Street, London SW3 3TZ (0171-867 8275, 0171-867 1103 Helpline). Provides a service of emotional support and practical information.

Brittle Bone Society, 112 City Road, Dundee DD2 2PW (01382-667603).

Camping for the Disabled, 20 Burton Close, Dawley, Telford, Shropshire (01952-507653 eve; 01743-761889 day). List of adapted campsites available.

Cancer, Association for New Approaches To, 5 Larksfield, Eaglefield Green, Egham, Surrey TW20 0RB (01784-433610). Information and advice on a range of comprehensive therapies.

Cancer Care Society, 21 Zetland Rd, Redland, Bristol BS6 7AH (0117-942 7419). National network of support groups, counselling, holiday accommodation for cancer patients, their families and friends.

Cancerlink, 17 Britannia St, London WC1X 9JN (0171-833 2451). Information resource, training, support centre for cancer support self help groups throughout UK (Asian Language service on 0171-713 7867).

Cancer Prevention Advice, Clinic for, 6 New Rd, Brighton, Sussex BN1 1US (01273-727213). Check-up including cholesterol, mammography, ultrasound Osteoporosis assessment, health counselling, HRT advice.

Cancer Relief, Macmillan Fund, 15–19 Britten St, London SW3 3TZ (0171-351 7811). Expert help and advice offered through nurses, day care and in-patient units.

Cancer United Patients, British Association of (BACUP), 3 Bath Place, London EC2A 3JR (0171-696 9003, Freephone 0800-181999). One to one counselling 0171 696 9000) Information, advice and support to cancer patients, families and friends.

Car Purchase, Disabled, 114 Commonwealth Rd, Caterham, Surrey CR3 6LS (01883-345298). Specialist vehicle supply and finance programme for disabled people and their families.

Care and Repair, Castle House, Kirtley Drive, Nottingham NG7 1LD (0115-979 9091).

Carers National Association, 20–25 Glasshouse Yard, London EC1A 4JS (0171-490 8818, Advice Line 0171-490 8898). Info and support for relatives/friends of sick, disabled and elderly people.

Cerebral Palsy – see also SCOPE (formerly The Spastics Society).

Chest, Heart and Stroke Association – see Stroke Association, The.

Children, Council for, Disabled, c/o National Childrens Bureau, 8 Wakley Street, London EC1V 7QE (0171-843 6000).

Children in Hospital – Action for Sick Children, Argyle House, 29–31 Euston Rd, London NW1 2SD (0171-833 2041).

Children with Heart Disorders, the Association for, Mrs G Hitchen, 26 Elizabeth Drive, Helmshore, Rossendale, Lancs BB4 4JB (01706-213632).

Children with Tracheostomies, Action for (ACT), 2 Dorset Way, Billericay, Essex CM12 0UD (01277-654425).

Children's Liver Disease Foundation, 138 Digbeth, Birmingham B5 6DR (0121-643 7282). Gives emotional family support.

Colitis and Crohn's Disease, National Association for, 98A London Rd, St Albans, Herts AL1 1NX (ansaphone: 01727-8 4296). Information booklets, newsletters, area groups, research and fund-raising.

Colostomy Association, British, 15 Station Rd, Reading, Berks RG1 1LG (01734-391537). Provide a free advisory service on having a colostomy and rehabilitation.

Communication for the Disabled, Foundation for, 25 High St, Woking, Surrey GU21 1BW (01483-727848/44). Charitable trading foundation independent of any manufacturers, with the object of making new technology available to disabled people.

Community Service Volunteers, 237 Pentonville Rd, London N1 9NJ (0171-278 6601). Full-time volunteers involved in independent living, home-based respite care, etc. UK wide.

Compassionate Friends, 53 North St, Bedminster, Bristol BS3 1EN. Organisation offering mutual friendship and understanding to bereaved parents.

Contact the Elderly, 15 Henrietta St, Covent Garden, London WC2E 8QH (0171-240 0630). Provides friendship for elderly housebound people living alone.

Contact a Family, 170 Tottenham Court Road, London W1 0HA (0171-383 3555). Provides advice and help for families caring for children with disabilities or special needs.

Continence Advisory Service, Dene Centre, Castles Farm Rd, Newcastle-Upon-Tyne NE3 1PH (Helpline 0191-213 0050).

Continence Foundation, 2 Doughty St, London WC1 (Helpline 0191-213 0050).

Counselling, British Association for, 1 Regent Place, Rugby, Warks CV21 2PJ (01788-578 328). Directory of counselling agencies available.

Crossroads Care Attendant Schemes Ltd. Association of, 10 Regent Place, Rugby, Warks CV21 2PN (01788-573653). Practical help for families with a disabled member.

Cruse, Bereavement Care, 126 Sheen Rd, Richmond, Surrey TW9 1UR (0181-940 4818, Bereavement Care Line 0181-332 7227). Bereavement counselling, social support and advice to all bereaved people.

CRYPT (Creative Young People Together), Forum Workspace, Stirling Rd, Chichester, W Sussex PO19 2EN (01243-786064). Opportunities for young people with disabilities to live in small group homes while studying creative arts.

Cued Speech, National Centre for, 29–31 Watling St, Canterbury CT1 2UD (01227-450757).

Cystic Fibrosis Trust, Alexandra House, 5 Blyth Rd, Bromley, Kent BR1 3RS (0181-464 7211).

Cystic Hygroma and Lymphangioma Support Group, Villa Fontane, Church Rd, Worth Crawley, W Sussex RH10 4RS (01293-883901). Contact between parents to share experiences, information, problems.

Deaf, Friends for the Young, East Court Mansion, College Lane, East Grinstead RH19 3LT (voice 01342-323444, minicom 01342-312639).

Deaf Association, The British, 38 Victoria Place, Carlisle CA1 1HU (01228-48844, voice and minicom, 01228-28719 vistel and minicom).

Deaf-Blind and Rubella Association, National (SENSE), 11–13 Clifton Terrace, London N4 (voice 0171-272 7774, minicom 0171-272 9648). Support, advice and services for deaf-blind children, young adults and their families.

Deaf Children's Society, National, 15 Dufferin Street, London EC1V 8PD (voice and minicom 0171-250 0123).

Deaf People, Royal Association in Aid of, 27 Old Oak Road, Acton, London W3 7HN (0181-743 6187).

Deaf People, Royal National Institute for (RNID), 105 Gower St, London WC1E 6AH (voice 0171-387 8033, minicom 0171-383 3154). Tinnitus Helpline (01345-090210). Text Users Help Scheme, Typetalk, National telephone relay service and text rebate scheme.

Deafened People, Link, The British Centre for, 19 Hartfield Rd, Eastbourne, E Sussex BN21 2AR (01323-638230). Residential courses for deafened adults together with their families.

Demonstration Centre, National, Pinderfields General Hospital, Wakefield, West Yorkshire WF1 4DG (01924-201688). Provides advice and information on disability to professionals and the public.

Depression Alliance, PO Box 1022, London, SE1 7QB (Answerphone 0171-721 7672). Self-help for depressives and their families.

Diabetic Association, British, 10 Queen Anne St, London W1M 0BD (0171-323 1531). Provides information and advice on living with diabetes and supports diabetic research.

Disability Equipment Register, 4 Chatterton Road, Yale, Bristol BS17 4BJ (01454-318818). Special service to help people obtain secondhand specialist equipment for the disabled.

Disabled Access to Technology Association, Broomfield Hse, Bolling Rd, Bradford BD4 7BG (01274-370019). Provides training in computing, business admin. and electronics for people with physical and/or sensory disabilities.

Disabled Christians Fellowship, 211 Wick Rd, Brislington, Bristol BS4 4HP (0117-977 6780). Fellowship by correspondence, cassettes, local branches, holidays, youth section.

Disabled Drivers Association, Ashwellthorpe, Norfolk NR16 1EX (01508-489 449). Self-help association aiming for independence through mobility.

Disabled Drivers Motor Club, Cottingham Way, Thrapston, Northants NN14 4PL (01832-734724). Offers advice on mobility problems, conversions, insurance, discounts.

Disabled Housing Trust, Head Office, Norfolk Lodge, Oakenfield, Burgess Hill, W Sussex RH15 8SJ (01444-239123). Long-term residential care to adults with physical disabilities or acquired brain injuries.

Disabled Motorists Federation, National Mobility Centre, Unit 2a, Atcham Estate, Shrewsbury SY4 4UG (01743-761889).

Disabled People, British Council of Organisation of, (BCODP), Litchurch Plaza, Litchurch Lane, Derby DE24 8AA (voice 01332-295551, minicom 01332-295581).

Disabled People, John Grooms Association for, 10 Gloucester Drive, Finsbury Park, London N4 2LP (0181-802 7272). Provides residential care, housing, holidays and work. Approximately 40 projects in England and Wales.

Disabled People, Queen Elizabeth's Foundation for, Leatherhead, Surrey KT22 0BN (01372-842204). Residential units for assessment, training, sheltered work, and holidays/convalescence, mobility and advice centre.

Disabled Professionals, Association of, Chair Sue Maynard, 170 Benton Hill, Wakefield Road, Horbury, West Yorkshire WF4 5HW (01924-270335).

Disabled Youth, National Star Centre, College of Further Education, Ullenwood, Cheltenham, Glos GL53 9QU (01242-527631). Specialist college for students who have a physical disability.

DISCERN (Disability Information Service for Sexuality Counselling, Education and Research Nottingham), Suite 6, Clarendon Chambers, Clarendon Street, Nottingham NG1 5LN (0115-947 4147).

Disfigurement Guidance Centre/Laserfair, PO Box 7, Cupar, Fife KY15 4PF (01334-839084). Information, help, publications.

Down's Syndrome Association, 155 Mitcham Rd, London SW17 9PG (0181-682 4001). Up to date advice, information and support on all aspects of Down's Syndrome.

Dyslexia Association, British, 98 London Rd, Reading, Berks RG1 5AU (01734-668271).

Dyslexia Institute, 133 Gresham Rd, Staines, Middx TW18 2AJ (01784-463851). Educational assessment, teaching, teacher-training and advice.

Dysphasic Adults, Action for, 1 Royal Street, London SE1 7LL (0171-261 9572). Advice and help for those speech impaired after stroke or head injury.

Dystonia Society, Weddel House, 13–14 West Smithfield, London EC1A 9JJ (0171-329 0797). Information and Support to sufferers of Dystonia, causing involuntary muscle spasms.

Dystrophic Epidermolysis Bullosa Research Association (DEBRA), Debra House, 13 Wellington Business Park, Dukes Ride, Crowthorne, Berks RG11 6LS (01344-771961). Support and advice for sufferers. Funds research into disease and treatment.

Eating Disorders Association, National Information Centre 44/48 Magdalen St, Norwich NR3 1JU (01603-621414). For help and understanding around anorexia and bulimia.

Eczema Society, National, 163 Eversholt Street, London, NW1 1BU (0171-388 4097).

Endometriosis Society, 35 Belgrave Square, London SW1 8PQ (0171-235 4137). Support, information and research.

Environments, Centre for Accessible, 60 Gainsford St, London SE1 2NY (0171-357 8182). Information on design of accessible buildings.

Epilepsy Association, British, Anstey House, 40 Hanover Sq, Leeds LS3 1BE (0113-2439393). National Information Centre – Helpline 0800-309030. Advice, information, education, mutual support groups, quarterly journal.

Epilepsy Federation, Stanley Mews, 71 Stanley Road, Thornton Heath, Surrey CRO 3QF (0181-665 1255). Information, support, sets up groups.

Epilepsy, National Society for, Chalfont St Peter, Gerrards Cross, Bucks SL9 0RJ (01494-873991). Assessment, rehabilitation, long-term care, research, education, advice and local groups.

Family Fund, PO Box 50, York, YO1 2ZX (01904-621115). Provides financial help to families caring for children who are severely disabled.

Family Service Units, 207 Old Marylebone Rd, London NW1 5QP (0171-402 5175). UK-Wide advice and support to families under pressure, network of projects UK-Wide.

Family Welfare Association, 501–505 Kingsland Rd, Dalston, London E8 4AU (0171-254 6251). Provides counselling and runs projects for people with social or emotional problems.

Friedreich's Ataxia – see Ataxia.

Gardening for Disabled Trust, Hayes Farmhouse, Hayes Lane, Peasmarsh, E Sussex TN1 6XR. Grants, advice and information, newsletter, garden club.

Gemma, BM Box 5700, London WC1N 3XX. National friendship network of lesbians and bisexual women with/without disabilities, all ages.

Growth Hormone Deficiency Group – see Turner Syndrome Society.

Guideposts Trust, Two Rivers, Witney, Oxon OX8 6BH (01993-772886). Provides care through day centres and nursing homes in the field of mental health.

Guillain Barre Syndrome Support Group, 'Foxley', Holdingham, Sleaford, Lincs NG34 8NR (01529-304615). Information and support.

Haemophilia Society, 123 Westminster Bridge Road, London SE1 7HR (0171-928 2020).

Handicapped Children's Aid Committee, c/o 9 Templars Drive, Harrow Weald, Middx HA3 6RX (0181-421 1222).

Handihols, 12 Ormonde Ave, Rochford, Essex SS4 1QW (01702-548257). Hospitality exchange holiday scheme for the disabled.

Headway, National Head Injuries Association Ltd, King Edward Court, 7 King Edward Street, Nottingham NG1 EW (0115-9240800). Gives help, information and support to patients and families in respect of problems created by head injuries.

Hearing Concern (British Association of the Hard of Hearing), 7/11 Armstrong Road, London W3 7JL (0181-743 1110, voice and minicom). Self-help clubs, advisory service for young people, social activities.

Heart Foundation, British, 14 Fitzhardinge St, London W1H 4DH (0171-935 0185).

Help for Health Trust, Highcroft Cottage, Romsey Road, Winchester SO22 5DH (0800-665544). Information service on health self-help groups.

Holiday Care Service, 2 Old Bank Chambers, Station Road, Horley, Surrey RH6 9HW (01293-774535). Free holiday information and advice for disabled people and others with special needs.

Home Farm Trust Ltd, Merchants House North, Wapping Road, Bristol BS2 4RW (0117-927 3746). Care and an individual service for people with learning disabilities.

Horticultural Therapy, Society for, Goulds Ground, Vallis Way, Frome, Somerset BA11 3DW (01373-464782). Advisory services to disabled gardeners.

Huntingtons Disease, Association to Combat, 108 Battersea High St, London SW11 3HP (0171-223 7000).

Hypothermia Prevention Service in Britain (COLDLINE), 31 Dalston Lane, London E8 3DF (0171-241 0440 office hours, 24 hour emergency 0171-241 2299).

Ileostomy Association of Great Britain and Ireland, PO Box 23, Mansfield, Notts NG18 4TT (01623-28099). Helps people return to active lives following ileostomy surgery. Seventy local groups.

In Touch Trust, 10 Norman Rd, Sale, Cheshire, M33 3DF (0161-905 2440). For parents of special needs children.

Incontinence, National Action on, 2 Doughty St, London WC1N 2PH (Helpline 0191-213 0050). Offers information and support on all aspects of incontinence.

Infantile Hypercalcaemia Foundation (incorporating Williams Syndrome), Mulberry Cottage, 37 Mulberry Green, Old Harlow, Essex CM17 0EY (01279-427214). Funds research. Parents association, advice and information.

Integration Alliance, Unit 2, 70 South Lambeth Road, London SW8 1RL (0171-735 5277). Campaigns for a national policy on integration by bringing together parents and teachers of children with disabilities.

Invalid Children's Aid Nationwide (I CAN), 1–3 Dufferin Street, London EC1Y 8NA (0171-374 4422).

Irritable Bowel Syndrome Network, c/o St Johns House, Hither Green Hospital, Hither Green, London SE13 6RU (0181-698 4611 ext. 8194).

Kidney Patient Association, British, Bordon, Hampshire GU35 9JZ (01420-472021/2). Financial help, advice and counselling. Holiday dialysis centres in the UK and abroad.

Kidney Research Fund, National, 3 Archers Court, Stukeley Road, Huntingdon, Cambs PE18 6XG (01480-454828). Funding kidney research, training doctors, providing equipment and supporting kidney patients.

Laryngectomy Clubs, National Association of, Ground Floor, 6 Rickett Street, Fulham, London SW6 1RU (0171-381 9993).

Law Society, 50 Chancery Lane, London WC2A 1PL (0171-242 1222). Group for solicitors with disabilities – contact Judith McDermott.

Learning Difficulties (Values into Action), Oxford House, Derbyshire St, London E2 6HG (0171-729 5436). Campaigns for people with learning difficulties rights to live in the community.

Learning Disabilities, British Institute of (Formally British Institute of Mental Handicap), Wolverhampton Road, Kidderminster, DY10 3PP (01562-850251).

Leonard Cheshire Foundation, 26–29 Maunsel St, London SW1P 2QN (0171-828 1822). Provides residential, respite, domiciliary care and independent living for people with physical or mental disability UK wide.

Leukaemia Research Fund, 43 Great Ormond St, London WC1N 3JJ (0171-405 0101).

Limbless Association, 31 The Mall, Ealing, London W5 2PX (0181-579 1758). Concerned with the welfare of people with limb loss.

Limbless Ex-Service Men's Association, British, Frankland Moore House, 185–187 High Rd, Chadwell Heath, Romford, Essex RM6 6NA (0181-590 1124).

Long Term Medical Conditions Alliance (LMCA), c/o Ms S Knibbs, British Diabetic Association, 10 Queen Anne Square, London W1M 0BD (0171-323 1531 ext.2085). Aims to improve the quality of life of people with long-term medical conditions.

ME – see Myalgic Encephalomyelitis.

Medic Alert Foundation, 12 Bridge Wharf, 156 Caledonian Rd, London N1 9UU (0171-833 3034). Provides 24 hour emergency identification for people with hidden medical problems.

MENCARE, 37 Sunningdale Park, Queen Victoria Road, New Tupton, Chesterfield S42 6DZ (01246-865069). Database of national services for people with mental health problems.

Meningitis Trust, The National, Fern House, Bath Rd, Stroud, Glos GL5 3TJ (24 hour helpline 01453-755049, admin 01453-751738). Raises money for research, provides info, and offers support to individuals and families.

Mental After Care Association (MACA), 25 Bedford Square, London WC1B 3HW (0171-436 6194). Provides a wide range of community services for people with mental health needs and their carers.

Mental Handicap, Care for People with a, 9 Weir Rd, Kibworth, Leicester LE8 0LQ (0116-279 3225).

Metabolic Diseases in Children, Research Trust for, Golden Gates Lodge, Western Road, Crewe CW1 1XN (01270-250221).

Microcephaly Support Group, c/o 43 Randall Rd, Northampton NN2 7DG (01604-713305).

Migraine Association, British, 178A High Rd, Byfleet, West Byfleet, Surrey KT14 7ED (01932-352468). Research, newsletter, leaflets, free information service. Membership £3 p.a.

Migraine Trust, 45 Great Ormond St, London WC1N 3HZ (0171-278 2676). Information, advice, clinics, research grants, helpline, regular newsletters.

Mobility Centre, Banstead, Damson Way, Orchard Hill, Queen Mary's Ave, Carshalton, Surrey SM5 4NR (0181-770 1151). Information service and assessment of disabled and elderly people for driving and 4/8mph pavement vehicles. Training courses, driving tuition and research.

Mobility for Disabled People, Joint Committee on, Woodcliff House, 51A Cliff Road, Weston-super-Mare, Avon BS22 9SE (01934-642313). National liaison and campaigning body on mobility, access and transport.

Mobility Information Service, National Mobility Centre, Unit 2a, Atcham Industrial Estate, Shrewsbury SY4 4UG (01743-761889). Information on all aspects of mobility. Driving assessment for disabled drivers.

Moebius Syndrome Contact Group, Mrs L Anderson, 21 Shields Rd, Whitley Bay, Tyne and Wear NE25 8UJ (0191-253 2090). Group providing contacts between parents to share problems and information.

Motability, Gate House, Westgate, Harlow, Essex CM20 1HR (01279-635666).

Motor Neurone Disease Association, PO Box 246, Northampton NN1 2PR (01604-22269, Helpline 0345-626262).

Mouth and Foot Painting Artists, 9 Inverness Place, London W2 3JF (0171-229 4491).

Mucopolysaccharide Diseases, The Society for, 55 Hill Avenue, Amersham, Buckinghamshire, Bucks HP6 6RU (01494-434156). Support to families, research newsletter and information booklets.

Multiple Sclerosis Society of Great Britain and Northern Ireland, 25 Effie Rd, London SW6 1EE (0171-736 6267, Helpline London 0171-371 8000, Midlands 0121-476 4229). Provides information and support for people affected by MS.

Muscular Dystrophy Group, 7–11 Prescott Place, London SW4 6BS (0171-720 8055).

Myalgic Encephalomyelitis Association, Stanhope House, High Street, Stanford-Le-Hope, Essex SS17 0HA (01375-642466, Helpline 01375-636013).

Myasthenia Gravis Association, Central Office, Keynes House, 77 Nottingham Rd, Derby DE1 3QS (01332-290219).

Narcolepsy Association UK, P. Saunders, South Hall, High St, Farningham, Kent DA4 0DE (01322-863056). Support to sufferers and their families, information and non-medical advice.

Neurofibromatosis Association, The (formally LINK), 120 London Road, Kingston upon Thames, KT2 6QJ (0181-547 1636/974 8707).

Noonan Syndrome Foundation (International), The, Chelsea House, Westgate, London W5 1DR (0181-862 0198). Promotes greater awareness, makes provision for, and co-ordinates research. Offers support for families.

Not Forgotten Association, 5 Grosvenor Cres, London SW1X 7EH (0171-235 1951). Provides televisions, holidays, outings for severely disabled ex-service people.

Occupational Pensions Advisory Service, 11 Belgrave Rd, London SW1V 1RB (0171-233 8080). An independent voluntary organisation giving free help to people concerned about pension rights.

Open University, Adviser on the Education of Disabled Students, Walton Hall, Milton Keynes MK7 6AA (01908-653442 Voice, 01908-655978 minicom). Multi-media distance learning. Higher Education, Continuing Education and training courses, especially suitable for disabled people.

Opportunities for People with Disabilities, 1 Bank Buildings, Princes St, London EC2R 8EU (0171-726 4961 voice 0171-726 4963 minicom). Employment service for job seekers and employers (nine regional offices).

Organic Acidaemias UK, Mrs E Priddy, 5 Saxon Rd, Ashford, Middx TW15 1QL (01784-245989). Arranges contacts between families whose children have protein metabolism related disorders.

OSCAR UK, Sickle Cell Community Centre, Tiverton Road, Tottenham, London N15 6RT (0181-802 0994; Helpline 0181-888 2148). Develops technology related employment opportunities for people with disabilities.

Paget's Disease, National Association for the Relief of, 207 Eccles Old Rd, Salford, Manchester M6 8HA (0161-707 9225).

Pain Concern (formerly Self Help in Pain: SHIP), 33 Kingsdown Park, Tankerton, Kent, CT5 2DT (01227-264677). Support and counselling available by phone to those in chronic pain.

Pain Society, The, 9 Bedford Sq, London WC1B 3RA (0171-636 2750).

Parkinson's Disease Society of the UK, 22 Upper Woburn Place, London WC1H 0RA (0171-383 3513). Provides information, advice and support via Head Office and local branches.

Partially Sighted Society, Queen's Rd, Doncaster, S Yorks DN1 2NX (01302-323132). London Office (0171-372 1551). Helps visually impaired people make best use of remaining sight.

Patients Association, 8 Guildford Street, London WC1N 1DT (0171-242 3460). Help and advice for patients. Leaflets and self-help directory.

People First, Instrument House, 207–215 King's Cross Rd, London WC1X 9DB (0171-713 6400). Independent self-advocacy organisation for people with learning difficulties.

Perthes Association, 42 Woodland Rd, Guildford, Surrey GU1 1RW (01483-306637).

PHAB, 12–14 London Rd, Croydon CR0 2TA (0181-667 9443). Clubs and holidays to bring disabled/able-bodied people together.

Phenylketonuria, National Society for, UK Limited, 7 Southfield Close, Willen, Milton Keynes MK15 9LL (01908-691653).

Phoebic Trust, 25a The Grove, Coulsden, Surrey CR3 2BH (0181-660 0332). Organises self-help groups and a phone contact scheme.

Polio Fellowship, British, Bell Close, West End Rd, Ruislip, Middx HA4 6LP (01895-639453). Provides welfare services to people who have had polio resident in the UK and Eire.

Portage Association, National, B Paul, 127 Monks Dale, Yeovil, Somerset, BA21 3JE. Home visiting teaching service for special needs children and parents.

Prader-Willi Syndrome Association UK, Rosemary Erskine, 2 Wheatleaf Close, Horsell, Woking, Surrey GU21 4BP (01483-724784). Help and support for people with Prader-Willi Syndrome and their families.

Primary Immunodeficiency Association, Alliance House, 12 Caxton Street, London, SW1H 0QS (0171-976 7640). Exists to improve quality of life through diagnosis, treatment and care.

Psoriasis Association, 7 Milton St, Northampton NN2 7JG (01604-711129).

Psychiatric Rehabilitation Association, Bayford Mews, Bayford St, London E8 3SF (0181-985 3570).

Raynaud's and Scleroderma Association Trust, 112 Crewe Rd, Alsager, Cheshire ST7 2JA (01270-872776). Support, advice, newsletters, publications.

Reac, 12 Wilson Way, Earl's Barton, Northamptonshire NN6 0NZ (01604-811041). An association for children with hand or arm deficiency.

Real Life Options, Tayson House, Methley Road, Castleford, West Yorkshire, (01977-556917). Provides Support and care for people with disabilities.

REMAP, J J Wright, Nat Organiser, 'Hazeldene', Ightham, Sevenoaks, Kent TN15 9AD (01732-883818). Makes or adapts aids for disabled people when not commercially available.

Remploy Ltd, 415 Edgware Road, Cricklewood, London NW2 6LR (0181-452 8020). Employers of 9000 severely disabled people in 96 factories throughout Great Britain.

Repetitive Strain Injury – see RSI Association.

Restricted Growth Association, PO Box 18, Rugeley, Staffordshire WS15 2GH (01889-576571). Provides information and support for people with restricted growth.

Retinitis Pigmentosa Society, British, PO Box 350, Buckingham, MK18 5EL (01280-860363, fax 01280-860515).

Rett Syndrome Association, UK, Admin Office, c/o C Freeman, 29 Carlton Road, Frien Barnet, N11 3EX (0181-361 5161). Support and information for parents, carers and professional advisers.

Rheumatism, British League Against, 41 Eagle Street, London WC1R 4AR (0171-242 3313).

Riding for the Disabled Association, Avenue 'R', National Agricultural Centre, Kenilworth, Warwicks CV8 2LY (01203-696510). Aims to provide the opportunity of riding and driving to disabled people.

RSI Association, Chapel House, 152 High Street, Yiewsley, West Drayton, Middx UB7 7BE.

Schizophrenia Association of Great Britain, Bryn Hyfryd, The Crescent, Bangor, Gwynedd LL57 2AG (01248-354048). Telephone helpline and information packs, researching causes of schizophrenia.

Scleroderma Research Organisation, Bretforton Hall Clinic, Bretforton, Vale of Evesham, Worcestershire WR11 5JH (01386-830537). Research into scleroderma and allied conditions, enquiries, treatment etc.

SCOPE (formerly The Spastics Society), 12 Park Cres, London W1N 4EQ (0171-636 5020, Helpline 0800-626216). Help and advice for children and adults with cerebal palsy and related disabilities.

Sex Education Team, Horizon Trust, Harperbury Hospital, Harper Lane, Radlett, Herts (01923-854861 ext. 4420). Direct work with people with learning disabilities, advice and training for staff.

Shaftesbury Society, 16 Kingston Rd, London SW19 1JZ (0181-542 5550, fax 0181-545 0605). Residential care centres/schools/FE colleges/holiday centres for people with learning or physical disabilities.

Sickle Cell Society, 54 Station Rd, London NW10 4UA (0181-961 7795).

Skin Disease Research Fund, c/o The Secretary, 3 St Andrew's Place, London NW1 4LB (0171-935 8576).

Snowdown Award Scheme, 22 Horsham Court, 6 Brighton Road, Horsham, West Sussex RH13 5BA (01403-211252). Bursaries to physically disabled young people for further education or training.

Special Educational Needs, The National Association for, 22 Warren Hill Road, Woodbridge, Suffolk, IP 12 1DU (01394-382 814).

Speech Impaired Children, Association for All, – see AFASIC.

Spinal Bifida – see ASBAH.

Spinal Injuries Association, Newpoint House, 76 St James's Lane, London N10 3DF (0181-444 2121, counselling line 0181-883 4296).

SPOD (The Association to Aid the Sexual and Personal Relationships of People with a Disability), 286 Camden Rd, London N7 0BJ (0171-607 8851).

Sports Association for the Disabled, British, Mary Glen Haig Suite, Solecast House, 13–27 Brunswick Place, London N1 6DX (0171-490 1919). Headquarters and Finance Office.

Stammerers, Association for, St Margaret's House, 21 Old Ford Rd, London E2 9PL (0181-983 1003).

Stroke Association, CHSA House, 123–127 Whitecross Street, London EC1Y 8JJ (0171-490 7999). Provides advice, publications, welfare grants and has local groups and volunteers.

Students with Disabilities, (SKILL), National Bureau for, 336 Brixton Rd, London SW9 7AA, (0171-274 0565). Telephone and minicom information service.

Tay Sachs and Allied Diseases Association, Dr S Simon, Room 26, Research Centre, Royal Manchester Childrens Hospital, Manchester M27 1HA (0161-794 4696 ext.2384) Information, advice, financial help.

Terrence Higgins Trust, The, 52/54 Grays Inn Rd, London WC1X 8JU (Admin 0171-831 0330, helpline 0171-242 1010, legal 0171-405 2381). Information, support, welfare rights and legal advice for everyone affected by HIV or AIDS.

Thalassaemia Society, UK, 107 Nightingale Lane, London N8 7QY (0181-348 0437). Education, information, counselling. Publicity available in Greek, Italian, Chinese, Turkish and the main Asian languages.

Thalidomide Society, UK, 19 Upper Hall Park, Berkhampstead, Herts, HP4 2NP (01442-864717).

Tinnitus Association, British, Room 6, 14–18 West Bar Green, Sheffield S1 2DA (0114-279 6600). Information, quarterly journal, self-help groups.

Tourette Syndrome (UK) Association, Valleymead, 27 Monkton Street, Ryde IOW PO33 2BY (Helpline 01983-568866). Supports people with Tourette Syndrome and their families.

Tracheo-Oesophageal Fistula Support, St George's Centre, 91 Victoria Rd, Netherfield, Nottingham NG4 2NN (0115-940694). Support for families of babies unable to swallow.

Tuberous Sclerosis Association of Great Britain, Mrs Janet Medcalf, Little Barnsley Farm, Catshill, Bromsgrove, Worcs B61 0NQ (01527-871898). Offers moral and practical support. Provides information, encourages research.

Turner's Syndrome Society, Child Growth Foundation, 2 Mayfield Ave, London W4 1PW (0181-994 7625). Support for girls with Turner's Syndrome and their parents from infants to adults.

Urostomy Association, 'Buckland', Beaumont Park, Danbury, Essex CM3 4DE (01245-224294). Provides support for people who have surgery for urinary diversion.

Vaccine Damaged Children, Association of Parents of, 2 Church St, Shipston-on-Stour, Warwick CV36 4AP (01608-661595).

Voluntary Organisations, National Council for, (NCVO), Regents Wharf, 8 All Saints St, London N1 9RL (0171-713 6161).

Wider Horizons, Ghyll Cottage, Ings, Kendal, Cumbria LA8 9PU (01539-821274). Publishes members' work bi-monthly, promotes friendships by post, wider interests for physically disabled people.

Winged Fellowship Trust, Angel House, 20–32 Pentonville Rd, London N1 9XD (0171-833 2594). Holidays and respite care for physically disabled people UK and abroad.

Writers, National Association of Disabled, 18 Spring Grove, Harrogate, N Yorkshire HG1 2HS (04213-563103). Researches political repression of writers.

Youth Exchange Centre, The British Council, 10 Spring Gardens, London SW1A 2BN (0171-389 4030). Administers grant aid for exchanges of groups of young people 15–25. Encourages participation of young people with disabilities.

B) Northern Ireland

Age Concern, Northern Ireland, 3 Lower Cres, Belfast BT7 1NR (01232-245729).

Age Concern Coleraine, 1 Waterside, Coleraine BT51 3DP (01265-57966).

Alzheimer's Disease Society, 11 Wellington Park, Belfast BT9 6DJ (01232-664100).

ANTS (Syringomyelia) Self-help Group, c/o T. Somers, 166 Battleford Rd, Armagh BT61 8BX.

Arthritis Care, R. Douglas, 31 New Forge Lane, Belfast BT9 5NW (01232-66988).

Blind, Royal National Institute for the, 40 Linenhall St, Belfast BT2 8BG (01232-663543). Services and advice available from the RNIB Northern Ireland Service Bureau and the RNIB Mobile Resource Unit Northern Ireland Wide.

Carers National Association, Northern Ireland, Regional Office, 113 University St, Belfast BT7 1HP (01232-439843).

Chest, Heart and Stroke Association Northern Ireland, Mrs M. Beggs, 21 Dublin Rd, Belfast BT2 7FJ (01232-320184). Help and advice on all aspects of chest, heart and stroke illnesses.

DIAL Belfast, 24–26 North Street Arcade, Belfast BT1 1PB (01232-322690).

Disability, Northern Ireland Council on, Malcolm Sinclair House, 31 Ulsterville Avenue, Belfast BT9 7AS (01232-666188). Provides training, accommodation and support to people with physical disabilities.

Disability Action, 2 Annadale Ave, Belfast BT7 3JR (01232-491011). Forum for over 130 organisations in N Ireland concerned with all forms of disability. Information service, support to groups, sheltered placement scheme, employment service, driver assessment and tuition, mobility information, transport services, advice about access.

Down's Syndrome Association Northern Ireland, J. McMaster, 2nd Floor, 28 Bedford St, Belfast BT2 7FE (01232-243266).

Epilepsy Association, British, Helen Hood, Old Postgraduate Medical Centre, City Hospital, Lisburn Rd, Belfast BT9 7AB (01232-248414).

Extra Care for Elderly People, 11A Wellington Park, Belfast BT9 6DJ (01232-683273). Free domiciliary care for carers of older people in most parts of Northern Ireland.

Families in Contact, E Belfast, 8 Lower Clara Cres, Belfast BT5 5ES (01232-457173) Parent/carer family support.

Haemophilia Society (Northern Ireland), 67 Woodavale Rd, Belfast BT13 3BN (01232-740001).

Huntington's Disease Support Group, W. Johnson, Dept of Medical Genetics, Floor A, West Podium Extension, Tower Block, Belfast City Hospital, Lisburn Road, Belfast BT9 7AB (01232-329241 ext. 2255).

ME Assoc, NI, 28 Bedford St, Belfast BT2 7FE (01232-439831). Support and information for Myalgic Encephalomyelitis sufferers and carers.

Mencap in NI, 4 Annadale Ave, Belfast (01232-691351). Information, support and services for people with a learning disability and their families.

Mental Health, Northern Ireland Association for, 80 University St, Belfast BT7 1HE (01232-328474). Information, advice services and support for those with mental health needs.

Multiple Sclerosis Society, 34 Annadale Ave, Belfast BT7 3JJ (01232-644914).

Polio Fellowship, Northern Ireland, J. Thompson, 198 Belvoir Drive, Belvoir Park, Belfast BT8 4PJ (01323-643367). Support for existing members.

Speech Impaired, Society for the, H. McClelland, 4 Malone View Pk, Belfast BT2 7FE (01232-614269).

C) Scotland

Aberdeen and NE Association for Mental Health, ACIS Centre, 100 Crown St, Aberdeen (01224-573892). Confidential counselling help with personal, emotional and mental health problems.

Aberdeen and North East Council on Disability, Chaplaincy Centre, 25 High St, Old Aberdeen AB2 3EE (01224-272141).

Action Group, 17 London Road, Edinburgh, EH7 5AT (0131-661 5818). Specialist information service on welfare rights to people with learning difficulties and carers throughout Lothian region.

Age Concern Scotland, 113 Rose Street, Edinburgh, EH2 3DT0 (0131-2203345).

Alcohol, Scottish Council on, 137–145 Sauchiehall St, Glasgow G2 3EW (0141-333 9677).

AIDS Monitor, Scottish, 26 Anderson Place Edinburgh EH6 5NP (0131-555 4850). Forum for AIDS issues in Scotland, also provides advice and runs helpline.

Alzheimer's Scotland, 8 Hill Street, Edinburgh, EH2 3JZ (0131-220 6155, advice 0131-220 6155). Provides information and support to people with dementia.

Care and Support after Diagnosis of Foetal Abnormality, Scottish Association for, (CARE), Stairhouse Farm, Stair, Manchline, Ayrshire KA5 5HW (01292-591741).

Chest, Heart and Stroke Scotland, 65 North Castle St, Edinburgh EH2 3TL (0131-225 6935, fax 0131-220 6313). Regional offices at Edinburgh (0131-225 5002). Glasgow (0141-633 1666); Inverness (01463-713433).

Citizens Rights Advice Service, 76 Frithside St, Fraserburgh (01346-515307).

Crossroads (Scotland) Care Attendant Schemes, 24 George Sq, Glasgow G2 1EG (0141-226 3793). Fifty area schemes providing flexible short-term respite care for carers in their own homes.

Deaf, Scottish Association for the, Moray House College, Holyrood Road, Edinburgh EH8 8AQ (0131-557 0591). Promotes interests/welfare of the deaf.

DIAL Scotland, Braid House, Labrador Avenue, Howden, West Lothian EH54 6BU (01506-433468, fax 0506-31201). Information service for the disabled and their carers.

Disability Action, 83, Blair Road, Coatbridge, Lanarkshire ML5 2EW (01236-426664).

Disability Information Service, FREEPOST, Grangemouth FK3 9BR (0324-665100).

Disability Resource Centre, 130 Langton Road, Pollock, Glasgow G53 (0141-883 2997).

Disability Scotland, 5 Shandwick Place, Edinburgh EH2 4RG (0131-229 8632). Information on all aspects of disability.

Disablement Income Group Scotland, 5 Quayside Street, Edinburgh EH6 6EJ (0131-555 2811).

Downs Syndrome Association, Scottish, 158/160 Balgreen Road, Edinburgh EH11 3AU (0131-313 4225). Provides support, information and advice. Local Groups offer a range of activities.

Dunfirmline Forum on Disability, W Gray, 14 Halbeath Road, Dunfirmline KY12 7QX (01383-731503). Minicom available.

Dyslexia Association, Scottish, The Flat, 7 Napier Road, Edinburgh EH10 5AX (0131-229 1865).

ENABLE (Scottish Society for the Mentally Handicapped), 6th Floor, 7 Buchanan Street, Glasgow G1 3HL (0141-226 4541).

Eplepsy Association of Scotland, (National Headquarters), 48 Govan Rd, Glasgow G51 1JL (0141-427 4911).

Fife Money Advice Project, 288 High Street, Kircaldy, Fife KY1 1LB (01592-643143). Grapevine, 8 Lochend Rd, Edinburgh EH6 8BR (tel/minicom 0131-555 4200). Disability information service.

Grampian Welfare Rights Service, 47 Belmont St, Aberdeen AB1 1JS (01224-648247).

Health Search Scotland, 0131-452 8666. Details of self-help groups in Scotland.

Huntingdon's Association, Scottish, Thistle House, 61 Main Road, Elderslie, Johnston PA5 9BA (01505-322245).

INFOBUS Mobile Advice Service, 59 Dundonald Road, Johnstone PA5 0NF (01505-324120).

LEAD – Scottish (Linking Education and Disability), Queen Margaret College, Clerwood Terr, Edinburgh EH12 8TS (0131-317 3439). Educational information and tuition for adults with disabilities.

Mental Health, Scottish Association for, Atlantic House, 38 Gardners Cres, Edinburgh EH3 8DQ (0131-229 9687).

Mental Health Foundation, Scotland, 24 George Street, Glasgow G2 1EG (0141-221 2092). Fund raising and grant making organisation in the field of mental health.

Mental Welfare Commission for Scotland, 25 Drumsheugh Gardens, Edinburgh EH3 7RB (0131-225 7034). Statutory independent body set up to protect the rights and interest of people with mental health problems.

Motor Neurone Disease Association, Scottish, 50 Parnie Street, Glasgow G1 5LS (0141-552 0507). Provides advice and support to patients and their families.

Multiple Sclerosis Society in Scotland, 2a North Charlotte St, Edinburgh EH2 4HR (0131-225 3600, Helpline 0131-226 6573).

Physically Disabled, Scottish Trust for the, Craigievar House, Edinburgh EH122 8YL (0131-317 7227). Considers grant applications from disabled people, all requests for help considered.

Red Cross Society, British, Scottish Branch, 204 Bath St, Glasgow G2 4HL (0141-332 9591). A limited range of equipment on loan; escort/transport services, holidays; home visiting.

SENSE in Scotland, Unit 5, 2–8 Elliott St, Glasgow G3 8EP (0141-221 7577). Support, advice and services for deaf-blind children, young adults and their families.

Sign Language Interpreters, Scottish Association of, 31 York Place, Edinburgh, EH1 3HP (0131-557 6370). Maintains register of interpreters, provides training and supplies interpreters for any assignment.

Spina Bifida Association, Scottish, 190 Queensferry Rd, Edinburgh EH4 2BW (0131-332 0743) Local branches throughout Scotland.

Spinal Injuries Scotland, Unit 22, 100 Elderpark St, Glasgow G51 3TR (0141-440 0960).

Strathclyde Forum on Disability, Room 21, 1st Floor, McIver House, 51 Cadogan St, Glasgow G2 7HB (0141-227 6125).

Thistle Foundation, 27a Walker St, Edinburgh EH3 7HX (0131-225 7282). Provides purpose-built family houses and residential accommodation for physically disabled people. Respite care unit gives relatives regular breaks from caring.

D) Wales

Action Aid for the Disabled, 3 Griffin St, Newport, Gwent NP9 1GL (01633-258212/3). Information, advice service, tribunal representation, confidential counselling service.

Agoriad Gif, Anels Plas-Y-Coed, Porth Renrhyn, Bangor, Gwynedd LL57 4HN (01248-361392/3). Employment agency dealing exclusively in supported employment for people with disabilities.

AIDS Advice Gwent: Caerleon (01633-422532).

AIDS Helpline and Clinic: Newport (01633-841901).

Computer Workshop, Coleg Glan Hafren, Trowbridge Rd, Cardiff CF3 8XZ (0222-794226). Employment initiative for people with special educational needs.

Cynon Valley Committee for Disabled People, R. Morgan, 63 Broniestyn Terr, Trecynon, Aberdare, Mid Glam CF44 8EG.

DIAL, Llantrisant and District (01443-237937). Merthyr Tydfil (01685-379769). Swansea (01792-587642).

Disablement Welfare Rights, Ground Floor, Bron Castell, Lower High St, Bangor, Gwynedd LL57 1YS (01248-352227).

Gwent Coalition of Disabled People, Stone Cottages, Sudbrook, Newport, Gwent NP6 4TA (01633-412270).

MIND Wales CYMRU (National Association for Mental Health), 23 St Mary St, Cardiff CF1 2AA (01222-395123).

SEQUAL Trust, The, (formerly Possum Users' Assoc), Ddol Hir, Glyn Ceirog, Llangollen, Clwyd (01691-72331, fax 0691-718331). Assessment and provision of communication aids.

Wales Council for the Blind, Shand House, 20 Newport Rd, Cardiff CF2 1YB.

Wales Council for the Deaf, Maritime Offices, Woodland Terr, Maesycoed, Pontypridd, Mid Glamorgan CF37 1DZ (01443-485687, minicom 485686).

3. Pressure groups working with an identified ethnic group
Afro Caribbean Society for the Blind, c/o DA Robinson, 12 Lilac Gardens, Shirley, Surrey CR0 8NR (0181-777 7352).

Afro Caribbean Mental Health Association, 35–37 Electric Avenue, Brixton, London, SW9 8JP (0171-737 3603). Counselling, legal, housing, advocacy and befriending.

Asian Peoples with Disability Alliance (APDA), The Disability Alliance Centre, The Old Refectory, Central Middlesex Hospital, Acton Lane, London NW10 7NS (0181-961 6773). Provides direct services: respite care, advice/information and advocacy/case work studies.

BHAN (Black HIV/Aids Network), 41 St Stephen House, Uxbridge Road, London W12 8LH (0181-749 2828, 0181-742 9223).

Black Disabled Persons Group, c/o GLAD, 336 Brixton Road, London SW9 7AA (0171-274 0107).

Blackliners, Unit 46, Eurolink Business Centre, 49 Effra Road, Brixton, London SW2 1BZ (0171-738 5274). AIDS advice and counselling for black people.

Blind Asians, Association of, 322 Upper Street, London N1 2XQ (0171-226 1950).

Chinese Mental Health Association, c/o Oxford House, Derbyshire Street, London E2 6HG (0171-613 1008).

Irish, Positively, St Marys House, 21 Old Ford Road, London E2 9PL (information 0181-983 0192 client, 0181-983 4293). Advice, information and referral service to Irish people affected by HIV/AIDS.

Jewish Blind and Physically Handicapped Society, 118 Seymour Place, London W1H 5DJ (0171-262 2003). Provides sheltered housing (flats), communal facilities and welfare services.

Jewish Care, Stewart Young House, 221 Golders Green Rd, London NW11 9DQ (0181-458 3282). Provides services for elderly, visually impaired, physically disabled, mentally ill people and families.

Jewish Society for the Mentally Handicapped – see Ravenswood Foundation.

Jewish Society for the Mentally Ill (JAMI), Elscot House, Arcadia Avenue, Finchley, London N3 2JU (0181-343 1111).

Naz Project, Palingswick House, 241 King St, London W6 9LP (0181-563 0205). HIV/AIDS education, prevention and support service for South Asian, Turkish, Irani and Arab communities.

Ravenswood Foundation (incorporating Jewish Society for the Mentally Handicapped), 17 Highfield Rd, Golders Green, London NW11 9DZ (0181-458 3282). A Jewish organisation caring for Jewish and non-Jewish children and adults with learning disabilities providing residential, community, recreational, educational and employment training services.

REFERENCES

Abberley, P. (1992), 'Counting us out: a discussion of the OPCS disability surveys'. *Disability, Handicap and Society 7*, 2, 139–155.

Abraham, A. (1995) 'Access with strings.' *Legal Action*, August at 8.

Arden, A. (1995) 'Homelessness: a Step Backwards.' *Legal Action*, August at 22.

Ashton, G. (1993) 'Residential care and mobility payments.' *Legal Action*, September at 18.

Audit Commission (1992) *Getting in on the Act: Provision for Pupils with Special Educational Needs: the National Picture.* London: HMSO.

Audit Commission (1994) *Finding a Place. Review of Mental Helth Services.*

Bagehot, W. (1867) *The English Constitution*, reproduced by Fontana Library, London in 1963 with Introduction by R.H.S. Crossman.

Barlow, W. and Hane, E. (1992) 'A practical guide to the Americans with disabilities act.' *Personnel Journal 71*, 6, 53.

Barnes, C. and Oliver, M. (1995) 'Disability rights: rhetoric and reality in the United Kingdom.' *Disability and Society 10*, 1.

Barron, A. and Scott, C. (1992) 'Citizens' charter programme.' *Modern Law Review 55*, 4, 526–546.

Barton, L. (1993) 'The struggle for citizenship: the case of disabled people.' *Disability, Handicap and Society 8*, 3, 235–248.

Bates, F. and Clements, L. (1996) 'New rights for carers.' *Legal Action*, Feb at 19.

Bates, P. (1994) 'Children in secure psychiatric units: Re K, W and H – Out of sight, out of mind?' *Journal of Child Law 6*, 3, at 131.

Bayefsky, A. (1990) 'The principle of equality and non-discrimination in international law.' 11 Human Rights Law Journal 1

Bayefsky, A. and Eberts, M (1985) *Equality Rights and the Canadian Charter of Rights and Freedoms.* Toronto: Carswell.

Bell, K. (1969) *Tribunals in the Welfare State.* London: Routledge, Kegan, Paul.

Berthoud, R., Lakey, J. and McKay, S. (1993) *The Economic Problems of Disabled People.* London: Policy Studies Institute.

Berthoud, R. (1995) 'The "medical" assessment of incapacity: a case study of research and policy.' *Journal of Social Security Law 2*, 61.

Bolderson, H. (1980) 'The origins of the disabled persons quota and its symbolic significance.' *Journal of Social Policy 9*, 2, 169.

Bonner, D. (1995) 'Incapacity for work: a new benefit and new tests.' *Journal of Social Security Law 2*, 86.

Bourne, P. (1995) 'Grants for renovation, improvement, and facilities for disabled people.' *Legal Action*, January at 20.

Bowen, A. (1995) 'Interpretation of European community law.' *Legal Action*, June at 10.

Brazier, M. (1992) *Medicine, Patients and the Law.* Harmondsworth: Penguin.

Brazier, M. and Lobjoit, M. (eds) (1991) *Protecting the Vulnerable: Autonomy and Consent in Health Care.* London: Routledge.

British Medical Association and the Law Society (1995) *Assessment of Mental Capacity Guidance for Doctors and Lawyers.* London: British Medical Association.

Brooke-Ross, R. (1984) 'The disabled in the Federal Republic of Germany.' *Social Policy and Administration 18,* 172.

Brooke-Ross, R. and Zacher, H.(1983) *Social Legislation in the Federal Republic of Germany.* London: Bedford Square Press.

Burgdorf, R. (1991) 'Equal members of the community: The public accommodations provisions of the ADA.' *Temple Law Review 64,* 551.

Campbell, C. (ed) (1980) *Do We Need a Bill of Rights?* London: Maurice Temple Smith.

Carney, T. (1988) 'The mental health, intellectual disability, Services and guardianship – acts: How do they rate?' *Legal Services Bulletin,* (June) 128.

Carson, D. and Wexler, D. (1994) 'New approaches to mental health law: Will the UK follow the US lead again?' *Journal of Social Welfare and Family Law* 79–96.

Chasty, H. and Friel, J. (1992) *Children with Special Needs, Assessment, Law and Practice.* London: Jessica Kingsley.

Child Poverty Action Group (1995) *National Welfare Benefits Handbook.* London: CPAG.

CPAG (1995) *Rights Guide to Non-Means Tested Benefits.* London: Child Poverty Action Group.

Clark, C. and Lapsley, I. (1995) *Planning and Costing Community Care.* London: Jessica Kingsley.

Clarke, L. (1994) *Discrimination, Law and Employment Series.* London: Institute of Personnel Management.

Clements, L. (1993) 'Community care legal structure.' *Legal Action* July at 10.

Clements, L. (1995) 'Community care update.' *Legal Action* December at 21.

Cooper, J. and Dhavan, R. (eds) (1986) *Public Interest Law.* Oxford: Basil Blackwell.

Cooper, J. (1991) 'Overcoming barriers to employment: the meaning of reasonable accommodation and undue hardship in the Americans with disabilities act.' *University of Pennsylvania Law Review 139,* 1431.

Cooper, J. (1994) *The Legal Rights Manual* (2nd Edition). Aldershot: Ashgate.

Coote, A. (ed) (1992) *The Welfare of Citizens.* London: Rivers Oram Press and the Institute for Public Policy Research.

Cornes, P. (1982) *Employment Rehabilitation: The Aims and Achievements of a Service for Disabled People.* London HMSO.

Craven, M. (1995) *The International Covenant on Economic, Social and Cultural Rights: A Perspective on its Development.* Oxford: Clarendon Press.

DAA (1995) *Information Kit on the United Nations Standard Rules on the Equalisation of Opportunities for Persons with Disabilities.* London: Disability Awareness in Action.

DAA (1995A) *Overcoming Obstacles to the Integration of Disabled People.* UNESCO sponsored report as a contribution to the World Summit on Social Development, Copenghagen. March 1995. London: Disability Awareness in Action.

Daunt, P. (1991) *Meeting Disability: a European Response.* London: Cassell.

Davenport, G.W. (1992) 'The ADA: An appraisal of the major employment-related compliance and litigation issues.' *Alabama Law Rev. 43,* 307.

Day, M., Balen, P. and McCool, G. (1995A) *Multi-Party Actions: A Practitioner's Guide to Pursuing Group Claims.* London: Legal Action Group.

Degener, T. (1995) 'Disabled persons and human rights: the legal framework.' In T. Degener and Y. Koster-Dreese (eds) *Human Rights and Disabled Persons: Essays and Relevant Human Rights Instruments. International Studies in Human Rights 40.* Dordrecht: Martinus Nijhoff.

Degener, T. and Koster-Dreese, Y. (eds) (1995) *Human Rights and Disabled Persons: Essays and Relevant Human Rights Instruments. International Studies in Human Rights 40.* Dordrecht: Martinus Nijhoff.

Dempsey, S. (1991) 'The civil rights of the handicapped in transportation: The ADA and related legislation.' *Transportation Law Journal 19,* 309.

Department of Health (1993A) *Fifth Report From the Health Committee, Session 1992–93.* Cm 2333. London: HMSO.

Department for Education (1992) *Special Educational Needs: Access to the System.* HMSO.

Department for Education (1992A) *Choice and Diversity – A New Framework for Schools.* Cmnd.2021. London: HMSO.

Department for Education (1994) *Code of Practice on the Identification and Assessment of Special Needs.* London: Department for Education.

Department of Education and Science (1978) *Special Educational Needs.* London: HMSO.

Department of Education and Science (1989) *Assessments and Statements of Special Educational Needs: Procedures – within the Educational, Health and Social Services.* Circular 22/89. London: DES.

Department of Health (1990) *The Case of Children. Principles and Practice in Regulations and Guidance.* London: HMSO.

Department of Health (1991) *The Children Act 1989 Guidance and Regulations, Volume 6, Children With Disabilities.* London: HMSO.

Department of Health (1993B) *Mental Health Review Tribunals for England.* Annual Report. London: HMSO.

Department of Health (1994) *A Framework for Local Community Care Charters.* London: Department of Health.

Department of Health (1994) First Report From the Health Committee, Session 1993–94. Better Off in the Community? The care of people who are seriously mentally ill. Vol 1. HMSO.

Department of Health, Home Office (1994) *Review of Health and Social Services for Mentally Disordered Offenders and Others Requiring Similar Services.* London: HMSO.

Department of Health and the Welsh Office (1991) *The Right to Complain: Practice Guidance in Complaints Procedures in Social Services Departments.* London: HMSO.

Department of Health and the Welsh Office (1993) *Code of Practice, Mental Health Act 1983.* London: HMSO.

Despouy, L. (1991) 'Human Rights and Disability, UN Document E/CN.4/Sub 2/1991/31, later published as (1993) Human Rights and Disabled Persons, Human Rights Study Series 6, New York: United Nations Press.

Disability Alliance (1987) *Poverty and Disability, Breaking the Link.* London: Disability Alliance.

Disability Alliance (1988) *Briefing on the Second OPCS Report.* London: Disability Alliance.

Disability Alliance/ERA (1995) *Disability Rights Handbook.* London: Disability Rights Alliance Educational Research Association.

Doyal, L. with Pennell, I. (1979) *The Political Economy of Health.* London: Pluto Press.

Doyle, B. (1987) 'Disabled workers, employment vulnerability and labour law.' In P. Leighton and R. Painter (ed) Vulnerable Workers in the UK Labour Market. *Employee Relations 9,* 5.

Doyle, B. (1987A) 'Employing disabled workers: The framework for equal opportunities.' *Equal Opportunities Review 12,* March/April.

Doyle, B. (1993) 'Employment rights, equal opportunities and disabled persons: the ingredients of reform.' *Industrial Law Journal 22,* 2, 89–103.

Doyle, B. (1995) *Disability, Discrimination and Equal Opportunities. A Comparative Study of the Employment Rights of Disabled Persons.* London: Mansell.

Doyle, B. (1996) *The Disability Discrimination Act 1995.* London: Mansell.

Dredger, D. (1989) *The Last Civil Rights Movement.* London: DPI, Hurst and Co.

DSS (1990) *The Way Ahead: Benefits for Disabled People.* London: Department of Social Security. Cmnd.917 HMSO.

DSS (1993) *The Growth of Social Security.* London: Department of Social Security. HMSO.

East, R. (1992) 'Housing benefit and unreasonable rent.' *Legal Action* October 18.

Eastman, M. (1984) *Old Age Abuse.* London: Age Concern.

Ehlermann, C. (1980) 'Accession of the European community to the European convention on human rights.' In Campbell (1980) at 114.

Eisenstein, H. (1985) 'Affirmative action at work in New South Wales.' In M. Sawer (ed) *Program for Change.* Sydney: Allen and Unwin.

ESCAP (1993) *Asian and Pacific Decade of Disabled Persons 1993–2002: The Starting Point.* New York: ESCAP.

European Commission (1994) *European Social Policy: a Way Forward for the Union. Directorate-General for Employment, Industrial Relations and Social Affairs.* European Commission, Brussels. COM (94) 333 27th July 1994.

Feldblum, C. (1991A) 'The ADA definition of disability.' *The Labour Lawyer 7,* 11.

Feldblum, C (1991B) 'Medical examinations and inquiries under the Americans with disabilities Act: a view from the inside.' *Temple Law Review 64,* 521.

Fennell, P. (1986) 'Law and psychiatry: The legal constitution of the psychiatric system.' *Journal of Law and Society 13,* 1, Spring 1986.

Fennell, P. (1988) 'Sexual suppressants and the Mental Health Act.' *Criminal Law Review* 660–676.

Fennell, P. (1989) 'The Beverley Lewis case: was the law to blame?' 139 *New Law Journal* 1557.

Fennell, P. (1991) 'Double detention under the Mental Health Act 1983: a case of extra-parliamentary legislation.' *Journal of Social Welfare Law 194.*

Fennell, P. (1993) 'The appropriate adult.' *Law Society's Gazette 90/19,* 19.5.93.

Finklestein, V. (1980) *Attitudes and Disabled People: Issues for Discussion.* New York: World Rehabilitation Fund.

Floyd, M., Gregory, E., Murray, H. and Welchman, R. (1983) *Schizophrenia and Employment.* London: Tavistock Institute of Human Relations, Occasional Paper No. 5.

Foley, C. (1995) *Human Rights, Human Wrongs, the Alternative Report on the United Nations Human Rights Committee.* London: River Orams Press.

Gaff, A. (1994) *The Human Rights of People with Disabilities.* West Bank: Al Haq, International Commission of Jurists.

Gaze, B. and Jones, M. (1990) *Liberty and Australian Democracy.* Sydney: The Law Book Company.

Gellner, D. and Galivan, T. (1995) 'Homelessness: a response.' *Legal Action,* September at 22.

Genn, H. (1994) 'The unrepresented tribunal applicant.' *Tribunals 1,* 1, 1, 8–11.

Genn, H. and Genn, Y. (1989) *The Effectiveness of Representation at Tribunals.* London: Lord Chancellor's Department.

Gibbons, J. (1993) 'A coach and horses?' *New Law Journal,* June 4th, 817.

Gooding, C. (1994) *Disabling Laws, Enabling Acts.* London. Pluto Press.

Gordon, P. (1992) 'The job application process after the ADA.' *Employee Relations LJ 18,* 185.

Gordon, R. (1993A) 'Challenging community care assessments.' *Legal Action,* August at 8.

Gordon, R. (1993B) *Community Care Assessments: a Practical Legal Framework.* Harlow: Longman.

Gostin, L (1983) 'Perspectives on mental health reform.' *Journal of Law and Society 10,* 1, 47.

Gostin, L. and Beyer, H. (1993) *Implementing the Americans with Disabilities Act: Rights and Responsibilities of All Americans.* Baltimore: Paul Brookes Publishing Company.

Grief, N. (1991) 'The domestic impact of the ECHR as mediated through community law.' *Public Law,* 555–67.

Griffith, A. (1995) 'The benefits of housing.' *Legal Action,* July at 9.

Griffith, R. (1988) *Community Care: An Agenda for Action.* London: HMSO.

Griffith, J. and Ryle, M. (1989) *Parliament.* London: Sweet and Maxwell.

Habeck, R., Galvin, D., Frey, W., Chadderton, L. and Tate, D. (1985) *Economics and Equity in Employment of People with Disabilities: International Policies and Practices.* East Lansing: University Centre for International Rehabilitation, Michigan State University.

Harper, M. and Momm, W. (1989) *Self Employment for Disabled People: Experiences from Africa and Asia.* Geneva: International Labour Office.

Harris, N. (1992) 'Special education and the law: Further progress? – Part 1.' *Journal of Child Law 104.*

Harris, N. And Wikeley, N. (1995) 'Disability working allowance.' (Editorial) *Journal of Social Welfare Law 2,* 276.

Harrison, K. (1995) 'Patients in the community.' *New Law Journal,* February 24, 276.

HCSL (1990) Mencap Evidence to House of Commons Select Committee 1990–1991.

Health Committee (House of Commons) (1993) Community Care: the Way Forward. 6th Report, 1992–1993, 3 Volumes.

HMSO (1989) *Caring for People: Community Care in the Next Decade and Beyond.* Cm 849. London: HMSO.

HMSO (1991) *Raising the Standard.* Cm 1599. London: HMSO.

Hoggett, B. (1990) *Mental Health Law.* London: Sweet and Maxwell.

Holt, A. and Viinikka, S. (1994) 'Living wills.' *Legal Action,* April 9.

Hornby, G. (1995) 'The code of practice: Boon or burden?' *British Journal of Special Education 2,* 3, 116.

Hough, B. (1988) '"Standing for Pressure Groups and the Representative Plaintiff".' *Dennning Law Journal 77.*

House of Commons Health Committee (1993) *Fifth Report of the House of Commons Health Committee,* vol.1 Community Supervision Orders.

Human Rights and Equal Opportunities Commission (1993) *Human Rights and Mental Illness. Report of the National Inquiry into the Human Rights of People with Mental Illness, Volumes 1 and 2.* Canberra: Australian Government Publishing.

IIAC (1981) *Report on Industrial Diseases.* London: Industrial Injuries Advisory Committee. Cmnd.8393. HMSO.

ILO (1968) The ILO and Human Rights. Report of the DG (Part 1) to the ILO Conference, 52nd session, Geneva: ILO.

ILO (1992) Job Creation for Disabled People: a Guide for Workers' Organisations.

Jefferson, T. (1776) *The American Declaration of Independence.*

Jenkin, P. (1990) *Policy Directions: People with a Physical Disability.* EEO Survey Report, 1990. Sydney, Australia.

Jochheim, K. (1985) 'Quota system policy in the federal republic of Germany' In R. Habeck, *et al.* (eds) *Economics and Equity in Employment of People with Disabilities.* East Lansing: Michigan State University.

Jones, M. (1992) 'Real estate impact of the ADA.' *Real Estate Law Journal 21,* 3.

Kemp, E. and Bell, C. (1991) 'A labour lawyer's guide to the ADA of 1990.' *Nova Scotia L.Rev. 15,* 31.

Kettle, M. and Massie, B. (1986) *Employers' Guide to Disabilities.* Cambridge: Woodhead Faulkner.

Kimber, C. (1993) 'Disability discrimination law in Canada.' In Quinn *et al.* (1993) *Disability Discrimination Law in the United States, Australia and Canada.* Dublin: Oak Tree Press.

Klerk, Y. (1987) 'Working paper on Article 2(2) and 3 of the International Covenant on Economic, Social and Cultural Rights.' *Human Rights Quarterly 9,* 250.

Kulkarni, M. (1981) *Quota Systems and the Employment of the Handicapped.* Michigan: Michigan University.

Lavery, R. and Lundy, L. (1994) 'The social security appointee system.' *Journal of Social Welfare and Family Law 313.*

Law Commission (1989) *Fourth Programme of Law Reform: Mentally Incapacitated Adults.* London: HMSO.

Law Commission (1991) *Mentally Incapacitated Adults and Decision-Making: An Overview. Consultation Paper No 119.* London: HMSO.

Law Commission (1993) Paper 130. Public Law Protection.

Law Commission (1993A) *Mentally Incapacitated Adults and Decision-Making: A New Jurisdiction, Consultation Paper No 128.* London: HMSO.

Law Commission (1993B) *Mentally Incapacitated Adults and Decision-Making: Medical Treatment and Research, Consultation Paper No 129.* London: HMSO.

Law Commission (1993C) *Mentally Incapacitated Adults and Decision-Making: Public Law Protection, Consultation Paper No 130.* London: HMSO.

Law Commission (1995) *Mental Incapacity No 231.* London: HMSO.

Law Commission (1995B) *Law Commission Report No 231 Mental Incapacity Summary of Recommendations.* London: HMSO.

Law Society (1989) *Decision Making and Mental Incapacity.* London: Law Society.

Leary, V. (1993) 'Implications of a right to health.' In K. Mahoney and P. Mahoney (eds) *Human Rights in the Twenty-First Century.* Dordrecht: Kluwer.

Leighton, P. and Painter, R. (eds) (1987) Vulnerable Workers in the UK Labour Market: Some Challenges for Labour Law, *Employee Relations 9* (5).

Lepofsky, M. and Bickenbach, J. (1985) 'Equality rights and the physically handicapped.' In M. Bayefsky and M. Eberts (eds) *Equality Rights and the Canadian Charter of Rights and Freedoms.* Toronto: Carswell.

Lewis, D. (1984) 'Legal rights and the workplace.' In J. Cooper (ed) *The Legal Rights Manual* (2nd Edition). Aldershot: Ashgate. Chapter Seven.

Light, R. (1995) *We have Become People: A Report on the Results of Federal Disability Legislation in the United States.* London: Disability Awareness in Action.

Lister, R. (1990) *The Exclusive Society.* London: Child Poverty Action Group.

Locke, J. (1698) *Two Treatises of Government.*

Lord Chancellor's Department (1996) *Press Notice 8.96.* London: Lord Chancellor's Department.

Lunt, N. and Thornton, P. (1993) *Employment Policies for Disabled People: a Review of Legislation and Services in Fifteen Countries. Research Paper Series Paper No. 16.* London: Department of Health.

Mahoney, K. and Mahoney, P. (eds) (1993) *Human Rights in the Twenty-First Century.* Dordrecht: Kluwer.

Mandelstam, M. (1995) *Community Care Practice and the Law.* London: Jessica Kingsley.

Martin, J., Meltzer, H. and Elliot, D. (1988) *Report 1, The Prevalence of Disability.* London: HMSO.

Mayerson, A. (1991) 'Title I – employment provisions of the ADA.' *Temple Law Review 61,* 499.

McDonagh, M. (1993) 'Disability discrimination law in Australia.' In G. Quinn *et al.* (eds) *Disability Discrimination Law in the United States, Australia and Canada.* Dublin: Oak Tree Press.

McGoldrick, D. (1991) *The Human Rights Committee: Its Role in the Development of the ICCPR.* Oxford: Clarendon Press.

Mental Health Act (1993) HMSO.

Mental Health Act Commission (1993) *5th Biennial Report.* HMSO.

Mikochik, S. (1991) 'The constitution and the ADA: some first impressions.' *Temple Law Review 64,* 619.

MIND (1993) *MIND's Policy on Black and Minority Ethnic People and Mental Health.* London: MIND.

Momm, W. and Konig, A. (1989) 'Community integration for disabled people: a new approach to their vocational training and employment.' *International Labour Review 128,* 4, 497.

Moreton, T (1992) 'European support for people with disabilities.' *Personnel Review 21,* 6, 74.

Morrell, J. (1990) *The Employment of People with Disabilities: Research into the Politics and Practices of Employers. Research Paper No. 77.* London: Department of Employment.

Murphy, J. (1992) 'W(h)ither adolescent autonomy?' *Journal of Social Welfare and Family Law* 529.

Murphy, R. (1991) 'Reasonable accommodation and employment discrimination under title I of the ADA.'S.' *Dakota Law Review 37,* 97.

National Audit Office (1994) *Looking after the Financial Affairs of People with Mental Incapacity.* London: HMSO.

Nelson-Jones, R. (1990) *Medical Negligence Case Law.* London: Fourmat Publishing.

Newman, F. (1995) 'Introduction.' In T. Degener T and Y. Koster-Dreese (1995).

Nicholas, H. (1975) *The United Nations as a Political Institution* (5th Edition). Oxford: Oxford Paperbacks.

Ogus, A., Barendt, E. and Wikeley, N. (1995) *The Law of Social Security.* London: Butterworths.

Oliver, M. (1990) *The Politics of Disablement.* London: Macmillan.

Oliver, M. and Zarb, G. (1989) 'The politics of disability: a new approach.' *Disability, Handicap and Society 4,* 3, 221–239.

Olson, S. (1984) *Clients and Lawyers: Securing the Rights of Disabled Persons.* Westport Connecticut: Greenwood Press.

O'May, N. and Biggs, N. (1993) 'Mentally disordered defendants.' *Legal Action,* January 11.

OPCS (1988) *The Financial Circumstances of Disabled Adults Living in Private Households.* London: Office of Population and Censuses and Surveys. HMSO.

Paine, T. (1791) *The Rights of Man.*

Parkin, A. (1991) 'Discretion and resources in mental health provision.' *New Law Journal,* October 25, 1453.

Parkin, A. (1995) 'The care and control of elderly and incapacitated adults.' *Journal of Social Welfare and Family Law 17,* 4, 431.

Petter, A. (1989) 'Canada's charter flight: Soaring backwards into the future.' *Journal of Law and Society 16,* 151.

Phelan, G. (1992) 'Essential functions of a Job under the ADA.' *Federal Bar News and Journal 39,* 1, 46.

Phillips, J. and Penhale, B. (eds) (1996) *Reviewing Care Management for Older People.* London: Jessica Kingsley Publications.

Pilling, D. and Watson, G. (eds.) (1995) *Evaluating Quality in Services for Disabled and Older People.* Disability and Rehabilitation Series 7. London: Jessica Kingsley Publications.

Pinet, G. (1990) 'Is the Law Fair to the Disabled?' Copenhagen: WHO Regional Publications, European Series No. 29.

Plant, R. (1992) 'Citizenship, rights and welfare.' In A. Coote (ed) (1992) at 15.

Powell, C. (1991) 'The ADA: the effect of Title I on employer/employee relations.' *Law and Psychology Review 15,* 313.

Poynter, R. and Martin. C. (1995) *Rights Guide to Non-Means Tested Benefits.* London: Child Poverty Action Group.

Preston, M. And Gregson, F. (1987) 'New deal for intellectually disabled.' *Law Institute Journal* (August) 800.

Public Law Project (1994) *Challenging Community Care Decisions.* London: Public Law Project.

Quinn, G. (1993) 'Disability discrimination law in the United States.' In G. Quinn, M. McDonagh and C. Kimber (1993) *Disability Discrimination Law in the United States, Australia and Canada.* Dublin: Oak Tree Press.

Quinn, G., McDonagh, M. and Kimber, C. (1993) *Disability Discrimination Law in the United States, Australia and Canada.* Dublin: Oak Tree Press.

RADAR (1981) *Putting Teeth into the Act.* London: Royal Association for Disability and Rehabilitation.

RADAR (1994) *Disabled People Have Rights. Final Report.* London: Royal Association for Disability and Rehabilitation.

RADAR (1994A) *Half Measures.* London: Royal Association for Disability and Rehabilitation.

RADAR (1995) *Be It Enacted: 25 Years of the Chronically Sick and Disabled Persons Act.* London: Royal Association for Disability and Rehabilitation.

Radford, G. (1985) 'Equal opportunity programs in the Australian public service.' In M. Sawer (ed) *Program for Change.* Sydney: Allen and Unwin.

Rasnic, C. (1992) A Comparative Analysis of Federal Statutes for the Disabled Worker in the Federal Republic of Germany and the United States' Arizona Journal of Comparative and International Law, 9 283.

Rawls, J. (1971) *A Theory of Justice.* Cambridge, Mass: Belknap Press.

Reed, J. (1994) *Review of Health and Social Services for Mentally Disordered Offenders and Others Requiring Similar Services,* vol.6. London: HMSO.

Report of the Committee of Administrative Tribunals and Enquiries. (1957) Cmnd.218. HMSO.

Ritchie, J. (1994) The Report of the Inquiry into the Care and Treatment of Christopher Clunis. London: HMSO.

Roberts, S. (1991) 'Mental incapacity.' *Legal Action*, October 17.

Robertson, A. and Merrills, J. (1993) *Human Rights in Europe* (3rd Edition). Manchester: Manchester University Press.

Robertson, S. (1989) *Disability Rights Handbook.* London: The Disability Alliance Educational and Research Association.

Robinson, J. (1994) 'Special education needs after the 1993 reforms.' *Education and the Law 6,* 1, 3.

Rogers, A. and Faulkner, A. (1987) *A Place of Safety.* London: MIND.

Roosevelt, E. (1948) Statement of Eleanor Roosevelt as Chairman of UN Committee on Human Rights 1948.

Rowlingson, K. And Berthoud, R. (1994) *Evaluating the Disability Working Allowance.* London: Policy Studies Institute.

Russell, P. (1994) 'The code of practice: New partnerships for children with special educational needs.' *British Journal of Special Education 21,* 2.

Sawer, M (ed) (1985) *Program for Change.* Sydney: Allen and Unwin.

Schwehr, B. (1995) 'Rational rationing of community care resources.' *Public Law,* 374.

Schwehr, B. (1995A) 'The Relevance of Resources – or a Lack of Resources – in Community Care.' 17 *Journal of Social Welfare and Family Law 2,* 195.

Scott, V. (1994) *Lessons from America: a Study of the Americans with Disabilities Act.* London: Radar.

Secretariat of European Day of Disabled Persons (1995) *Disabled Persons' Status in the European Treaties: Invisible Citizens.* Brussels.

Secretary General UN, Implementation of the World Programme of Action Concerning Disabled Persons and the UN Decade of Disabled Persons, UN-DOC. A/47/415, 11 September 1992, para.15.

Seed, P. and Kaye, G. (1994) *Handbook for Assessing and Managing Care in the Community.* London: Jessica Kingsley.

Sharp, C. (1991) *Problems Assured: Private Renting After the 1988 Housing Act.* London: SHAC/Joseph Rowntree Foundation.

Smith, B., Povall M. and Floyd, M. (1991) *Managing Disability at Work: Improving Practice in Organisations.* London: Jessica Kingsley and The Rehabilitation Resource Centre.

Smith, R. (1986) 'How good are test cases?' In J. Cooper and R. Dhavan (eds) *Public Interest Law.* Oxford: Basil Blackwell.

Social Security Advisory Committee (1988) *Benefits for Disabled People: A Strategy for – Change.* London: Social Security Advisory Committee. HMSO.

Social Services Inspectorate (1994) Letter from Chief Inspector to Directors of Social Services. CI(94)2.

Social Services Inspectorate (1994a) *Report of the National Inspection of Local Authority Services to Disabled Children And Their Families.* London: Social Services Inspectorate.

Social Services Inspectorate Department of Health (1993) *No Longer Afraid: The Safeguard of Older People in Domestic Settings.* London: HMSO.

Solomon, C. (1992) 'What the ADA means to the non-disabled.' *Personnel Journal 71,* 6, 70.

SSI (1993) *Progress on the Rights to Complain: Monitoring Social Services Complaints Procedures, 1992–1993.* London: Department of Health.

SSISWSG (1991A) *Care Management and Assessment Practitioner's Guide.* London HMSO.

SSISWSG (1991B) *Care Management and Assessment Manager's Guide.* London HMSO.

Stace, S. (1987) 'Vocational rehabilitation for women with disabilities.' *International Labour Review 126*, 3, 301.

Stine, M. (1992) 'Reasonable accommodation and undue hardship under the ADA of 1990s.' *Dakota Law Rev. 37*, 97.

Stone, J. (1995) 'Medical treatment and mental incapacity.' *Solicitors Journal* 24th March.

Strauss, K. and Richardson, R. (1991) 'Breaking down the telephone barrier: Relay services on the line.' *Temple Law Review 64, 583.*

Szasz, T. (1974) *Law, Liberty and Psychiatry.* London: Routledge and Kegan Paul.

Thornburgh, D. (1991) 'The American with disabilities act: what it means to All Americans.' *Temple Law Review 64,* 375.

'Too little too late.' *Community Care 5–10,* January 1996.

TUC (1995) *Report on the Access to Work Scheme.* London: TYC Equal Rights Department.

Tucker, B. (1992) 'The ADA: an overview.' *University of New Mexico L.Rev 13*, 34.

Vernon, S. (1994) *Social Worker and the Law* (Second Edition) London: Butterworths.

Waddington, L. (1995) 'Disabled People are Invisible in the Treaties.' In Secretariat of European Day of Disabled Persons.

Wade, H. (1988) *Administrative Justice.* Oxford: Clarendon Press.

Wadham, J. and Leach, P. (1995) 'Protecting human rights in the United Kingdom' 146 – (6706) *New Law Journal* 1133–6.

Wagner, G. (1988) *Residential Care: A Positive Service.* London: HMSO.

Wallace, R. (1992) *International Law* (2nd Edition). London: Sweet and Maxwell.

Wansborough, N. and Cooper, P. (1979) *Open Employment after Mental Illness.* London: Tavistock Press.

Ward, M. and Zebedee, S. (1995–1996) *Guide to Housing Benefit.* London SHAC/Institute of Housing.

Warnock, M. (1992) 'Special case in need of reform.' Schools Report, *The Observer* 18 October 1992.

Weirich, C. (1991) 'Reasonable accommodation under the Americans with disabilities act.' *The Labour Lawyer 7,* 27.

Whitehorn, N. (1991) *Heywood and Massey's Court of Protection Practice.* London: Sweet and Maxwell.

WHO (1990) *Is the Law Fair to the Disabled? A European Survey.* Copenhagen: World Health Organisation.

Wikely, N. and Young, R. (1993) 'The marginalisation of lay members in social security appeal tribunals.' *Journal of Social Welfare and Family Law,* 127–142.

Youngs, R. (1994) *Sources of German Law.* London: Cavendish.

Zappa, J. (1991) 'The ADA 1990: Improving Judicial Determinations of Whether an Individual is Substantially Limited.' *Minnesota L.Rev. 75,* 1303.

Zebedee, J. (1993–1994) *Guide to Council Tax.* London: SHAC.

THE INTERNATIONAL COVENANT ON ECONOMIC, SOCIAL, AND CULTURAL RIGHTS

PREAMBLE
THE STATES PARTIES TO THE PRESENT COVENANT

Considering that, in accordance with the principles proclaimed in the Charter of the United Nations, recognition of the inherent dignity and of the equal and inalienable rights of all members of the human family is the foundation of freedom, justice and peace in the world.

Recognizing that these rights derive from the inherent dignity of the human person,

Recognizing that, in accordance with the Universal Declaration of Human Rights, the ideal of free human beings enjoying freedom from fear and want can only be achieved if conditions are created whereby everyone may enjoy his economic, social and cultural rights, as well as his civil and political rights,

Considering the obligation of States under the Charter of the United Nations to promote universal respect for and observance of, human rights and freedoms,

Realizing that the individual, having duties to other individuals and to the community to which he belongs, is under a responsibility to strive for the promotion and observance of the rights recognised in the present Covenant,

Agree upon the following articles:

Part I

Article 1

1. All peoples have the right to self-determination. By virtue of that right they freely determine their political status and freely pursue their economic, social and cultural development.

2. All peoples may, for their own ends, freely dispose of their natural wealth and resources without prejudice to any obligations arising out of international economic co-operation, based upon the principle of mutual benefit, and international law. In no case may a people be deprived of its own means of subsistence.

3. The States Parties to the present Covenant, including those having responsibility for the administration of Non-Self-Governing and Trust Territories, shall promote the realization of the right of self-determination, and shall respect that right, in conformity with the provision of the Charter of the United Nations.

Part II

Article 2

1. Each State Party to the present Covenant undertakes to take steps, individually and through international assistance and co-operation, especially economic and technical, to the maximum resources, with a view to achieving progressively the full realization of the rights recognized in the present Covenant by all appropriate means, particularly the adoption of legislative measures.

2. The States Parties to the present Covenant undertake to guarantee that the rights enunciated in the present Covenant will be exercised without discrimination of any kind as to race, colour, sex, language, political or other opinion, national or social origin, property, birth or other status.

3. Developing countries, with due regard to human rights and their national economy, may determine to what extent they would guarantee the economic rights recognized in the present Covenant to non-nationals.

Article 3

The States Parties to the present Covenant undertake to ensure the equal rights of men and women to the enjoyment of all economic, social and cultural rights set forth in the present Covenant.

Article 4

The States Parties to the present Covenant recognise that, in the enjoyment of those rights provided by the State in conformity with the present Covenant, the State may subject such rights only to such limitations as are determined by law only in so far as this may be compatible with the nature of those rights and solely for the purpose of promoting the general welfare in a democratic society.

Article 5

1. Nothing in the present Covenant may be interpreted as implying for any State, group or person any right to engage in activity or to perform any act aimed at the destruction of any of the rights or freedoms recognized herein, or at their limitation to a greater extent than is provided for in the present Covenant.

2. No restriction upon or derogation from any of the fundamental human rights recognized or existing in any country in virtue of law, conventions, regulations or custom shall be admitted on the pretext that the present Covenant does not recognize such rights or that it recognizes them to a lesser extent.

Part III

Article 6

1. The States Parties to the present Covenant recognize the right to work, which includes the right of everyone to the opportunity to gain his living by work which he freely chooses or accepts, and will take appropriate steps to safeguard this right.

2. The steps to be taken by a State Party to the present Covenant to achieve the full realization of this right shall include technical and vocational guidance and training pro-grammes, policies and techniques to achieve steady economic, social and cultural development and full and productive employment under conditions safeguarding fundamental political and economic freedoms to the individual.

Article 7

The States Parties to the present Covenant recognize the right of everyone to the enjoyment of just and favourable conditions of work which ensure, in particular:

(a) Remuneration which provides all workers as a minimum with:
   (i) Fair wages and equal remuneration for work of equal value without distinction of any kind, in particular women being guaranteed conditions of work not inferior to those enjoyed by men, with equal pay for equal work;
   (ii) A decent living for themselves and their families in accordance with the provisions of the present Covenants;
(b) Safe and healthy working conditions;
(c) Equal opportunity for everyone to be promoted in his employment to an appropriate higher level, subject to no consideration other than those of seniority and competence;
(d) Rest, leisure and reasonable limitation of working hours and periodic holidays with pay, as well as remuneration for public holidays.

Article 8

1. The States Parties to the present Covenant undertake to ensure:
   (a) The right of everyone to form trade unions and join the trade union of his choice, subject only to the rules of the organization concerned, for the promotion and protection of his economic and social interests. No restrictions may be placed on the exercise of this right other than those prescribed by law and which are necessary in a democratic society in the interests of national security or public order or for the protection of the rights and freedoms of others;
   (b) The right of trade unions to establish national federations or confederations and the right to the latter to form or join trade-union organizations;
   (c) The right of trade unions to function freely subject to no limitations other than those prescribed by law and which are necessary in a democratic society in the interests of national security or public order or for the protection of the rights and freedoms of others;
   (d) The right to strike, provided that it is exercised in conformity with the laws of the particular country.
2. This article shall not prevent the imposition of lawful restrictions on the exercise of these rights by members of the armed forces or of the police or of the administration of the State.
3. Nothing in this article shall authorize States Parties to the International Labour Organization Convention of 1948 concerning Freedom of Association and Protection of the Right to Organize to take legislative measures which would prejudice, or apply the law in such a manner as would prejudice, the guarantees provided for in that Convention.

Article 9

The States Parties to the present Covenant recognize the right of everyone to social security, including social insurance.

Article 10

The States Parties to the present Covenant recognize that:

1. The widest possible protection and assistance should be accorded to the family, which is the natural and fundamental group unit of society, particularly for its establishment and while it is responsible for the care and education of dependent

children. Marriage must be entered into with the free consent of the intending spouses.

2. Special protection should be accorded to mothers during a reasonable period before and after childbirth. During such period working mothers should be accorded paid leave or leave with adequate social security benefits.

3. Special measures of protection and assistance should be taken on behalf of all children and young persons without any discrimination for reasons of parentage or other conditions. Children and young persons should be protected from economic and social exploitations. Their employment in work harmful to their morals or health or dangerous to life or likely to hamper their normal development should be punishable by law. States should also set age limits below which the paid employment of child labour should be prohibited and punishable by law.

Article 11

1. The States Parties to the present Covenant recognize the right of everyone to an adequate standard of living for himself and his family, including adequate food, clothing and housing, and to the continuous improvement of living conditions. The States Parties will take appropriate steps to ensure the realization of this right, recognizing to this effect the essential importance of international co-operation based on free consent.

2. The States Parties to the present Covenant, recognizing the fundamental right of everyone to be free from hunger, shall take, individually and through international co-operation, the measures, including specific programmes, which are needed:

   (a) To improve methods of production, conservation and distribution of food by making full use of technical and scientific knowledge, by disseminating knowledge of the principles of nutrition and by developing or reforming agrarian systems in such a way to achieve the most efficient development and utilization of natural resources:

   (b) Taking into account the problems of both food-importing and food-exporting countries, to ensure an equitable distribution of world food supplies in relation to need.

Article 12

1. The States Parties to the present Covenant recognize the right of everyone to the enjoyment of the highest attainable standard of physical and mental health.

2. The steps to be taken by the States Parties to the present Covenant to achieve the full realization of this right shall include those necessary for:

   (a) The provision for the reduction of the stillbirth-rate and of infant mortality and for the healthy development of the child;

   (b) The improvement of all aspects of environmental and industrial hygiene;

   (c) The prevention, treatment and control of epidemic, endemic, occupational and other diseases;

   (d) The creation of conditions which would assure to all medical service and medical attention in the event of sickness.

Article 13

1. The States Parties to the present Covenant recognize the right of everyone to education. They agree that education shall be directed to the full development of the human personality and the sense of its dignity, and shall strengthen the

respect for human rights and fundamental freedoms. They further agree that education shall enable all persons to participate effectively in a free society, promote understanding, tolerance and friendship among all nations and all racial, ethnic or religious groups, and further the activities of the United Nations for the maintenance of peace.

2. The States Parties to the present Covenant recognize that, with a view to achieving the full realization of this right:

   (a) Primary education shall be compulsory and available free to all;

   (b) Secondary education in its different forms, including technical and vocational secondary education, shall be made generally available and accessible to all by every appropriate means, and in particular by the progressive introduction of free education;

   (c) Higher education shall be made equally accessible to all, on the basis of capacity, by every appropriate means, and in particular by the progressive introduction of free education;

   (d) Fundamental education shall be encouraged or intensified as far as possible for those persons who have not received or completed the whole period of their primary education;

   (e) The development of a system of schools at all levels shall be actively pursued, an adequate fellowship system shall be established, and the material conditions of teaching staff shall be continuously improved.

3. The States Parties to the present Covenant undertake to have respect for the liberty of parents and, when applicable, legal guardians to choose for their children schools, other than those established by the public authorities, which conform to such minimum educational standards as may be laid down or approved by the State and to ensure the religious and moral education of their children in conformity with their own convictions.

4. No part of this article shall be construed so as to interfere with the liberty of individuals and bodies to establish and direct educational institutions, subject always to the observance of the principles set forth in paragraph 1 of this article and to the requirement that the education given in such institutions shall conform to such minimum standards as may be laid down by the State.

Article 14

Each State Party to the present Covenant which, at the time of becoming a Party, has not been able to secure in its metropolitan territory or other territories under its jurisdiction compulsory primary education, free of charge, undertakes, within two years to work out and adopt a detailed plan of action of the progressive implementation, within a reasonable number of years, to be fixed in the plan, of the principle of compulsory education free of charge for all.

Article 15

1. The States Parties to the present Covenant recognize the right of everyone:

   (a) To take part in cultural life;

   (b) To enjoy the benefits of scientific progress and its applications;

   (c) To benefit from the protection of the moral and material interests resulting from any scientific, literary or artistic production of which he is the author.

2. The steps to be taken by the States Parties to the present Covenant to achieve the full realization of this right shall include those necessary for the conservation, the development and the diffusion of science and culture.

3. The States Parties to the present Covenant undertake to respect the freedom indispensable for scientific research and creative activity

4. The State Parties to the present Covenant recognize the benefits to be derived from the encouragement and development of international contacts and co-operation in the scientific and cultural fields.

Part IV

Article 16

1. The States Parties to the present Covenant to submit in conformity with this part of the Covenant reports on the measures which they have adopted and the progress made in achieving the observance of the rights recognized herein.

2. (a)   All reports shall be submitted to the Secretary-General of the United Nations, who shall transmit copies to the Economic and Social Council for consideration in accordance with the provisions of the present Covenant;

    (b) The Secretary-General of the United Nations shall also transmit to the specialized agencies copies of the reports, or any relevant parts therefrom, from State Parties to the present Covenant which are also members of these specialized agencies in so far as there reports, or parts therefrom, relate to any matters which fall within the responsibilities of the said agencies in accordance with their constitutional instruments.

Article 17

1. The States Parties to the present Covenant shall furnish their reports in stages, in accordance with a programme to be established by the Economic and Social Council within one year of the entry into force of the present Covenant after consultation with the States Parties and the specialized agencies concerned.

2. Reports may indicate factors and difficulties affecting the degree of fulfilment of obligations under the present Covenant.

3. Where relevant information has previously been furnished to the United Nations or to any specialized agency by any State Party tot he present Covenant, it will not be necessary to reproduce that information, but a precise reference to the information so furnished will suffice.

Article 18

Pursuant to its responsibilities under the Charter of the United Nations in the field of human rights and fundamental freedoms, the Economic and Social Council may make arrangements with the specialized agencies in respect of their reporting to ti on the progress made in achieving the observance of the provisions of the present Covenant falling within the scope of their activities. These reports may include particulars of decisions and recommendations on such implementation adopted by their competent organs.

Article 19

The Economic and Social Council may transmit to the Commission on Human Rights for study and general recommendation or, as appropriate, for information the reports concerning human rights submitted by States in accordance with articles 16 and 17, and those concerning human rights submitted by the specialized agencies in accordance with article 18.

Article 20

The States Parties to the present Covenant and the specialized agencies concerned may submit comments to the Economic and Social Council on any general recommendation under article

19 or reference to such general recommendation in any report of the Commission on Human Rights or any documentation referred to therein.

Article 21

The Economic and Social Council may submit from time to time to the General Assembly reports with recommendations of a general nature and a summary of the information received from the States Parties to the present Covenant and the specialized agencies on the measures taken and the progress made in achieving general observance to the rights recognized in the present Covenant.

Article 22

The Economic and Social Council may bring to the attention of other organs of the United Nations, their subsidiary organs and specialized agencies concerned with furnishing technical assistance any matters arising out of the reports referred to in this part of the present Covenant which may assist such bodies in deciding, each within its field of competence, on the advisability of international measures likely to contribute to the effective progressive implementation of the present Covenant.

Article 23

The States Parties to the present Covenant agree that international action for the achievement of the rights recognized in the present Covenant includes such methods as the conclusion of conventions, the adoption of recommendations, the furnishing of technical assistance and the holding of regional meetings and technical meetings for the purpose of consultation and study organized in conjunction with the Governments concerned.

Article 24

Nothing in the present Covenant shall be interpreted as impairing the provisions of the Charter of the United Nations and of the constitutions of the specialized agencies which define the respective responsibilities of the various organs of the United Nations and of the specialized agencies to the matters dealt with in the present Covenant.

Article 25

Nothing in the present Covenant shall be interpreted as impairing the inherent right of all people to enjoy and utilize fully and freely their natural wealth and resources.

Part V

Article 26

1. The present Covenant is open for signature by any State Member of the United Nations or member of any of its specialized agencies, by any State Party to the invited by the General Assembly of the United Nations to become a party to the present Covenant.
2. The present Covenant is subject to rectification. Instruments of ratification shall be deposited with the Secretary-General of the United Nations.
3. The present Covenant shall be open to accession by any State referred to in paragraph I of this article.
4. Accession shall be effected by the deposit of an instrument of accession with the Secretary-General of the United Nations.
5. The Secretary-General of the United Nations shall inform all States which have signed the present Covenant or acceded to it of the deposit of each instrument of ratification or accession.

Article 27

1. The present Covenant shall enter into force three months after the date of the deposit with the Secretary-General of the United Nations of the thirty-fifth instrument of ratification or instrument of accession.
2. For each State ratifying the present Covenant or acceding to it after the deposit of the thirty-fifth instrument of ratification or instrument of accession, the present Covenant shall enter into force three months after the date of the deposit of its own instrument of ratification or instrument of accession.

Article 28

The provision of the present Covenant shall extend to all parts of federal States without any limitations or exceptions.

Article 29

1. Any State Party to the present Covenant may propose an amendment and file it with the Secretary-General of the United Nations. The Secretary-General shall thereupon communication any proposed amendments to the States Parties to the present Covenant with a request that they notify him whether they favour a conference of States Parties for the purpose of considering and voting upon the proposals. In the event that at least one third of the States Parties favours such a conference, the Secretary-General shall convene the conference under the auspices of the United Nations. Any amendments adopted by a majority of the States Parties present and voting at the conference shall be submitted to the General Assembly of the United Nations for approval.
2. Amendments shall come into force when they have been approved by the General Assembly of the United Nations and accepted by a two-thirds majority of the States Parties to the present Covenant in accordance which they have accepted.
3. When amendments come into force they shall be binding on those States Parties which have accepted them, other States Parties still being bound by the provisions of the present Covenant and any earlier amendment which they have accepted.

Article 30

Irrespective of the notifications made under article 26, paragraph 5, the Secretary-General of the United Nations shall inform all States referred to in paragraph 1 of the same article of the following particulars:
(a) Signatures, ratifications and accessions under article 26;
(b) The date of entry into force of the present Covenant under article 27 and the date of entry into force of any amendments under article 29.

Article 31

1. The present Covenant, of which the Chinese, English, French, Russian and Spanish texts are equally authentic, shall be deposited in the archives of the United Nations.
2. The Secretary-General of the United Nations shall transmit certified copies of the present Covenant to all States referred to in article 26.

SIMPLE GUIDE TO THE RULES

In this section of the booklet, you will find:

- a list of the contents of the Standard Rules
- an outline of some of the major points.

The introduction to each Rule is given in 'speech marks' and *'italic'* text. These are direct options quotations from the Rules.

For the full text, which may contain some very important points relevant to your particular situation, you need to get a copy of the Standard Rules themselves.

See page 32 for where you can get them.

CONTENTS OF THE STANDARD RULES

INTRODUCTION

Background and current needs
Previous international action
Towards Standard Rules
Purpose and content of the Standard Rules on the Equalisation of Opportunities for Persons with Disabilities
Fundamental concepts in disability policy

PREAMBLE

I. PRECONDITIONS FOR EQUAL PARTICIPATION

Rule 1. Awareness-raising
Rule 2. Medical care
Rule 3. Rehabilitation
Rule 4. Support services

II. TARGET AREAS FOR EQUAL PARTICIPATION

Rule 5. Accessibility
Rule 6. Education
Rule 7. Employment
Rule 8. Income maintenance and social security
Rule 9. Family life and personal integrity
Rule 10. Culture
Rule 11. Recreation and sports
Rule 12. Religion

III. IMPLEMENTATION MEASURES

Rule 13. Information and research
Rule 14. Policy-making and planning
Rule 15. Legislation
Rule 16. Economic policies
Rule 17. Coordination of work
Rule 18. Organisations of persons with disabilities
Rule 19. Personnel training
Rule 20. National monitoring and evaluation of disability programmes in the implementation of the Rules
Rule 21. Technical and economic cooperation
Rule 22. International cooperation

IV. MONITORING MECHANISM

BRIEF GUIDE TO THE RULES

INTRODUCTION

The Introduction to the Rules gives a short description of the status of disabled people worldwide and outlines the history of disability policy during the last thirty years.

The Introduction also outlines the content and aim of the Standard Rules: to make sure that disabled women and men, girls and boys, as citizens of their societies, have the same rights and duties as others.

The Introduction points out that is up to United Nations' Member States to take action to remove the barriers that stop disabled people from using their rights and freedoms and being able to take part in society. It also stresses that organisations of disable people should play an active role as partners in this process.

Special attention should be given to women, children, older people, poor people, migrant workers, people with more than one impairment, indigenous people, refugees and ethnic minorities.

PREAMBLE

The Preamble to the Standard rules mention basic aims of States to promote higher standards of living, full employment and economic and social progress for all citizens.

It reaffirms commitment to human rights and fundamental freedoms, social justice and the dignity and worth of the human person.

It states the reasons that the Standard Rules have been adopted:

(a) *To stress that all action in the field of disability presupposes adequate knowledge and experience of the conditions and special needs of persons with disabilities;*

(b) *To emphasise that the process through which every aspect of societal organisations is made accessible to all is a basic objective of socio-economic development;*

(c) *To outline crucial aspects of social policies in the field of disability, including, as appropriate, the active encouragement of technical and economic cooperation;*

(d) *To provide for the political decision-making process required for the attainment of equal opportunities, bearing in mind the widely differing technical and economic levels, the fact that the process must reflect keen understanding of the cultural context within which it takes place and the crucial role of persons with disabilities in it;*

(e) *To propose national mechanisms for close collaboration among States, the organs of the United Nations system, other intergovernmental bodies and organisations of persons with disabilities;*

(f) *To propose an effective machinery for monitoring the process by which State seek to attain the equalistion of opportunities for persons with disabilities.'*

I. PRECONDITIONS FOR EQUAL PARTICIPATION

This is where the rules themselves start, giving four basic activities which must be happening before equal participation can be achieved.

Rule 1. Awareness-raising

'States should take action to raise awareness in society about persons with disabilities, their rights, their needs, their potential and their contribution.'

There are nine recommendations under this Rule. Some of the things recommended are that information should be available in accessible forms; that information campaigns on disabled people should be supported; that positive portrayals of disabled people in the media should be encouraged; that disabled people should be educated about their rights and potential.

Rule 2. Medical care

'States should ensure the provision of effective medical care to persons with disabilities.'

There are six recommendations under this Rule. Some of the things recommended are that there should be programmes that prevent, reduce or get rid of functional limitations; that local community workers should be trained to take part in such programmes and that organisations of disabled people should be involved; that disabled people should have the same level of medical care within the same system as other members of society and should have the treatment they require; that medical and paramedical personnel should have access to relevant treatment methods and technology and ongoing training.

Rule 3. Rehabilitation

'States should ensure the provision of rehabilitation services to persons with disabilities in order for them to reach and sustain their optimum level of independence and functioning.'

There are seven recommendations under this Rule. These include that national rehabilitation programmes for all disabled people should be developed, based on individual needs and the principles of full participation and equality; programmes should include a wide range of activities, for the development of self-reliance, assessment and guidance; disabled people and their families should be empowered; rehabilitation should be available in the local community; disabled people and their families should be involved in rehabilitation, for example as trained teachers, instructors or counsellors; the expertise of organisations of disabled people should be used when setting up or evaluating rehabilitation programmes.

Rule 4. Support services

'States should ensure the development and supply of support services, including assistive devices for persons with disabilities, to assist them to increase their level of independence in their daily living and to exercise their rights.'

There are seven recommendations under this Rule, all of which support rights-based services – including, among other things, support for cheap and simple technical aids, available free or at low-cost; the involvement of disabled people in design and support of personal assistance programmes and interpreter services to support integrated living.

II. TARGET AREAS FOR EQUAL PARTICIPATION

This part of the Standard Rules sets out goals in various areas of life. Meeting these goals will help ensure equal participation and equal rights for disabled people.

Rule 5. Accessibility

'States should recognise the overall importance of accessibility in the process of the equalisation of opportunities in all spheres of society. For persons with disabilities of any kind, States should (a) introduce programmes of action to make the physical environment accessible; and (b) undertake measures to provide access to information and communication.'

There are eleven recommendations under his Rule. Some of the things recommended are programmes of action, laws, consultation wit organisations of disabled people and the provision of accessible information and Sign Language interpretation services.

Rule 6. Education

'States should recognise the principle of equal primary, secondary and tertiary educational opportunities for children, youth and adults with disabilities, in integrated settings. They should ensure that the education of persons with disabilities is an integral part of the education system.'

There are nine recommendations under this Rule. Some of the things recommended are the support of integrated education through provision of interpreters and other support services; the involvement of parents and organisations of disabled people; making sure that services are available to very young disabled children and to disabled adults, particularly women.

Rule 7. Employment

'States should recognise the principle that persons with disabilities must be empowered to exercise their human rights, particularly in the field of employment. In both rural and urban areas they must have equal opportunities for productive and gainful employment in the labour market.'

There are nine recommendations under this Rule. They include making sure that employment laws and regulations do not discriminate and taking action to support disabled people in open employment.

Rule 8. Income maintenance and social security

'States are responsible for the provision of social security and income maintenance for persons with disabilities.'

There are seven recommendations under this Rule, aimed at ensuring that disabled people and their supporters get an adequate income covering the extra costs of disability and outlining action to be taken.

Rule 9. Family life and personal integrity

'States should promote the full participation of persons with disabilities in family life. They should promote their right to personal integrity and ensure that laws do not discriminate against persons with disabilities with respect to sexual relationships, marriage and parenthood.'

There are four recommendations under this rule, all focused on making sure that disabled people can be full and active members of a family and have an equal personal life to their peers. There are also recommendations to prevent abuse and to improve negative attitudes.

Rule 10. Culture

'States will ensure that persons with disabilities are integrated into and can participate in cultural activities on an equal basis.'

This Rule has three recommendations, including full access to places of culture and the support of disabled people to use their creative, artistic and intellectual potential in the whole community.

Rule 11. Recreation and sports

'States will take measures to ensure that persons with disabilities have equal opportunities for recreation and sports.'

This Rule has five recommendations, covering full access to recreational and sporting venues and the encouragement of all tourist authorities to provide services to everyone, including disabled people.

Rule 12. Religion

'States will encourage measures for equal participation by persons with disabilities in the religious life of their communities.'

This Rule has four recommendations which emphasise the right of disabled people to take part in religious activities of their choice and show ways of achieving this.

III. IMPLEMENTATION MEASURES

This section outlines ways in which the Standard Rules can be carried out effectively.

Rule 13. Information and research

'States assume the ultimate responsibility for the collection and dissemination of information on the living conditions of persons with disabilities and promote comprehensive research on all aspects, including obstacles that affect the lives of persons with disabilities.'

This Rule, with its seven recommendations, says that research should not just emphasise numbers of disabled people but reveal their status within their communities.

Rule 14. Policy-making and planning

'States will ensure that disability aspects are included in all relevant policy-making and national planning.'

This Rule has five recommendations. It goes further than the World Programme of Action in making sure that disabled people are involved in general policy-making, as well as having separate policies and also ensures action at the local level.

Rule 15. Legislation

'States have a responsibility to create the legal bases for measures to achieve the objectives of full participation and equality for persons with disabilities.'

This Rule includes four recommendations, emphasising the need for legislation to support the rights of disabled people and the need to include organisations of disabled people in drafting and evaluating legislation.

Rule 16. Economic policies

'States have the financial responsibility for national programmes and measures to create equal opportunities for persons with disabilities.'

This Rule has four recommendations to ensure that disability policies are part of the regular budgets of national, regional and local authorities, and that economic measures are considered to encourage and support equal opportunities for disabled people, particularly at the grassroots.

Rule 17. Coordination of the work

'States are responsibilities for the establishments and strengthening of national coordinating committees, or similar bodies, to serve as a national focal point on disability matters.'

This Rule has four recommendations and gives independent, permanent and legal status to national disability coordinating committees, with organisations of disabled people as the major influence and enough funds to fulfil its responsibilities.

Rule 18. Organisations of disabled people

'States should recognise the right of the organisations of persons with disabilities to represent persons with disabilities at national, regional and local levels.'

This Rule has eight recommendations and goes into much greater detail than the World Programme of Action on the importance of the direct representation of disabled people in disability policy-making and development, including at the local community level.

Rule 19. Personnel training

'States are responsible for ensuring the adequate training of personnel, at all levels, involved in the planning and provision of programmes and services concerning persons with disabilities.'

This Rule has four recommendations, covering the training of personnel working work with disabled people. The Rule emphasises that training must be based on the principles of full participation and equality, and should involve disabled people, their families and other community members.

Rule 20. National monitoring and evaluation of disability programmes in the implementation of the Standard Rules

'States are responsible for the continuous monitoring and evaluation of the implementation of national programmes and services concerning the equalisation of opportunities for persons with disabilities.'

This Rule has five recommendations which look at how Member States can monitor and evaluate their work on equal opportunities for disabled people, in close cooperation with organisations of disabled people.

Rule 21. Technical and economic cooperation

'States both industrialised and developing, have the responsibility to cooperate in and take measures for the improvement of the living conditions of persons with disabilities in developing countries.'

This Rule has six recommendations. It looks at the issues of development and technical and economic cooperation, making sure that, as a priority, disabled people are involved as full and equal participants and recipients in the process.

Rule 22. International cooperation

'States will participate actively in international cooperation concerning policies for the equalisation of opportunities of persons with disabilities.'

This Rule has four recommendations, outlining how Member States can cooperate internationally through the development of policy, inclusion of disability in general standards, policies and activities, and the dissemination of information.

IV. MONITORING MECHANISM

This section of the Standard Rules outlines the aim of the international monitoring mechanism – to make the carrying out of the Standard Rules effective. Monitoring the progress made by governments to meet the Standard Rules is very important. The international monitoring of the Standard Rules will take place through the United Nations Commission for Social Development.

What Has Happened So Far?

The main developments to the monitoring mechanism have been the appointment of a Special Rapporteur and a Panel of Experts.

Special Rapporteur

International monitoring is begin carried out by a Special Rapporteur, appointed by the United Nations Secretariat.

In March 1994, the Secretary General of the United Nations announced his intention to appoint Mr. Bengt Lindqvist as Special Rapporteur. Mr. Lindqvist is visually-impaired. He is an ex-minister for Social Services and has been active in organisations of disabled people nationally and internationally for many years.

The first part of the monitoring process takes place between July 1994 and June 1997. The Rapporteur reported to the Commission on Social Development as its session in 1995 and will do so again in 1997.

The Special Rapporteur has sent questions to States, bodies within the United Nations system and intergovernmental and non-governmental organisations, including organisations of disabled people.

Panel of Experts

The Standards Rules require the Special Raporteur to have a Panel of Experts, set up by the international non-governmental organisations, to advise him on his work. It has been decided that there will be ten experts, two each from Disabled Peoples' International, the International League of Societies for Persons with Mental Handicap, the World Blind Union and the World Federation of the Deaf and one each from Rehabilitation International and the World Federation of Psychiatric Users.

Index